Royal Commissions and Departmental Committees in Britain

A Case-Study in
Institutional Adaptiveness
and Public Participation
in Government

T. J. Cartwright

HODDER AND STOUGHTON
LONDON SYDNEY AUCKLAND TORONTO

034083

Acknowledgements

We are grateful to the following for permission to use copyright material: *New Society*, the weekly review of the social services, 128 Long Acre, London W.C.2 (for extracts from an article by David Donnison in *New Society*, 18 April 1968); Her Majesty's Stationery Office (for extracts from *Committee Procedure*); the Royal Statistical Society (for extracts from an article by Lord Kennet in the *Journal of the Royal Statistical Society* for 1937).

ISBN 0 340 17602 4

Printed and bound in Great Britain for
Hodder and Stoughton Educational,
a division of Hodder and Stoughton Ltd,
St Paul's House, Warwick Lane, London EC4P 4AH,
by Hazell Watson & Viney Ltd, Aylesbury, Bucks

Contents

034083

Foreword

Coming as it does at the end of a long and sometimes weary road, a foreword is a pleasure to write. But this one is doubly so because of the opportunity it provides to acknowledge a few of the many sources of help and encouragement I have received over the years it has taken to complete this study.

My first thanks must go to the Warden and Fellows of Nuffield College, Oxford, for electing me to a Studentship and to the Warden (Sir Norman Chester) in particular for supervising the thesis which eventually turned into this book.

Secondly, I should like to thank my trans-Atlantic 'coach' and friend for nearly a decade, Professor Michel Chevalier, for his inspiration and assistance in so many ways.

A good deal of the information on which the present study is based reflects the willingness of literally hundreds of people – former chairmen and members of committees, former committee secretaries and other civil servants – to take the time to talk to me and to answer my numerous queries. To them I owe sincere thanks. Others too have helped, often perhaps in ways they scarcely realized, but also through specific acts of kindness. Among these are friends and present and former colleagues on the research staffs of two Canadian royal commissions (especially Meyer Brownstone, who read a draft at a crucial stage); and at Magdalen College, Oxford (especially my tutor, Kenneth Tite), the Institut d'Urbanisme, Université de Montréal, and the Faculty of Environmental Studies, York University, Toronto.

I should like also to record the fact that this study has been possible only through the generous support of the Canada Council, first by means of a predoctoral fellowship and then through a research grant.

Finally, my thanks to a patient and long-suffering wife – who, until now, has never known a husband unpreoccupied with royal commissions and departmental committees in Britain!

Nuffield College
Oxford
July 1974

1
Introduction

Royal commissions and departmental committees are *ad hoc* advisory committees appointed by virtue of non-statutory powers of the Crown and its ministers respectively. As such, they represent one of the oldest and most numerous of all the institutions of government in Britain. In this century alone, approximately sixteen hundred royal commissions and departmental committees have been appointed, more than six hundred of them since the end of the war. Yet, in spite of their popularity, there has been no systematic study of what they are and how they work.

Royal commissions and departmental committees possess two other major characteristics which make them worthy of closer study. First of all, as an institution of government, they demonstrate a quite remarkable degree of flexibility in being able to adapt to the wide range of situations in which they are appointed. Secondly, as part of the governmental process, royal commissions and departmental committees provide a unique channel through which private individuals and interest groups can participate directly in the making of public policy.

Previous Studies

Royal commissions and departmental committees are a good deal more significant than might be thought from the kind of attention paid to them in the scholarly writing on British government. This is partly because, as W. J. M. Mackenzie remarked of pressure groups, they are 'a subject wrapped in a haze of common knowledge'.[1] All the same, the existing literature on royal commissions and departmental committees leaves a good deal to be desired. Much of it is now out-of-date and some of it is frankly partisan, but the major inadequacy is that there is no single study of royal commissions and departmental committees as a special kind of committee.[2] Either royal

---

1 W. J. M. Mackenzie, 'The Articulation of Pressure-Group Demands', in Richard Rose (ed.), *Studies in British Politics* (London: Macmillan, 1966), p. 204.

2 The only book to treat both royal commissions and departmental committees (at least by implication) as a governmental institution *sui generis* is a series of case-studies edited by Richard A. Chapman, *The Role of Commissions in Policy-Making* (London: Allen and Unwin, 1973).

commissions are examined alone, with scarcely a word about departmental committees; or royal commissions and departmental committees are considered together with several other kinds of committees, so that the special characteristics of each are lost sight of. In the first category are two books on royal commissions, one of them written by two American professors in 1937 and the other (a flagrantly partisan defence) written by an American business-man in 1965.[3] There have been only three other books on committees in general which also touch on royal commissions and departmental committees. One of these was written by a Tory pamphleteer in 1849, another by a group of intellectuals in Oxford in 1939, and the third (and probably best known) by Sir Kenneth Wheare in 1955.[4] As for articles and monographs, these can at best provide little more than new illustrations of old themes or limited new hypotheses.[5] In fact, most articles tend to deal with specific committees and the substantive (rather than the institutional) issues they entail. This all adds up to an astonishing dearth of material.

Those who write about royal commissions and departmental committees tend to reflect one of two basic attitudes towards their topic. For some (like Charles J. Hanser, for example), the institution would be difficult to improve. In a typical passage, Hanser declares that

> No other country has produced anything comparable in effectiveness to the Royal Commission of Great Britain as an agency to which an appeal can be made for a definitive determination of controversial facts and for a trustworthy judgement on a complex public problem.[6]

For others (like Sir Alan Herbert, for example), the appointment of a royal commission or a departmental committee is *prima facie* evidence of a failure to govern. Government departments, he argues, are supposed to be expert in

---

3 H. M. Clokie and J. W. Robinson, *Royal Commissions of Inquiry* (Stanford University Press, 1937); and C. J. Hanser, *Guide to Decision: the Royal Commission* (Totowa, N. J.: Bedminster Press, 1965).

4 J. Toulmin Smith, *Government by Commissions Illegal and Pernicious* (London: Sweet, 1849); R. V. Vernon and Nicholas Mansergh (eds.), *Advisory Bodies* (London: Allen and Unwin, 1940); and K. C. Wheare, *Government by Committee* (London: Oxford University Press, 1955).

5 See, for example, W. H. Moore, 'Executive Commissions of Inquiry', *Columbia Law Review*, XIII (June 1913), pp. 500–23; H. F. Gosnell, 'British Royal Commissions of Inquiry', *Political Science Quarterly*, XLIX (March 1934), pp. 84–118; Watson Sellar, 'A Century of Commissions of Inquiry', *Canadian Bar Review*, XXV (1947), pp. 1–28; R. M Jackson, 'Royal Commissions and Committees of Inquiry', *The Listener* (14 April 1956), pp. 388–9; A. P. Herbert, 'Anything but Action? A Study of the Uses and Abuses of Committees of Inquiry', in Ralph Harris (ed.), *Radical Reaction: Essays in Competition and Affluence*, 2nd (rev.) ed. (London: Hutchinson, 1961); Eric Lubbock, 'Have Royal Commissions Had Their Day?' *The Times* (13 December 1966); David Donnison, 'Committees and Committeemen', *New Society* (18 April 1968), pp. 558–61; and William Plowden, 'An Anatomy of Commissions', *New Society* (15 July 1971), pp. 104–7.

6 Hanser, *op. cit.*, p. 221.

their respective areas of responsibility; they are 'full of men who are paid to know, or to find out, what is for the best'.

> When, therefore, they [the departments] set up committees and commissions of private citizens, who are *not* paid to do any such thing, to ascertain and report what is for the best, may there not be something wrong? Have our rulers failed in capacity, or in energy and duty? Or are there some tasks which Parliament, with all its powers and committees, Whitehall with all its ministers and civil servants, cannot be fairly expected to do without private, unpaid, assistance from outside?[7]

This debate between supporters and opponents of royal commissions and departmental committees has been focussed largely on two basic questions: Why are these committees appointed? and What effects do they have? Supporters tend to argue that most royal commissions and departmental committees are appointed for good and sufficient reasons and that, in some cases at least, they have a significant effect on the outcome of the policy-making process. Opponents, on the other hand, tend to argue that royal commissions and departmental committees are usually appointed for some essentially 'political' or otherwise improper reason and that they rarely have any real effect on decisions made by the government. In fact, of course, evidence can usually be found to support both points of view. For the true cause and effect of a royal commission or a departmental committee – as, indeed, of any political event – is always problematical, always open to different interpretations, and always a matter for debate.

The Present Study

The implication of the foregoing argument is that the focus of traditional debate about royal commissions and departmental committees may be somewhat misplaced. The reasons why royal commissions and departmental committees are appointed and the effects they have are important questions, of course, and need to be examined and discussed (as they are in some of the chapters below). But the fact that these questions are ultimately irresolvable suggests that there may be some more profitable line of inquiry.

Thus the present study takes a somewhat different approach. Questions of cause and effect are not ignored, but they do not enjoy the central place which others have accorded them. The main purpose of the present study is neither to praise nor to condemn royal commissions and departmental committees: rather it is to describe how they work. From this description, however, emerge three important characteristics which instead form the basic themes for this study. These are: 1 that royal commissions and departmental committees constitute a unique but ubiquitous institution of government;

---

7 A. P. Herbert 'Anything but Action?', *op cit.*, p. 263; see also his poem about the 'Royal Commission on Kissing', 'Sad Fate of a Royal Commission', in *Mild and Bitter* (London: Methuen, 1936).

2 that, as such, they demonstrate a quite remarkable degree of flexibility and adaptiveness; and 3 that they provide a unique kind of mechanism for public participation in government.

Royal commissions and departmental committees form a unique institution of government for two reasons. First of all, royal commissions and departmental committees are distinct from all other kinds of committees in government. No other committees are *ad hoc* advisory committees appointed by the Crown or its ministers by virtue of non-statutory powers. Secondly, royal commissions are similar to departmental committees in all important respects. What differences there are turn out, upon examination, to be either differences merely of degree or, if differences of kind, then of little significant kind nowadays. Together, therefore, royal commissions and departmental committees constitute what is a unique institution of government.

A study of royal commissions and departmental committees in Britain is a study of the major issues of public policy. Almost all important subjects of government concern – and some others besides – have been examined at one time or another by a royal commission or a departmental committee. From the maintenance of lighthouses to the slaughter of horses, from nuclear physics to public health and welfare, royal commissions and departmental committees have ranged over the entire spectrum of government responsibilities. Examples of their use can be traced back nearly a thousand years; their subsequent history has reflected the broader political and constitutional development of the British system of government. The frequency of their use, especially over the past century, testifies to a belief in their importance and their usefulness. Few other institutions of government have enjoyed such consistent or such widespread popularity. Royal commissions and departmental committees are only one of many different institutions involved in the formation of public policy in Britain, of course, but they are a ubiquitous one.

The second main theme of this study is based on the fact that royal commissions and departmental committees are not *bureaucratic* forms of organisation. Bureaucracy, in government as elsewhere, is essentially a structured set of responses to a number of preconceived challenges.[8] In other words, bureaucracy is based ultimately on stereotypes. It is these assumptions about its environment that are in turn the basis for the success and efficiency of bureaucracies – but only as long as those assumptions conform to reality, only as long as the challenges a bureaucracy *actually* faces correspond to those it was *designed* to face. When that relationship changes, a bureaucracy's source of strength becomes a source of weakness. For a bureaucracy is ill-equipped to cope with a 'new' kind of challenge, except by forcing it into the mould of the kind it knows how to deal with.

Thus, there is an inherent dilemma in designing bureaucracies. The more

8 Max Weber, *The Theory of Social and Economic Organization*, ed. A. M. Henderson and T. Parsons (New York: Free Press, 1947), pp. 328–40, is the classic reference; but see also Michel Crozier, *The Bureaucratic Phenomenon* (London: Tavistock Publications, 1964).

closely a bureaucracy is tailored to responding to a specific kind of challenge, the more efficient it can be but the less able it will be to deal with other kinds of challenges. On the other hand, the more a bureaucracy is designed to be able to respond to challenges on a broad front, the less it can be tailored to meeting one specific kind of challenge with maximum efficiency. A bureaucracy, rather like a suit of clothes, may fit better if it is 'made to measure'; but one which is 'ready made' is likely to fit a wider variety of cases.

If an organisation faces a rapidly changing environment or if it is likely to face a lot of different kinds of challenges, then this dilemma can be a serious one. One way to reduce the risks involved is to design a form of organisation which does not depend on environmental stability to the same extent as does a bureaucracy. Such an organisation would deliberately be made flexible enough to be adapted – or, better still, to be able to adapt itself – to a variety of different kinds of challenges from its environment. Organisations of this kind may be said to be *adaptable* or, if the capacity is inherent in the organisation itself, *adaptive* in nature.

One of the main themes of this study is that royal commissions and departmental committees embody precisely this sort of flexibility as an institution of government. Their adaptability and even adaptiveness are reflected not only in their structure but also at every step of their operation – in fact, from the moment they are first conceived and discussed in government circles and outside until the final report of the committee is delivered to the minister or ministers who appointed it. To show the extent to which this is so is the second main theme of this study.

The last major theme of this study has to do with what is usually referred to as the participation of the governed in their government. Participation seems to form an increasingly important part of contemporary discussions of democracy.[9] In general, two different kinds of arguments seem to be advanced in support of participation. One is that participation should be conceived as an end in itself. According to this view, participation is an essential part of a democratic system of government. The other argument is that participation need be conceived only as a means to other ends. Thus, participation is not necessarily essential in a democracy, but it may be (and usually is) useful for certain purposes (such as arousing public interest, getting information, promoting agreement on what to do, and so on); moreover, its usefulness for any such purpose may well vary from one situation to another. Either as an end in itself or as a means to other ends, therefore, participation is to a greater or lesser degree a feature of most democracies.

Public participation in government in Britain already occurs in a variety of ways. A private individual can participate either on his own or as the member of an organised interest group of some kind. He can participate by

9 As even one of the committees within the scope of this study illustrates: see the report of the Skeffington Committee, *People and Planning* (London: HMSO, 1969). See also Carole Pateman, *Participation and Democratic Theory* (Cambridge University Press, 1970).

taking an active role in the electoral process; by lobbying his Member of Parliament, a minister or a civil servant; by taking on some appointed public office; and in other ways as well. The issue, therefore, is not whether to have participation, but rather the nature of the mechanisms through which it can and should occur.

Royal commissions and departmental committees offer a unique mechanism for public participation in British government. At no other point in the political process is there a comparable opportunity for private individuals or interest groups to take part in the making of public policy. To show how this opportunity is built into both the structure and the operation of royal commissions and departmental committees is the third main theme of the present study.

These three themes are reflected in the organisation of this study. The next two chapters are devoted to establishing the uniqueness (Chapter 2) and the popularity (Chapter 3) of royal commissions and departmental committees. (The first of the appendices describes some of the difficulties involved in obtaining accurate historical data.) The next eight chapters form the central part of the study, which amounts to a detailed analysis of 358 of the most important committees appointed between the beginning of 1945 and the end of 1969. (The data on these committees are summarised in the second appendix, and brought up to the present date in the third appendix.) The analysis covers the appointment of these committees (Chapter 4), their membership (Chapter 5), their terms of reference (Chapter 6), their procedures (Chapter 7), their evidence (Chapter 8), their research (Chapter 9), their reports (Chapter 10), and their adjournment (Chapter 11). Finally, Chapter 12 concludes the study by describing some of the strengths and weaknesses of this unique institution, and – rather like a report of the very committees it has been examining – makes a few recommendations of its own.[10]

Government today, not only in Britain but in other countries as well, faces growing demands for more effective government and also for greater participation in it.[11] Some institutions are criticised for not providing good government, others for not providing open government. Royal commissions and departmental committees have the advantage of being able to provide both. Undoubtedly it is this which has contributed most to their consistent popularity in the past and which will ensure their continued use in the years to come.

10 Throughout this study, reports of committees are identified only by their Command numbers or (in the case of reports not published as Command papers) by the year in which they were published. Further information can be found in the Appendices, which list most of the royal commissions and major departmental committees appointed since 1945 in order of their Command numbers.
11 A. H. Hanson, 'Public Administration and the Social Order in Twentieth-Century Britain' in *Planning and the Politician, and Other Essays* (London: Routledge and Kegan Paul, 1969).

2
A Unique Institution of Government

One of the distinguishing features of any political system is the way in which it is organised into different kinds of institutions. Among the institutions of government in Britain are various kinds of committees, and among these various committees are some which are called royal commissions and some which are called departmental committees. These royal commissions and departmental committees, it is argued, constitute a unique institution of government.

To establish the uniqueness of royal commissions and departmental committees means showing first that they are distinct from all other kinds of committees and then that they are similar to each other in all important respects. The key step in this argument is to classify all the various kinds of committees found in British government.

Committees in Government

Government nowadays appoints a great many committees, and their abundance makes the task of classifying them as difficult as it is important.[1] There are obviously several different ways of attacking the problem; however, the most generally accepted system of classification is one based on the question of who appoints the committee. Seven different persons or bodies are commonly said to appoint committees in British government. These are:

a Parliament
b the Privy Council

1 For a discussion of the meaning of the word 'committee', see K. C. Wheare, *Government by Committee* (London: Oxford University Press, 1955), Chapter 1; and W. J. M. Mackenzie, 'Committees in Administration', *Public Administration*, XXXI (1953), pp. 235–44. The major point of controversy about the definition of a committee seems to be over its minimum size, Wheare arguing for two members and Mackenzie for three. Whatever the general merits of each position may be, the fact remains that there are committees of one appointed in government; so no lower limit on the size of a committee has been assumed in this study.

c the Cabinet
d the Crown
e ministers (including their departmental officials)
f non-departmental organisations of various kinds, and
g local authorities

In a sense it may be argued that some of these distinctions are artificial, since it is 'really' the Cabinet which appoints Crown and Privy Council committees, for example, and the Chief Whip who 'really' appoints Parliamentary committees. Nevertheless, the formal distinction remains, and it provides a convenient and widely accepted basis for classifying committees in government.

Reference here is to committees in *British* government only. No attempt has been made to deal with committees appointed by any other government, including governments devolving from or dependent upon Westminster (such as the government of Northern Ireland, colonial or territorial governments). In particular, Irish Vice-Regal Commissions, which were appointed (until 1922) by the Lord-Lieutenant of Ireland as representative of the Crown, are not included.[2] Secondly, two Australian royal commissions, one on the 1904 Navigation Bill and the other on Old-Age Pensions in 1905, were published as British Parliamentary Papers, but they are not included here since they were appointed by the Australian government.[3] At the same time, it must be remembered that the British government has appointed committees which dealt wholly or partly with matters pertaining to Ireland, Australia or other countries; however, these committees are still British government committees.

Of all the committees in British government, Parliamentary committees are the only ones not appointed by the executive branch. The most familiar Parliamentary committees are probably the select and standing committees appointed each session by the House of Commons, but the House of Lords also appoints similar committees. All of them, including joint committees of both Houses, are formally appointed by means of a simple resolution of the respective chambers.[4] There is also a special kind of committee chaired by the Speaker of the House of Commons, called a Speaker's Conference,

---

2 Details of Irish Vice-Regal Commissions since 1900 are given in David Butler, *British Political Facts, 1900–1968*, 3rd ed. (London: Macmillan, 1969), p. 180.

3 See the reports of these committees (Cd. 3023 and Cd. 3341 respectively).

4 See Lord Campion, *The Procedure of the House of Commons*, 3rd ed. (London: Macmillan, 1958), Chapter 7; and Eric Taylor, *The House of Commons at Work*, 6th ed. (Harmondsworth: Penguin, 1967), Chapter 5. There is no recent study of Parliamentary committees in general, but there have been two excellent case-studies: David Coombes, *The Member of Parliament and the Administration: the Case of the Select Committee on Nationalised Industries* (London: Allen and Unwin, 1966); and Nevil Johnson, *Parliament and Administration: the Estimates Committee, 1945–65* (London: Allen and Unwin, 1966). On standing committees, see C. B. Koester, 'Standing Committees in the British House of Commons', *The Parliamentarian*, XLIX 2 (April 1968), pp. 64–72.

which comes into existence upon an announcement by Mr Speaker acting at the request of the Prime Minister.[5]

Parliament may also appoint committees by means of an Act of Parliament. Most committees appointed under an Act of Parliament are, in fact, only indirectly Parliamentary in nature, inasmuch as Parliament usually passes enabling legislation which (as will be discussed below) permits or requires the Crown, a minister, a non-departmental organisation or a local authority to appoint a committee. Occasionally, however, Parliament does appoint committees directly by statute. Two such committees deserve special mention, since they are sometimes confused with royal commissions. These are the committees appointed by the Special Commissions (Dardanelles and Mesopotamia) Act, 1916 'to inquire into the origin, inception and conduct of war' in the Dardanelles and in Mesopotamia respectively.[6] Committees like these, however, are very rare.

Committees appointed by the Privy Council are now largely of historical interest but there have been a few important ones since the war.[7] Two of these dealt with matters concerning the constitutional status of the Channel Islands, and another with the procedures authorised for interrogating suspected terrorists.[8] It should be noted, however, that not all committees composed of Privy Councillors are in fact committees of (i.e. appointed by) the Privy Council – just as a committee composed of professors, for instance, need not be appointed by a university. Thus, the Prime Minister appointed two Committees of Privy Councillors in the mid-1950's to deal with certain questions affecting national security.[9]

5 See Nicholas Mansergh, 'The Use of Advisory Bodies in the Reform of the Machinery of Government', in R. V. Vernon and Nicholas Mansergh, eds., *Advisory Bodies* (London: Allen and Unwin, 1940), pp. 31–85, for a discussion of some prewar Speaker's Conferences. See also the final report of the last Conference (Cmnd. 3550).

6 6 & 7 Geo. V, Chapter 34. The standard work on royal commissions, H. M. Clokie and J. W. Robinson, *Royal Commissions of Inquiry* (Stanford University Press, 1937), confuses these special commissions with royal commissions; and even the official *General Index to Parliamentary Papers, 1900 to 1948–9* (London: HMSO, 1960) lists the Dardanelles Commission report (Cmd. 371) as that of a 'Commission' and the Mesopotamia Commission report (Cd. 8610) as that of a 'Royal Commission'.

7 Of particular historical interest is the Privy Council Committee for Trade and Foreign Plantations (later the Board of Trade), appointed by Order-in-Council on 23 August 1786 and which last met 'as a collective entity' on 23 December 1850. Since that time (according to one former President of the Board of Trade), 'The Board of Trade does meet. The quorum consists of one person – myself' (quoted in Roger Prouty, *The Transformation of the Board of Trade, 1830–1855* (London: Heinemann, 1957), pp. 107–8). Another important Privy Council committee was the Judicial Committee, which played a significant part in the constitutional evolution of the Empire; see, for example, G. P. Browne, *The Judicial Committee and the British North America Act* (University of Toronto Press, 1967).

8 They were committees under the chairmanship of James Chuter Ede on Proposed Reforms in the Channel Islands (Cmd. 7074) and on the Island of Alderney (Cmd. 7805), and the recent Committee (Cmnd. 4901) under Lord Parker of Waddington.

9 They were the Salisbury Committee on Security (Cmd. 9715) and the Birkett Committee on the Interception of Communications (Cmnd. 283).

Not much information is available on committees appointed by the Cabinet. Details of their existence remain, like the operations of the Cabinet generally, a matter of secrecy. There appear to be at least two kinds of Cabinet committees: standing committees, which deal with continuing issues like defence or foreign affairs, and *ad hoc* committees, which deal with specific matters of temporary concern.[10] It should be noted that Cabinet committees are appointed by the Cabinet itself, not by the Crown or an individual minister on behalf of the Cabinet.

Before dealing with committees appointed by the Crown and by ministers, it is worth looking briefly at committees appointed by non-departmental organisations and by local authorities. The line between departments of the central government and non-departmental organisations is not always clear, but departments are normally defined as those bodies for which a minister has 'full and direct responsibility to an elected body, usually Parliament'.[11] Thus, committees appointed by non-departmental organisations would include committees appointed by bodies such as the Agricultural Research Council, the Council for Wales and Monmouthshire, the Medical Research Council, the National Parks Commission, and so on.[12] They would also include committees appointed by nationalised industries. For example, the Advisory Committee on the Organisation of the National Coal Board, under the chairmanship of Sir Alexander Fleck, was appointed by the National Coal Board in 1953.[13]

Committees are also appointed by local authorities, by either elected or appointed officials pursuant to their respective powers and duties.[14] Committees of local authorities may be standing or *ad hoc* in nature and may

10 There are several general studies of the Cabinet which touch upon its committee system, including Hans Daalder, *Cabinet Reform in Britain, 1914–1963* (Stanford University Press, 1963); J. P. Mackintosh, *The British Cabinet*, 2nd ed. (London: Stevens and Sons, 1968); and Patrick Gordon Walker, *The Cabinet* (London: Jonathan Cape, 1970). For the evolution of one particular (standing) committee of Cabinet, see F. A. Johnson, *Defence by Committee: The British Committee of Imperial Defence, 1885–1959* (London: Oxford University Press, 1960).

11 D. N. Chester, 'Public Corporations and the Classification of Administrative Bodies', *Political Studies*, 1 (1953), pp. 34–52.

12 Some of these are described in Political and Economic Planning, 'Government by Appointment', *P.E.P.*, XXVI 443 (25 July 1960), pp. 207–25; reprinted in W. J. Stankiewicz (ed.), *Crisis in British Government* (London: Collier-Macmillan, 1967), pp. 282–300.

13 See J. R. Nelson, 'The Fleck Report and the Area Organisation of the National Coal Board', *Public Administration*, XLIII (1965), pp. 41–57.

14 In general, see R. M. Jackson, *The Machinery of Local Government*, 2nd ed. (London: Macmillan, 1965), Chapter 5. More specifically, see L. Hagestadt, 'Local Advisory Committees', *Public Administration*, XXX (1952), pp. 215–19; Enid Harrison, 'Local Advisory Committees', *Public Administration*, XXXI (1953), pp. 65–75; Peter Hutchison, 'The Committee System in East Suffolk', *Public Administration*, XXXVIII (1959), pp. 393–402; and R. Greenwood *et al.*, 'Recent Changes in the Internal Organisation of County Boroughs; Part I: Committees', *Public Administration*, 48 (1970), pp. 151–67.

include selected or appointed officials (or both) as well as members of the general public in some cases.

Finally, there are committees appointed by the Crown and committees appointed by ministers or their departmental officials. Both Crown and ministerial committees are normally divided into three kinds, depending on the nature of the relationship between the committee and the body or bodies which appoint it. These three kinds are called internal committees, tribunals and external or (more commonly) advisory committees.

Although there is fairly general agreement on these distinctions, their precise nature is not so clear.[15] The main element in the difference between internal and advisory committees arises out of their membership. As Professor K. C. Wheare has pointed out,

> ... although committees are often composed of a selection from the members of a larger body, they need not be so composed. It is true that committees of the House of Commons do in fact consist only of members of that House; the same is true usually, but not always, of committees set up by town and county councils. But committees or commissions may be appointed by ministers or ... by the sovereign ... and in these cases their members may be chosen from a variety of places.[16]

To be more precise, members of Crown and ministerial committees may come from either inside or outside the Civil Service.[17] In general, internal committees consist of civil servants, while advisory committees draw their members wholly or partly from outside the Civil Service.

However, there are exceptions to this rule, and it is necessary to look at the nature of the activities and recommendations of a committee as well. Internal committees are essentially the private affairs of the bodies which appoint them; whereas advisory committees can be announced with fanfare, can hear evidence in public sessions, can take part in open debate, and can issue detailed public reports of their findings and recommendations. Another related difference between internal and advisory committees lies in the

15 Both Vernon and Mansergh, *op. cit.*, and Political and Economic Planning, *Advisory Committees in British Government* (London: Allen and Unwin, 1960), make this distinction; however, the first includes two Speaker's Conferences (see pp. 55ff.) and the second (in spite of its title) proceeds to limit itself to 'standing advisory committees' (see pp. xi–xii).

16 Wheare, *op. cit.*, p. 9.

17 There is no official definition of the Civil Service, but it is normally held to include '... servants of the Crown, other than holders of political or judicial office, who are employed in a civil capacity and whose remuneration is paid wholly and directly out of moneys voted by Parliament'. This is the definition which was proposed originally by the Tomlin Royal Commission on the Civil Service (Cmd. 3909) in 1929–31: it was subsequently adopted by both the Priestley Royal Commission on the Civil Service (Cmd. 9613) and the Fulton Committee on the Civil Service (Cmd. 3638). See also W. J. M. Mackenzie, 'The Civil Service, the State and the Establishment', in Bernard Crick (ed.), *Essays on Reform, 1967: a Centenary Tribute* (London: Oxford University Press, 1967), pp. 182–202. The membership of committees is discussed in Chapter 5 below.

responsibility of ministers for these committees. Ministers have consistently refused in Parliament to be bound by the findings of advisory committees, whereas ministers are responsible for internal committees in the same way that they are for individual civil servants.[18]

Tribunals are similar to advisory committees in some respects and like internal committees in others. Like advisory committees, tribunals operate essentially outside the regular machinery of Whitehall; their members are often from outside the Civil Service and their existence and operations are a matter of public record. However, tribunals, unlike advisory committees, may have powers to make decisions; thus, ministers cannot in Parliament disclaim all responsibility for the actions of tribunals. In this respect, they are closer to internal committees than to advisory committees. Tribunals are by definition statutory committees, but they may be either standing committees (in which case they are usually called administrative tribunals) or *ad hoc* committees (sometimes called Tribunals of Inquiry).[19]

Committees in government, therefore, are of seven principal kinds, depending on the nature of the body or bodies formally appointing them. Table 2.1 shows the various kinds of committees in summary form. Royal commissions are appointed by the Crown and departmental committees are appointed by ministers; so they are different from Parliamentary committees, Privy Council committees, Cabinet committees, committees of non-departmental organisations, and committees of local authorities. Royal commissions and departmental committees are also both advisory committees in the sense described here; they are not internal committees or tribunals. This means that their members are normally drawn from outside the Civil Service, that they usually conduct their activities openly and issue public reports of their findings, and that ministers are not responsible for and need not accept their recommendations. As such, royal commissions and departmental committees are different from the other committees discussed so far.

18 See Chapter 11 below for a discussion of ministerial reactions to reports of royal commissions and departmental committees. On ministerial responsibility in general, see Geoffrey Marshall and G. C. Moodie, *Some Problems of the Constitution*, 3rd ed. (London: Hutchinson, 1964), Chapters 3, 4, 5 and 8. Very little has been written about the working of internal committees in central government. There are very brief descriptions in some of the general studies of the civil service (e.g. T. A. Critchley, *The Civil Service Today* (London: Gollancz, 1951), and G. A. Campbell, *The Civil Service in Britain* (Harmondsworth: Penguin, 1955)). But the most useful information is still to be found in case-studies, such as those in the two volumes by F. M. G. Willson and Gerald Rhodes respectively, *Administrators in Action* (London: Allen and Unwin, 1961 and 1965).

19 See R. W. S. Pollard, *Administrative Tribunals at Work* (London: Stevens, 1950); and H. J Elcock, *Administrative Justice* (London: Longman, 1969), who describes the workings of a number of administrative tribunals as well as the role of the Council on Tribunals, which was established under the Tribunals and Inquiries Act, 1958 (6 & 7 Eliz. II, Chapter 66). See also N. D. Vandyck, *Tribunals and Inquiries* (London: Oyez Publications, 1965), for a guide to the procedure of 'over 2,000 administrative tribunals'. Tribunals of Inquiry are appointed under the Tribunals of Inquiry (Evidence) Act, 1921 (11 Geo. V, Chapter 7).

Table 2.1 The principal kinds of committees in British government

Parliamentary committees	Committees of the House of Commons*	Standing committees Select committees Speaker's Conferences
	Committees of the House of Lords*	Standing committees Select committees
	Statutory Parliamentary committees	
Committees of the Privy Council	Standing committees *Ad hoc* committees	
Cabinet Committees	Standing committees *Ad hoc* committees	
Committees appointed by the Crown	Internal committees Tribunals of Inquiry Advisory committees (see fig. 2.1)	
Committees appointed by ministers	Internal committees	Standing committees *Ad hoc* committees
	Tribunals	Administrative tribunals Tribunals of Inquiry
	Advisory committees (see fig. 2.1)	
Committees of non-departmental organisations	Standing committees *Ad hoc* committees	
Committees appointed by local authorities	Committees of Council	Standing committees *Ad hoc* committees
	Other local committees	Standing committees *Ad hoc* committees

* Joint Parliamentary committees are appointed separately by both Houses.

Advisory Committees

Although royal commissions and departmental committees are both advisory committees, they are not the only kinds of advisory committees. Thus, some further distinctions are necessary in order to demonstrate that royal commissions and departmental committees are *sui generis*. As before, there are various possible ways of classifying advisory committees, but custom and convenience suggest two basic criteria:

a the nature of the power by virtue of which a committee is appointed, and
b the duration of its mandate.

The first criterion for classifying advisory committees lies in the nature of the power by virtue of which they are appointed. Broadly speaking, such power can come from one of two possible sources: either it may be granted by Parliament (by means of an Act) or it may derive from royal prerogative (in the case of the Crown) or convention (in the case of ministers).[20] Statutory powers may be further divided into those which authorise the appointment of an unspecified number of committees of a general kind and those which authorise the appointment of a specific committee.

One further observation should be made. Statutory power to appoint a committee can be either mandatory or discretionary. This leads to something of a paradox, however, since statutory authority to appoint a committee is, strictly speaking, redundant when that power is merely discretionary. Neither the Crown nor a minister actually needs this power, for their own prerogative and conventional powers are adequate to any occasion. Professor W. A. Robson has called this 'one of the most curious features of British constitutional practice'. He goes on to say that it

> cannot be explained by saying that statutory authorisation is necessary . . . [to] enforce the attendance of witnesses, [to] examine them on oath, or to compel the attendance of witnesses; for by no means all legislation which provides for [statutory] inquiries confers these powers, though much of it does. Nor can it be explained by saying that statutory enactment is passed in order to impose a duty on a Minister . . . For many of the enactments are permissive and do not impose a duty. There appears, indeed, to be no logical distinction between the statutory and the non-statutory inquiry.[21]

20 A. B. Keith, *The British Cabinet System* (London: Stevens and Sons, 1952), stresses the constitutional freedom of ministers to seek advice from any quarter (p. 156). On the meaning and significance of conventional powers in general, see K. C. Wheare, *Modern Constitutions*, 2nd ed. (London: Oxford University Press, 1966), Chapter 8, and Marshall and Moodie, *op. cit.*, Chapter 2. Both prerogative and conventional powers to appoint advisory committees have been challenged at various times in the past, but it would be hard to sustain such an argument nowadays (see Chapter 12 below).

21 W. A. Robson, 'Public Inquiries as an Instrument of Government', *British Journal of Administrative Law* (now *Public Law*), I (1954), pp. 79–80.

In spite of these logical difficulties, however, there is a clear and useful distinction to be made between advisory committees appointed under statutory powers (be they general or specific) and those appointed under non-statutory powers.

The second criterion for classifying advisory committees, the duration of the mandate, refers to its expected life-span. On the one hand, an advisory committee may be appointed to deal on a continuing basis with such matters, usually within some general category, as may be referred to it from time to time. This kind of advisory committee is usually called a standing committee. On the other hand, an advisory committee may be appointed for a limited and temporary purpose. This purpose (which may range from the very narrow to the very broad) is put before the committee when it is appointed; when it has accomplished this purpose, the committee ceases to exist *ipso facto* (unless a new mandate is issued reappointing the committee). This kind of advisory committee is usually called an *ad hoc* committee.

It should be added that the distinction between standing and *ad hoc* committees is not based on the actual length of time for which a committee is in existence, with the more long-lived ones being called standing and the more short-lived ones *ad hoc*. Although this is the pattern which usually occurs, it is not always true. Some standing committees have been disbanded after a relatively short period of time, and some *ad hoc* committees have taken years to complete their inquiries. The distinction between the two lies rather in the fact that a standing committee tends to have specific tasks referred to it from time to time, so that its adjournment requires an explicit act, whereas an *ad hoc* committee is appointed for a limited and temporary purpose and automatically comes to an end when that purpose is accomplished. Advisory committees, therefore, are

> divisible into two classes – standing and non-standing [or *ad hoc*]. The former exist to offer advice on some subject as it develops, either at regular or irregular intervals, and are appointed either for some stated length of time or until they are explicitly dissolved. The latter, on the other hand, exist for the purpose of making a single report (though it may not, of course, be issued all at one time) and automatically dissolve whenever that report is presented.[22]

Advisory committees appointed by the Crown or by ministers may, therefore, be divided into those which are standing committees and those which are *ad hoc* committees; and also into those which are appointed by virtue of statutory powers (which may be either specific or general in their authorisation) and those which are appointed by prerogative or conventional powers. Combining these two distinctions yields six different types of advisory committees (see Figure 2.1):

22 A. J. Brown, 'The Use of Advisory Bodies by the Treasury' in Vernon and Mansergh, *op. cit.*, p. 89. The duration of royal commissions and departmental committees, as well as the manner of their adjournment, is discussed in detail in Chapter 11 below.

Figure 2.1 A typology of advisory committees

| | Committees appointed by virtue of statutory powers | | Committees appointed by virtue of prerogative or conventional powers |
	general powers	*specific powers*	
Standing committees	Ia	Ib	II
Ad hoc committees	IIIa	IIIb	IV

Types I and II: Standing (advisory) committees
Type III: Statutory or public inquiries
Type IV: Royal commissions and departmental committees

Ia   standing committees appointed by virtue of general statutory powers.
Ib   standing committees appointed by virtue of specific statutory powers.
II   standing committees appointed by virtue of prerogative or conventional powers.
IIIa *ad hoc* committees appointed by virtue of general statutory powers.
IIIb *ad hoc* committees appointed by virtue of specific statutory powers.
IV   *ad hoc* committees appointed by virtue of prerogative or conventional powers.

In practice, advisory committees of Types I and II are usually referred to as standing advisory committees or just standing committees. Similarly, committees of Type III may be called statutory advisory committees; however, the more common practice is to call those of Type IIIa statutory or public inquiries and those of Type IIIb administrative tribunals. Finally, advisory committees of Type IV are called royal commissions if they are appointed by the Crown and departmental committees if they are appointed by ministers.

With this typology, advisory committees appointed by the Crown are relatively easy to classify. Almost all of them are of a single type (Type IV); that is to say, most Crown advisory committees are royal commissions. The exceptions are largely of Type II, although there have also been a few of Type III.[23] Since the turn of the century, however, the total number of these exceptions is only seventeen (see Table 2.2).

Thirteen of these exceptions have been standing committees appointed by

23 Some would argue that these exceptions should also be classified as royal commissions since they are always called 'Royal Commissions' and because their appointment is by means of a royal act which may be termed a commission. This seems to be the position adopted by C. J. Hanser, *op. cit.*, although Hanser distinguishes Type II Crown committees as 'semi-permanent' or 'operating' commissions. On the other hand, commissions are issued by the Crown for many other purposes besides the appointment of committees; see W. R. Anson, *Law and Custom of the Constitution*, Volume 2, 4th ed. by A. B. Keith (London: Oxford University Press, 1935), pp. 62–72 and Appendices 2 and 3. Thus, Clokie and Robinson, *op. cit.*, refer (as we do) only to Type IV committees when they talk of royal commissions.

Table 2.2 Advisory committees appointed by the Crown since 1900, excluding royal commissions (Type IV)

committee	type	date of appointment	date of adjournment	report
Property of the Free Church of Scotland	IIIb	Aug 1905	Feb 1910	Cd. 5060
Election in Worcester in 1906	IIIa	Jul 1906	Nov 1906	Cd. 3268
Ancient and Historical Monuments and Constructions of Scotland	II	Feb 1908		Cmnd. 4808
Ancient Monuments and Constructions of Wales and Monmouthshire	II	Aug 1908		Cmnd. 2551
Ancient and Historical Monuments and Constructions of England	II	Oct 1908		Cmnd. 5578
Supply of Sugar	II	Aug 1914	Apr 1921	Cmd. 1300
Defence of the Realm Losses	II	Mar 1915	Nov 1920	Cmd. 1044
Supply of Paper	II	Feb 1916	Feb 1918	—
Supply of Wheat	II	Oct 1916	Jul 1925	Cmd. 2462
Awards to Investors	II	Mar 1919	Nov 1937	Cmd. 5594
Coal Industry	IIIb	Apr 1919	Jun 1919	Cmd. 360
Compensation for Suffering and Damage by Enemy Action	II	Aug 1921	Feb 1924	Cmnd. 2066
Fine Art	II	May 1924		Cmnd. 4832
Fine Art for Scotland	II	Aug 1927		Cmnd. 5343
Indian Government	IIIb	Nov 1927	May 1930	Cmd. 3568
Awards to Investors	II	May 1946	Apr 1956	Cmd. 9744
Environmental Pollution	II	Feb 1970		Cmnd. 5054

Note: Absence of adjournment date means that the committee is still in existence; in these cases, the report shown is the last issued. A dash indicates that no report was issued.

Source: Reports of the various committees; for the Royal Commission on the Supply of Paper, see *House of Commons Debates*, 21 February 1916 and 21 February 1918.

virtue of the royal prerogative (Type II). Six of them are still in existence, along with two left over from the previous century (the Royal Commission on the Exhibition of 1851, appointed in January 1850, and the Royal Commission on Historical Manuscripts, appointed in 1869). The seven which have been dissolved were all associated in one way or another with the two World Wars. Three were appointed during the First War to manage the scarce resources of sugar, paper and wheat in Britain; naturally these came to an end once the shortages of wartime had disappeared and an international market had been re-established.[24] The other four committees were appointed to award compensation for war-time losses and inventions, three for the

24 See the reports of the Commissions on Sugar (Cmd. 1300) and on Wheat (Cmd. 2462). The Paper Commission, which started life as a regular royal commission but was then invited to administer the Paper Restriction (Posters and Circulars) Order, never issued any report; see *House of Commons Debates* for 21 February 1916 and 21 February 1918.

period of the First War and one for the period of the Second. The Defence of the Realm Losses Commission, appointed in 1915, was reconstituted in 1920 as the War Compensation Court; the other three came to a natural end following the imposition of a deadline for the claims which the committees had each been appointed to hear.[25] The six Crown-appointed standing committees still in existence deal with ancient monuments, fine arts and environmental pollution.[26] Finally, the present Labour government is reported to be considering the appointment of two more similar committees, one on the distribution of income and another on corruption in business and public life.

The other group of Crown advisory committees which are not classified as royal commissions are *ad hoc* rather than standing committees but are appointed by virtue of statutory rather than prerogative powers (Type III). Only four such committees have been appointed since 1900 (and none since 1927), three of them by means of specific statutory powers and one by means of general statutory powers. The three commissions specifically appointed by statute were: a commission appointed under the Churches (Scotland) Act, 1905, to divide the property of the Free Church of Scotland between the Free Church and the new United Free Church;[27] the well-known Sankey Commission, appointed under the Coal Industry Commission Act, 1919, which provided that

> His Majesty shall have power to appoint Commissioners, consisting of a chairman, who shall be a judge of the Supreme Court, a vice-chairman, and such other persons as His Majesty may think fit, for the purpose of inquiring into the position of, and conditions prevailing in, the coal industry . . .;[28]

and the Indian Statutory Commission chaired by Sir John Simon, which was provided for in the Government of India Act, 1915, when, after a period of ten years from the entering into force of the Act, the King was empowered to 'approve a commission proposed by the Secretary of State [for India]'.[29] The fourth statutory *ad hoc* committee appointed by the Crown was appointed

---

25 The War Compensation Court was established under the Indemnity Act, 1920 (10 & 11 Geo. V, Chapter 48); while the deadlines on claims for compensation or awards were imposed by supplementary royal warrants (see the Commissions' final reports, Cmd. 2066, Cmd. 5594 and Cmd. 9744 respectively).

26 For a brief description of the work of the Fine Arts Commissions, see E. N. Gladden, *British Public Service Administration* (London: Staples Press, 1961), pp. 198ff. The Scottish Commission did not issue its first report (Cmnd. 982) until February 1960, more than thirty years after its appointment.

27 5 Edw. VII, Chapter 12. The royal warrant of appointment is reproduced in the Commission report (Cd. 5060).

28 9 Geo. V, Chapter 1. See also the report of the Commission (Cmd. 360). Note that the subsequent Samuel Commission on the Coal Industry was appointed by virtue of prerogative power (Type IV); see the report of that Commission (Cmd. 2600).

29 5 & 6 Geo. V, Chapter 61, Section 84A, as amended. See the report of the Commission (Cmd. 3568).

under the provisions of a general statute. This was the Royal Commission on the Election in Worcester in 1906, the last of a series of committees appointed under the Election Commissioners Acts, 1842–1949, for the purpose of investigating allegations of extensive electoral irregularities.[30]

There is one more Crown committee which might appear to be a statutory committee but which actually is not. This is the Macmillan Royal Commission on Lunacy and Mental Disorder (Cmd. 2700), an *ad hoc* committee appointed by the Crown by virtue of its prerogative powers (Type IV), but which was subsequently granted certain powers under an Act of Parliament.[31] In spite of acquiring statutory powers in this way, however, the Macmillan Commission was appointed by virtue of prerogative, not statutory, powers.

Advisory committees appointed by the Crown are, therefore, predominantly of a single type: Type IV. Apart from only seventeen exceptions (listed in Table 2.2), all Crown-appointed advisory committees in this century have been royal commissions. All of them have been so designated, too, except only for the Esher Committee on the Osborne Estate (Cd. 1384) appointed in 1904 'to consider the disposition of His Majesty's Osborne Estate in the Isle of Wight'.

Advisory committees appointed by ministers are not so straightforward, for there are large numbers of every one of the six types of advisory committees described above.

Standing committees (Types I and II) are probably very numerous. Detailed information is lacking, but the most recent estimate is that there were at least 484 of them in existence in 1958.[32] There is little to suggest that the number has declined much since then. Some of these committees are appointed by virtue of the conventional powers of ministers (Type II): for example, the Consultative Committee for Industry, the Agricultural Improvement Council for England and Wales, the Advisory Council on Scientific Policy, and the Television Advisory Committee.[33] Other standing committees are appointed by statute (Type I). In fact,

it has become common for Acts developing new social services or other Government functions to contain provision for a standing advisory com-

---

30 See the report of the Commission (Cd. 3268). See also Erskine May, *The Law, Privileges, Proceedings and Usage of Parliament*, 17th ed. (London: Butterworth, 1964), pp. 188–9, for details of the relevant statutes, the last of which is still in force although as yet unused.

31 Reference is to the Tribunals of Inquiry (Evidence) Act, 1921 (11 Geo. V, Chapter 7). The Act has also been extended by statutory reference to a number of statutory committees (Type III): see Robson, *op. cit.*, for examples and further details.

32 Political and Economic Planning, *Advisory Committees in British Government* (*op. cit.*), Special Study V, pp. 198–217, lists 484 standing advisory committees as of March 1958.

33 *ibid.*, Special Study II, pp. 132–85, for detailed descriptions of these and a number of other committees like them. For a description of the use of such committees in connection with industry, see J. W. Grove, *Government and Industry in Britain* (London: Longman, 1962), *passim*.

mittee as a matter of course. By 1958 the number of [standing] advisory committees with a statutory basis had reached over a hundred.[34]

In some cases, the statutory basis is general (Type I*a*); for example, the Women's Consultative Committee on Labour and other similar committees were appointed under the provisions of the Employment and Training Act, 1948.[35] In other cases, the statutory basis is specific (Type I*b*); for example, the Central Advisory Water Committee, which has been appointed by the Ministry of Housing and Local Government, was provided for in the Water Act, 1945.[36]

Ministers also appoint *ad hoc* advisory committees by means of statutory powers. Most are appointed under general statutory powers (Type III*a*) and are usually referred to as statutory committees, statutory inquiries, or public inquiries. In fact, this is the most numerous kind of committee to be found in British government. According to Professor H. W. R. Wade,

> Statutory inquiries are now so common that it is unusual to find a statute concerned with planning control or with the acquisition of land, or indeed with any important social service or scheme of control, which does not provide this machinery [for appointing statutory committees] for one or more purposes. Acts concerned with housing, town and country planning, new towns, roads, agriculture, health, transport, aviation, rivers, police, local government – these are merely a few examples to show the range of subjects covered by what has now become a standard technique. Many inquiries have to be held in cases of compulsory acquisition, as, for example, where land is taken for roads, schools, hospitals, airfields, housing estates, town development, open spaces and playing fields, swimming baths, cemeteries, children's homes, markets, slaughterhouses, small-holdings, drainage schemes. There are also many planning inquiries. The Ministry of Housing and Local Government, which arranges inquiries concerning local authorities and some central departments, as well as its own cases of housing and planning ... [is] responsible for about 8,000 inquiries a year.[37]

In addition, statutory inquiries investigate various kinds of accidents (railway accidents, factory and mines accidents, shipwrecks, aircraft disasters, and so

34 *ibid.*, p. 21. One especially interesting recent development has been the use of these committees for regional economic planning. See A. V. Peterson, 'The Machinery for Economic Planning', *Public Administration*, XLIV (1966), pp. 29–41; and Brian C. Smith, *Advising Ministers: the South West Economic Planning Council* (London: Routledge and Kegan Paul, 1969).

35 11 & 12 Geo. VI, Chapter 46, Section 1(2).

36 8 & 9 Geo. VI, Chapter 42, Section 2.

37 H. W. R. Wade, *Administrative Law*, 2nd ed. (London: Oxford University Press, 1967), p. 200.

on); various matters connected with transport and commerce; and certain kinds of disputes arising out of labour-management relations.[38]

The remaining group of ministerial advisory committees are *ad hoc* committees appointed by virtue of ministers' conventional powers: i.e. Type IV. Such committees are referred to generically as departmental committees; however, not all committees which are departmental committees (i.e. committees of Type IV) are called 'Departmental Committees'. In fact, more than two dozen different names have been used – although not all these names are equally common. The most common designation is plain 'committee'; roughly half of all departmental committees are so called. Other common terms are 'Inquiry' or 'Committee of Inquiry' and 'Departmental' or 'Interdepartmental Committee'.[39] Apart from these five common names, there are all sorts of others, including combinations of the previous titles (such as 'Departmental Committee of Inquiry') as well as 'Joint Working Party', 'Advisory Committee', 'Investigation', 'Committee of Privy Councillors', 'Group', 'Panel', 'Technical Committee of Inquiry', 'Public Enquiry', 'Tribunal of Inquiry', 'Board of Inquiry', 'Independent Committee of Inquiry', 'Commission of Inquiry', 'Legal Committee', 'Independent Committee', 'Technical Evaluation Committee', and several others besides.

None of these names, moreover, can be relied upon to indicate anything definite about the nature of the departmental committee to which it is applied. Not even 'Departmental Committee' and 'Interdepartmental Committee' can be counted on. It is true that most 'Interdepartmental Committees' are appointed by more than one department and may have officials from more than one department as members, but this is not always the case.[40] The opposite assumption – that 'Departmental Committees' are always appointed by only one department and do not have officials from more than one department as members – is even less reliable.[41] Similarly,

38 There is a fairly extensive list of statutes under which inquiries are and have been held in R. E. Wraith and G. B. Lamb, *Public Inquiries as an Instrument of Government* (London: Allen and Unwin, 1973), pp. 357–74; some other examples are given in Robson, *op. cit.*, and Wade, *op. cit.*, Chapter 6.

39 There seems to be no marked preference for either 'inquiry' or 'enquiry'. Both spellings occur in official publications, even in the same document. See also the amusing dilemma of the Beveridge Committee on Broadcasting (Cmd. 8116): should the B.B.C. be referred to as 'it' or 'them'?

40 For example, the Herbert Interdepartmental Committee on Slaughterhouses and the Handford Interdepartmental Committee on Slaughterhouses in Scotland were both appointed by only one department each, the Ministry of Food and the Department of Health for Scotland respectively, although they did have officials from more than one department as members; see the reports of these Committees (Cmd. 9542 and Cmd. 9376 respectively).

41 For example, the Waverley Departmental Committee on Coastal Flooding (Cmd. 9165) was appointed by the Home Office, the Department of the Secretary of State for Scotland, the Ministry of Housing and Local Government, and the Ministry of Agriculture, Fisheries and Food; while the Beveridge Committee on Broadcasting (Cmd. 8116) included officials from more than one department.

most of the committees which are called 'Inquiries' have only one member (the chairman), but not all of them do.[42] Sometimes a 'Tribunal of Inquiry' has been granted special powers under the Tribunals of Inquiry (Evidence) Act, 1921, but this is not always true.[43] The term 'Working Party' seems to have carried a special meaning in the immediate postwar period when the Labour government set up a series of fifteen tripartite Working Parties representative of employers, employees and government for the purpose of reorganising and making more efficient various sectors of private industry; but this particular meaning does not seem to have been retained.[44]

It is true that some of the more esoteric names are probably chosen for specific reasons. For example, it was the 'Legal Committee' on Medical Partnerships (Cmd. 7565) in order to emphasise its exclusive concern with the legal aspects of partnerships under the National Health Service Act of 1946. It was the Plowden 'Group' on Public Expenditure (Cmnd. 1432) possibly in order to indicate that it was not to be an ordinary departmental committee with respect to the manner in which it conducted its inquiries. The 'Advisory Committee' on Publicity and Recruitment for the Civil Defence and Allied Services (Cmd. 9131) may have been so called in order to avoid having a departmental committee appear to be telling a more junior branch of government how to do its own job. The 'Independent Committee' on Security Procedures in the Public Service (Cmnd. 1681) was probably so called to emphasise the fact that it was a committee of objective laymen. Finally, it was the Cohen 'Panel' on the Composition of Flour (Cmd. 9757) and the Fleck 'Technical Evaluation Committee' on Windscale Piles (Cmnd. 471), probably in order to emphasise the essentially scientific nature of the inquiries concerned. But these are isolated examples. In general, the name of a departmental committee can serve as only an occasional guide to its nature.

To summarise, therefore, very few advisory committees appointed by the Crown are not royal commissions (Type IV), and all but one of them have been called 'Royal Commissions' by name. Among advisory committees appointed by ministers, however, the situation is more complicated. Many of

42 Two recent Inquiries have had two and three members each: the Bridges Inquiry into Security at the National Gallery (Cmnd. 1750) had two members including the chairman, and the Lang Inquiry into the Pricing of Ministry of Aviation Contracts (Cmnd. 2581) had three members including the chairman.

43 The Adams Tribunal of Inquiry into the Accident to the *Sea Gem* (Cmnd. 3409), for example, had no such powers.

44 See *House of Commons Debates*, 414 (15 October 1945) and 420 (11 March 1946). The reports of these postwar Working Parties which were published appeared as Non-Parliamentary Papers, but the Jones Working Party on China Clay (Cmd. 6748) in 1945–6 was clearly within the same tradition. On the other hand, the Brittain-Hall Joint Working Party on the Economy of Northern Ireland (Cmnd. 1835) in 1961–2 clearly was not.

them are not departmental committees (Type IV) and, even of those which are, many are not actually called 'Departmental Committees' by name.

From this somewhat confusing picture emerges the peculiar nature of royal commissions and departmental committees. First of all, they are appointed by the Crown and its ministers respectively, not by any other agency of government. Secondly, they are both advisory committees, not internal committees or tribunals. Thirdly, they are both *ad hoc* committees, not standing committees, appointed by virtue of prerogative and conventional powers respectively, not statutory powers. Royal commissions and departmental committees may, therefore, be regarded as being distinct from all other kinds of committees in British government.

Royal Commissions and Departmental Committees

So far it has been argued that, because they are formally appointed in a distinctive way, royal commissions and departmental committees are different from all other committees in government. The next step is to see how different these committees are from each other – to see whether they represent two distinct institutions of government or just one.

The difference between royal commissions and departmental committees lies in the fact that the former are appointed by the Crown and the latter by ministers. The evolution of the British constitution has, however, rendered this distinction obsolete. The Crown has completely surrendered its prerogative powers in this respect to the Home Secretary (or, in Scotland, the Secretary of State for Scotland) in his capacity as 'residuary legatee' of the powers of the Crown.

Although the Crown did in the past appoint royal commissions on its own initiative, such a step would no longer be permitted. In his detailed study of the powers of the Crown, Professor Berriedale Keith discloses how King Edward VII proposed a royal commission to examine 'foreign tariffs and the growth of trusts'; however, his unsolicited advice was ignored.[45] Since that time, it has been accepted that the Crown cannot independently exercise the prerogative power to appoint committees. Nowadays, the royal warrant of appointment for a royal commission is prepared for the signature of the Crown by the Home Secretary or, in Scotland, the Secretary of State for Scotland, and the monarch has no choice but to sign the warrant. In the words of a former Permanent Under-Secretary at the Home Office,

> When the appointment of a Royal Commission has been decided on and its personnel settled, the Home Office submits to the King for his signature the warrant naming the commissioners and prescribing the terms of reference. The Royal Commission sends its report when completed to the

45 A. B. Keith, *The King and the Imperial Crown* (London: Longmans Green, 1936), pp. 236–7. On the legal status of the royal prerogative, see R. F. V. Heuston, *Essays in Constitutional Law* (London: Stevens and Sons, 1961), Chapter 3.

Home Secretary who submits it to the King and afterwards presents it to Parliament. [Moreover] royal commissions frequently consult the Home Office on questions as to their powers and procedures.[46]

Thus royal commissions and departmental committees are effectively appointed by the same persons: namely, ministers of the Crown.

Royal commissions, it is true, are formally appointed by only one minister – the Home Secretary (or the Secretary of State for Scotland) – whereas the appointment of a departmental committee may involve more than one minister. This difference is probably more one of appearance than reality. Although only one minister actually signs the warrant of appointment of a royal commission, it would be difficult to believe that other ministers besides the Home Secretary have not been closely involved in the appointment of at least some royal commissions. For example, the Minister of Housing and Local Government, and probably other ministers too, must have participated in the establishment of the three postwar Royal Commissions on local government.[47] Similarly, the Royal Commission on the Taxation of Profits and Income twice consulted the Chancellor of the Exchequer – not the Home Secretary – about the implications of its terms of reference.[48] The fact that royal commissions are never formally appointed by several ministers acting together does not, therefore, indicate a significant difference from departmental committees.

It should be added that both royal commissions and departmental committees are formally appointed by specific ministers acting individually, not on behalf of the Cabinet. Apparently, the appointment of a royal commission is traditionally brought before the Cabinet for approval, but the secrecy in which all Cabinet procedures are shrouded makes it impossible to know whether this practice was followed even in such relatively straightforward cases as the Salmon Royal Commission on Tribunals of Inquiry (Cmnd. 3121) or the Todd Royal Commission on Medical Education (Cmnd. 3569). Equally, it seems highly probable that at least some of the more important or more contentious departmental committees may also for one reason or another have been discussed in Cabinet, although again it is impossible to be certain. For example, the Radcliffe Committee on the Working of the Monetary System (Cmnd. 827) and the Plowden Group on the Control of Public Expenditure (Cmnd. 1432) could well have come before the Cabinet. In any case, even if they do come before the Cabinet for approval, royal

---

46 Sir Edward Troup, *The Home Office*, Whitehall Series (London: Putnam, 1925), pp. 38–9.

47 Reference is to the Herbert Royal Commission (Cmnd. 1164), the Maud Royal Commission (Cmnd. 4040) and the Wheatley Royal Commission (Cmnd. 4150) on local government in Greater London, in England and in Scotland respectively. See Chapter 4 below for further details of jointly appointed committees.

48 See the report of the Commission (Cmd. 9474) and *House of Commons Debates*, 483 (6 February 1951), Columns 1529–31.

commissions and departmental committees are both appointed by specific ministers and not by the Cabinet.

The result is that there are no hard and fast rules for ministers and their officials as to when a committee should be appointed as a royal commission and when as a departmental committee. As will be shown in the next few paragraphs, the formal appointment of royal commissions by the Crown has only two direct consequences, and both of these turn out to have little significance in practice. As for indirect consequences, subsequent chapters will show that royal commissions function in substantially the same way as departmental committees. Neither Prime Ministers nor the Treasury seem ever to have established guidelines about the appointment of royal commissions as opposed to departmental committees or about the relative numbers of each which might be appointed. Thus, the choice between a royal commission and a departmental committee is probably based on two other factors: tradition and prestige.

One of the direct consequences of formal appointment by the Crown is that royal commissions enjoy a more secure constitutional position than do departmental committees. It is possible that the existence of a departmental committee could be challenged following a change of government or even a change of minister, whereas such changes would not affect the position of bodies appointed by the Crown. In practice this extra security has meant little, since there is no evidence of departmental committees having been brought to a premature end for political reasons (see Chapter 11 below).

The other direct consequence of formal appointment by royal warrant is that these warrants invariably provide for the granting of certain subpoena powers to royal commissions. Departmental committees, on the other hand, must acquire such powers through the provisions of an Act of Parliament. Again, this distinction has meant little in practice, since no royal commission has ever exercised these powers and it is doubtful that they could now be used at all (see Chapter 9 below).

As far as their activities are concerned, royal commissions and departmental committees function in substantially the same way. Both may or may not call for evidence, may or may not hold public hearings, may or may not publish minutes of evidence, may or may not undertake research, and so on. There are no important differences between what each may do. It is true that royal commissions tend to be bigger, more expensive and more publicised undertakings than are departmental committees: on average, royal commissions take a longer time, have more meetings (including more public hearings), receive more evidence from a larger number of witnesses, undertake more research, make more recommendations, write longer reports and publish more evidence than do departmental committees.[49] But these are only tendencies. There are significant exceptions among both kinds of com-

49 These points are all covered in much greater detail in the chapters to come.

mittees on every one of these points. It is impossible, therefore, to draw any clear and fixed distinctions between royal commissions and departmental committees on the basis of their activities.

The choice between royal commission and departmental committee is thus based on less tangible factors than these. One such factor is probably tradition. Over the past one hundred and fifty years, history has established a certain pattern from which departures need to be justified. In most cases, the presumption is that a committee should be a departmental committee unless special considerations suggest otherwise. There is, however, a category of matters which seem to be regarded as appropriate for treatment by royal commission unless special considerations suggest otherwise. Among this select category is the machinery of local government – but only when the whole system is under scrutiny. Thus, the reorganisation of local government in Greater London, in England and in Scotland has been assigned to three royal commissions within the past fifteen years, whereas the examination of local authority social services was recently given to a departmental committee.[50] Should it become necessary to review the whole system of local government in Wales, for example, the presumption is that such a review would be assigned to a royal commission. The laws relating to marriage and divorce have been examined by royal commissions on at least four occasions: in 1850, 1853, 1912 and 1955.[51] The laws relating to betting, lotteries and gaming have twice been the subject of inquiries by royal commissions in this century, as have Justices of the Peace, the police and the press.[52] Precedents such as these indicate that there are certain subjects which should be investigated by royal commissions and not by departmental committees.

There is at least one important subject omitted from the above list of precedents, and this leads to the second factor at work in the choice between royal commission and departmental committee. The Civil Service has been the subject of no less than five royal commissions in the past one hundred years: namely, the Playfair Commission (C. 1317) in 1875, the Ridley Commission (C. 6172) in 1884–90, the Macdonell Commission (Cd. 7832) in 1910–14, the Tomlin Commission (Cmd. 3909) in 1929–31 and the Priestley Commission (Cmd. 9613) in 1953–55. But there have also been a number of

50 Reference is to the Herbert Commission (Cmnd. 1164), the Maud Commission (Cmnd. 4040), the Wheatley Commission (Cmnd. 4150), and the Seebohm Committee (Cmnd. 3703) respectively.

51 Reference is to the 1850 Commission (Command 1203), the Campbell Commission (Command 1604), the Gorell Commission (Cd. 6478), and the Morton Commission (Cmd. 9678) respectively.

52 Reference is to the Rowlatt Commission (Cmd. 4341) and the Willink Commission (Cmd. 8190) on betting, lotteries and gaming; the James Commission (Cd. 5250) and the du Parcq Commission (Cmd. 7463) on Justices of the Peace; the Lee Commission (Cmd. 3297) and the Willink Commission (Cmnd. 1728) on the police; and the Ross Commission (Cmnd. 7700) and the Shawcross Commission (Cmnd. 1811) on the press. A third royal commission on the press has just been appointed under the chairmanship of Mr Justice Finer (see *House of Commons Debates*, 2 May 1974).

departmental committees on the Civil Service. It might be supposed that, as in the case of local government, comprehensive inquiries are reserved to royal commissions while less than comprehensive ones are assigned to departmental committees. Such an explanation is not adequate in this case. The Priestley Royal Commission in the mid-1950's dealt only with the conditions of employment of civil servants. On the other hand, among recent departmental committees on the Civil Service was the Fulton Committee (Cmnd. 3638), which undertook a full-scale examination of the 'structure, recruitment and management' of the Civil Service.[53] In short, if tradition establishes a norm, then there must also be some other factor to explain departures from that norm.

It is probably a question of prestige – of which royal commissions enjoy substantially more than departmental committees. The greater prestige of royal commissions derives not just from their greater pomp and tradition; nor just from the fact that, in this century at least, there have been a great many fewer royal commissions than departmental committees; nor even just from the fact that royal commission reports are certain to be presented to Parliament as Command Papers whereas departmental committee reports are more likely to be merely Non-Parliamentary Papers – although all these characteristics are quite true.[54] The main thing is probably that royal commissions tend to be identified with the government as a whole, whereas departmental committees are linked to specific ministers or departments. In any case, the result is that royal commissions are regarded as a higher order of government institution. As R. V. Vernon and Nicholas Mansergh wrote some thirty years ago, 'The distinction between a Royal Commission and a [departmental] committee is of some theoretical importance, but does not today amount in practice to very much more than a question of prestige.'[55]

It is important to realise that the greater prestige of royal commissions can be of more than just symbolic value to ministers and officials intending to appoint a committee. Prestige may help attract a chairman and members of sufficient ability to serve on the committee in what is, after all, an unremunerative capacity. The prestige of a royal commission can also help to strengthen the position of the chairman vis-à-vis strong-minded members of his committee. Prestige may enable the committee to get a better press than it would do as a departmental committee. Prestige may induce more interest groups to take the time and make the effort necessary to present their views in a serious and careful manner. The prestige of a royal commission may permit it to take a stronger position with respect to its witnesses, including

53 There was also the Gladstone Committee on Recruitment to the Civil Service after the War in 1918–19 (Cmd. 34) and the Tennant Committee on the Organisation of the Scientific Civil Service in 1964–5 (Non-Parliamentary Paper, 1965).

54 For the distinction between Command and Non-Parliamentary Papers, as well as details of the number of committees appointed each year, see Chapter 3 below.

55 Vernon and Mansergh, *op. cit.*, p. 24.

government departments. Prestige may help a committee to 'sell' its findings to the general public, to interested parties, to officials and to cabinet ministers. If, in short, a minister feels that it will be useful to have people believe that his committee is more important than most, then he is likely to want to have it appointed as a royal commission.

Conversely, the extra prestige associated with a royal commission may in certain circumstances be regarded as a liability. Appointing a royal commission automatically means the involvement of the Home Secretary (or the Secretary of State for Scotland) and probably the Prime Minister as well.[56] If the committee is expected to prove politically controversial, its appointment is more likely to cause lengthy discussion in Cabinet if it is to be a royal commission. The result is that a royal commission inevitably takes longer to appoint than a departmental committee. Moreover, service on a royal commission will probably seem to prospective members to demand a greater commitment of time and energy than will service on a departmental committee. The procedures of a royal commission will be more in the public eye and thus more likely to provoke controversy among and even 'posturing' by some of the committee members and some of the interest groups involved. The whole enterprise will be more formal and will probably take longer; it will have to be conducted in such a manner that it will not only be judicious but also be seen to be judicious. Finally, a minister and his officials may feel they do not really have to 'sell' anyone on what the committee is likely to propose. They may feel, on the contrary, that much could be lost through unnecessary publicity; they may want nothing more than to be able to go ahead with the implementation of whatever the committee recommends with as little fuss as possible. Thus, there are certain circumstances in which it is desirable to play down the existence and activities of a committee. In such a case, the committee is not likely to be appointed as a royal commission but rather as a departmental committee.

A number of other factors are sometimes held to be involved in the distinction between royal commissions and departmental committees. In particular, it is often argued that royal commissions are reserved especially for issues of major public importance, for matters which cut across many departmental jurisdictions, and for questions about which widespread public discussion is desired. Although none of these beliefs turns out to be very accurate, they all serve to reinforce the notion that royal commissions carry more prestige than do departmental committees.

56 Naturally, this is less of a restraint for the Home Secretary himself. When the Home Secretary appoints a committee, there is obviously no more inter-ministerial co-ordination necessary for a royal commission than for a departmental committee. Thus, it is probably significant that the percentage of postwar royal commissions which dealt with Home Office matters – and which would, therefore, have been appointed by the Home Secretary even if they had been departmental committees (48%) – is much higher than the percentage of departmental committees which actually were appointed in the same period either jointly or singly by the Home Office (22%). See Table 4.2 below.

One popular belief is that royal commissions are appointed to deal with exceptional issues of widespread public or national importance, while more ordinary problems are consigned to departmental committees.[57] Unfortunately, the evidence just does not bear this out. For one thing, royal commissions are in fact slightly less likely to deal with an issue of national importance than are departmental committees (see Chapter 6 below). For another thing, there are all sorts of exceptions on the basis of the relative importance of the subject of the committee. Royal commissions have examined university education in Dundee and the remuneration of doctors and dentists among other things; while these may be vital issues for some sections of the population, they would scarcely rank as exceptional issues of major public importance.[58] Among the subjects which have been assigned to departmental committees, on the other hand, are leasehold reform, foot-and-mouth disease, higher education, decimal coinage and so on.[59] Such issues, on the contrary, probably could be classed as major issues of national concern; yet they were dealt with by departmental committees. Moreover, the proposed generalisation gives rise to several particular anomalies: the taxation of profits and income deserved a royal commission but the working of the monetary system did not, tribunals of inquiry did but administrative tribunals and inquiries did not, and the remuneration of doctors and dentists did but that of ministers and Members of Parliament did not.[60] In short, the more important issues of major public concern may or may not be assigned to royal commissions.

Another belief is that royal commissions are appointed for issues which involve not just two, three or even four government departments, but six, eight or more. In other words, they are used for issues which are highly 'interdepartmental' in scope. For example, the organisation of local government could easily involve not only the Ministry of Housing and Local Government, but the Home Office, the Treasury and the Ministries of Agriculture, Fisheries and Food, of Education, of Health, of Transport, of Labour, and perhaps others as well. Thus, as has been shown, committees on local government tend to be royal commissions. Similarly, the Balfour Royal Commission on Scottish Affairs (Cmd. 9212) implicated all of the home departments of

---

57 This is the qualified view of K. C. Wheare, *Government by Committee, op. cit.*, p. 69.

58 Reference is to the Tedder Commission (Cmd. 8514) and the Pilkington Commission (Cmnd. 939) respectively. In 1902, there was even a Royal Commission on Physical Training in Scottish Schools (Cd. 1507).

59 Reference is to the Uthwatt-Jenkins Committee on Leasehold (Cmd. 7982), the Gowers and the Northumberland Committees on Foot-and-Mouth Disease (Cmd. 9214 and Cmnd. 4225 respectively), the Robbins Committee on Higher Education (Cmnd. 2154), and the Halsbury Committee on Decimal Coinage (Cmnd. 2145).

60 Reference is to the Cohen-Radcliffe Commission (Cmd. 9474) and the Radcliffe Committee (Cmnd. 827); the Salmon Commission (Cmnd. 3121) and the Franks Committee (Cmnd. 218); and the Pilkington Commission (Cmnd. 939) and the Lawrence Committee (Cmnd. 2516) respectively.

government, and so it was a royal commission. Unfortunately, however, this theory is as fallible as the previous one. There are royal commissions which could hardly be called interdepartmental at all; for example, the Gowers Royal Commission on Capital Punishment (Cmd. 8932) and the Willink Royal Commission on the Police (Cmnd. 1728) scarcely concern more than the Home Office and perhaps the Lord Chancellor's Department. On the other hand, there are departmental committees which could surely be construed as being just as interdepartmental as many royal commissions; for example, the Halsbury Committee on Decimal Currency (Cmnd. 2145) and the Hunt Committee on Intermediate Areas (Cmnd. 3998) obviously dealt with issues which could have concerned a great many departments. Royal commissions, therefore, are not necessarily appointed for problems which cut across a great many departmental jurisdictions.

A third belief is that royal commissions are appointed in cases where the committee is expected to sound out the opinion of the general public in a particularly extensive way. This would explain royal commissions on betting and gaming, for example, or on marriage and divorce or capital punishment. But again, there are cases of royal commissions which, by this standard, ought to have been departmental committees and departmental committees which similarly ought to have been royal commissions.

Although all of these popular beliefs are misleading, they nevertheless serve to reinforce the idea of royal commissions having a greater prestige than departmental committees. On the basis of numbers, royal commissions are obviously the exception and departmental committees the rule; so there must be something special about a committee for it to be appointed as a royal commission. Where a minister and his officials feel that their committee can work better without such distinction, they will be satisfied with a departmental committee.

It is probably considerations like these which explain anomalies such as the ones described in the paragraphs above. In the case of the Gowers Royal Commission on Capital Punishment (Cmd. 8932) or the Pilkington Royal Commission on Doctors' and Dentists' Remuneration (Cmnd. 939), for example, it must have been felt that the added prestige of a royal commission would make the committee more effective. In the case of the Wolfenden Committee on Homosexual Offences and Prostitution (Cmnd. 247), the Lawrence Committee on the Remuneration of Ministers and M.P.s (Cmnd. 2516) and the Fulton Committee on the Civil Service (Cmnd. 3638), it was probably felt that their operations would benefit more from a low-key approach, and so they were not appointed as royal commissions.

Thus, the difference between royal commissions and departmental committees is difficult to pin down, for in all important structural and functional respects they appear to be similar. Considerations of tradition and prestige go a long way towards accounting for the choice actually made between a royal commission and a departmental committee. Historically, certain subjects have come to be regarded as matters for examination by royal commissions, while others have not. Departures from this norm are governed by a desire for more or less prestige. In a sense, therefore, a royal commission is simply the 'big brother' of a departmental committee and, together, they constitute a single and distinct institution of government.

3
A Historical Perspective

Committees are as old as government. Indeed, it can be argued that political power, the power to govern, includes by definition the power to delegate, which is the essence of a committee.[1] This would imply that committees in England must be very ancient indeed, royal commissions as old as the monarchy and departmental committees as old as government departments. Although their precise date of origin is lost in the incompletely recorded past, advisory committees in English government can be assumed to have existed at least as far back as the eleventh century, when William I appointed some of his barons and justices to make the inquiries which resulted in the Domesday Book of 1086.[2] Since then the use of advisory committees has broadly reflected the constitutional development of the executive branch as a whole.

Origin and Development up to 1800

Royal commissions were not widely used during the Norman period, but they became quite common during the reigns of Henry I and Henry II.[3] The Inquest of Sheriffs in 1176, for example, involved panels of justices commissioned by the Crown to inquire into allegations of abuse and injustice by sheriffs and other local officials.[4] Similarly, some of the legal reforms under Edward I were the result of royal commissions, including the extension of the common law to Wales in 1284, the Mortmain regulations for church lands in 1279, and new police and arms regulations laid down in the Statute of Winchester in 1285. By the reign of Edward III, however, opposition to these unfettered royal inquiries led Parliament to demand an end to them, except where they conformed to law or were explicitly sanctioned by Parliament.

---

1 K. C. Wheare, *Government by Committee* (London: Oxford University Press, 1955), pp. 5–6.

2 Extracts can be found in William Stubbs, *Select Charters . . . of English Constitutional History*, 8th ed. (London: Oxford University Press, 1905), pp. 85–91, and in H. M. Clokie and J. W. Robinson, *Royal Commissions of Inquiry* (Stanford University Press, 1937), Appendix A.

3 Clokie and Robinson, *op. cit.*, Chapter 2.

4 D. J. Medley, *English Constitutional History*, 3rd ed. (Oxford: Blackwell, 1902), pp. 364–5, provides some details.

The result was a gradual decline in the use of royal commissions until the accession of Henry VII in 1485.[5]

Under the Tudors and Stuarts, the royal commission established itself as a regular institution of government. During this period, there were numerous inquiries into questions as varied as the partition of the 'debatable lands' along the northern borders of England in 1550 and the conduct of Lord Lisle in Calais in 1539. By this time, moreover, royal commissions had come to be composed of Privy Councillors, officials and outsiders all at the same time.[6] In addition, by the early part of the sixteenth century, there began to be inquiries into the causes and effects of what we would now call social problems; for example, the Commission on Enclosures was appointed in 1517 to investigate the gradual enclosure of land and its withdrawal from cultivation and the consequent depopulation of the countryside. But it was really the breach with the Church of Rome in 1534 that produced the widest extension until then of the practice of appointing royal commissions; there was a commission for the valuation of benefices in 1535, one for the regulation of divorce and one for the collection of lead, plate and ornaments from churches in 1551–2.[7] 'From this time', comments Sir William Ashley, 'the idea of a royal commission was never absent from the mind of politicians'.[8]

During the seventeenth century,

> the early and mid-1630's saw a series of attempts at administrative reform, few of which were carried through with sustained resolution. . . . [At the same time], Royal Commissions proliferated, many with a reforming purpose . . .[9]

Unfortunately, however, these commissions were not always very effective, and 'very little was achieved'. Between 1629 and 1634, for example, a series of royal commissions on the Ordinance Office found grave cases of maladministration, but their recommendations led only to the adoption of stricter oaths of office for officers of the Navy and Ordinance Office.[10] Following this came a long period of relative unpopularity for royal commissions, a period which lasted through the rest of the seventeenth century and most of the eighteenth as well.

5 Other examples of royal commissions appointed up to the end of the fourteenth century can be found in T. F. Tout, *Chapters in the Administrative History of Mediaeval England*, six volumes (Manchester University Press, 1920–37); see, for example, Volume III, pp. 347–58.

6 G. E. Aylmer, *The King's Servants: the Civil Service of Charles I, 1625–1642* (London: Routledge and Kegan Paul, 1961), p. 22.

7 Clokie and Robinson, *op. cit.*, Chapter 2.

8 Sir William Ashley, *An Introduction to English Economic History and Theory* (London: Rivington, 1888–93), quoted in Clokie and Robinson, *op. cit.*, p. 39.

9 Aylmer, *op. cit.*, p. 62.

10 *ibid.*, p. 145.

The reasons for this decline are not hard to find. As the active exercise of power by the Crown declined, so did the appointment of royal commissions. They became unpopular again for their apparently extra-legal status and procedures. No less a person than Sir Edward Coke argued that royal commissions were illegal, and even William Blackstone was critical of their use.[11] During this time, however, royal commissions were not abolished or even non-existent. Although statutory commissions were preferred for some kinds of issues, royal commissions were used repeatedly for others, such as those involving the partition or enclosure of land. By the end of the eighteenth century, therefore, the royal commission was firmly established as a regular institution of government, but one that was not as widely or as frequently used as it had been some two centuries earlier.

Another reason for the relative decline of royal commissions during the eighteenth century must have been the gradual development of first one and then a second important competitor. First, Parliament had begun to make much greater use of its own investigatory committee, the select committee.[12] Secondly, by the end of the century, departmental committees had begun to appear.

Departmental committees are a much more modern development than royal commissions – if only because government departments in England are a relatively recent development. It is true that there were high executive offices of the Crown at least from the Middle Ages onwards, even from the end of the reign of Henry III in 1272; that, at least as early as the seventeenth century, the Privy Council began to appoint bodies which were the forerunners of both the Cabinet and modern departments; and that these bodies began to appoint committees almost as early.[13] But it was not until the late eighteenth and early nineteenth centuries that officials in these various offices were converted from being servants of ministers to being servants of the Crown paid by Parliament.[14] And it was not until this distinction emerged

---

11 See Sir Edward Coke, *Institutes*, Book II, Sections 4, 78 and 165, and William Blackstone, *Commentaries*, Book I, Section I, Paragraphs 7 and 8; both cited in Clokie and Robinson, *op. cit.*, pp. 45, 47 and 53. Nineteenth-century opponents of Whig royal commissions were fond of quoting Coke in their support: see, for example, the arguments in Joshua Toulmin Smith, *Government by Commissions Illegal and Pernicious* (London: Sweet, 1849).

12 Josef Redlich, *The Procedure of the House of Commons* (London: Constable, 1908), Volume II, pp. 203–14, has a note on the history of select committees in the House of Commons. See also Lord Campion, *The Procedure of the House of Commons*, 3rd ed. (London: Macmillan, 1958), Chapter 7.

13 W. J. M. Mackenzie and J. W. Grove, *Central Administration in Britain* (London: Longman, 1957), Chapter 11; and R. G. S. Brown, *The Administrative Process in Britain* (London: Methuen, 1970), Chapter 1.

14 Emmeline Cohen, *The Growth of the British Civil Service, 1780–1939* (London: Allen and Unwin, 1941), Chapters 1 and 2; H. J. Hanham, *The Nineteenth-Century Constitution, 1815–1914: Documents and Commentary* (Cambridge University Press, 1969), pp. 314ff; and R. H. Gretton, *The King's Government: a Study of the Growth of the Central Administration* (London: Bell and Sons, 1913).

between the political office of minister and the permanent office of civil servant that it becomes possible to distinguish departmental committees from what we would now call Cabinet or Privy Council committees. Even so, departmental committees in the nineteenth century were still quite likely to consist largely of government officials.[15] As one recent study explains:

> In the first place, not all Privy Councillors had departmental responsibilities; thus until the Cabinet was clearly differentiated from the Privy Council, both the Privy Council itself and committees composed of its members included some who would now be regarded as Ministers and some who would now be regarded as outsiders. In the second place, Ministers, until in some cases the last quarter of the nineteenth century, carried out functions which would now be carried out by their administrative or even executive civil servants.[16]

Thus, departmental committees cannot really be said to have come into existence much before the beginning of the nineteenth century. Some exceptions can be found, such as the Committee of Magistrates respecting Middlesex Prisons, in 1798–9, but this is the only recognisable departmental committee listed in the Abbot Collection of Parliamentary Papers.[17] There was also apparently a Committee of Inquiry into the management of the Post Office mail-packet service in 1788, which found that its management had become 'an unbounded source of expense and peculation'.[18] These two examples must be among the earliest departmental committees ever appointed.

Development since 1800

By the beginning of the last century, therefore, royal commissions had had a long and even illustrious history. They had fallen somewhat into disuse and disrepute for several generations; however, they had not completely disappeared. There were also signs of the emergence of a new kind of committee quite similar to the royal commission; namely, the departmental committee. From that time to the present, royal commissions and departmental committees have been a permanent feature of British government.

Reliable detailed information from 1800 to the present can be obtained only in the case of royal commissions; in the case of departmental committees, detailed information is available only from 1900 onwards. Prior to

15 Leonard Courtney, *The Working Constitution of the United Kingdom and Its Outgrowths* (London: Dent, 1901), p. 135.

16 Political and Economic Planning, *Advisory Committees in British Government* (London: Allen and Unwin, 1960), p. 2.

17 The Abbot Collection, which is described in Appendix A below, covers the period from 1731 to 1800, but it is an incomplete record; the report of the Committee of Magistrates can be found in Volume 48 of the Collection.

18 Sir Evelyn Murray, *The Post Office*, Whitehall Series (London: Putnam, 1927), p. 18.

Table 3.1 Royal commissions and departmental committees, 1800–1969 (by decades), by number appointed and average annual number in existence

decades	royal commissions only		all committees	
	total number appointed	*average annual number in existence*	*total number appointed*	*average annual number in existence*
1800–9	11	—	—	—
1810–9	19	—	—	—
1820–9	20	—	—	—
1830–9	46	—	—	—
1840–9	51	—	—	—
1850–9	75	—	—	—
1860–9	59	17	—	—
1870–9	43	14	—	—
1880–9	40	14	—	—
1890–9	35	13	—	—
1900–9	44	15	209	47
1910–19	24	9	269	57
1920–9	25	6	239	52
1930–9	16	5	167	42
1940–9	6	2	252	54
1950–9	10	4	269	65
1960–9	10	4	206	59
1800–99	399	—	—	—
1860–99	177	15	—	—
1900–69	135	8	1,611	54
1800–1969	534	—	—	—
1945–69	24	3	640	64

Notes: A dash indicates that there are no data available. Data for the years 1953–69 are based on estimated numbers of departmental committees.
Source: For full details, see Appendix A.

1800, the records are simply inadequate for yielding any reasonably accurate list of royal commissions; and, prior to 1900, the records cannot be relied upon for departmental committees.[19] In any case, even if detailed information were available from earlier periods, its significance would be questionable. For the relationship between the executive and legislative branches of government was so different before 1800 from what it is now, and the extent of government activity so different before 1900, that changes in the use of

19 See Appendix A, p. 227 for further details on the historical sources of information for this study.

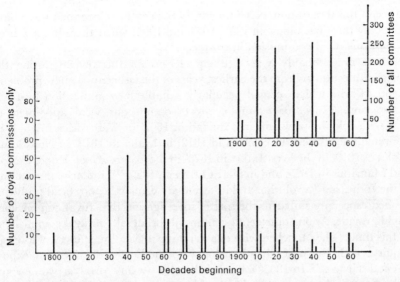

Figure 3.1 Royal commissions and departmental committees, 1800–1969 (by decades) by number appointed and average annual number in existence

Source: See Table 3.1

royal commissions and departmental committees become overshadowed by other, more fundamental changes in the system of government as a whole.

There are at least two different ways of measuring the use of royal commissions and departmental committees over time: by the number of committees appointed each year and by the number of committees in existence each year. The first method is the more common one, even though it gives a somewhat distorted view of the use of committees, in the sense that each committee is recorded only once and at the time of its appointment regardless of how long the committee is actually in operation. The second method, therefore, gives a more realistic measure of the use of committees over time. In any case, Table 3.1 and the accompanying figure show both the number of committees appointed and the average annual number of committees in existence in each decade since the beginning of the last century.

Royal commissions had fallen somewhat out of favour by the end of the eighteenth century, but they were destined for a dramatic change of fortune. Early in the nineteenth century, royal commissions were being appointed at the rate of about one each year. By the middle of the century, the rate had increased more than sevenfold; in 1859, no fewer than thirteen royal commissions were appointed in a single year.[20] This period has been called the 'Golden Age' of royal commissions, and the data here clearly reveal the

20 This record number included royal commissions on popular education, naval recruitment, the condition of the militia, and the siting and maintenance of nautical lights and beacons; see Clokie and Robinson, *op. cit.*, Chapter 3.

justice of this description. Nevertheless, in the century since then there have been only three occasions (in 1963, 1967 and 1968) when there has not been at least one royal commission in existence.

There are probably a good many reasons for this revival during the nineteenth century. From the earliest years of the last century, new problems began to arise which seemed peculiarly suitable for examination by royal commission. Thus, for example, royal commissions were appointed to deal with colonial problems in Trinidad in 1802, in West Africa in 1811, in the remaining American colonies in 1812, in Malta in 1812, in New South Wales in 1819, in the West Indies in 1825, in the Cape of Good Hope, Ceylon and Mauritius in 1825, and in Sierra Leone in 1825.[21] Similarly, the coming of the Industrial Revolution and its attendant economic and social problems seemed especially suited to the sort of investigation that royal commissions could provide. As one nineteenth-century historian said of royal commissions at this time, 'They touched with one hand the ancient machinery of forensic inquiry, with the other hand the new methods of inductive and experimental science.'[22] In 1833, for example, after twenty years of two new appointments each year or so, suddenly eleven new commissions were appointed in the space of a single year: three to examine municipal corporations in England, Scotland and Ireland and eight others on a variety of matters, including the conditions of employment for children in factories, the poor in Ireland, a digest of the criminal law, and the Department of Excise.[23] Gradually, moreover, the opportunities for royal commissions grew, not only owing to the emergence of new problems but also owing to ever more extensive demands for government to play an active role in the management of society. Both these factors led inevitably to a marked increase in the use of royal commissions.

Other factors were at work as well. With the continued passing of powers from the Crown to Parliament, some of the old unpopularity surrounding royal commissions began to wear off. It became recognised that commissions were no longer merely creatures of the Crown, but were normally appointed *de facto* by the elected representatives of the people. Moreover, the previous favourites, Parliamentary committees, began to find that they had to face criticisms of their own, which led in turn to a curtailment of their activities.[24]

---

21 The reports of some of these commissions 'formed the basis for many important decisions in the years that followed'. (G. M. Young, *The Colonial Office in the Early Nineteenth Century* (London: Longman, 1961), p. 37; see *ibid.*, pp. 37 and 72 for details of the commissions cited).

22 William Cory, *A Guide to Modern English History*, Part II (London: Kegan Paul, French, 1882), p. 366.

23 Clokie and Robinson, *op. cit.*, Chapter 3; and H. W. C. Davis, *The Age of Grey and Peel* (London: Oxford University Press, 1929), pp. 162ff.

24 Clokie and Robinson, *op. cit.*, Chapter 3. See also K. B. Smellie, *A Hundred Years of English Government*, 2nd ed. (London: Duckworth, 1950), *passim*.

As for departmental committees, the other possible rival, the available evidence suggests that they did not become a serious threat to the popularity of royal commissions until later in the century.

When the decline came, it came gently. In the 1870s, the economic depression prompted the appointment of royal commissions on the problems of industry and agriculture, but a smaller total number of royal commissions was being appointed. Through the 1860s, there had been an average of nearly six new appointments per year. In the '70s and '80s this rate fell back to about four new appointments per year, and in the '90s it fell below four for the first time in seven decades. Royal commissions did not, however, revert to anything like their position of relative obscurity in the eighteenth century. They remained an important institution of government. In 1884, for example, there was a Royal Commission on the Housing of the Poor which included the Prince of Wales, Cardinal Manning, Lord Salisbury and many other leading politicians of the day. As one historian has explained, 'The era of royal commissions during the last twenty years of the nineteenth century was fertile in ideas but deficient in achievement'.[25]

There seems to have been a slight recovery in the popularity of royal commissions during the first decade of the present century. Most of this can be traced to the sudden appointment of eleven new royal commissions in 1906, more than in any other single year since the record number in 1859. These eleven included royal commissions on canals, the metropolitan police, mines, coast erosion, lighthouses and vivisection.[26] The decennial average fell more abruptly from 1910. This cannot really be explained as simply the effect of the World War, since no fewer than ten royal commissions were actually appointed during the war. Nevertheless, 1915 was the first year for nearly a century in which no new royal commission was appointed. During the '20s the appointment of royal commissions remained at an average of about three per year. National economic conditions in the early '30s probably caused the decline to go still further in this decade to an average rate of appointment of well under two per year. Then the Second World War, unlike the First, did lower the rate of appointment of royal commissions in the '40s to a level lower than any in two centuries. The '50s and '60s have not yet seen much in the way of a recovery; since the war, the situation seems to have stabilised at an average of approximately one new royal commission each year.

The gradual decline in the number of royal commissions during the late Victorian era as well as the more abrupt change after 1910 are almost certainly related to the growing popularity of departmental committees, a

---

25 Hanham, *op. cit.*, p. 297.

26 The most complete list of all the royal commissions appointed since 1900 is to be found in David Butler, *British Political Facts, 1900–1968*, 3rd ed. (London: Macmillan, 1969), pp. 175–9.

popularity which rapidly surpassed that of royal commissions by a large margin. During the last century, the use of departmental committees grew in step with the gradual development of what are now recognised as government departments. Perhaps the use of departmental committees in the mid-century was curtailed to some extent by the popularity of royal commissions at the time, but it is difficult to know exactly what happened since no detailed information has yet been compiled on departmental committees before 1900. By 1900, however, it is known that departmental committees were being appointed at the rate of thirteen per year – already more than the highest number of royal commissions ever appointed in a single year except for 1859.

Since the beginning of this century, more than fourteen hundred departmental committees have been appointed: an average of more than twenty new committees every year. Their appointment has been marked by two bursts of activity and two relatively quiet periods. The two bursts of activity followed the two world wars. Forty five new committees were appointed in 1919 and forty two in 1948. Like that of royal commissions, the appointment of departmental committees fell off during the troubled '30s, when first economic conditions and then the outbreak of war curtailed many of the activities of government. The use of departmental committees declined again in the early 1960s, probably due at least in part to renewed economic difficulties, but the decline was not quite as marked as the previous one. In fact, except for a period during the Second World War, the number of departmental committees in existence per year has never fallen below the level first set in 1900. Moreover, the average annual number of committees in existence was higher during the '50s than in any other decade. Departmental committees, therefore, are much more numerous than royal commissions are or ever have been, and they have not yet suffered any sustained decline in popularity.

A fairly clear and consistent picture emerges from an examination of the use of royal commissions and departmental committees together (see Figure 3.1). Since 1900, between two hundred and two hundred and seventy of these committees have been appointed each decade except in the '30s. As has been suggested, national political and economic conditions readily account for these exceptions. In only eight of the first seventy years of this century have there been fewer than forty committees of both kinds in existence. The annual average for the whole century is fifty three, of which twenty three are new appointments and thirty are appointed in previous years.

One result of this consistent popularity is that the institution of royal commissions and departmental committees has been exported to many of the former British dominions.[27] In particular, Canada and Australia have

27 A. H. Cole, *A Finding-List of Royal Commission Reports in the British Dominions* (Cambridge, Mass.: Harvard University Press, 1939) lists royal commissions appointed up to 1939 by the governments of Australia, Canada, Newfoundland, New Zealand, South Africa and Southern Rhodesia.

adopted the practice of appointing these committees at both federal and provincial or state levels.[28] In Canada, for example, the federal government alone appointed no less than 344 royal commissions between 1870 and 1969; in Britain, there were only 253 appointed during the same period.[29] In Australia, ninety six royal commissions were appointed between 1945 and 1967, seven by the Commonwealth government and eighty nine by the various State governments; in Britain, twenty four were appointed in the same period.[30] Before the last war, some dominion royal commissions even 'imported' commissioners from Britain.[31] Perhaps the most interesting point, however, is that, outside Britain, royal commissions and departmental committees are appointed under the provisions of a statute and not by prerogative or conventional powers.[32] Nevertheless, the spread of royal commissions and departmental committees through the Empire is further testimony to their usefulness in government.

It is worth noting, too, that one of the casualties of the continued popularity of royal commissions and departmental committees in Britain since the turn of the century has been the select committee of Parliament. Professor

28 *Ibid.*; Watson Sellar, 'A Century of Commissions of Inquiry', *Canadian Bar Review*, XXV (1947), pp. 1–28; and Alexander Brady, 'Royal Commissions in the Dominions', *University of Toronto Quarterly*, VIII (1939), pp. 284–92.

29 Data on Canadian royal commissions are from John Courtney, 'In Defence of Royal Commissions', *Canadian Public Administration*, XII 2 (Summer 1969), pp. 198–212. The other major sources on Canadian royal commissions are: T. K. Ramsay, *Government Commissions of Inquiry* (Toronto: no information, 1863); J. E. Hodgetts, 'Royal Commissions of Inquiry in Canada: a Study in Investigative Technique', unpublished M.A. thesis (University of Toronto, 1940); J. E. Hodgetts, 'Royal Commissions of Inquiry in Canada', *Public Administration Review*, IX (1949), pp. 22–9; K. B. Callard, 'Commissions of Inquiry in Canada: 1867–1949', Special Report prepared for the Privy Council (Ottawa: mimeo, 1950); J. E. Hodgetts, 'The Role of Royal Commissions in Canadian Government', *Proceedings of the Third Annual Conference on the Institute of Public Administration of Canada*, ed. Philip Clark (Toronto: mimeo, 1951), pp. 351–67; Gordon Bennett, 'An Administrator Looks behind the Scenes of a Royal Commission', unpublished M.A. thesis (Ottawa: Carleton University, 1964); John Courtney, 'Canadian Royal Commissions of Inquiry 1946 to 1962', unpublished Ph.D. thesis (Durham, N.C.: Duke University, 1964); G. F. Henderson, *Federal Royal Commissions in Canada, 1867–1966: a Checklist* (University of Toronto Press, 1967); G. B. Doern, 'The Role of Royal Commissions in the General Policy Process and in Federal-Provincial Relations', *Canadian Public Administration*, X 4 (December 1967), pp. 415–28; H. R. Hanson, 'Inside Royal Commissions', *Canadian Public Administration*, XII 3 (Fall 1969), pp. 356–64; and C. E. S. Walls, 'Royal Commissions – Their Influence on Public Policy', *ibid.*, pp. 365–71.

30 National Library of Australia, 'Royal Commissions Appointed by the Commonwealth and by the States since 1945' (Canberra: typescript, December 1967).

31 Hodgetts, 'Royal Commissions of Inquiry in Canada' (1940), *op. cit.*, pp. 4–5.

32 In Canada, see the Inquiries Act, 1952 (*Revised Statutes of Canada*, 1952, Chapter 154), as well as the various provincial statutes. In Australia, see the Royal Commissions Act, 1902 (*Commonwealth Acts*, 1902, No. 12), as amended, as well as the various State statutes. In New Zealand, see the Commissions of Inquiry Act, 1908 (*Statutes of New Zealand*, 1908, No. 25), as amended.

Bernard Crick has pointed out that

> from 1867 to the end of the century there were – on a rough average – something like thirty three Select Committees [of the House of Commons] sitting each session . . . of which about three-fifths sat to consider matters of general public interest. But a similar count from 1945–61 shows an average of only fifteen Select Committees a year . . . of which only six, or seven at best, could be said to have been of public interest and not simply concerned with the domestic affairs of the House.[33]

While, in short, royal commissions and departmental committees have flourished, select committees of the House of Commons have withered. Professor Crick concludes sadly that it is symptomatic of 'Ministerial willingness to be advised on policy by Whitehall a hundred times more gladly than by the House'.

At the same time, one might well ask why the use of royal commissions and departmental committees has not in fact shown more growth than it has done since 1900. After all, the expansion of government activities in the nineteenth century was marked by a dramatic increase in the number of royal commissions. Why was a similar expansion in the present century not reflected by a corresponding growth in the use of royal commissions and departmental committees? There is no obvious answer to this question, unless perhaps it is that there is an upper limit to the use of this kind of advisory committee. It may be that government and the society it serves can cope with no more than fifty or sixty royal commissions and departmental committees at a time. Beyond this point, perhaps, committees begin to lose their credibility. They can no longer attract people to serve on them, interest groups to present evidence to them, Parliament to pay any attention to their recommendations, and so on. This saturation point, if such it is, was reached as early as 1906 and has been maintained more or less consistently ever since.

In any event, royal commissions and departmental committees have grown into an important and ever-present institution of government in Britain over the past century and a half. There have been some periods of greater use than others, but these swings can readily be accounted for by wars or temporary national economic conditions. Royal commissions seem to have gradually given way to departmental committees as the century has unfolded, but together they are as popular as they have ever been.

The Period since 1945

Over six hundred royal commissions and departmental committees were appointed in the twenty five years from 1945 to 1969. Table 3.2 distributes these committees according to the year in which each was appointed and the

33 Bernard Crick, *The Reform of Parliament* (London: Weidenfeld and Nicolson, 1964), pp. 94–5 and Appendix A; see also his own contribution, 'Parliament and the Matter of Britain', in Bernard Crick (ed.), *Essays on Reform* (London: Oxford University Press, 1967), pp. 203–22.

Table 3.2 Royal commissions and departmental committees, 1945–69, by number appointed and in existence per year

year	number of committees appointed	number of committees in existence
1945	26	65
1946	34	63
1947	38	71
1948	42	88
1949	27	80
1950	18	66
1951	29	66
1952	25	66
1953	29	73
1954	25	73
1955	25	62
1956	16	40
1957	44	71
1958	31	70
1959	27	66
1960	12	52
1961	21	46
1962	15	49
1963	31	58
1964	25	63
1965	20	65
1966	22	60
1967	27	69
1968	16	67
1969	17	62
1945–69	640	64 (mean)

Notes: See Table 3.1.

Source: See Appendix A.

years in which each existed; Figure 3.2 provides an illustration of the results. The data show that royal commissions and departmental committees have been appointed at an average rate of twenty five per year – or more than two every month – since the war. Over the same period, there was an average of sixty four committees in existence each year, more than during any decade prior to this time.

Within this period, the number of new appointments per year has in fact fluctuated widely. Over forty new appointments were recorded in 1948 and 1957, while only about a dozen were made in 1960. In general, there

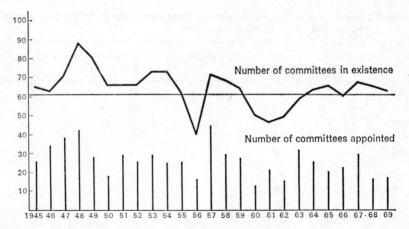

Figure 3.2: Royal commissions and departmental committees, 1945-69, by number appointed and in existence per year

Source: See Table 3.2

have been two major periods of activity. Above-average rates of appointment occurred principally during the immediate postwar years (1945–9), when the rate rose steadily for four years before dropping off; and then again during the years 1957–9, when the rate suddenly shot up from sixteen per year in 1956 to forty four the following year and then gradually subsided. The pattern becomes clearer if one examines the data on the number of royal commissions and departmental committees in existence per year. The postwar boom appears to have given way to a fairly stable level of activity during the 1950s – apart from the exceptional year of 1956. There is a decline in activity during the early '60s, but it is not sustained after 1963. To summarise, therefore: expansion immediately postwar; levelling off in the '50s at a slightly above-average rate (except for 1956); clear decline in the early '60s; and recovery in the mid-60's.

This pattern can fairly easily be explained. The immediate postwar boom was the offspring of a newly elected and relatively active Labour government. As the ardour of the government wore off and as the prospect of retaining power for another five years became less certain, the number of new appointments declined in 1949 and 1950. Successive Tory governments during the 1950s enjoyed relatively stable political conditions for most of the decade (except in 1956, the year of Suez). During this time, the various governments appointed an above-average number of committees every year (except for 1956). Contemporary national economic conditions probably account for the relatively low number of appointments in the early '60s. The change in fortune occurring in 1963 and 1964 came with the expectation of better things under first Sir Alec Douglas-Home and then Harold Wilson.

This explanation is based on the assumption that the appointment of royal commissions and departmental committees is sensitive to broad economic and political conditions in the country. In other words, committees tend to reflect changes in the overall level of activity of a government. This is because they are, in a sense, economic and political luxuries. Thus, when economic conditions restrict government activities or when political problems preoccupy ministers, fewer royal commissions and departmental committees are appointed. When, on the contrary, economic conditions are favourable and political problems under control, then more committees are likely to be appointed. In short, committees seem to be creatures of stability not crisis.[34]

The Major Postwar Committees

There have been, therefore, at least two thousand different royal commissions and departmental committees appointed in Britain. Well over six hundred have been appointed since 1945 alone. These committees have varied enormously, of course, in terms of their relative importance. Some of them, in fact, have been quite insignificant; on the other hand, it would be hard to exaggerate the importance of some others. To make a more detailed study of the structure and operation of these committees, a selection has been made of some of the more important ones appointed in the twenty five years immediately following the Second World War. This selection consists of a total of 358 committees, including twenty four royal commissions and 334 departmental committees. This set of committees is referred to throughout the rest of the study as the 'major postwar committees'.

The twenty-five-year period selected runs from the beginning of 1945 to the end of 1969. Thus, the major postwar committees were all appointed on or after 1 January 1945 and on or before 31 December 1969. Within this period, the major committees are defined as consisting of:

a   all royal commissions; and
b   all departmental committees which
  i   dealt with matters of direct concern to the government of Britain, and
  ii had their reports published as Command Papers rather than Non-Parliamentary Papers.

In brief, the effect of the last two criteria is to include (as near as can be determined[35]) just over half of all the departmental committees actually appointed in the period from 1945 to 1969.

The purpose of the first criterion is essentially to omit all committees having exclusively to do with colonies and dependent territories (though not

34 Interestingly enough, Hodgetts, 'Royal Commissions of Inquiry in Canada' (1940), *op. cit.*, p. 10, indicates that, 'in both Canada and Australia there has been a tendency to increase the use of [royal] commissions, especially in times of stress such as war, depression or rapid expansion'.

35 See Appendix A, p. 227.

with Britain's international relations). Northern Ireland presents something of a special case in this connection. Committees of the Ulster government are not included in any case (see p. 8), but a great many committees of the British government are appointed to consider matters as they exist throughout the United Kingdom (including Northern Ireland) and some even deal with matters limited to Northern Ireland. All these committees are considered here as being of direct concern to Britain and (subject to the second criterion) are classed as major committees.

The second criterion of a major committee is that its report (or at least one of its reports in cases where there is more than one) must be published as a Command Paper. At first glance, it may seem rather odd to base the selection on this kind of technical distinction, even though it is one which is very easy to apply in practice. In fact, however, the distinction has become more than just a technical one. It is used to indicate official documents which are considered by the government or a minister to be relatively important for present and future public policy.

Official papers may be published as either Parliamentary or Non-Parliamentary Papers. In general, papers and documents arising from activities inside the Houses of Parliament – that is, Journals, Votes, Act Papers, Orders, Reports from Committees of either House, etc. – are published as Parliamentary Papers, and papers and documents arising from activities outside Parliament are published as Non-Parliamentary Papers.[36]

There is, however, one important exception: the Command Paper. The Command Paper provides a means of publishing a document that arises from activities outside Parliament as a Parliamentary Paper and thereby bringing it directly to the attention of the two Houses. What this means is that reports of royal commissions and departmental committees can be published in one of two different ways, either as Non-Parliamentary Papers or as Parliamentary (i.e. Command) Papers.

The formal distinction between Command Papers and other Parliamentary Papers lies in the fact that the former are 'Presented to Parliament by Command of the Crown', whereas the latter are simply 'Ordered by the House of Commons to be printed'.[37] This difference is underlined by the fact that Command Papers have their own distinct numbering system. Since 1833 they have been numbered according to the date of their publication (not, incidentally, according to the date of their presentation to Parliament) in five series:

36 On the historical development of Parliamentary Papers, see P. Ford and G. Ford, *A Guide to Parliamentary Papers* (Oxford: Blackwell, 1955), Part II, and Josef Redlich, *The Procedure of the House of Commons*, Volume II (London: Constable, 1908), pp. 47–50. See also Appendix A, p. 227.

37 For the differences in procedure involved in presenting the various kinds of Parliamentary Papers, see Erskine May, *The Law, Privileges, Proceedings and Usage of Parliament*, 17th ed. (London: Butterworth, 1964), pp. 261–76.

> from   1 (in 1833) to   4222 (in 1868–9),
> from   C. 1 (in 1870) to   C. 9550 (in 1899),
> from   Cd. 1 (in 1900) to   Cd. 9239 (in 1918),
> from   Cmd. 1 (in 1919) to Cmd. 9889 (in 1956), and
> from Cmnd. 1 (in 1956) which is still in effect.

Other Parliamentary Papers have sessional series of numbers, while Non-Parliamentary Papers have no formal numbering system beyond an internal system of code numbers used by HMSO. There have been about seven thousand Command Papers since the beginning of 1945. Command Papers, therefore, are readily distinguishable from other Parliamentary Papers as well as from Non-Parliamentary Papers.

This technical distinction is relatively unimportant in itself but it has assumed a certain significance since 1921. It is normally up to the minister or ministers involved to decide whether to publish the report of a committee as a Command Paper or as a Non-Parliamentary Paper.[38] Originally, virtually all official papers arising from activities outside Parliament were presented to Parliament by Command; however, since 1921

> there has been a fundamental change in the situation. The immediate cause of this was the difficulties which arose from the Free List. The House and Command Papers, known together as the *Sessional Papers*, were distributed free to Members of Parliament and to a number of bodies and organisations both at home and abroad, and the expense of this practice had engaged the attention of many committees on Printing and Publications. This was brought to a head in the economy campaigns of the Government after the 1914–18 war, when the Treasury issued the important Circular No. 38/21.[39]

This Circular instructed departments to reduce the number of their Command Papers. It put the onus on departments to be able to justify the publication of any document as a Command Paper – that is, of proving that 'the matter dealt with was likely to be the subject of early legislation or the papers were otherwise essential to Members of Parliament as a whole to enable them to discharge their responsibilities'.[40] The immediate effect of the Circular was a reduction in the number of Command Papers and the transfer of many of the regular and routine papers (such as annual reports, statistical returns, etc.) to the Non-Parliamentary series.

> But the long-run effects were more far-reaching and went beyond what seems to have been originally contemplated, for not only were regular,

38 A former committee chairman told me he had insisted on having photographs in his final report. This nearly cost him Command-Paper status since papers presented by Command normally do not contain photographs!

39 Ford and Ford, *op. cit.*, pp. 16–17.

40 *ibid.*, p. 17.

routine reports . . . affected, but also policy documents of major importance. For the Treasury rule had to be interpreted and applied to the
greatly increasing flow of reports from these outside investigating bodies –
the Departmental, Advisory and Consultative Committees, etc. The
result has been greatly to reduce the number and proportion . . . presented
[by Command].[41]

Since 1921, the Treasury does not appear to have offered any further
guidance on the question of Command Papers. Thus, the decision still rests
in principle upon the anticipated importance of the document for public
policy. Command Papers are generally

restricted to matters of Government policy likely to be the subject of
debate or legislation, Commonwealth and foreign affairs and treaties, and
reports on the work of government departments.[42]

Official papers not concerned with the matters specified above are normally
published as Non-Parliamentary Papers.

Traditionally, the reports (though not necessarily the minutes of evidence)
of royal commissions are always published as Command Papers, but as far as
departmental committees are concerned, it is more difficult to assess the
impact of the Command-Paper criterion. Since the Treasury ruling on
Command Papers is still rather vague and since its application has involved
a large number of different ministers and officials over many years, there
have quite naturally been some paradoxical results. For example, one may
well wonder whether some of the following committees were not sufficiently
important to warrant having their reports published as Command Papers
instead of as Non-Parliamentary Papers: the Morison Committee on the
Probation Service (1962), the Buchanan Committee on Traffic in Towns
(1963), the Hole Committee on a Third London Airport (1963), the Platt
Committee on the Reform of Nursing Education (1964), the Geddes Committee on Road Haulage (1965), the Tennant Committee on the Organisation of the Scientific Civil Service (1965), and the Maud Committee on the
Management of Local Government (1967).[43] Conversely, one may equally
well wonder how some of the committees which did have their reports published as Command Papers were felt to be sufficiently important. In spite of
both of these difficulties, it is still reasonable to say that, in general, the more

41 *loc. cit.*

42 Norman Wilding and Philip Laundy, *An Encyclopaedia of Parliament*, rev. ed. (London:
Cassell, 1961), p. 118; see also Marjorie Ogilvy-Webb, *The Government Explains* (London:
Allen and Unwin, 1965), p. 25.

43 One compromise has been to publish an 'Explanatory Memorandum' by the government
as a Command Paper at the same time as the committee report appears as a Non-
Parliamentary Paper: e.g., Cmnd. 5364 and the report of the Nugent Committee on
Defence Lands (Non-Parliamentary Paper, 1974).

important departmental committees have their reports published as Command Papers, and thus to use this as a basis for selecting the major postwar committees.

Most of the rest of this study is based on an analysis of the 358 major postwar committees chosen in the way described above. These committees are all listed in Appendix B, along with detailed information about their structure and operation. It should be emphasized again that these committees are not the only ones to have been appointed since the war – although the list does include all postwar royal commissions. Some postwar departmental committees are not included because they did not deal with matters of direct concern to the government of Britain or because their reports were not published as Command Papers. There have also been royal commissions and departmental committees appointed since the end of the twenty-five-year postwar period used here (i.e. since 1969), and some of these have already published reports. None of these is included in the selection of major postwar committees, although the major ones which have issued reports at the time of going to press are listed briefly in Appendix C.

4
Appointing a Committee

Royal commissions and departmental committees come into existence through the action of government ministers or their officials. The precise nature of the action required to bring a committee officially into existence can vary all the way from the most formal kind of government document to no more than a letter addressed to the intended chairman. Different committees reflect a variety of different usages.

The appointment of a royal commission or departmental committee, moreover, reflects a decision which is both governmental and departmental in nature. There is the general question of how willing and able a given government is to appoint committees of this kind, and there is the particular question of the extent to which a given department is prepared to appoint such committees. Broadly speaking, there tends to be little variation in the use of committees by different governments. On the other hand, royal commissions and departmental committees are quite clearly more popular with some government departments than with others.

The Mechanics of Appointment

The formal distinction between royal commissions and departmental committees (described in Chapter 2) is perpetuated principally by a basic difference in the mechanics of their appointment. If the committee is to be a royal commission, then it will invariably be appointed by means of a royal warrant prepared by the Home Secretary or the Secretary of State for Scotland and signed by the monarch. If the committee is to be a departmental committee, a royal warrant is not used. Instead, there are several alternatives, some of them nearly as formal as a royal warrant and others much less so, all of which are signed by ministers or their officials and not by the Crown.

Royal warrants proclaim in a rather grandiloquent manner that the Queen sends 'Greeting' to certain of her subjects; informs them that she deems it 'expedient that a Commission should forthwith issue' to inquire into some particular matter for which the terms of reference are specified; and, 'reposing great trust and confidence in your knowledge and ability', proceeds 'by these Presents to authorise and appoint you . . . to be our Commissioners for the purpose of the said inquiry. . . .' Finally, the warrant is 'given at Our

Court at St. James' and is signed 'by Her Majesty's Command' by the Home Secretary or the Secretary of State for Scotland.[1]

Formal appointment of departmental committees is accomplished by means of what are called warrants of appointment and minutes of appointment. By means of a warrant of appointment, the minister or ministers whose signatures appear on the warrant 'hereby appoint' one or more people named in the warrant 'to be a committee' to inquire into some particular matter according to specified terms of reference. A minute of appointment is not, strictly speaking, a device for making an appointment, although it often serves as such; rather it is the formal record of an appointment. Thus, it is signed not by a minister but by an official of his department. It states that, 'in accordance with' some policy or statement of policy to which reference is made, a minister or ministers has appointed one or more people named in the minute 'to be a committee' to inquire into some particular matter, and again the terms of reference are specified.[2] Royal warrants, incidentally, specify the name of the chairman, whereas warrants and minutes of appointment do not always do so. On the other hand, warrants and minutes of appointment (unlike royal warrants) often name committee staff (secretaries, assessors, etc.) as well.

Finally, some departmental committees are appointed in a quite informal manner, without a warrant or a minute or anything else except a letter from the minister. The Lewis Committee on Army and Air Force Courts-Martial (Cmd. 7608), for example, reported that it was appointed by means of a 'War Office letter dated 4 November 1946' sent to each of its members. Similarly, the Cameron Inquiry into the Complaint Made by the National Union of Bank Employees to the International Labour Organisation (Cmnd. 2202) reported that it was appointed by means of only a 'note' dated 9 April 1963. It should be added that ministers may take advantage of Parliamentary Questions (some of them no doubt 'inspired') not only to draw attention to committees which have already been appointed by some more formal device, but also to announce more or less officially the existence of committees which have been appointed in the informal ways just described.

Among departmental committees, it is easy to say when but hard to say why one form of appointment is preferred to another. Not all committees describe how they were appointed; but of the major postwar committees

---

1 There are minor variations in the wording of these warrants, but this is typical. See also A. B. Keith, *The King and the Imperial Crown* (London: Longmans, Green, 1936), pp. 68–76, for a description of the various kinds of royal acts, including royal warrants and commissions.

2 The wording of warrants and minutes of appointment is again fairly standard, but there is more variety than among royal warrants. For specific examples of each of the former, see the reports of the Littlewood Committee on Cruelty to Animals (Cmnd. 2641) and the McCorquodale Committee on the Assessment of Disablement (Cmnd. 2487) respectively.

which did, three-quarters date their official existence from a formal document of some kind. Among these, warrants are slightly more common than minutes. In addition, a fairly high proportion of the one-man committees were appointed by warrant but none of them by minute. Most of the other departmental committees which stated how they were appointed were simply announced in Parliament, although even the Press is used occasionally as a forum for announcing the appointment of a committee.[3] In general, it is the relatively more important committees which are appointed by the more formal devices, but there are exceptions. For example, the Plowden Group on the Control of Public Expenditure (Cmnd. 1432) – which could scarcely be regarded as an unimportant committee – was not appointed formally by either warrant or minute of appointment; perhaps this was because of the confidential nature of this committee.

From a constitutional point of view, this variety is of little practical consequence. The appointment of a departmental committee represents the exercise of conventional powers by ministers. Thus, as long as there is some document signed by a minister or one of his officials attesting to the existence of a committee, it may be deemed to have a legitimate constitutional existence. On the other hand, this means that the defeat of a government raises a nice constitutional point: do committees appointed under one government continue to exist when a new government takes its place after an election? (Royal commissions are, of course, above this controversy as they are formally appointed by the Crown.) In practice, no major committee appears to have ever been disbanded or even brought to a premature end following a change in government, even though this must at times have entailed a fairly radical change in ministerial attitude. On the other hand, the constitutional question remains; and, following the election of a Conservative government in 1951, two committees did in fact report that they had been invited explicitly to continue by their new ministers.[4] Moreover, plans to appoint committees have been abandoned following a change of government. For example, there were rumours in 1970 that had the Labour government been re-elected, a committee under the chairmanship of Lord Annan would have been appointed to inquire into the future of broadcasting; with the return of Labour in 1974, such a committee has in fact been appointed. Nevertheless, no serious problem has yet arisen over the status of a departmental committee following a change of government.

3 Most Parliamentary announcements occur in the House of Commons; but the Somervell Committee on State Immunities (Cmd. 8460) reported that it was first announced in the House of Lords. The appointment of the Birkett Committee on the Interception of Communications (Cmnd. 283) was announced in *The Times* on 29 June 1957.
4 The Nathan Committee on Charitable Trusts was appointed by Prime Minister Attlee; it reported (Cmd. 8710) that 'In November, 1951, you [Prime Minister Churchill] invited us to continue this inquiry'. Similarly, the Ridley Committee on Fuel and Power Resources reported (Cmd. 8647) that 'You [the new Minister of Fuel and Power] asked us to continue the inquiry begun at your predecessor's request. . . .'

Appointment by Different Governments

Every government and, at one time or another, virtually every department of government has appointed and been advised by a royal commission or a departmental committee. As such, the appointment of these committees reflects ideas about the nature of government and the role which various departments perceive themselves as having. It is worthwhile, therefore, to see which governments and which departments have been relatively more active in appointing committees.

On the face of it, there are things about royal commissions and departmental committees to appeal to both Conservative and Labour governments. For Conservatives, committees may be regarded as combining decentralisation of government with greater participation by those members of society who are best qualified to do so. For Labour supporters, on the other hand, royal commissions and departmental committees may be regarded as non-partisan devices for achieving more informed and more democratic government.[5] Accordingly, it seems reasonable to expect that the incidence of committee appointments will not vary much according to the party in power.

Instead, the rate of appointment of committees is more likely to vary from one particular government to another. For one thing, individual governments often face distinctive kinds of economic and political conditions. For another thing, each government has its own specific programme of reform to carry out. Thus, it seems likely that, for example, the first Attlee government, with its image of postwar revival, would have felt a greater need for royal commissions and departmental committees than, say, the Wilson governments, with their image of a government technocracy at work.

Table 4.1 shows how many major royal commissions and departmental committees have been appointed by each government since the war. Each government is in power for a different length of time, of course, and so the figures for each government cannot be compared without taking this into account. In order to permit such comparisons, a hypothetical annual rate of appointment has been calculated for each government.

There is little evidence in the data to support the view that one political party has a greater tendency to appoint committees than the other. Conservative governments have been in power for slightly longer than Labour governments in the postwar period and, if this is taken into account, there is very little difference in the behaviour of the two parties. Only among royal commissions alone does any difference emerge. Fourteen of the twenty four major royal commissions were appointed by the four Labour governments, and ten by the seven Conservative governments. Conservatives, therefore, are slightly less disposed towards creating royal commissions, apparently being more content with the lower-key approach of departmental committees.

5 One of the best recent discussions of party ideologies in Britain can be found in S. H. Beer, *Modern British Politics* (London: Faber and Faber, 1965).

Table 4.1 Major royal commissions and departmental committees, 1945–69, by appointing governments

government	total number of committees appointed (including royal commissions)		hypothetical annual rate of appointment
National Government		7	17
Churchill (23 May '45)		4	24
Attlee (26 Jul '45)*	80		17
Attlee (24 Feb '50)*	22		13
Attlee		102 (7)	16
Churchill (26 Oct '51)*		51 (4)	15
Eden (6 Apr '55)	3		18
Eden (27 May '55)*	17		11
Eden		20 (1)	11
Macmillan (10 Jan '57)	54		19
Macmillan (9 Oct '59)*	43		11
Macmillan		97 (4)	14
Douglas-Home (19 Oct '63)		15 (1)	16
Wilson (15 Oct '64)*	21		14
Wilson (31 Mar '66)*	41		11
Wilson (to end of '69)		62 (7)	12
Total		*358 (24)*	*14*
National Government		7	17
Conservative Governments		187 (10)	14
Labour Governments		164 (14)	14

Notes: The dates in parentheses refer to the date of formation of the governments shown; an asterisk denotes a government formed after a general election. The numbers in parentheses refer to royal commissions only. The hypothetical annual rate of appointment for each government is found by dividing its number of appointments by the number of years and months during which it held power. Conservative governments were in power for 13 years 1 month and Labour for 11 years 6 months.

Source: See Appendix B.

Among the various individual governments (apart from the short-lived ones in 1945 and 1955), the highest rate of appointment (nineteen committees per year) was achieved during Harold Macmillan's first term as Prime Minister. The first government under Clement Attlee was a close second, followed by Sir Alec Douglas-Home's brief government. The lowest rate of appointment (ten per year) was recorded by the second government of Harold Wilson. The government under Sir Anthony Eden following the election of May 1955 and (oddly enough in view of its earlier performance) the second Macmillan government also appointed relatively few committees. Thus, the evidence suggests that royal commissions and departmental committees suit the style of some governments (such as Macmillan's first) better than that of others (such as Wilson's second). On the other hand, it is interesting to see that, of the committees they did appoint, governments under Harold Wilson were more than twice as likely as any others to appoint royal commissions in preference to departmental committees.

In conclusion, neither political party exhibits a stronger tendency than the other to appoint committees, although Labour governments on the whole seem to like royal commissions slightly more than do Conservative governments. Among individual governments, differences are more marked, in that some governments have been quite a bit more prolific than others. In line with earlier conclusions, these differences must partly reflect the different sets of economic and political conditions facing the various postwar governments. But the differences must also reflect, to some extent at least, different styles of government. The idea of relying – and being seen to rely – on bodies of people outside ordinary government circles will appear more attractive to some governments than it will to others. A government which sees a degree of complementarity between its own responsibilities to govern and the involvement of others in that process will probably show a greater tendency to appoint royal commissions and departmental committees than will a government which sees a conflict between these two principles. In short, the appointment of a committee is just like any other political action. It is the response of a particular actor to a particular situation; hence, the cause of that action lies partly in the nature of the actor and partly in the nature of the situation.

Appointment by Different Departments

Royal commissions and departmental committees are appointed by a multitude of different departments as well as by different governments, and there is a much clearer pattern to departmental behaviour than there was to governmental. Almost every department of government appointed or helped to appoint at least one major postwar committee, but most of them were appointed by a group of eight specific departments. At one extreme, there is the Chancellor of the Duchy of Lancaster who appointed only two of the major postwar committees.[6] At the other extreme, there is the Home Office which has been involved in more than one out of every four major committee appointments since the war.

Most committees are appointed by a single department acting on its own. Of the major postwar committees, fewer than one quarter of them were

6 The Hopkins Committee on Cotton Import (Cmd. 8510) was appointed jointly with the President of the Board of Trade, while the Upjohn Committee on the Court of Record for the Hundred of Salford (Cmd. 8364) was appointed by the Chancellor of the Duchy of Lancaster alone.

formally appointed by more than one minister. The most 'co-ordinated' appointment was that of the Swann Committee on the Use of Antibiotics in Animal Husbandry and Veterinary Medicine (Cmnd. 4190), which was appointed by no less than five ministers: the Minister of Health, the Minister of Agriculture, Fisheries and Food, the Secretary of State for Social Services, the Secretary of State for Scotland, and the Minister of Agriculture for Northern Ireland. These joint appointments occur largely in cases where the subject of the committee impinges on the responsibilities of more than one department. Co-ordination short of formal interdepartmental participation in the appointment may also occur, as it did in the case of the Runciman Committee on the Taxicab Service (Cmd. 8804), which reported that its appointment by the Chancellor of the Exchequer had been 'in consultation with [his] colleagues, the Home Secretary, the Secretary of State for Scotland and the Minister of Transport'. As many as half of the postwar royal commissions may also have been appointed in a similar way. On the other hand, formal joint appointment may be just a courtesy, as in cases where the same minister is simultaneously head of two departments. For example, Henry Brooke was the Minister for Housing and Local Government and the Minister for Welsh Affairs when 'both' ministers jointly appointed the Reading Committee on the Consolidation of the Highway Law (Cmnd. 630). In spite of both these factors (which tend to offset each other in any case), roughly three quarters of all committee appointments are independent acts by individual departments.

More detailed comparisons of the number of committees appointed by various departments over a period of twenty five years depend upon making certain assumptions about the nature of those departments over time. Government departments are not static; they appear and disappear from year to year, shedding some functions and acquiring new ones along the way. Several departments, for example, were not in existence throughout the period between 1945 and 1969.[7] Or if they were, their jurisdictions have changed.[8] Some committees have even found, like the Monckton Committee on Alternative Remedies (Cmd. 6860), that they have been transferred in mid-operation from one department to another along with a transfer of jurisdiction. The Monckton Committee recorded laconically:

7 For example, the Ministry of Production was absorbed by the Board of Trade between May and December 1945, the Ministry of Materials was created in July 1951 and disbanded in August three years later, the wartime Ministry of Supply lasted until October 1959 when it became the Ministry of Aviation, and the Ministry of Overseas Development was set up in October 1964. For further details, see D. N. Chester and F. M. G. Willson, *The Organisation of British Central Government, 1914–1964*, 2nd ed. (London: Allen and Unwin, 1968).

8 In 1946, an Act was passed permitting the transfer of functions from one department to another by means of Orders-in-Council: the Ministers of the Crown (Transfer of Functions) Act, 1946 (9 & 10 Geo. VI, Chapter 31).

Since our appointment by the Home Secretary, the Ministry of National Insurance has been established, and it has, we understand, been agreed that we should make our report to you [the Minister of National Insurance].

The result is a very real difficulty in knowing how to classify committees appointed by departments which no longer exist or which have only just been created, as well as committees which obviously would have been appointed by another department if they had occurred some years earlier or some years later.

Clearly some sort of compromise has to be found between recording every minor change in departmental name and jurisdiction on the one hand, and trying to tie every committee to a single set of departments (such as those in existence in 1945 or 1969) on the other hand. The first procedure would create rather pointless distinctions between, for example, committees appointed by the Ministry of Pensions and those appointed by the Ministry of National Insurance, and between both of these and committees appointed by the combined Ministry after it was created in August 1953. The second procedure would require intricate conjectures about which department would have appointed a committee had it been appointed at a time different from when it actually was appointed. The slaughter of animals, for example, has been under the jurisdiction of the Ministry of Food since January 1953 and the Ministry of Agriculture, Fisheries and Food since April 1955; but before that time committees such as the Herbert Committee on Slaughter-houses in England and Wales (Cmd. 9542) and the Handford Committee on Slaughterhouses in Scotland (Cmd. 9376) would probably have been appointed by the Home Office, the Ministry of Housing and Local Government, and/or the Ministry of Health.

Finding a suitable balance between these two extremes requires a certain amount of judgement. In practice, this has meant grouping departments only to the extent that it helps to maintain certain departmental 'cores'. For in the final analysis, it is real organisations which appoint committees: namely, Whitehall departments, each with its own identity and its own values, traditions and practices. On this basis, the major postwar royal commissions and departmental committees were distributed among twenty two different departments, and the results are shown in Table 4.2.

The first point which emerges from this analysis is that the Home Office and the Scottish Office are each involved in the appointment of nearly three times as many committees as any other department. They have each had a hand in the appointment of more than one quarter of all committees. Another half-dozen departments – the Lord Chancellor's Department, the Board of Trade, the Prime Minister's Office, the Treasury, and the Ministries of Agriculture, Fisheries and Food and of Health – fall into a second class of departments which are each involved in the appointment of between five and

Table 4.2 Appointments of major royal commissions and departmental committees, 1945–69, by appointing department(s)

appointing department	total number of appointments	number of single appointments	single as a percentage of total
Home Office	100	66	66
Lord Chancellor's Department	34	24	71
Board of Trade[1]	27	25	93
Prime Minister's Office	24	23	96
Treasury[2]	24	20	83
Agriculture, Fisheries and Food[3]	23	8	35
Health	20	3	15
Education and Science[4]	17	7	41
Power[5]	14	12	86
Employment and Productivity[6]	14	13	93
Housing and Local Government[7]	13	4	31
Transport[8]	11	9	82
Defence	11	11	100
Social Services[9]	6	5	83
Foreign Office[10]	5	5	100
Welsh Office	5	1	20
Postmaster General	4	3	75
Public Buildings and Works	2	1	50
Duchy of Lancaster	2	1	50
Civil Service Department	1	1	100
Master of the Rolls	1	0	0
Scottish Office	93	37	40
Total Committees	*358*	*279*	*78*
Scottish Office[11]			
Home Department	65	29	45
Agriculture and Fisheries	26	6	23
Health Department	22	6	27
Education Department	6	4	67

Notes: Columns do not add to the total number of committees because of joint appointments. Royal commissions are divided between the Home Office (21) and the Scottish Home Department (3).

1 includes Materials and Overseas Trade.
2 includes the Department of Economic Affairs.
3 includes Agriculture and Fisheries and Food separately.
4 includes Education and Science separately and the Office of the Lord President of the Council.
5 includes Fuel and Power.
6 includes Labour and Labour and National Service.
7 includes Town and Country Planning and Land and Natural Resources.
8 includes Supply, Civil Aviation, and Transport and Civil Aviation.
9 includes Pensions and National Insurance, separately and together.
10 includes the Colonial Office and Technical Cooperation.
11 is subdivided into the four departments shown even though (a) the Home Department and the Department of Health were combined in June 1962, and (b) a Scottish Development Department has emerged largely from the Home Department. Scottish figures do not add up to the totals for the Scottish Office because of joint appointments between departments within the Scottish Office.

No departments not mentioned above (such as Technology or Overseas Development) have appointed any major committees.

Source: See Appendix B, p. 239.

ten percent of all committees. This represents an average of about one committee appointment per year, compared to the three or four per year by the Home Office and the Scottish Office. Apart from these eight, all other departments of government are involved only occasionally in the appointment of committees.

The second point emerging from this analysis is that the Home Office is really in a class by itself, since the Scottish Office figures are actually 'inflated' by two special factors. One is that a relatively high proportion of the Scottish Office committees are appointed jointly with other departments, usually those having corresponding responsibilities south of the border. The second is that the scope of responsibilities of the Scottish Office is equivalent to several 'English' departments. To some extent, Home Office figures are also 'inflated' due to its responsibility for appointing all royal commissions (except Scottish ones): eleven of the twenty four royal commissions probably would not have been appointed by the Home Office if they had been departmental committees. Taking all these factors into account, the Home Office is clearly the most important source of committee appointments.

Among the more prolific departments (including the Home Office and the Scottish Office), there is a clear distinction between those which tend to appoint committees on their own and those which tend to appoint committees jointly with other departments. Broadly speaking, departments appoint either more than sixty five or less than forty five percent of their committees on their own. There is no middle ground. On the one hand, the Home Office, along with most of the other leading departments, is relatively independent in its behaviour. On the other hand, the Scottish Office, along with the Ministries of Agriculture, Fisheries and Food and of Health, is relatively dependent. The interrelationship among these three dependent departments is self-explanatory when the sub-departmental figures for the Scottish Office are considered: its most dependent sectors are precisely Agriculture and Fisheries and Health. On the basis of single appointments alone, the Home Office is nearly twice as prolific as its nearest rival, the Scottish Office. Moreover, if the Scottish Office is considered not just as one department but as four, the position of the Home Office is again unrivalled. For Home Office appointments clearly exceed those of the Scottish Home Office (the leading Scottish sub-department), whether all appointments or only single appointments are considered.

There is one other factor worth mentioning here in connection with Scottish committees. That is the tendency to appoint independent but 'matching' committees; these are committees appointed by the Scottish Office alone but which, in effect, duplicate contemporary English committees.[9] One of the most recent examples involves the Perks Committee on Criminal Statistics (Cmnd. 3448) and the Thomson Committee on Criminal

9 Scottish interests may also be represented through the appointment to a committee of a 'Scottish member' (see Chapter 5, p. 62).

Statistics in Scotland (Cmnd. 3705): each of these committees was appointed independently by the Home Office and the Scottish Home Department respectively within six months of the other; they had virtually identical terms of reference; and they reported within eight months of each other. Actually, cases of matching Scottish committees are not as common as might be thought. There are only five other examples among the 358 major postwar committees; and, in one of these cases, it was in fact the Scottish committee which was appointed first.[10] This means that of the ninety three major postwar committees which the Scottish Office appointed or helped appoint, fifty six were in conjunction with English departments (so that a committee's mandate might be extended to Scotland), six were committees 'matching' similar English ones, and only thirty one were independent committees on particular Scottish problems.

To summarise, then, the Home Office is involved in the appointment of more committees than any other department: roughly one in every four. Close behind comes the Scottish Office, but many of its committees are joint appointments with other departments, since its activities range over the equivalent of several English departments, and a few committees are appointed merely to 'match' English committees. Next, there are the Lord Chancellor's Department, the Board of Trade, the Prime Minister's Office, the Treasury, and the Ministries of Health and of Agriculture, Fisheries and Food; these departments each appoint approximately one new committee per year. All other departments of government appoint committees only occasionally if at all.

The main reasons for the activity of some departments and not others are fairly straightforward. To begin with, some departments do things for which royal commissions and departmental committees are not really suitable. It is not surprising, for example, to find that the Ministry of Defence and the Foreign Office appoint relatively few committees and that not one of them was a joint appointment. Secondly, some of the older, better established departments have a tradition of appointing committees, a tradition which newer departments naturally do not have. This tradition would obviously make it easier to justify the appointment of committees. Thirdly, 'big' departments, with large areas of responsibility and correspondingly large

10 These were: the Curtis Committee on the Care of Children (Cmd. 6922) and the Clyde Committee on Homeless Children (Scotland) (Cmd. 6911); the Rushcliffe Committee on Legal Aid and Advice (Cmd. 6641), which was actually appointed before the beginning of the postwar period, and the Cameron Committee on Legal Aid and Advice in Scotland (Cmd. 6925); the Morton Committee on the Law of Intestate Succession (Cmd. 8310) and the Mackintosh Committee on the Law of Succession in Scotland (Cmd. 8144), in which case the Scottish Committee was appointed more than a year before the English Committee; the Herbert Committee on Slaughterhouses (England and Wales) (Cmd. 9542) and the Handford Committee on Slaughterhouses (Scotland) (Cmd. 9376); and the recent Maud Royal Commission on Local Government in England (Cmnd. 4040) and the Wheatley Royal Commission on Local Government in Scotland (Cmnd. 4150).

annual appropriations, are likely to be able to appoint committees more readily than smaller departments with smaller budgets. Fourthly, more powerful departments can rely on their ministers to be able to defend the appointment of a committee if the need arises and also to ensure their own independence of the committee should its recommendations (in the view of the department) go astray. In short, the appointment of committees offers greater possibilities and holds fewer risks for some departments than for others, and it is those departments which tend to appoint most committees.

There is, therefore, something of a pattern to committee appointments by department if not by government. This in turn points to the fact that the initiative and the decision to appoint a committee normally comes from specific departments rather than from the Cabinet or the Prime Minister. Some exception has to be made in the case of royal commissions, and probably some of the major departmental committees as well, as these do traditionally go before Cabinet for approval. But, in general, the evidence suggests that royal commissions and departmental committees are conceived and appointed by a number of individual ministers. These are chiefly the Home Secretary, the Secretary of State for Scotland, and six others.

5
Choosing the Right People

One of the most striking characteristics of royal commissions and departmental committees is that, although similar in kind, they are highly diversified in form. From appointment to adjournment, royal commissions and departmental committees exhibit a quite extraordinary degree of variety. One source of this variety is the nature of the people chosen to fill the positions of chairman, member, and staff.

The same two basic factors seem to be involved in choosing people for all of these positions. On the one hand, choices are based to some extent on the nature of the committee in question. Ministers and their officials will naturally try to ensure that the committee shares and reflects some of their own ideals and expectations. As one observer once put it,

> The statesman who nominates the Commission can almost always determine the course that it is going to take, since he will have a pretty good knowledge beforehand of the minds of the experts whom he puts on it, while, of course, avoiding any appearance of 'packing' his team.[1]

This is a bit of an overstatement, since few people will consent to serve on committees as merely departmental or ministerial puppets and because opponents will be only too anxious to point out that a committee has been 'packed' if there is even the slightest suspicion of such an intention; but there is some truth to the statement. On the other hand, if committees are to serve any useful purpose at all, departments will want to appoint – and be seen to be appointing – individuals of recognised ability and experience to serve on their committees. Thus, people appointed to a committee represent a careful balance between amenability to departmental views and credibility as suitably qualified individuals.

Impartial, Expert and Representative Committees

Right from the start, a minister and his officials will probably have some idea of the sort of committee they want. In general, the nature of a royal commis-

1 Wilhelm Dibelius, *England*, translated from the German by Mrs Mary Hamilton M.P. (London: Jonathan Cape, 1930), p. 254.

sion or a departmental committee may usefully be classified as being either impartial, expert or representative.[2] A committee is deemed to be representative if there appears to be a pattern in its membership as a whole such that it suggests the deliberate representation of two or more (often counterbalanced) interests related to the subject of the committee's mandate. Representatives of interests are also normally regarded as experts on the subject in question, since they have more than average knowledge of that subject; but if there is no apparent pattern of representation in the expertise, then the committee is classified as expert but not representative. Finally, impartial committees are composed of people, often referred to as 'intelligent laymen', who can be expected to possess only an average knowledge of the subject under study by the committee.

Representative committees often make a practice of indicating as much by giving details of the backgrounds of their members in the first few pages of their reports. Thus, the Wheatley Committee on the Teaching Profession in Scotland (Cmnd. 2066) revealed its representative nature when it declared that its membership included two senior officials from the Scottish Education Department; representatives of the Scottish Secondary Teachers' Association, the Educational Institute of Scotland, the Association of County Councils in Scotland, the Scottish Council for the Training of Teachers, and the Glasgow and Edinburgh Education Committees; and six headmasters, principals and teachers. The first major postwar committee appointed, the Newson-Smith Committee on Training for Business Administration (Cmd. 6673), was also a representative committee. In addition to the chairman, who was a businessman, there were seventeen members as follows: one official from each of the Ministry of Education, the Board of Trade, and the Ministry of Labour and National Service; several executives of Imperial Tobacco, John Lewis, Allied Supplies, Anglo-Iranian Oil and Dunlop Rubber; officers of the London Chamber of Commerce, the Retail Distributive Trades Conference, the British Employers' Confederation, the National Amalgamated Union of Shop Assistants, Warehousemen and Clerks, the Trades Union Congress and the Co-operative Union; and the Director of the City of London College and the Vice-Chairman of the Nuffield Organisation. Among these members were also a woman and a Member of Parliament. Other examples of representative committees include the Cohen-Radcliffe Royal Commission on the Taxation of Profits and Income (Cmd. 9474), which was the only representative royal commission; the Nugent Committee on London Roads (Cmnd. 812); and the Wilson Committee on the Problem of Noise (Cmnd. 2056). Another particularly interesting example is the Working Committee on

2 C. J. Hanser, *Guide to Decision* (Totowa, N.J.: Bedminster Press, 1965), uses the same three categories in his analysis of twentieth-century royal commissions; but he makes no effort to explain how he uses the terms. We differ from his analysis at only one point in the postwar period, however, and that is the case of the Percy Royal Commission on Mental Illness and Deficiency (Cmnd. 169), which Hanser classifies as impartial and we as expert.

China Clay (Cmd. 6748), which was chaired by Professor W. R. Jones and had two members, one representative of the trades union (Transport and General Workers) and one representative of industry (Carpalla United China Clay Company). Finally, it should be noted that in a few cases 'Scottish members' have been appointed for the explicit purpose of representing the particular interests of Scotland on national committees, as they were on the Reith Committee on New Towns (Cmd. 6876), for example.

Expert committees which are not also representative can be illustrated by three related committees appointed in October 1957. These committees, all three under the chairmanship of Sir Alexander Fleck, were appointed to inquire into various aspects of an accident which occurred in one of the Windscale Piles operated by the Atomic Energy Authority. Besides the chairman, who was then head of Imperial Chemical Industries, there were among the members of the three committees four university professors in fields related to atomic energy, one of the Members of the Atomic Energy Authority (who was also a director of Courtaulds), the Director of the Atomic Weapons Research Establishment, the Chief Inspector of Factories of the Ministry of Labour and National Service, and the Chief Alkali Inspector of the Ministry of Housing and Local Government.[3] Another expert but non-representative committee was the three-man Lawrence Committee on the Remuneration of Ministers and Members of Parliament (Cmnd. 2516). The chairman, Sir Geoffrey Lawrence, was then also Chairman of the National Incomes Commission, and his two colleagues on the committee were the Deputy Chairman of the Commission and a Professor of Government (W. J. M. Mackenzie) from the University of Manchester. Finally, the recent Todd Royal Commission on Medical Education provides an excellent example of an expert royal commission: among its sixteen original members, thirteen (including the chairman) were connected directly with the medical profession (Cmnd. 3569).

Impartial committees are composed of members who cannot be said to have more than an average interest in and knowledge of the subject under study by the committee. Essentially, this has to be a residual category. If committee members do *not* have special interests or knowledge, then the committee is said to be impartial.

It is not always easy, of course, to make these distinctions, to assess whether a particular person does have special interests or expert knowledge – to say nothing of whether he was appointed because of it rather than for some other reason (such as previous experience in committee work). Similarly, in cases where a committee is obviously more than a group of intelligent

---

3 The three Committees dealt with the organisation and staffing of certain parts of the Authority (Cmnd. 338), health and safety conditions throughout the Authority (Cmnd. 342), and the technical aspects of Windscale Piles and the controlled release of Wigner energy (Cmnd. 471).

Table 5.1 Major royal commissions and departmental committees, 1945–69 by nature (impartial, expert or representative)

nature	royal commissions only	all committees
impartial	14	188
expert (including representative)	10	169
expert only	9	139
representative	1	30
no information	0	1
total	24	*358*

Source: see Appendix B.

laymen, the line between an expert and a representative committee is not always easy to draw.

Nor are these difficulties just difficulties of analysis, for they can cause acute problems for the people concerned. Rather like a Member of Parliament, a committee member may wonder whether his duty is to speak his own mind or to try to represent the interests of a particular constituency. In some cases, departments resolve this dilemma by making clear what is expected of their committee members. For example, the Cope Committee on Medical Auxiliaries (Cmd. 8188) reported that,

> In the letter of invitation received by the Chairman it was explained that those who had been asked to serve as members were people with special experience chosen as individuals and not as representatives of any organisation.

Similarly, it was made clear to the Kennet Committee on the Draft Customs and Excise Bill (Cmd. 8453) that thirteen organisations 'were directly represented on the Committee' by its thirteen members. Nevertheless, declarations of intent such as these are more the exception than the rule.

With these reservations, the major postwar royal commissions and departmental committees are distributed in Table 5.1 among the three kinds of committees just described. The results show that slightly more than half of the committees were impartial and slightly less than half expert. Of the expert committees, only one out of five was representative. Very similar tendencies are reflected in royal commissions taken by themselves, except that representative royal commissions are even less frequent.[4]

Representative committees are the least common kind of committee, constituting less than ten percent of all the major postwar committees. More

4 Hanser, *op. cit.*, pp. 247–53, performs a similar analysis for 137 royal commissions from 1900 to 1965, and finds that 49 percent were impartial and 51 percent expert (of which one in three was representative).

than half of them were in fact appointed by the Labour governments during the immediate postwar years. The principal reason for this degree of unpopularity must be that many of the subjects dealt with by royal commissions and departmental committees simply cannot be resolved into competing interests, either because the matter is too technical, because there is no public controversy about it, or for other reasons. Even where several well-defined interests do exist, representative committees will probably work best in cases where the lack of consensus among the interests is due primarily to a lack of communication or to inadequate co-ordination. For example, a successful representative committee was the recent Wilcox-Donaldson Committee on Herbage Seed Supplies, in which representatives of the seed growers, the seed users and the seed trade were brought together.[5] In such cases, where lack of consensus does not necessarily mean fundamental conflict, committee members are more likely to be able to resolve their own views with those of their constituents. In the words of one representative committee, the Ramsden Committee on Exhibitions and Fairs (Cmd. 6782),

> We have . . . consistently sought to give expression to our personal views on the matters before the Committee, and not to those of any representative body to which we might belong, while still endeavouring to offer proposals which we believe will be acceptable to industry throughout the country.

Where, on the other hand, the lack of consensus is due to fundamental and even well-understood disagreement, it seems unlikely that the appointment of a representative committee will *ipso facto* resolve those differences of opinion and produce a consensus.

The choice between an impartial, expert or representative committee is a very significant one, for it sets the whole tone and direction of a committee's activities. This is reflected in the kind of chairman and members who are appointed to serve on a committee, and it is these choices to which the study now turns.

Choosing a Chairman

The choice of chairman is particularly important. His position in a royal commission or a departmental committee is potentially pre-eminent, and a determined chairman can more or less run his committee as he wishes. Not all chairmen do, of course, and the influence each one exerts can depend on many different things, including his own personality and the personalities of his members, his position outside the committee, his personal status and experience, and his relations with officials, with the members of his committee and with important witnesses. Departments cannot hope to control or even

5 The sixteen-man committee also included a civil servant, two 'independent members', a member of the Sports Turf Research Institute and a member of the Welsh Plant Breeding Station; see the report of the Committee (Cmnd. 3748).

foresee the significance of all these factors, but they will generally take great care in selecting a chairman.

Ministers select their committee chairmen in a variety of ways and for a variety of reasons. The choice may be based on little more than ministerial whim. A minister meets a great many people in the course of his political career as well as his official duties, some of whom may impress him as suitable committee material. He has advisers, both official and unofficial, who are always ready to suggest the names of people who might be useful in some capacity or another. Finally, he has political debts to pay and a committee appointment is one way of discharging such a debt.[6]

On the other hand, a minister may decide to leave the whole problem to his officials. The selection of a chairman may then become the result of a complicated process of careful calculation and negotiation with other departments or with outside interest groups. In particular, the Treasury may be asked for advice. In evidence to the Franks Committee on Administrative Tribunals and Inquiries (Cmnd. 218), a senior civil servant explained that the reason why the Treasury was often consulted about the appointment of chairmen was 'because they have a comprehensive list of likely people to be used for this and other kinds of public service'.[7] In fact, the list (facetiously called the 'Book of the Great and the Good') is reputed to be somewhat less than comprehensive in scope, and to be composed more of people technically qualified in certain specialised fields than of people known to make good committee chairmen as such. Thus, Treasury advice is probably more likely to be sought in the case of specialised inquiries. Finally, officials, like ministers, will have their own networks of professional and personal contacts to whom they can refer for the names of suitable people.

A variety of procedures is adopted. The minister may decide to write formally in the first instance to the candidate inviting him or her to accept the chairmanship of a particular committee. Alternatively, the minister may prefer to have preliminary soundings made on an informal basis. Such approaches can be made to one candidate at a time or to several, since invitations may not always be accepted. Invitations are refused for several reasons, such as poor health or recent bereavement, a lack of time, or sometimes just a conviction that previous public service has not led to any significant action by the government. For such reasons, the chairmanships of the Jennings Royal Commission on Common Land (Cmnd. 462) the Radcliffe Committee on the Working of the Monetary System (Cmnd. 827), and the Pilkington Committee on Broadcasting (Cmnd. 1753), for example, are all rumoured to have been refused by the people asked first. There is a certain

6 P. G. Richards, *Patronage in British Government* (London: Allen and Unwin, 1963), Chapter 6.

7 Sir Gilmour Jenkins, then Permanent Secretary in the Ministry of Transport; see *Oral Evidence* (Non-Parliamentary Paper, 1957), Fourth Day, question no. 931. See also Samuel Brittan, *The Treasury under the Tories, 1951–1964* (Harmondsworth: Penguin, 1964), p. 58.

Table 5.2 Chairmen of major royal commissions and departmental committees, 1945–69, by previous committee experience

previous experience	royal commission chairmen only	chairmen of all committees
with experience as chairman or member	13	143
experience as chairman	13	110
experience as member only	0	33
with no experience at all	10	199
no information	0	11
total	23	353

Notes: The data apply only to first chairmen in cases where committees have had two successive chairmen. Committee experience is defined as including service on any kind of ad hoc committee, whether appointed by statute, prerogative or convention, whether Parliamentary or executive, and whether dealing with British or colonial affairs. Standing committee experience is not included.

Source: Who's Who for the years from 1945 to 1970.

amount of prestige attached to being a committee chairman, especially of a potentially important one such as the recent Maud Royal Commission on Local Government in England (Cmnd. 4040), and certain incentives, such as the promise of a research staff, can also be offered; but invitations are still not always accepted. Finally, it should be added that even once a chairman has been appointed, it may subsequently become necessary to replace him due to his death or resignation. Resignations occur on account of poor health, changes in other activities which make it inappropriate for one reason or another to continue as chairman, and simply 'pressure of other commitments'.[8] In such cases, a new chairman can sometimes be found among the remaining members of the committee, but more often than not the process of finding a chairman has to be repeated.

There is fairly clear evidence that departments look for experience on previous committees in their choice of chairmen for new ones. The data in Table 5.2 show that about forty percent of the major postwar committees were chaired by people who had been on previous committees. Interestingly enough, three quarters of the chairmen with previous experience have been not just members but actually chairmen at least once before. Among chairmen of royal commissions, who are in any case more likely to be experienced,

8 Fourteen major postwar committees have changed chairmen, none of them more than once. This does not include the Committee on Broadcasting in 1949, in which 'the Chairman first announced, Lord Radcliffe, was unable to take up his duties owing to his appointment as a Lord of Appeal in Ordinary. The appointment of our present chairman [Lord Beveridge], completing the Committee, was announced in the House of Commons on the 21st of June [1949].' See the report of the Committee (Cmd. 8116).

the emphasis on experience as a chairman is even stronger. Some individuals
– such as Lord Radcliffe, Lord Salmon, Sir Henry Willink and others – have
each reappeared as chairmen of several different committees, but it would be
a misconception to conclude that chairmen are chosen exclusively or even
mainly from a small circle of official favourites and an exaggeration to speak
of committees as 'government by Radcliffery'.[9] There is undoubtedly a
certain premium placed on experience, but the majority of committee chairmen come to their jobs with none.

The most obvious characteristics of committee chairmen are that they are
almost all men and that most of them have reached a relatively advanced age.
Just before the war a historian of the role of women in government wrote
optimistically,

> It is now widely recognised, that in addition to the contributions which
> women can make to those questions which particularly affect women and
> children, their special qualities and gifts can be used and indeed are
> needed on all sides of government work.[10]

The fact is, however, that women stand very little chance of becoming chairmen of committees. No royal commission has ever been chaired by a woman,
and only three major postwar departmental committees have had female
chairmen – and these were precisely committees 'which particularly affect
women and children'.[11] The inescapable conclusion is that women are not
regarded as making suitable chairmen except in a few cases where they may
be presumed to have special knowledge of the subject matter by virtue of
their sex.

Similarly, very few young men are selected as committee chairmen. As the
data in Table 5.3 indicate, nearly eighty five percent of the chairmen of major
postwar committees were over fifty years of age when they were appointed,
and half of all the chairmen were over sixty. The average age was fifty eight,
but the most common age was sixty two. The youngest chairman (at thirty
eight and the only chairman under forty) was the Duke of Northumberland
when he was appointed chairman of the Committee on the Slaughter of
Horses (Cmd. 8925). In this case, his relative youth must have been regarded
as outweighed by his close interest in equine affairs. The oldest chairmen were
Lord Macmillan and Sir Gerald Hurst, who, at seventy five years of age,
were respectively appointed to chair committees on Land Registration in

9 The phrase is Sir Alan Herbert's. Mary Morgan, *British Government Publications, 1941–66*
   (London: Library Association, 1969), gives a listing of government committees from 1941
   to 1966 by the name of the chairman. See also Richard Rose, *Politics in England* (Boston:
   Little, Brown, 1964), pp. 102ff. and 118ff.

10 Hilda Martindale, *Women Servants of the State* (London: Allen and Unwin, 1938), p. 10.

11 Miss Myra Curtis was chairman of the Committee on the Care of Children (Cmd. 6922),
   the Countess of Albemarle was chairman of the Committee on the Youth Service in
   England and Wales (Cmnd. 929), and Miss Jean Graham Hall was chairman of the
   Committee on Statutory Maintenance Limits (Cmnd. 3587).

Table 5.3 Chairmen of major royal commissions and departmental committees, 1945–69, by age on appointment

age on appointment	number of chairmen
under 35	0
35–39	1
40–44	6
45–49	41
50–54	52
55–59	76
60–64	87
65–69	55
70–74	20
75–79	2
80 or more	0
no information	18
total	*358*
mean age	58 years
modal age	62 years

Note: The data are for first chairmen only and apply to their age at the time of the appointment of the committee.

Source: Who's Who for the years from 1945 to 1970.

Scotland (Cmd. 7451) and (somewhat ironically!) the Adoption of Children (Cmd. 9248).

Younger men, it is true, may tend to decline the honour of serving as chairmen because they cannot afford the time required. Older men are more likely to have retired from full-time employment and to have reached a position of some financial independence. This is important, since service on royal commissions and departmental committees is financially unremunerative – although it can count towards earning life peerages or other honours! Traditionally, chairmen of royal commissions receive as an honorarium a replica of the silver George IV inkstand which graces the desk of the Chancellor of the Exchequer, but chairmen of departmental committees as well as members of both get nothing but thanks for their efforts.[12] On the other hand,

12 One former royal commission chairman, who had already chaired a previous royal commission, apparently let it be known that he would prefer a good pair of field glasses to another inkstand, and he got the field glasses! Expenses are, of course, reimbursed according to the normal standards set by the Treasury for the civil service. In addition, an honorarium appears exceptionally to have been paid to the chairman of the Inquiry into the Disaster at Bolton Wanderers' Football Ground on 9 March 1946 (Cmd. 6846), according to information supplied in a private communication from the former secretary. The practice in some other countries (such as Canada) is to pay chairmen and members a *per diem* honorarium: see K. B. Callard, 'Commissions of Inquiry in Canada, 1867–1949', Special Report prepared for the Privy Council (Ottawa: mimeo, 1950), p. 31, and Appendix D.

these constraints do not appear to discourage younger men from becoming members of committees. Nor do the constraints apply in any case to chairmen drawn from within the various branches of government, especially Members of Parliament and those who hold judicial office. Such people can relatively easily arrange to be released temporarily from their ordinary functions without any threat to their income or their prospects for advancement. Thus, it seems unlikely that the predisposition towards relatively old chairmen can be accounted for entirely by the lack of remuneration. It must be as much a result of deliberate departmental choice.

Finally, it is interesting to examine the backgrounds of committee chairmen. There are several different yardsticks which can be used for this purpose, but two factors should be kept in mind. First of all, it is interesting to see if there is any truth in the popular conception of chairmen as being peers, judges or lawyers. At the same time, a more systematic analysis of the ordinary occupations of chairmen is desirable in order to find out exactly what kinds of background they have.

The results of analysing the major postwar committees (see Table 5.4) lend some support to the belief that chairmen tend to be peers, judges or lawyers. Nearly one chairman in four is a peer (mostly life peers) and, if royal commissions are taken on their own, the proportion jumps to one in two. The Duke of Northumberland, for example, has chaired three of the major postwar committees, all of them connected in some way with the welfare of animals.[13] Most of the peers who chair committees, however, are law lords like Lord Justice Salmon who recently chaired both a royal commission (Cmnd. 3121) and a departmental committee (Cmnd. 4078) dealing with Tribunals of Inquiry. Judges (including Law Lords) chaired more than one third of all committees. There is a good deal of overlapping among these categories, of course; Law Lords, for example, are both peers and judges and may well be Q.C.'s as well. Nevertheless, more than half of all committee chairmen are either peers, judges or lawyers; among royal commissions alone, the proportion is closer to two thirds.

It is also worth noting that Members of Parliament, unlike peers, are relatively rarely named as chairmen of committees. Among the major committees since the war, only six sitting M.P.'s, one of them a junior minister, ever sat as chairmen, and none ever chaired a royal commission.[14] The last time an M.P. was appointed chairman was in 1957. Former M.P.'s have chaired about ten percent of the major postwar committees, but two thirds of them had become peers before doing so.

13 The three Committees were on the Slaughter of Horses (Cmd. 8925), Recruitment for the Veterinary Profession (Cmnd. 2430), and Foot-and-Mouth Disease (Cmnd. 4225).

14 G. R. H. Nugent, M.P., Joint Parliamentary Secretary to the Minister of Transport and Civil Aviation, chaired the Committee on London Roads (Cmnd. 812). Other committees chaired by M.P.'s dealt with electoral registration (Cmd. 7004), discipline in an Approved School (Cmd. 7150), civil aviation personnel (Cmd. 7746), the Territorial Army (Cmd. 9523) and the Army Cadet Force (Cmnd. 268).

Table 5.4 Chairmen of major royal commissions and departmental committees, 1945–69, by occupation and background

occupation and background	royal commission chairmen only	chairmen of all committees
judiciary[1]	7	118
civil service[2]	0	14
retired central government[3]	4	34
other government (active or retired)[4]	1	25
legal profession	1	26
university, school, research, etc.	7	53
business, finance, industry	3	52
medical profession	0	2
trade unions	0	3
other	0	10
none apparent or no information	1	20
total	24	358
Made up of: peers[5]	12	85
senior barristers[6]	10	144
Members of Parliament	0	6
former Members of Parliament	7	35
no information	0	2
none of the above	6	144

Notes: The data refer to first chairmen only and apply (a) to their principal occupation prior to appointment and (b) to any aspect of their background up to the time of their appointment.

1 includes judges, sheriffs, magistrates, recorders, etc., but not justices of the peace.
2 does not include part-time or temporary (war-time) service.
3 includes retired members of the judicial and legislative branches.
4 includes military, local government, nationalised industry, etc.
5 does not include peers created after the date of appointment of the chairman.
6 refers to barristers who have taken silk (i.e. become Q.C.s).

Source: Who's Who for the years from 1945 to 1970.

A more systematic analysis of the principal occupations of committee chairmen permits some elaboration of the above conclusions. Members of the judiciary are by far the most common kind of chairman, accounting for over one third of all appointments. No other category is even half as common. The nearest rivals are academics and businessmen, each with about one chairman in seven. For example, Professor R. G. D. Allen chaired the Committee of Inquiry into the Impact of Rates on Households (Cmnd. 2582); and Lord Beeching, then deputy-chairman of Imperial Chemical Industries Ltd, was chairman of the Royal Commission on Assizes and Quarter Sessions (Cmnd. 4153). Moreover, the likelihood of an academic chairman is twice as high among royal commissions; for example, Lord Todd, Professor of

Organic Chemistry at Cambridge University, was chairman of the Royal Commission on Medical Education (Cmnd. 3569). One chairman in ten is a retired civil servant or other member of central government, and even a few active civil servants have chaired committees.[15] Relatively few chairmen are practising lawyers or come from non-central government positions. Perhaps the most astonishing thing, however, is the very small number of chairmen *not* accounted for by the above categories. One practising doctor, three trade unionists and eight other professionals are the only exceptions, and none of these chaired a royal commission.[16]

Thus, although peers, judges and lawyers are common among committee chairmen, it would be more accurate to describe chairmen as being likely to be either judges, academics, businessmen, or persons formerly or presently connected with government in some full-time capacity: this accounts for nearly ninety percent of all committee chairmen. The fact that service on committees is part-time and unpaid probably goes a long way towards explaining the kind of people who become chairmen. It is judges, academics, persons formerly or presently connected with government, and even business-men who are the sort of people who can render part-time public service most conveniently. The salaries of judicial officials are paid by the state in any case and they can be released on a temporary or part-time basis from their normal duties. University people often regard service on government committees as falling within the scope of their academic duties and, for their part, univer-sities are often willing to countenance reduced teaching or research respon-sibilities in order to facilitate such work. A retired civil servant is often free and even eager to come back into contact with official circles for a brief period as a committee chairman. Big corporations in business and industry can make it possible for their directors and even some of their senior execu-tives to chair committees, especially when 'invisible' benefits may well accrue to their firms as a result. For example, Courtaulds Ltd was prepared to allow Sir Alan Wilson, its Managing Director, to be chairman of the Committees on Coal Derivatives (Cmnd. 1120) and on the Problem of Noise (Cmnd. 2506). It is true that some chairmen are indeed peers or lawyers, but this is probably

15 For example, Sir William Douglas agreed to be chairman of the Committee on Purchase Tax/Utility (Cmd. 8542) almost immediately after he retired from the Civil Service in 1951. Among active civil servants who have chaired committees are Sir Eric Bamford who was chairman of the Committee on Taxation and Overseas Minerals (Cmd. 7728) while he was still Chairman of the Board of Inland Revenue, and C. H. M. Wilcox, who was chairman for the first six months of the Committee on Herbage Seed Supplies (Cmnd. 3748) while he was an Under-Secretary in the Ministry of Agriculture, Fisheries and Food.

16 The only practising doctor was Dr Zachary Cope who chaired the Committee on Medical Auxiliaries (Cmd. 8188). Lord Westwood and Lord Crook, both former trade unionists, each chaired a committee on Mineral Development (Cmd. 7732) and the Statutory Registration of Opticians (Cmd. 8531) respectively. Most of the others in this group were accountants, such as Sir Harold Howitt, who chaired committees on Unpatented Inven-tions and Defence Contracts (Cmd. 9788) and on the British Transport Commission Cmnd. 262).

only incidental. Their choice as chairmen is more likely to have been based on their other qualifications.

Choosing Members

Although it may not appear so from the formal procedures of appointment, the selection of members for a committee is normally an incremental process. Members are recruited to new committees one by one, rather than all at once, *en bloc*; and the committee membership takes shape in a gradual, piecemeal fashion.

Even if he had no special nominee for chairman of the committee, a minister is quite likely to have some suggestions for members. In this he may have all sorts of motives, from the assessment of a person's ability to the repayment of political debts. There may be larger political considerations, too, such as the desirability of having representatives of the two main parties sitting on a committee, as was the case of the Percy Royal Commission on Mental Illness and Mental Deficiency (Cmnd. 169). The chairman himself is sometimes consulted and he may well want to propose some professional colleagues whom he admires or some other people with whom he has been able to work particularly well in the past. He may also have violent objections to one or two of the proposed members! As a gesture towards common sense and a successful practical outcome to the committee's labours, it must often be felt wise to include among the members (whatever the nature of their mandate) a lawyer, a trade unionist, a woman, or some other such stereotype. Finally, various organisations and interest groups need to be placated by having 'their' man on a committee. They may even be invited to nominate committee members themselves, especially when the members are intended to be representative of those organisations but also in other cases too. For example, all the members of the expert Cohen Panel on the Composition and Nutritive Value of Flour 'were nominated at the request of the Minister of Agriculture, Fisheries and Food by the President of the Royal Society (Lord Adrian O.M.) . . .' (Cmd. 9757). In short, many of the same contacts and sources that served in the selection of a chairman may be called upon again in the search for suitable members. Officials and sometimes the minister (if the committee is important enough or if it is close to his personal interests) assess these suggestions as they are received. In most cases, they first make soundings and then issue formal invitations. Some invitations are accepted and a few are refused, but gradually the committee takes shape. Thus, a good deal of behind-the-scenes activity usually precedes the appointment of the members to a committee.

There are, of course, many cases of the same person being appointed to several committees, but it would be quite wrong to regard committee members as coming mostly from a select group of favourites. Rather it is a question of departments being understandably willing to reappoint people who have made an effective contribution to the work of a committee on a previous occasion. It is rare to find someone sitting on two committees concurrently, but there have been a number of recent examples. The Payne Committee on the Enforcement of Judgement Debts (Cmnd. 3909) had one member who was also a member of the Winn Committee on Personal Injuries Litigation (Cmnd. 3691) and another who was also a member of the Hall Committee on Statutory Maintenance Limits (Cmnd. 3587).[17] Secondly, the Perks Committee on Criminal Statistics (Cmnd. 3448) and the Thomson Committee on Criminal Statistics in Scotland (Cmnd. 3705) had one member in common, while the secretary of the former was also a member of the Adams Committee on Civil Judicial Statistics (Cmnd. 3684). It is easy to see how, in these particular cases, concurrent appointments could have contributed to co-ordinating the efforts of committees which were dealing with closely related matters. Nevertheless, concurrent appointments are rare.

Drawing on his own experiences as a committee member, Professor David Donnison has described the juggling act which occurs each time a committee is appointed:

> Interests will be carefully balanced: the right professional and administrative groups; Scotland and Wales; the north and the south; women and men; the left and the right – all will be carefully matched, though the representatives of each generally come from the middle of the political road.[18]

He then goes on to warn of the dangers inherent in this procedure, of the risks of losing sight of more important considerations.

> Whitehall is politically sophisticated but alarmingly ignorant about people, particularly if they live more than an hour's journey from London. It is too easy to pick the willing horses, already known and trusted. To the official selection there will generally be added a sprinkling of more eccentric names chosen by the minister and his friends. Among them will be found some of the best members of the committee, and some of the worst.

The variety and diversity of people who are appointed to royal commissions and departmental committees is one of their most interesting features. All in all, nearly 2,900 members have been appointed to the major postwar committees; so it is not an easy matter to do justice to the variety of their qualifications in relation to each committee on which they sat. What can be done is to stipulate a series of characteristics and then see how often they are represented among the members of committees. The results of such an analysis can then be compared with the characteristics found in committee chairmen.

17 Incidentally, the two 'concurrent' members of the twelve-man Payne Committee were the only ones who did not add reservations to their signature of the Committee report!

18 D. V. Donnison, 'Committees and Committeemen', *New Society* (18 April 1968), p. 558.

Table 5.5 Major royal commissions and departmental committees, 1945–69, by selected characteristics of members (excluding chairmen)

characteristics	royal commissions only	all committees
peers	15	65
Members of Parliament	6	51
civil servants	3	54
members of the judiciary[1]	5	108
senior barristers[2]	11	74
professors and doctors	19	180
local government officers[3]	6	47
businessmen	11	72
trade unionists	6	33
women	21	144
one or more of the above	24	301
none of the above or no information	0	24
chairmen only (i.e. no members)	0	33
total	*24*	*358*

Notes: The data apply to members only, not to chairmen. Thus, no account is taken of one-man committees which have a chairman but no members. It should also be noted that several characteristics may be represented by a single member.

1 includes justices of the peace.
2 refers to barristers who have taken silk (i.e. become Q.C.s).
3 includes elected and appointed officers.

Source: Reports of the various committees often give details about their members, and this was supplemented by reference to *Who's Who* for the years from 1945 to 1969 and by various private communications.

The most striking point about the members of the major postwar committees (see Table 5.5) is the frequency with which professors, doctors and women were appointed as members. The last is particularly interesting in view of the apparent reluctance to appoint women as committee chairmen (see Table 5.4). The popular reference to a 'statutory woman' member on every committee is a bit overdrawn (unless it is confined to royal commissions), but there were women members on well over forty percent of the major postwar committees.[19] In fact, it would be more accurate to speak of a 'statutory intellectual' among the members of a committee, since professors

19 The only two postwar royal commissions which did not have woman members were the Salmon Royal Commission on Tribunals of Inquiry (Cmnd. 3121) and the Beeching Royal Commission on Assizes and Quarter Sessions (Cmnd. 4153). The appointment of Mrs Grace Wyndham Goldie to the Verdon-Smith Committee on Meat Marketing and Distribution (Cmnd. 2282) is probably a good example of the appointment of a 'statutory woman' committee member.

and doctors sat on more than half of the committees. This, too, represents a distinct contrast with the practice in so far as chairmen are concerned, where only about one in seven is chosen from a similar group. The feeling seems to be that women and intellectuals make good members of committees but poor chairmen!

There are other differences as well between suitable members and suitable chairmen. Peers were less common as members (except on royal commissions) but Members of Parliament were more common.[20] Civil servants, officers of local government and trade unionists were also more likely to be members than they were to be chairmen. The members of the Bamford Committee on Taxation and Overseas Minerals (Cmnd. 7728) and the Nugent Committee on London Roads (Cmnd. 812) were all either civil servants or local government officers. On the other hand, although they were still fairly common as committee members, senior barristers, judges and other members of the judiciary were more likely to be appointed as chairmen than as members.

To generalise still further, the evidence suggests that committee chairmen tend to be chosen for their abilities as chairmen, whereas members tend to be chosen more for their ability to contribute to the substance of the matter to be examined by the committee. The criteria may not be very sophisticated – judges make good chairmen and women make poor ones – but this does leave the selection of members free to reflect whatever substantial abilities and interests are deemed essential to the effective operation of the committee. There is a story about one committee nearly ready for appointment but which was still felt to lack both a Scottish representative and a spokesman for the Church. Conscious also of the desirability of a woman member as well, officials invited the otherwise undistinguished wife of a Scottish minister to sit on the committee!

The Size of Committees

The result of these procedures for selecting chairmen and members is that committees vary widely in size. There are committees of one and committees of more than twenty. Secondly, the size of a committee emerges as a relatively unimportant consideration. There may be some preconceived idea of keeping the committee relatively small or of making it relatively large, but that is all. Size is more often a result than a determinant of membership.

The sizes of the major postwar royal commissions and departmental committees have varied from one to as much as twenty four (see Table 5.6). The largest committee (twenty four members) was the Evershed Committee

---

20 Nevertheless, there are still complaints that not enough M.P.s are appointed to royal commissions and departmental committees: see D. McI. Johnson, *A Cassandra at Westminster* (London: Johnson, 1967), p. 75, who adds that even finding out how many M.P.s had served on committees in the past 'threw the P.M.'s office out of gear for about a fortnight'.

Table 5.6 Major royal commissions and departmental committees, 1945–69, by size

number of members	royal commissions only	all committees
1	0	33
2	0	2
3	0	25
4	0	6
5	1	35
6	0	32
7	3	41
8	0	28
9	4	35
10	0	19
11	2	20
12	4	23
13	1	12
14	1	14
15	2	9
16	4	13
17	1	3
18	1	2
19	0	1
20	0	0
21	0	2
22	0	1
23	0	0
24	0	1
no information	0	1
total committees	*24*	*358*
mean size	13 members	8 members
modal size		7 members

Note: Size includes the chairman and the members as at the date of appointment of the committee.

Source: See Appendix B, p. 239.

on Supreme Court Practice and Procedure (Cmd. 8878), which sat for over six years. The average size of all the committees is eight members (thirteen in the case of royal commissions alone); however, the standard deviation from this mean is over fifty percent.

Committees seem to fall into four classes. Small committees consist of one, two, three or four members. Medium-sized committees range from five to nine members each. Large committees contain ten, eleven or twelve members, and extra-large ones thirteen or more. To give some idea of their relative importance, it is probable that, in any six committees, one will be small, three medium-sized, one large and one extra large. Thus, half of all committees are medium-sized, having five, six, seven, eight or nine members; and the rest are more likely to be bigger than smaller. This is more or less what might have been expected; what is interesting, though, is that there does not in fact seem to be any more precise preference insofar as size is concerned.

Thus, size emerges as a not very significant factor in the appointment of royal commissions and departmental committees. This must be due at least in part to the way in which committees are appointed. The incremental nature of this process would make it very difficult to keep to any precise guidelines even if this were thought desirable. For instance, it does not seem likely that departmental officials would refuse to add to the membership of a committee someone whom they felt could contribute to its work simply because his appointment raised the size of the committee above some predetermined level. It is more likely that departments have only a rough idea of what size committee they expect to appoint. If they do think in terms of categories similar to the ones revealed in the data, it is probably not out of any sense of the intrinsic value of such categories.

There is one further point to make, and that concerns the pattern of appointing committees of an odd number of members and an even number. Among small committees, sizes of one and three are much more common than sizes of two and four. To give some examples, one of the two two-man committees was the Bridges Inquiry into Security at the National Gallery (Cmnd. 1750), and one of the six four-man committees was the Henderson Committee on Security at Broadmoor (Cmd. 8594). Even among medium-sized committees, any odd size seems to be preferred to an even size. To the extent that there is any preference among the large and extra-large committees, it is in the opposite direction, in favour of even sizes; but the tendency is not as pronounced as the others.

The reason for these tendencies is probably fairly straightforward. Chairmen of committees of any kind conventionally have an extra tie-breaking vote. On the smaller committees, such a vote would be less easy to exercise without offending other members; so it is built into the committee by appointing an odd number of people. Conversely, on a larger committee, interests are more likely to be balanced off against each other, and it is probably felt that a chairman needs the additional authority of a potential extra vote.

Secretaries and Assessors

Staff of various kinds are appointed to assist committees in carrying out their mandates. There are three basic kinds of staff: secretaries, assessors and research staff. Since the appointment of a research staff usually occurs after the committee itself has been appointed, further discussion is postponed to

Chapter 9 below. Of the other kinds of staff, virtually every committee has a secretariat, but only a few have assessors. The secretariat is responsible for organising the work of the committee, including scheduling meetings, organising witnesses, and sometimes drafting the report. The secretariat acts throughout at the direction of the chairman and the committee but, as the principal link between a committee and its appointing department, the secretariat may enjoy a position of some influence (see also Chapters 7 and 9 below). Assessors are appointed on occasions when it is thought desirable to provide committees with expert advice and assistance of their own.

Various arrangements within the secretariat are possible, ranging from one man on a part-time basis to a full-time staff of dozens. Clerical services are normally provided from the ordinary resources of the department (or departments) appointing the committee, but sometimes clerical staff will be formally attached to the committee. The most important part of the secretariat, however, is the secretary or secretaries. The ordinary practice is to appoint a single secretary, but two 'joint secretaries' or a secretary plus an assistant secretary are also common. One of the most lavish complements of secretaries was recorded by the recent Brown Committee on Labour in Building and Civil Engineering (Cmnd. 3714), which had a Secretary and three Assistant Secretaries. In most cases of a committee jointly appointed by two or more departments, this is reflected in the appointment of two or more secretaries; however, committees appointed by only one department may also have more than one secretary. Three quarters of all the major postwar royal commissions, for example, had the secretary-plus-assistant arrangement. There do not seem to be any other significant patterns in the organisation of committee secretariats.

Most secretaries are civil servants and most of them come from the department or departments which appointed the committee. There are cases, though, of committees with secretaries from outside the appointing departments and even from outside the Civil Service altogether. Sixteen major postwar committees (about one in twenty) drew their secretaries from outside the Civil Service, as in the case of the Payne Committee on the Enforcement of Judgment Debts (Cmnd. 3909), whose secretary came from the British Institute of International and Comparative Law. Another twenty seven committee secretaries came from outside appointing departments (usually from the Treasury). Most committees, however, drew their secretaries entirely from their appointing departments. Of the civil servants appointed as secretaries, most are Principals, but there are also significant numbers of Assistant Secretaries (especially on royal commissions) and of scientific, professional and executive officers (largely for committees dealing with technical questions). The typical committee secretary, though, is a civil servant of the rank of Principal from the department which appointed the committee.

As was suggested above, the criteria for choosing secretaries are not really clear. Undoubtedly committee work is considered a good training-ground for civil servants aspiring to higher rank in the administrative class: hence, the tendency to appoint young Principals who still have their careers in front of them. But it can also be an exacting job requiring a high level of both administrative and technical skill. Most civil servants would probably feel that appointment as secretary of a royal commission or a departmental committee was a sign of esteem, but there are some former secretaries who doubt that it has had much significance except in a few cases. Certainly, it must often mean a good deal of extra work, for secretaries are not always relieved of their normal duties (except perhaps in the case of royal commissions and the more important of the departmental committees) and still more rarely formally seconded to their new jobs. The job of secretary to a committee is regarded as simply a regular part of the duties of a civil servant. In conclusion, the former secretary of the Somervell Committee on State Immunities (Cmd. 8460) may be quoted, explaining his selection from the Cabinet Office to be secretary of a Foreign Office committee:

> To be perfectly honest, I was never really quite clear why I got the job; it could equally well have been done by a Foreign Office man, for the work of the Committee was primarily a Foreign Office concern. The fact remains, however, that it ranged over the field of responsibility of a good many departments; so it was perhaps no bad idea that we in the Cabinet Office were involved.[21]

To assist committees in dealing with expert evidence, they are sometimes also provided with 'assessors' or similar advisers. Assessors are experts from within the Civil Service or from outside. They are appointed by the appointing departments and usually attend committee meetings. The practice of appointing assessors to committees, though not a common procedure, is probably not a new one. It goes back at least to the time of the Samuel Royal Commission on the Coal Industry (Cmd. 2600) in 1925. Assessors are at the disposal of the committee and provide advice, assist in examining witnesses and occasionally brief or prepare technical papers for the committee. Since 1945, approximately one committee in five has made use of assessors or some similar kind of assistance. The Robbins Committee on Higher Education (Cmnd. 2154), for example, had four assessors: the Chairman of the University Grants Committee, plus representatives of the Treasury, the Ministry of Education and the Scottish Education Department. The Halsbury Committee on Decimal Coinage (Cmnd. 2145) had five assessors: the Deputy Master of the Royal Mint, the Under Secretary in charge of the Home Finance Division of the Treasury, the Deputy Chief Cashier at the Bank of England, the Deputy Principal Accountant of the Post Office Contracts Department, and the Manager of the Office Machines Repair Service of H.M. Stationery Office.

21 From a private communication.

Sometimes assessors may replace secretaries, as in the case of the Adams Inquiry into the Accident to the Drilling Rig *Sea Gem* (Cmnd. 3409): this Inquiry had two assessors, one a civil servant and one a university professor. Sometimes assessors are nominated by interested parties, as in the case of the Rees Committee on Night Baking (Cmd. 8378) whose four assessors were nominated by baking employers and operatives in England and Wales and Scotland; and the Cameron Inquiry into the Complaint by the National Union of Banking Employees to the International Labour Organisation (Cmnd. 2202), which had three assessors, one each nominated by the Committee of London Clearing Banks, the Central Council of Bank Staff Associations and the National Union of Bank Employees.

Sometimes assistants are appointed for special jobs: the Rochdale Committee on the Major Ports (Cmnd. 1824) and the Radcliffe Committee on the Working of the Monetary System (Cmnd. 827) each had a 'Statistical Adviser', and the Verdon-Smith Committee on Meat Marketing and Distribution (Cmnd. 2282) had a 'Liaison Officer for Northern Ireland'. The assistant to the Sinclair Committee on the Financial Structure of the Colonial Development Corporation (Cmnd. 786) was an accountant from Peat, Marwick, Mitchell and Company. The 'Military Adviser' to the Wolfenden Committee on the Employment of National Service Men (Cmnd. 35) was a major-general. Two of the four assessors of the Hill Watson Committee on the Drainage of Trade Premises in Scotland (Cmd. 9117) were simply expected to give 'an account of the experience in England'! Finally, special mention should be made of the twelve 'Assistant Commissioners' – four each for Scotland and Wales and Northern Ireland – appointed (by a separate royal warrant) to help the recent Royal Commission on the Constitution (Cmnd. 5460) in 'evaluating evidence' presented to the Commission.

Normally, however, assessors and other advisers have no such specific functions but are at the general disposition of committee. In this way, they can also act as an added insurance for the appointing departments. As one experienced committee man has explained,

> Committee members, once a report is signed, go back to their job – or to other public service – but the department has to cope with the outcome of their inquiry. Its officials will be asking whether the committee is likely to reach sound conclusions and back them with effective arguments. Will the report disrupt their work – or even redistribute precious bits of it among other departments? Will it hang an albatross around the department's neck for years to come? The assessors attached to the committee by the department can steer the committee off dangerous ground and re-phrase its proposals more acceptably.[22]

Both secretaries and assessors can help keep a committee on the tracks, but ultimately it is the chairman and members – and especially the chairman –

22 Donnison, *op. cit.*, p. 559.

who determine the effectiveness of a committee. Hence it is those positions which departments must fill with care. They cannot afford to rely entirely on indirect channels of communication once the committee is appointed, for these devices cannot make an effective committee out of ill-chosen members.

The chairman is the single most important part of a royal commission or a departmental committee. Insofar as the major postwar committees are concerned, departments have tended to be relatively conservative in their choices. They seem to look for experience and age, and they clearly favour men who are judges, academics or businessmen and who are or have been connected with government in some capacity. These tendencies in the selection of chairmen are counterbalanced to some extent by greater diversity in the choice of members. Members come from a broader range of occupations and backgrounds. They are often chosen to make up for characteristics lacking in the chairman or in other members: thus the references to so-called 'statutory' women, academics, Scotsmen, politicians, and so on – although these are in fact unlikely to appear all on the same committee.

The process of selecting a chairman and members for a royal commission or departmental committee poses departments with a very difficult problem. But it is a problem which will repay the efforts spent on its solution, for in it lie the seeds of the ultimate success or failure of the committee.

6
Why Committees are Appointed

One of the perennially fascinating questions about royal commissions and departmental committees is why they are appointed. In fact, there is an enormous variety of such reasons, and there may even be several different ones explaining the appointment of a single committee. But all these various reasons may be divided into two basic categories: reasons which are overt or 'substantial' in nature and reasons which are instrumental or 'political' in nature.

On the one hand, a committee may be said to have been appointed for the purpose of gathering information and making recommendations about some particular matter, such as housing in Scotland, or local government in England, or foot-and-mouth disease, and so on. To explain the existence of a committee in terms like these is to offer an overt or substantial reason for its appointment.

On the other hand, a committee – even the same committee – may be said to have been appointed for one or more reasons of the following kind: to postpone the need for further action, to placate vociferous interest groups, to defuse a controversial issue, to provide a mechanism for co-ordinating the action of several government departments, to legitimate a decision already taken, and so on. To explain the existence of a committee in terms such as these is to offer an instrumental or political reason for its appointment.

There is, of course, nothing 'wrong' with trying to explain the appointment of a committee in terms of either substantial or political reasons. The important thing is to recognise that there are those two different types of explanation possible. Nevertheless, ever since the first book on the subject more than a century ago, there has been a tendency to concentrate on only one type of explanation: namely, the political reasons.[1]

1 Joshua Toulmin Smith, *Government by Commissions Illegal and Pernicious* (London: Sweet, 1849), sees royal commissions as little more than a device for extending government (especially Whig government) control over the people to the point where (as he put it) they would soon 'direct every man at what time he might rise, at what time go to bed, when and what he might eat, when and what he might drink and when and how he might discharge every office of life' (pp. 17–18).

Political reasons for government actions are extremely important, of course, not only in the narrow party-political sense of the term but also in the broader contextual sense used here. Certainly, it would be difficult if not impossible to deny that there are such reasons for appointing royal commissions and departmental committees.[2] The problem is, however, that it is difficult to say very much about the political motives for the appointment of a committee, beyond the fact that such motives do exist. It is a simple matter to draw up a list of the sort of political purposes which committees (as well as other institutions of government) may serve, but it is a good deal more difficult to say which of these reasons explains the appointment of any specific committee. For one thing, it depends on whose point of view is to be taken. The minister or ministers concerned may have one motive, departmental officials another, and the chairman and members of the committee possibly still others. For another thing, the political reasons for appointing a committee may well change as time goes by. A committee may be appointed for one such reason (for example, to postpone or even obviate the need for further action), yet eventually have its recommendations accepted for precisely the opposite reason (i.e. because its effect has been to keep alive public interest when it might otherwise have died out). Finally, political motives can be ascribed to almost any act of government, but the effect of concentrating on such motives is ultimately to say more about the political system in which the act occurs than about the act itself. Royal commissions and departmental committees are not in any sense 'outside' politics, but to place too much emphasis on this fact is to risk turning a truth into a truism.

Emphasising the political reasons why committees are appointed also tends to detract from the equally important substantial reasons for their existence. Every royal commission or departmental committee has an explicit job which it is expected to perform. This job is described succinctly in its terms of reference. It is useful, therefore, to examine this statement and to try to discover on that basis why committees are appointed.

Terms of Reference

At the time of its appointment – in fact, as an intrinsic part of its appointment – every committee is given a clear statement of what it is expected to do. The importance to a committee of its terms of reference is described by one former committee member in this way:

> The government tells committees of inquiry what they are to do. . . . Terms of reference give all concerned a sense of purpose and urgency, and ensure that other people know the kind of help the committee needs. . . .

2 There is one book – C. J. Hanser, *Guide to Decision: the Royal Commission* (Totowa, N.J.: Bedminster Press, 1965) – which so minimises the importance of political motives as to come close to denying their existence (e.g. p. 221); see my review in the *Canadian Journal of Economics and Political Science*, 33 (1967), pp. 482–4.

Committees need terms of reference. They always complain about those they are given, but without them their job could be neither defined nor completed.[3]

Terms of reference are normally quite straightforward, but they can be very short or very long, very simple or very complicated.[4] For example, the terms of reference of the Clapham Committee on the Provision for Social and Economic Research (Cmd. 6868) were simply 'to consider whether additional provision is necessary for research into social and economic questions'. By contrast, the McCorquodale Committee on the Assessment of Disablement (Cmnd. 2487) was invited to

> examine Schedule 1 and Schedule 3, Table 1, to the Royal Warrant of 24th May, 1949 (Cmd. 7699) and Schedule 2 to the National Insurance (Industrial Injuries) (Benefit) Regulations, 1964 (S.I. 1964 No. 504) which relates to the assessment of certain disablements, and
>
> *i* to consider, in the light of any relevant developments since 1948, whether any, and if so what, modification in the lists of specified disablements, or variation in the assessments of such disablements, is desirable; and
>
> *ii* to consider whether there is any case for special provision by way of supplementary compensation confined to disablement due to amputation, either generally or in relation to advancing age;

and to report. In general, committee terms of reference tend to be more often like the first than the second of these two examples. That is, terms of reference are likely to be relatively short and uncomplicated and, in general, not too restrictive.

Royal commissions and departmental committees have been appointed in virtually every field of government activity. At the same time, there are certain classes of subjects which are more commonly assigned to these committees. There is obviously a clue to what these subjects might be in the pattern of appointment by government departments (see Chapter 4 above). Since the Home Office is the leading source of appointments, and since it is followed by the Scottish Office (notably the Scottish Home Department) and the Lord Chancellor's Department, then it would be reasonable to expect a relatively high proportion of royal commissions and departmental committees to be appointed to deal with matters which fall within the responsibilities of these

---

3 David Donnison, 'Committees and Committeemen', *New Society* (18 April 1968), p. 559. The formal appointment of royal commissions and departmental committees is described in Chapter 4 above.

4 Here and throughout this chapter, formal amendments (if any) are considered as part of a committee's original terms of reference: they are discussed separately in the next chapter.

departments.[5] One would expect committees to be charged with problems related to the legal process, the process of government, crime and punishment, the police, marriage and divorce, the welfare of young people, and so on. Broadly speaking, these expectations are fulfilled.

Thus, Table 6.1 on the next two pages illustrates both the fact that royal commissions and departmental committees have in the postwar period been involved in all the principal fields of government activity and at the same time that committees are much more likely to deal with some subjects than with others. In broad terms, two thirds of all the major postwar committees were concerned with what are called 'general government services' (Item 1) and 'economic services' (Item 8). Committees on all other subjects combined account for only one third of the total number appointed. Within these broad categories, the largest single group of committees consists of those concerned with matters of public order (Item 1.4): approximately one committee in five is of this single kind. Other significant numbers of committees dealt with general government administration (Item 1.1), agriculture (Item 8.2) and transportation (Item 8.6). Committees on matters of health, education, welfare and environmental services, on the other hand, account for less than one quarter of the total. The remainder considered matters related to defence and security, research and science, and disasters and calamities.

Using such broad categories as these, however, it is impossible to convey much of the real nature and breadth of the range of subjects which committees have been asked to consider. For this, there is no substitute to summarising as briefly as possible the subject of the terms of reference of all the major postwar royal commissions and departmental committees. Although it may seem rather tedious, a survey of all the major postwar committees can convey, as no set of categories can by itself, the enormous variety of subjects which are thought suitable for assigning to committees. As will become clear, a study of royal commissions and departmental committees is truly a study of virtually every aspect of public policy.

GENERAL GOVERNMENT SERVICES

Committees of this kind were asked to consider five main groups of subjects (see Table 6.1): namely, general administration; external affairs; property and tenancy; public order; and police, prisons and punishments.

Committees on matters of general government administration can in turn be subdivided into five groups. Nine major postwar committees have been

5 The responsibilities of these departments are described in D. N. Chester and F. M. G. Willson, *The Organisation of British Central Government 1914–1964*, 2nd ed. (London: Allen and Unwin, 1968); and in more detail in Sir Frank Newsam, *The Home Office* (London: Allen and Unwin, 1954), and Sir David Milne, *The Scottish Office* (London: Allen and Unwin, 1957).

Table 6.1 **Major royal commissions and departmental committees, 1945–69, by the subject of their terms of reference**

subject of terms of reference	number of committees		
1 GENERAL GOVERNMENT SERVICES			**136**
1.1 *General administration*		39	
1.1.1 Parliament and the Civil Service	9		
1.1.2 organisation of government	13		
1.1.3 local government	8		
1.1.4 records and statistics	6		
1.1.5 miscellaneous	4		
1.2 *External affairs*		8	
1.3 *Property and tenancy*		14	
1.3.1 property	9		
1.3.2 tenancy	5		
1.4 *Public order*		63	
1.4.1 public law	16		
1.4.2 judicial institutions	15		
1.4.3 legal procedures	17		
1.4.4 records and statistics	5		
1.4.5 alleged miscarriages of justice	10		
1.5 *Police, prisons and punishments*		11	
1.5.1 police and related services	5		
1.5.2 prisons and punishments	6		
2 DEFENCE AND SECURITY			**17**
2.1 *Armed Forces*		10	
2.2 *Security*		7	
3 RESEARCH AND SCIENCE			**13**
3.1 *General administration*		6	
3.2 *Specific research*		7	
4 EDUCATION			**17**
4.1 *Schools, universities, etc.*		3	
4.2 *Professional education*		10	
4.3 *Special investigations*		4	
5 HEALTH			**18**
5.1 *General administration*		3	
5.2 *Individual health services*		6	
5.3 *Conditions of employment*		9	
6 SOCIAL SECURITY AND WELFARE			**21**
6.1 *Services to children*		11	
6.2 *Other social services*		5	
6.3 *Legal aid and related services*		5	

subject of terms of reference		number of committees	
7 ENVIRONMENTAL SERVICES			**26**
7.1	*Housing*	5	
7.2	*Town and country planning*	11	
7.3	*Recreation and culture*	10	
8 ECONOMIC SERVICES			**105**
8.1	*General administration*	15	
8.1.1	economic policy	11	
8.1.2	industrial relations	4	
8.2	*Agriculture*	20	
8.3	*Fishing and hunting*	7	
8.4	*Mining and manufacturing*	13	
8.5	*Power*	11	
8.6	*Transportation*	20	
8.6.1	aviation	7	
8.6.2	shipping, waterways and ports	8	
8.6.3	roads and traffic	5	
8.7	*Communications and the media*	9	
8.8	*Finance and commerce*	10	
9 DISASTERS AND CALAMITIES			**5**
total			*358*

Note: The classification of subjects is adapted from United Nations Economic and Social Council, *Proposals for Revising the Standard National Accounts,* ref. no. E/CN.3/345 (New York: UN Publications, 1966), Table 2, pp. 67–73.

Source: Terms of reference of committees listed in Appendix B.

asked to look into questions involving Parliament and the Civil Service. Five of these dealt with the Civil Service, including a royal commission (Cmd. 9613), the well-known Fulton Committee (Cmnd. 3638), the Masterman Committee on the Political Activities of Civil Servants (Cmd. 7718), a committee on Higher Civil Service Remuneration (Cmd. 7635), and another on the 'Method II' selection of civil servants for the administrative class (Cmnd. 4156).[6] Two other committees looked into cases of misconduct, one arising

6 The report of the Fulton Committee (Cmnd. 3638) is discussed in R. A. Chapman, 'The Fulton Committee on the Civil Service', in Chapman (ed.), *The Role of Commissions in Policy-Making* (London: Allen and Unwin, 1973), Chapter 2; in T. J. Cartwright, 'The Fulton Committee on the Civil Service in Britain', *Canadian Public Administration,* XII (1969), pp. 89–107; and in articles by Sir William Armstrong, Sir James Dunnett, W. G. Harris and Sir Maurice Dean in 'The Fulton Report', *Public Administration,* 47 (1969), pp. 1–63.

out of the Crichel Down case in the 1950's (Cmd. 9220) and the other from the misuse of certain official facilities by M.P.s (Cmnd. 583).[7] The remaining two advised on improved methods of electoral registration (Cmd. 7004) and the remuneration of ministers and M.P.s (Cmnd. 2516).[8]

Thirteen more committees were asked to consider various aspects of the organisation of government. Among these were the Balfour Royal Commission on Scottish Affairs (Cmd. 9212), the Franks Committee on Administrative Tribunals and Inquiries (Cmnd. 218), the Plowden Group on the Control of Public Expenditure (Cmnd. 1432), the Salmon Royal Commission on Tribunals of Inquiry (Cmnd. 3121), and the Crowther-Kilbrandon Royal Commission on the Constitution (Cmnd. 5460).[9] Five others dealt with government procurement and disposal procedures regarding land at Crichel Down (Cmd. 9176), unpatented inventions (Cmd. 9788), the British Transport Commission (Cmnd. 262), the London Electricity Board (Cmnd. 605), and Ministry of Aviation contracts (Cmnd. 2581). The remaining three looked at the costs of the various home information services of the government (Cmd. 7836); recognition of certain organised post office workers (Cmd. 8740); and local organisation in the Ministry of Agriculture, Fisheries and Food (Cmd. 9732).

The best known of the eight major postwar committees on local government are probably the three royal commissions on local government in Greater London (Cmnd. 1164), in England (Cmnd. 4040) and in Scotland (Cmnd. 4150).[10] The others have dealt with rating of property – in Scotland (Cmd. 9244), of charities (Cmnd. 831) and of commercial establishments (Cmnd. 4366) – with the consolidation of local government law generally in Scotland (Cmd. 8993), and with the question of expenses for members of local authorities (Cmd. 7126).

Five more committees have dealt with government records – one on the

---

7 On the Crichel Down affair, see C. J. Hamson, 'The Real Lesson of Crichel Down', *Public Administration*, XXXII (1954), pp. 383–7; D. N. Chester, 'The Crichel Down Case', *ibid.*, pp. 389–401; J. A. G. Griffith, 'The Crichel Down Affair', *Modern Law Review*, XVII (1955), pp. 557–70; R. D. Brown, *The Battle of Crichel Down* (London: Bodley Head, 1955); and the comments in R. E. Wraith and S. B. Lamb, *Public Inquiries as an Instrument of Government* (London: Allen and Unwin, 1971), pp. 202ff.

8 Some of these 'top salaries' are now dealt with by a standing Review Body (Type II) under the chairmanship of Lord Boyle of Handsworth (see its reports, Cmnd. 4836 and Cmnd. 5001).

9 On the Plowden Group report (Cmnd. 1432), see Ursula Hicks, 'Plowden, Planning and Management in the Public Service', *Public Administration*, XXXIX (1961), pp. 299–312; and articles by D. N. Chester, R. W. B. Clarke, W. W. Morton and J. E. Wall in 'The Plowden Report', *Public Administration*, 41 (1963), pp. 1–50.

10 The report of the London Royal Commission (Cmnd. 1164) is discussed in: W. A. Robson, 'The Reform of London Government', *Public Administration*, XXXIX (1961), pp. 59–71; L. J. Sharpe, 'The Report of the Royal Commission on Local Government in Greater London', *ibid.*, pp. 73–92; Peter Robshaw, 'Another View on the London Government Royal Commission', *ibid.*, pp. 247–50; and Peter Self, 'The Herbert Report and the Values

form of government accounts (Cmd. 7969) and another on departmental records (Cmd. 9163) – and statistics, including three committees on the censuses of production and distribution (Cmd. 6687, Cmd. 6764 and Cmd. 9276) and one on Scottish financial and trade statistics (Cmd. 8609).

The last four committees dealing with general government administration are a mixed group. There was a committee on intermediaries, or people who were making a business of acting for other people in the obtaining of various licences and permits (Cmd. 7904); another looked into allegations concerning public-house operators in the Carlisle and District State Management Scheme (Cmnd. 168); a third committee considered the whole question of Crown land (Cmd. 9483); and the fourth looked into statutory smallholdings provided by the Minister of Agriculture, Fisheries and Foods, by County Councils and by other authorities in England and Wales (Cmnd. 3303).

The second main group of committees on general government services includes those concerned with external affairs. Of the eight major postwar committees in this group, two dealt with overseas representation (Cmnd. 2276 and Cmnd. 4107), two with foreign investment (Cmnd. 786 and Cmnd. 3516), one with state immunities (Cmd. 8460), and one with the government's overseas information services (Cmd. 9138).[11] The two other committees were a royal commission on East Africa (Cmd. 9475) and a committee on the damage and casualties in Port Said following the military action there in 1956 (Cmnd. 47).

The third group of committees consists of those concerning property and tenancy. Of the first, two dealt with charges on land (Cmd. 8440 and Cmd. 9825), three with the registration of land in Scotland (Cmd. 7451, Cmnd. 2032 and Cmnd. 4137), and four with a variety of matters: namely, common land (Cmnd. 462), rights of light (Cmnd. 473), positive covenants affecting land (Cmnd. 2719) and conveyancing (Cmnd. 3118). Of the committees dealing with tenancy, three concerned the tenure of shops and business premises in Scotland (Cmd. 7285, Cmd. 7903 and Cmnd. 472), and two leases and leasehold in England and Wales (Cmd. 7982) and in Scotland (Cmd. 8657).

The fourth (and largest) group of committees on general government services concerned matters of public order. Sixteen major postwar committees dealt with specific matters of public law. There were three on marriage and

---

of Local Government', *Political Studies*, X (1962), pp. 146–62. The report of the English Royal Commission (Cmnd. 4040) is discussed by Jeffrey Stanyer, 'The Redcliffe-Maud Royal Commission on Local Government' in Chapman, *The Role of Commissions in Policy-Making, op. cit.*, Chapter 5. On the report of the Scottish Royal Commission (Cmnd. 4150), see John Mackintosh, 'The Royal Commission on Local Government in Scotland, 1966–69', *Public Administration*, 48 (1970), pp. 49–56.

11 The report of the Committee on Representational Services Overseas (Cmnd. 2276) is discussed in articles by Max Beloff and K. E. Robinson in 'Another Plowden Report', *Public Administration*, 42 (1964), pp. 415–22.

divorce (Cmd. 9678, Cmnd. 3587 and Cmnd. 4011), three on the law of succession (Cmd. 8114, Cmd. 8310 and Cmnd. 3051), two on cremation and death certification (Cmd. 8009 and Cmnd. 4810 respectively), and two on matters relating to cruelty to and damage by animals (Cmd. 8266 and Cmd. 8746 respectively). The remaining six committees examined a variety of different matters: namely, weights and measures legislation (Cmd. 8219), homosexual offences and prostitution (Cmnd. 247), human artificial insemination (Cmnd. 1105), the law on Sunday observance (Cmnd. 2528), the legal status of the Welsh language (Cmnd. 2785) and the age of majority (Cmnd. 3342).

Another fifteen major postwar committees examined the functioning of various legal institutions. All but four of these looked at specific courts: namely (in order of the appearance of their reports), county courts (Cmd. 7668), the Court of Record for the Hundred of Salford (Cmd. 8364), the Supreme Court (Cmd. 8878), a proposed new criminal court for South Lancashire (Cmd. 8955), the Supreme Court of Northern Ireland (Cmnd. 227), the criminal courts generally (Cmnd. 1289), magistrates' courts in London (Cmnd. 1606), the Court of Criminal Appeal (Cmnd. 2755), the Sheriff Court in Scotland (Cmnd. 3248), assizes and quarter sessions (Cmnd. 4153) and the Supreme Court of Judicature of Northern Ireland (Cmnd. 4292). The other four dealt with Justices of the Peace (Cmd. 7463), proceedings before examining Justices (Cmnd. 479), the office of the Public Trustee (Cmd. 9755), and Chancery Chambers and the Chancery Registrar's Office (Cmnd. 967).

There were also seventeen major postwar committees concerned with various legal procedures not necessarily peculiar to any one court but instead related more to the nature of the subject of the litigation. They form a somewhat disparate group. There were two dealing with procedures in matrimonial causes (Cmd. 7024 and Cmnd. 638) and one on conflicts of jurisdiction affecting children (Cmnd. 842). There were three committees on the procedures of various kinds of tribunals and appeal boards (Cmnd. 1033, Cmnd. 3387 and Cmnd. 4078). There were committees on the limitation of legal actions (Cmd. 7740), on the limitation of actions for personal injury (Cmnd. 1829) and on personal injuries litigation in general (Cmnd. 3691). There were two committees on matters connected with jury trials, one on their use in civil suits in Scotland (Cmnd. 851) and one on jury service generally (Cmnd. 2627). There were also committees on depositions (Cmd. 7639), the law of diligence governing the attachment of the property or person of a debtor (Cmnd. 456) and the enforcement of judgement debts (Cmnd. 3909). Finally, there were committees on the grounds for new trials in criminal cases (Cmd. 8150), the summary trial of minor offences like traffic violations (Cmd. 9524), and the administration of funds in court (Cmnd. 818).

Records and statistics formed the subject of concern for another five major postwar committees. Two of them dealt with court records, one with their preservation (Cmnd. 3084) and the other with the mechanical recording of court proceedings (Cmnd. 3096). The other three committees were asked to advise on the keeping of criminal statistics (Cmnd. 3448 and Cmnd. 3705) and civil judicial statistics (Cmnd. 3684).

The final group of committees dealing with matters of public order were appointed to consider individual cases where it was thought that a miscarriage of justice might have occurred. Each of these ten committees (Cmd. 6736, Cmd. 6783, Cmd. 6933, Cmd. 7049, Cmd. 7061, Cmd. 8522, Cmd. 8896, Cmnd. 2319, Cmnd. 2526 and Cmnd. 3101) deals with its own particular case; the best known are probably the two which reviewed the conviction of Timothy John Evans (Cmd. 8896 and Cmnd. 3101).

The fifth and final group of committees concerned with general government services dealt with matters relating to police, prisons and punishments. Of the five major postwar committees on the police and other services, two dealt with conditions of service in the police (Cmd. 7831 and Cmnd. 1728), one with a specific police force (Cmnd. 251), one on the Prison Services (Cmnd. 544) and one on the Probation Service (Cmnd. 1800).[12] Of the six major postwar committees on prisons and punishments, two dealt with punishments – both of them royal commissions (Cmnd. 8932 and one which did not issue any report) – three with prisons (Cmd. 8594, Cmnd. 503 and Cmnd. 3175), and one with both – that is, with punishments in prisons (Cmd. 8429).

DEFENCE AND SECURITY

Committees of this second major kind fall into two groups: those concerned with some aspect of the armed forces and those concerned with national security. Of the ten major postwar committees in the first group, three were focussed on the special problems of young servicemen (Cmd. 9433, Cmnd. 268 and Cmnd. 4509) and two on questions of discipline (Cmd. 7608 and Cmd. 8119). Two more dealt with recruitment (Cmd. 8845 and Cmnd. 545) and three others with certain somewhat peripheral issues: namely, the Territorial Army (Cmd. 9523), civil defence (Cmd. 9131) and the employment of national service men on leaving the services (Cmnd. 35).

Of the seven major postwar committees concerned with national security, three dealt with specific cases – the so-called Vassal case (Cmnd. 1871), the Profumo case (Cmnd. 2152) and the Bossard and Allen cases (Cmnd. 2773).[13] The other four committees looked at security generally (Cmd. 9715), security in the public service (Cmnd. 1681), the government's powers to intercept

---

12 On the Willink Royal Commission (Cmnd. 1728), see Jennifer Hart, 'Some Reflections on the Report of the Royal Commission on the Police', *Public Law*, IX (1963), pp. 283–304.

13 In connection with the Profumo case, see Clive Irving *et al.*, *Scandal '63: a Study of the Profumo Affair* (London: Heinemann, 1963) and Wayland Young, *The Profumo Affair: Aspects of Conservatism* (Harmondsworth: Penguin, 1963).

communications in the interests of security (Cmnd. 283), and the 'D' Notice system (Cmnd. 3309).

RESEARCH AND SCIENCE

Major postwar committees of this kind can be divided into those concerned with general issues of administration (six) and those carrying out investigations into specific matters (seven). In the first group there have been two on social studies (Cmd. 6868 and Cmnd. 2660), two on the role of science in government and of government in science (Cmd. 9734 and Cmnd. 2171), one on the supply of and demand for scientific manpower (Cmd. 6824), and one on experiments on animals (Cmnd. 2641).[14] The second group of committees considered a wide range of subjects: namely, the storage of celluloid (Cmd. 7929); the composition and nutritive value of flour (Cmd. 9757); solid smokeless fuels (Cmnd. 999); coal derivatives (Cmnd. 1120); the composition of milk (Cmnd. 1147); the use of antibiotics in animal husbandry and veterinary medicine (Cmnd. 4190); and the medical and toxicological aspects of orthochlorobenzylidene malononitrile or, as it is more commonly known, CS gas (Cmnd. 4775).

EDUCATION

Seventeen major postwar committees were appointed to deal with some aspect of education. Three of them dealt with higher education, including a royal commission on university education in Dundee (Cmd. 8514), a committee on grants to students (Cmnd. 1051) and the well-known Robbins Committee on Higher Education (Cmnd. 2154). Another ten of them were concerned with professional education of various kinds: business administration (Cmd. 6673), teaching in Scotland (Cmd. 9419 and Cmnd. 2066), agriculture (Cmnd. 614 and Cmnd. 2419), law (Cmnd. 1255 and Cmnd. 4595), medicine (Cmnd. 3569), veterinary medicine (Cmnd. 2430) and technical training (Cmnd. 4335). Finally, there were four committees charged with investigating three specific incidents at Approved Schools (Cmd. 7150, Cmnd. 937 and Cmnd. 3367) and an educational dispute in Durham (Cmnd. 4152).

HEALTH

Eighteen major postwar committees have dealt with matters related to public health, three of them with the health service generally, six with specific health services and nine with conditions of employment in the health services. The first three concentrated on the industrial health services (Cmd. 8170), the cost of the National Health Service (Cmd. 9663) and the provision of general medical services in the Highlands and Islands of Scotland (Cmnd. 3257).[15]

14 In connection with the Committees on a Department of Scientific and Industrial Research (Cmd. 9734) and on the Organization of Civil Science (Cmnd. 2171), see H. Melville, *The Department of Scientific and Industrial Research* (London: Allen and Unwin, 1962).

15 The report of the Committee on the Cost of the National Health Service (Cmd. 9663) is discussed in T. E. Chester, 'The Guillebaud Report', *Public Administration*, XXXIV (1956), pp. 199–210.

The six more specific committees looked at the problems of disablement (Cmd. 7076, Cmd. 9833 and Cmnd. 2847), industrial diseases (Cmd. 7557 and Cmd. 9584), and mental illness and mental deficiency (Cmnd. 169). Finally, there were nine committees on conditions of employment: four of them dealt with the remuneration of certain categories of people (Cmd. 6810, Cmd. 7402, Cmd. 7420 and Cmnd. 939), one with recruitment to the dental profession (Cmd. 9861), two with the regulation of certain medical activities (Cmd. 7565 and Cmd. 8531), one with the special problems of medical auxiliaries (Cmd. 8188) and another with the special problems of social workers in the mental health services (Cmd. 8260).

SOCIAL SECURITY AND WELFARE

Twenty-one major postwar committees have focused on questions relating to social security and social welfare. Among these are eleven concerned with children. There were two pairs of 'matching' English and Scottish committees on homeless children in 1945-6 (Cmd. 6911 and Cmd. 6922) and on children and young people generally in the late 1950's and early 1960's (Cmnd. 1191 and Cmnd. 2306). There were also the Albemarle Committee on the Youth Service (Cmnd. 929), two committees on the adoption of children (Cmd. 9248 and Cmnd. 5107), and one committee to investigate a specific case of boarding-out children (Cmd. 6636). Finally, two committees dealt with the employment of children in entertainments (Cmd. 8005) and in the potato harvest (Cmd. 9738), and another looked at the effect of the cinema on children (Cmd. 7945).

In addition, there were five committees on certain aspects of other kinds of social services: namely, the question of making grants available for marriage guidance (Cmd. 7566), the issue of taxing provisions made for retirement (Cmnd. 9063), the problems of providing for old age (Cmnd. 9333), the provision of personal social services by local authorities (Cmnd. 3704) and the problems of one-parent families (Cmnd. 5629).[16] Finally, there were five more committees in this group, three of them on legal aid (Cmd. 6925, Cmnd. 1015 and Cmnd. 2934), one on discharged prisoners' aid societies (Cmd. 8879) and one on compensation for victims of crimes of violence (Cmnd. 1406).

ENVIRONMENTAL SERVICES

In this group are twenty six major postwar committees, five concerned with housing, eleven with town and country planning and ten with recreation and culture. The five housing committees considered the selling price of houses (Cmd. 6670), the use of caravans as homes (Cmnd. 872), the impact of rates on households (Cmnd. 2582), housing in Greater London (Cmnd. 2605) and the various Rent Acts (Cmnd. 4609). The eleven planning committees dealt with new towns (Cmd. 6876) and the qualifications of planners (Cmd. 8059);

16 On the last of these, see N. M. Thomas, 'The Seebohm Committee on Personal Social Services' in Chapman, *The Role of Commissions in Policy-making, op. cit.*, Chapter 6.

with land drainage in Scotland (Cmd. 7948), the drainage of trade premises (Cmd. 9117) and coastal flooding (Cmd. 9165); with the preservation of the Regent's Park Terraces (Cmd. 7094) and of Downing Street (Cmnd. 457); with building legislation in Scotland (Cmnd. 269) and the fire service (Cmnd. 4371); and with the problems of air pollution (Cmd. 9322) and noise pollution (Cmnd. 2056). Finally, there were ten committees on recreation and culture: two dealt with betting and gaming (Cmd. 8190 and Cmnd. 1003), two with the licensing of public houses (Cmnd. 2021 and Cmnd. 2709), two with museums and galleries (Cmd. 8604 and Cmnd. 1750), two with libraries (Cmnd. 660 and Cmnd. 4028), one with a new concert hall (Cmd. 9467) and one with the protection of field monuments (Cmnd. 3904).

ECONOMIC SERVICES

Committees dealing with economic services of various kinds from the second largest group of the nine identified in Table 6.1, comprising 105 major postwar committees in all. These committees may in turn be subdivided according to the industry involved, with a general category of matters extending across the economy as a whole.

In this general category are fifteen committees, eleven of them dealing with economic policy and four with industrial relations. Seven of the economic policy committees dealt with taxation in one form or another (Cmd. 8189, Cmd. 8452, Cmd. 8453, Cmd. 8784, Cmd. 8830 and Cmnd. 2300), including the Cohen-Radcliffe Royal Commission on the Taxation of Profits and Income in 1951–5 (Cmd. 9474). The other four dealt with somewhat broader issues: namely, the working of the monetary system (Cmnd. 827), the economy of Northern Ireland (Cmnd. 1835), decimal currency (Cmnd. 2145), and economic growth in intermediate areas (Cmnd. 3998). Among the four committees on industrial relations, the most significant was probably the Donovan Royal Commission on Trade Unions and Employers' Associations (Cmnd. 3623).[17] The others dealt with employment in specific kinds of work (Cmd. 7664 and Cmnd. 3714) and the circumstances surrounding a complaint made by a British union to the International Labour Organisation (Cmnd. 3623).

Twenty major postwar committees have dealt with some aspects of agriculture. Eight of these concerned livestock, five its slaughter (Cmd. 7888, Cmd. 8925, Cmd. 9376, Cmd. 9542 and Cmnd. 154), one the question of pig production (Cmd. 9588), another the experimental importation of Charollais cattle (Cmnd. 1140), and another the general welfare of livestock (Cmnd. 2836). Four more committees were concerned with diseases to animals, including two on foot-and-mouth disease (Cmd. 9214 and Cmnd. 4225), one on anthrax (Cmnd. 846), and one on fowl pest (Cmnd. 1664). Four more committees looked at crofting conditions (Cmd. 9091), the utilisation of grasslands (Cmnd. 547), supplies of herbage seeds (Cmnd. 3748) and the use and role of allotments (Cmnd. 4166). Finally, there were another four com-

17 See Robert Kilroy-Silk, 'The Donovan Royal Commission on Trade Unions', in Chapman, *The Role of Commissions in Policy-Making, op. cit.*, Chapter 3.

mittees concerned with the marketing and distribution of agricultural produce: milk (Cmd. 7414 and Cmnd. 1597), horticulture (Cmnd. 61) and meat (Cmnd. 2282).

Committees on various aspects of fishing and hunting account for another seven committees. There was one on hunting – the question of a 'close season' for deer in Scotland (Cmd. 9273) – and six on fishing: illegal fishing in Scotland (Cmd. 7917), salmon and freshwater fisheries (Cmnd. 1350 and Cmnd. 2691), inshore fisheries in Scotland (Cmnd. 4453), the fishing industry (Cmnd. 1266), and trawler safety (Cmnd. 4114).

Committees on mining and manufacturing make up a group of thirteen, four on mining and nine on manufacturing. Of the first, two dealt with mining overseas (Cmd. 7728 and Cmnd. 2351), one with mining subsidence (Cmd. 7637), and one with mineral development generally (Cmd. 7732). The nine committees on manufacturing looked at the china clay industry (Cmd. 6748), double day-shift working (Cmd. 7147), night baking (Cmd. 8378), the importation of cotton (Cmd. 8510 and Cmd. 8861), hallmarking and assaying (Cmnd. 663), industrial design (Cmnd. 1808), the pharmaceutical industry (Cmnd. 3410), and the patent system and patent law (Cmnd. 5629).

A related group of eleven committees considered questions relating to different kinds of power, chiefly electrical power. Just after the war, there was a committee on the general use of fuel and power resources in Britain in the postwar period (Cmd. 8647) and, some time later, a committee on the distribution costs of coal (Cmnd. 446); still later there was a committee on steam boilers (Cmnd. 1173). There were five committees on the generation and distribution of electricity (Cmd. 7464, Cmd. 9672, Cmnd. 695, Cmnd. 1895 and Cmnd. 3960) and (following an accident at a generating station) three closely interrelated committees on nuclear power (Cmnd. 338, Cmnd. 342 and Cmnd. 471).

The twenty major postwar committees bearing on matters related to transportation may conveniently be divided among those dealing with aviation (seven); those dealing with shipping, waterways and ports (eight); and those dealing with roads and traffic (five). The first group consists of committees on Tudor aircraft (Cmd. 7478), the certification of civil aircraft (Cmd. 7705), civil aviation personnel (Cmd. 7746), procedures for the landing and taking off of aircraft (Cmd. 8147), local objections to Gatwick as a second London airport (Cmd. 9215), the aircraft industry as a whole (Cmnd. 2853) and the civil air transport industry (Cmnd. 4018). Most of the maritime committees dealt with the port transport industry (Cmnd. 1824 and Cmnd. 2734), especially its problems of labour relations (Cmd. 8236, Cmd. 9813 and Cmnd. 3104); but there were also committees on inland waterways (Cmnd. 486), on shipbuilding (Cmnd. 2937) and on shipping (Cmnd. 4337). The five committees concerned with surface transport considered: the taxicab trade, especially in London (Cmd. 8804 and Cmnd. 4483); evasions of petrol rationing after the war (Cmd. 7372); the consolidation of highway law (Cmnd. 630); and roads in London (Cmnd. 812).

Communications and the media form the subject of the next group of nine committees. Chief among these are probably the two royal commissions on the press (Cmd. 7700 and Cmnd. 1811) and the three committees on broadcasting (Cmd. 8116, Cmnd. 39 and Cmnd. 1753, of which the second dealt exclusively with broadcasting in Wales).[18] There were also two committees on matters related to films (Cmd. 7361 and Cmd. 7838), one on Welsh language publishing (Cmd. 8661) and one on copyright law (Cmd. 8662).

Finally, ten committees looked at questions related to finance and commerce. There were committees on exhibitions and fairs (Cmd. 6782) and charitable trusts (Cmd. 8710); committees on company law (Cmnd. 1749) and certain of its aspects (Cmd. 9112 and Cmnd. 221); committees on the endorsement of cheques (Cmnd. 3), consumer protection (Cmnd. 1781) and consumer credit (Cmnd. 4596); and committees on resale price maintenance (Cmd. 7696) and small firms (Cmnd. 4811).

DISASTERS AND CALAMITIES

The final group of major postwar committees dealt with natural disasters and calamities, three of them fires in different parts of the country (Cmd. 6877, Cmd. 7048 and Cmd. 7440), one the collapse of a football stadium (Cmd. 6846), and the most recent an accident to a drilling rig in the North Sea (Cmnd. 3409). That there are so few committees on such subjects implies neither that there are few disasters and calamities nor that there are few inquiries into them, but that most such inquiries are carried out by statutory committees (Type IIIa, usually known as public inquiries) rather than by royal commissions or departmental committees.[19]

The Scope of the Mandate

It will be clear from the preceding survey of terms of reference that a committee's mandate can vary not only in terms of its subject matter but also in terms of its geographical scope. Some committees dealt with matters affecting the whole of Britain while others were confined to matters affecting only Scotland, London or even a specific institution (such as an approved school or a prison). It is interesting to look briefly at this source of variation, too.

In fact, the majority of committees are given mandates which are national in scope, but about one committee in three is likely to find that its terms of reference confine its attention to only a part of the country. Surprisingly, royal commissions are more likely than departmental committees to be less than national in the scope of their terms of reference. No fewer than ten (out of twenty three) postwar royal commissions were given mandates which did not extend to affairs in the entire country. All the same, most of the major

18 Another Royal Commission on the Press has just been announced (*see House of Commons Debates*, 2 May 1974) under the chairmanship of Mr Justice Finer.

19 Wraith and Lamb, *op. cit.*, pp. 146–54.

Table 6.2 Major royal commissions and departmental committees, 1945–69, by the geographical scope of their terms of reference

geographical scope		number of committees
National		223
England and Wales only		56
England and Wales as a whole	31	
England and Wales excluding London	3	
England as a whole	0	
England excluding London	6	
London	12	
Wales	4	
Scotland only		41
Northern Ireland only		4
essentially local (excluding London)		27
unclassifiable		7
total		*358*

Source: Terms of reference of committees listed in Appendix B.

postwar committees were asked to consider a matter as it affected the whole of Great Britain and (where appropriate) Northern Ireland (see Table 6.2).

Just over one committee in ten dealt with some question peculiar to Scotland. As the earlier analysis of appointing departments suggested (Chapter 4 above), almost all of these committees were appointed by the Scottish Office on its own, but occasionally an English department will be involved even in a purely Scottish affair. For example, the Ministry of Food participated in the appointment of the Handford Committee on Slaughterhouses in Scotland (Cmd. 9376). On the other hand, committees dealing with some question as it applies in Scotland as well as the rest of the country are not necessarily appointed jointly by the Scottish Office, even in matters for which the Scottish Office is responsible. For example, when the Minister of Agriculture, Fisheries and Food appointed the recent Northumberland Committee on Foot-and-mouth Disease (Cmnd. 4225) 'to review the policy and arrangements for dealing with foot-and-mouth disease in Great Britain', he did so without the formal participation of the Scottish Department of Agriculture and Fisheries.

More committees dealt exclusively with England and Wales (fifty six) than dealt exclusively with Scotland (forty one), and only six of each were actually 'matching' pairs of English and Scottish committees. Sometimes a committee is clearly in a dilemma as to whether it should extend its investigations to include the situation in Scotland. For example, the Working Party on Compensation for Victims of Crimes of Violence (Cmnd. 1406), which was appointed independently by the Home Office, reported having decided finally that:

R.C.—4*

In the interests of simplicity, our report is for the most part written in terms appropriate to England and Wales. Insofar as special consideration might be thought, or appear to us, to apply to a scheme of compensation in Scotland, these are discussed in Appendix A to the report.

The cases of Wales and Northern Ireland provide interesting contrasts with Scotland. Wales, of course, enjoys nothing like the same privileged administrative position as Scotland. Unless a committee deals with a peculiarly Welsh matter (and not always even then), the Welsh Office is very rarely involved in a formal way.[20] It has appointed only one major postwar committee entirely on its own: namely, the Parry Committee on the Legal Status of the Welsh Language (Cmnd. 2785).

Northern Ireland, on the other hand, has a good deal more constitutional and administrative autonomy than Scotland or Wales, and this applies as much to the appointment of committees as it does to other aspects of home rule. Nevertheless, there were four committees in our sample which were formally appointed from Westminster alone and which dealt with purely Irish matters. Two of these were concerned with the Supreme Court of Northern Ireland, which, strictly speaking, was created by an Act of Parliament in London in any case.[21] Another, on the Economy of Northern Ireland (Cmnd. 1835), was described as 'a joint Working Party of senior officials of the United Kingdom and Northern Ireland departments concerned, under a chairman from outside the public service'. Finally, the Robson Committee on Coal Distribution Costs (Cmnd. 446) was adapted in a unique way to serve the needs of both Britain and Northern Ireland. The Committee was originally appointed by the Minister of Fuel and Power with jurisdiction 'in Great Britain'; however, as soon as the Committee was appointed in London, it was 'also appointed by the Minister of Commerce, Northern Ireland, to conduct a similar inquiry in Northern Ireland. . . .' No separate report was issued on Northern Ireland. More recently, however, there has been a committee formally appointed on a joint basis by the two governments: the Minister of Agriculture for Northern Ireland was formally involved in the appointment of the Swann Joint Committee on the Use of Antibiotics in Animal Husbandry and Veterinary Medicine (Cmnd. 4190).

20 When the Welsh Office is involved in the appointment of a committee dealing with a question not peculiar to Wales, it may be simply because the Minister for Wales happens to be also Minister of Housing and Local Government (as in the case of the Reading Committee on the Consolidation of Highway Law (Cmnd. 630)) or Home Secretary (as in the case of the Mabane Committee on Civil Defence (Cmd. 9131)). On the other hand, a committee dealing with a matter peculiar to Wales may not involve the Welsh Office, as in the case of the Ince Committee on Welsh Broadcasting which was appointed by the Postmaster General alone, although he did so with 'the concurrence of the . . . Minister for Welsh Affairs' (Cmnd. 39).

21 These were the Black-Sheil Committee (Cmnd. 227) and the MacDermott Committee (Cmnd. 4292). The statutory reference is to the Government of Ireland Act, 1920 (10 and 11 Geo. V, Chapter 67), Sections 38ff. See also Nicholas Mansergh, *The Government of Northern Ireland* (London: Allen and Unwin, 1936).

Finally, there is a group of twenty seven committees appointed to consider questions of an essentially local nature (apart from those dealing with the particular problems of London). Examples of such committees are the Moelwyn Hughes Enquiry into the Disaster at the Bolton Wanderers' Football Ground on March 9, 1946 (Cmd. 6846), and the Gibbens Inquiry into the Administration of Punishment at Court Lees Approved School (Cmnd. 3367). These committees dealt with local issues which could have occurred anywhere in Britain.

In both the nature and the scope of their terms of reference, therefore, royal commissions and departmental committees tend broadly to reflect the responsibilities and concerns of the departments which have appointed them. The result is that there are very few areas of government in which committees have not been appointed.

The Purposes of Committees

Why, then, are royal commissions and departmental committees appointed? From the preceding discussion, some of what were called at the beginning of this chapter the substantial (as opposed to the political) reasons for appointing committees have now appeared. In general, most committees are appointed to deal with questions of general government services (including matters of public order and government organisation) and questions of economic services (especially those related to agriculture, transportation and economic policy generally). Only about one committee in four is likely to be asked to deal with a matter of health, education, welfare or environmental services. Moreover, the majority of committees deal with national issues, although the numbers which do not are by no means insignificant. But there is still an important element missing from this explanation of why committees are appointed, and that is the question of what they are actually expected to *do* about the matters assigned to them.

The basic purpose of any royal commission or departmental committee is to offer advice to the government, advice about any of its various functions. Accordingly, the purposes of these committees may conveniently be classified in terms of the functions of government about which they are asked to give advice.

There are many ways of describing the functions of government. Walter Bagehot, for example, wrote about the 'elective', 'expressive', 'teaching', 'informing' and 'legislation' functions of the House of Commons.[22] Other descriptions are equally possible, but one proposed by Professor Herbert Simon is particularly useful. Simon argues that any decision-making process can be divided into three principal 'phases':

> The first phase of the decision-making process – searching the environment for conditions calling for decision – I shall call *intelligence* activity

22 Walter Bagehot, *The English Constitution*, ed. R. H. S. Crossman (London: Collins, 1963), Chapter 4.

(borrowing the military meaning of intelligence). The second phase – inventing, developing, and analysing possible courses of action – I shall call *design* activity. The third phase – selecting a particular course of action from those available – I shall call *choice* activity.[23]

In terms more appropriate to the governmental process, these three 'phases' of decision-making can be translated into three basic functions of government: i obtaining information, ii formulating policy, and iii proposing specific action.

To set out a series of governmental functions like this does not imply that, in practice, all government decisions pass neatly from the first (information) stage through the second (policy) stage and into the third (action) stage; or indeed that decisions follow any particular sequence. A set of functions does not describe how government works in practice, merely how its various activities may be classified. Nor are the distinctions between what is information, what policy and what action always quite unambiguous, although one possible source of ambiguity can be removed by making clear that 'information' includes both facts (e.g. from experts) and opinion (e.g. from interest groups). Any one of the above three functions can have implications for the other two, and it may require a certain amount of discretion to determine how important these implications are. Finally, there are obviously other ways of classifying the functions of government.[24] The proposal here is not necessarily better or worse than any others, but it is useful for describing the purposes for which royal commissions and departmental committees are appointed.

The purposes of a royal commission or a departmental committee can be described in terms of these three functions of government. In other words, a committee may be appointed just to help provide *information* to the government about the existing state of affairs with regard to some particular matter, or it may be expected to make recommendations for *action* as well or instead. A committee may be asked to advise the government on what sort of *policy* ought to be adopted, or it may be told to take questions of policy as given and

---

23 H. A. Simon, *The Shape of Automation for Men and Management* (New York: Harper Torchbooks, 1963), p. 54. The nature of these three activities within various organisations is described in greater detail in James G. March and H. A. Simon, *Organisations* (New York: Wiley, 1958), Chapters 6 and 7. For further information, see Harold Wilensky, *Organizational Intelligence* (New York: Basic Books, 1967), on the intelligence activity; H. A. Simon 'The Science of Design' in *The Sciences of the Artificial* (Boston: M. I. T. Press, 1969), Chapter 3, on the design activity; and David Braybrooke and C. E. Lindblom, *A Strategy of Decision* (New York: Free Press, 1963), on the choice activity.

24 For those inclined more towards a systems view of government, it may be noted that the three categories above can readily be translated into: i 'inputs', ii 'transformations' and iii 'outputs'. See, for example, David Easton, *A Framework for Political Analysis* (Englewood Cliffs: Prentice-Hall, 1965), and H. V. Wiseman, *Political Systems* (London: Routledge and Kegan Paul, 1966).

Table 6.3 Major royal commissions and departmental committees, 1945–69, by purpose

purpose	royal commissions only	all committees
information (I)	1	56
information and policy (IP)	2	45
policy (P)	0	1
policy and action (PA)	0	0
action (A)	0	4
information and action (IA)	8	115
information, policy and action (IPA)	14	137
total	24	358

Source: See Appendix B.

to propose what action should be taken to implement that policy. In fact, if the functions of government are defined in the manner described above, there are seven possible purposes for royal commissions and departmental committees:

a to obtain information (I)
b to obtain information and formulate policy (IP)
c to formulate policy (P)
d to formulate policy and propose action (PA)
e to propose action (A)
f to obtain information and propose action (IA)
g to obtain information, formulate policy and propose action (IPA)

Any royal commission or departmental committee – indeed, any institution of government – can be classified as having one of these seven different kinds of purposes.

Table 6.3 provides an analysis of the major postwar royal commissions and departmental committees. It must be recognised immediately, of course, that there is probably some element of subjectivity in this analysis; however, even allowing for this, there is a clear and significant pattern to the results. Broadly speaking, seven out of every ten committees (including all but three royal commissions) were more or less equally likely to be in two of the seven categories and most of the remaining committees fell into two others. No postwar royal commissions at all and only five major postwar departmental committees have belonged in the other three categories.

To be more precise, over one third of the committees were appointed to obtain information, to formulate policy and to propose specific actions (IPA). No committee could be assigned a broader purpose than this, for such a purpose parallels that of government itself. A committee with an 'IPA' purpose may in effect pretend to be a 'mini-government' insofar as the subject of its mandate is concerned – although, of course, no government is bound to accept its findings on all or any aspects of its mandate (see Chapter 11 below). Nearly another third of the committees were appointed for the purpose of gathering information and, on the basis of it, advising the government on specific actions for implementing a predetermined policy (IA). Such committees are appointed in cases where departments have already decided more or less what to do but not how best to do it.

Nearly all the rest of the major postwar committees fall more or less evenly into two other categories. Either they are fact-finding bodies appointed purely and simply to obtain information (I) – although their findings may sometimes seem to have quite clear implications for policy and action. Or they may be asked to gather information and to advise on some of its implications for policy (IP). Less than two percent of all committees are appointed for the other three purposes (P, PA and A), which are all distinguished by the fact that they do not require committees to make any special efforts to obtain information.

Four important conclusions can be drawn from all this. 1 The typical royal commission or departmental committee is virtually certain to be appointed at least partly for the purpose of obtaining *information* about a certain matter. This information may concern matters of fact, matters of opinion, or both. 2 The typical committee is also very likely to be expected to make proposals for specific *action*, proposals which are ready for implementation by departments through legislation, by ministerial order, or in some other direct way. 3 About one committee out of every six, on the other hand, is purely an information-gathering or fact-finding body, with no overt responsibility for either formulating policy or proposing suitable actions for implementing it. 4 Finally, committees are unlikely to be entrusted with the question of formulating policy except as part of a 'package deal' – i.e. unless they are also asked first to obtain information and then to propose suitable means for implementing the policy.

The most significant of these conclusions about the purposes of committees is probably the first. Ninety eight percent of the major postwar royal commissions and departmental committees were fact-finding bodies. Most of them had more to do than just to obtain information, but the requirement to obtain information was common to nearly every single committee examined.

7
Getting down to Work

Committees normally begin work as soon as they are appointed. In most cases, a committee will hold its first meeting within a month or two of the date of its appointment. Longer delays tend to occur in cases when committees (especially larger ones) are appointed during or just before the summer.

Even before the first meeting, however, members of a committee need not be idle. Usually, there is a good deal of preparatory work whch can be done As the Treasury indicates in a set of 'Notes' prepared for the guidance of civil servants appointed to committees,

> Some weeks often elapse between the appointment of a committee and the date of its first meeting. This interval can appropriately be used by the members in reading such material as may be immediately available. In most cases, certain facts, historical and descriptive and for the most part non-controversial, form the background to the inquiry, and it is best to get these facts narrated at the outset in one continuous story. The department which deals with the subject should therefore, as soon as the committee is set up, be invited to supply a written statement of these facts.[1]

At the same time, the secretary will probably circulate a paper describing the precise terms of reference and the membership of the committee as well as a list of important official documents and other papers bearing on the task at hand.

The next step is to arrange for the first meeting of the committee. The Treasury suggests the following procedure:

> The chairman may now wish to get the committee's agreement to a plan of work, and a preliminary meeting should usually be held for this purpose. The subjects to be discussed at such a meeting will vary, but may be sufficiently complex to warrant a chairman's note circulated beforehand in order to focus discussion. They are likely to include:

1 *Committee Procedure*, Treasury Notes on Government Procedure, No. 20 (London: HMSO 1958), Paragraph 3: this booklet is for official use and is not an HMSO sale item. See also the comments in the report (Cmnd. 3409) of the Adams Tribunal of Inquiry into the Accident to the Drilling Rig *Sea Gem*.

 i the meaning of the terms of reference, any possible ambiguities, the circumstances in which the committee has been set up, any limiting factors, etc.

 ii what kind of information the committee requires

 iii how this information should be obtained and in what order, whether by written statement or oral evidence or both, by members paying visits or by special investigations by persons working for the committee

 iv the frequency, length, times and dates of meetings

 v procedure at meetings[2]

Not all of these matters are likely to be resolved at the first meeting, of course, but most of them are likely to be discussed.

Interpreting the Mandate

The first job of any committee is to decide how it is going to interpret its mandate. Normally this is a step which produces little serious controversy, but it is a step which needs to be taken if the members of a committee are to establish any common framework for action. It is also a step which provides royal commissions and departmental committees with another important element of flexibility.

 Committees are often given deliberately broad terms of reference in the expectation that they will be refined by the committee in the course of its work. As the Robbins Committee on Higher Education (Cmnd. 2154) commented, 'Our terms of reference cover a wide field and would justify an investigation of almost any circumstances relevant to the future of higher education'. Similarly, the Rochdale Committee on the Major Ports of Great Britain (Cmnd. 1824) reported that

> The terms of reference which we were given were widely drawn; indeed the Minister of Transport made it clear in reply to questions in the House of Commons that no subject affecting the major ports of Great Britain was to be excluded from our purview.

Mandates like this leave committees a good deal of room for interpretation, and committees have to decide at their first few meetings exactly what they are going to do.

 For one thing, the scope of a committee's mandate may be adjusted in the light of some of the 'interests' relevant to the inquiry. The Hutchison-Maclean Committee, for instance, was asked 'to examine and report upon the general administration of the Territorial Army and upon the functions of the Territorial and Auxiliary Forces Associations . . .' The Committee noted in its report (Cmd. 9523) that the terms of reference could be construed in such a way as to include the Royal Auxiliary Air Force; nevertheless, the R.A.A.F. was included only by agreement with the Air Council, which then

---

2 *Committee Procedure, op. cit.,* Paragraph 5.

insisted that 'an Air Ministry representative should serve as a member of the Committee, with the particular task of advising on proposals which might affect the Royal Auxiliary Air Force'. Departmental officials may also be ready to have a committee look at some issue which they had intended to ignore if, for example, this would enable the committee to respond to some long-standing demand for an inquiry or if it were to help make an unpalatable inquiry more acceptable. Similarly, officials may be ready to omit some particularly contentious issue which they had intended a committee to deal with if, for example, its inclusion is likely to lead to a boycott by certain important interests. Finally, there may be unforeseen aspects of the problem which arise in the course of a committee's inquiry and which make adjustment of the terms of reference essential *en route*. The result of all these factors is that terms of reference tend in general to grant a fairly wide degree of discretion to each committee in carrying out its inquiries.

In most cases, officials do not interfere and committees are left to themselves to make what they think best out of their terms of reference. Their terms of reference, reported one committee (Cmnd. 1781), 'were particularly comprehensive, and in some respects leave us to judge for ourselves what is appropriate and practicable to investigate'. In making this judgement, committees can choose to place either a broad and all-inclusive or a narrow and exclusive construction upon their terms of reference. Some committees take the first course, and allow themselves free rein in their inquiries. The Blagden Committee on Bankruptcy Law Amendment (Cmnd. 221) explained that it had interpreted its terms of reference as broadly as it could, broadly enough 'to direct our attention to the whole of the Bankruptcy Acts and the Deeds of Arrangement Act'. Nevertheless, it is more common for a committee to try to reduce the scope of its terms of reference, paring them down in such a way as to produce the most effective and the most useful results. The Cook Committee (Cmnd. 1147), for example, was asked 'to consider the composition of milk . . . from the standpoint both of human nutrition and of animal husbandry . . .' After carefully discussing these terms of reference, the Committee decided that it would consider only the chemical (and not the bacteriological) composition of milk; that it would confine its inquiries to the natural components (and not other chemicals, such as strontium 90, or those used for the treatment of dairy cattle); and that it would examine scientific, legal and economic factors only insofar as they were directly related to the composition of milk.

Sometimes, there are fairly obvious reasons why a committee feels it has to reduce the scope of its terms of reference as they stand. For one thing, it may find it has to strike a balance between two different objectives. For example, the Runciman Committee on the Taxicab Service (Cmd. 8804) was mandated 'to consider the effect of the present economic and fiscal circumstances on the taxicab service (particularly in London)'; in the end, the Committee decided to concentrate 'our main attention on London while bearing in mind the effect our recommendations might have in other places'. The same result may stem from a committee having to define some of the words in its mandate. The Chorley Committee on Higher Civil Service Remuneration (Cmd. 7635), for example, was asked to advise 'as to the general level of remuneration of the higher posts of the Civil Service – administrative, professional, scientific and technical . . .' Faced with the problem of defining the 'higher posts' of the Service, the Committee decided to consider only posts of or above that of Under Secretary or its equivalent; it was felt that these were 'the grades above the "normal career level" which carry exceptional responsibility and are reached only by outstanding men'. Thirdly, there may be fairly obvious historical limits required, as in the case of the Birkett Committee (Cmnd. 283) which decided to confine their 'detailed investigations [of the executive power to intercept communications through the mails] to the interception of communications over the last twenty years . . .' Fourthly, a committee may obviously have to make certain assumptions about future government policy. The Herbert Committee on the Electricity Supply Industry (Cmd. 9672) decided that it should view its terms of reference entirely 'in the light of the Government's decision that the industry would not be de-nationalised, and we have examined no suggestion which would conflict with that decision'. Something of all these arguments must have prompted the Peech Committee on Solid Smokeless Fuels (Cmnd. 999) to restrict its inquiries to the domestic sector of demand for such fuels, to ignore the possibility of any significant changes in technology, and to plan for only five years ahead.

Probably the cruellest dilemma of all faces the committee appointed to deal with the legal or administrative aspects of a social issue. Such a committee has to decide how far it is going to pay attention to the moral aspects of its recommendations about law or administration. Sometimes a committee chooses to ignore these implications. For example, the Hodson Committee on Conflicts of Jurisdiction Affecting Children (Cmnd. 842) pointed out that its object – uniformity in the treatment of children in the various courts and in the various parts of the country – would inevitably entail substantial as well as merely procedural changes in the law at some points. After some discussion among its members, the Committee decided to ignore this problem; the Committee reasoned that it was not a body suitable for making social judgements, which 'should only follow upon a much wider inquiry by a body of a more widely representative character [than our own]'. Another and opposing argument was put forward by the Littlewood Committee on Experiments on Animals (Cmnd. 2641). This Committee decided it could not ignore the wider implications of its mandate, and explained the decision thus:

> A few members of the public wrote to us condemning all animal experiments on what they felt to be compelling moral grounds. Representatives of the anti-vivisection societies . . . though prepared to discuss stricter

measures of control as interim steps, also urged that there is a powerful moral argument for the prohibition of experiments involving animals. Although our terms of reference directed us specifically to the present statutory and administrative control, it was inevitable, and we believe proper, that we should regard moral criteria and the availability of other methods of research as relevant to our field of study . . . Anyone who makes use of an animal in research incurs a moral responsibility to justify his action and a duty to avoid or at least to limit pain and give proper care. This [principle] has governed our approach throughout and underlies the whole of our Report.

For a number of reasons, then, committees have to work out at their first few meetings how they are going to interpret their terms of reference.

Sometimes committees will seek guidance on this point from officials. Treasury advice on this point is quite clear: at the first meeting of a committee, the chairman should report

the upshot of any discussions he may have had with the department sponsoring the committee. If ambiguities in the terms of reference become apparent at any stage, or if it should be desired to ask for some alteration in them, reference should be made to the department.[3]

Thus, for example, the Streatfield Committee on the Business of the Criminal Courts (Cmnd. 1289) consulted the Home Secretary and the Lord Chancellor (joint appointers of the Committee) and were informed that

our terms of reference should be construed as including questions of machinery and jurisdiction, but not the basic procedures for determining the soundness of charges made against an accused person.

Similarly, the Holmes-Bateson Committee on the Employment of Children (Cmd. 8005) asked for advice on its terms of reference soon after its first meeting; it was informed that its mandate included all types of performances by children in entertainments.

Committees may also rely on statements in Parliament to convey some idea of what is expected of them. When the appointment of a committee is announced in Parliament, the minister may be drawn into making a short statement about it. When the Piercy Committee on Disabled Persons (Cmd. 9833) was announced, for example, 'the Minister [of Labour and National Service] stated that it was not intended to limit the terms of reference in any way and that the review was to cover disabled persons of all kinds'. Shortly before the appointment of the Herbert Committee on Slaughterhouses (Cmd. 9542), a statement was made by the Minister of Food which 'we have regarded as being complementary to our terms of reference'. Similarly, the Nathan Committee on Charitable Trusts (Cmd. 8710) took guidance from a

3 *Committee Procedure, op. cit.,* Paragraph 6.

debate in the House of Lords, especially in connection with the problem of distinguishing 'charitable' trusts from other kinds.

Parliament, moreover, represents an avenue for interests outside the government and the committee to push for minor changes in a committee's mandate. In response to a Parliamentary Question in October 1950, for example, the Chancellor of the Exchequer agreed to extend the terms of reference of the Tucker Committee on the Taxation of Provisions for Retirement (Cmd. 9063) to include the treatment for tax purposes of purchased annuities. Similarly, the Home Secretary was asked in the House whether the Littlewood Committee on Experiments on Animals (Cmnd. 2641) was considering the question of the supply of animals for experimental purposes; as a result, reported the Committee, 'We were informed that our terms of reference were wide enough to allow us to examine this question . . .'

Sometimes these various *de facto* changes are reflected in formal amendments to the terms of reference. A good example is provided by the Denning Committee on Legal Records. Four months after it had been appointed, its terms of reference were informally extended by the Committee with the agreement of the Minister (the Lord Chancellor) to include several other kinds of legal records besides those mentioned specifically in the original minute of appointment. Nearly a year later, a second minute was issued confirming the previous informal extension of the terms of reference to include

1 records created in matrimonial matters, and
2 records created in non-contentious probate matters,

and extending the terms of reference to include still more classes of records, namely

3 records of the Court of Criminal Appeal and the Courts-Martial Appeal Court;
4 records of criminal cases tried at Assizes, the Central Criminal Court and the Crown Courts of Liverpool and Manchester;
5 records of Quarter Sessions;
6 records of Magistrates' Courts.

The result was to enlarge the scope of the Committee's terms of reference to include nearly all types of legal records of the realm (estimated at more than seven hundred different types).[4] Similarly, the terms of reference of the Somervell Committee on State Immunities (Cmd. 8460) were formally extended from a concise 'whether the law of the United Kingdom in regard to diplomatic immunity is . . . wider than is necessary or desirable' to a thirteen-line, three-paragraph mandate which gave a much more precise direction to the Committee.

Formal changes in the terms of reference of a committee normally come at its own instigation. The Pilcher Committee, for example, was appointed to deal with 'the administration of justice under the court-martial system based

4 See the report of the Committee (Cmnd. 3084). The Evershed Committee on Supreme Court Practice and Procedure (Cmd. 8878) provides another similar example.

on the Naval Discipline Act'; however, the Committee reported (Cmd. 8119) that 'a preliminary survey of our task satisfied us' that the terms of reference were too narrow as they stood and so they were enlarged by omitting the words, 'the court-martial system based on'. Similarly, the terms of reference of the Harman Committee on Chancery Chambers (Cmnd. 967) were also extended formally at the request of the Committee:

> In the course of our deliberations we found it impracticable to divorce from matters under consideration allied questions relating to practice and procedure in the Chancery Division. We requested you [the Lord Chancellor] to extend our terms of reference to enable us to entertain some of the proposals we have received [on these matters].

On the other hand, some committees are quite frankly asked by the minister to do more than was originally asked of them, although these subsequent additions are not usually very substantial. The Jones Working Committee on China Clay (Cmd. 6748), for example, reported that, in addition to suggesting ways of increasing china clay production (as requested in their terms of reference), the Committee had also been asked to give 'their opinion concerning the Board of Trade's decision to de-concentrate the industry as from 31st December 1945'. The Westwood Committee on Mineral Development (Cmd. 7732) reported that 'At the Minister's request we have conducted three special enquiries since our appointment which necessitated more detail[ed] . . . investigations than our terms of reference envisaged'. Another clear case arises in the report of the Hancock Committee on the Assessment of Disablement due to Specified Injuries: in a separate 'Addendum' to the report (Cmd. 7076), signed by the Chairman 'on behalf of the Committee', the Committee explained:

> We were asked by the Minister of National Insurance, as a matter outside our terms of reference, to comment on the provision which it is proposed to make by Regulations under the National Insurance (Industrial Injuries) Act for the assessment of unspecified minor injuries.

Interpretation of the terms of reference does not always go the way a minister may intend. One very clear example is the Ormond Committee on Legal Education (Cmnd. 4595), which was in fact asked to act not as a departmental committee but as a standing advisory committee. Its terms of reference read in part:

> To advance legal education in England and Wales by furthering co-operation between the different bodies now actively engaged upon legal education . . . [and by making] recommendations upon such other matters relating to legal education as the Lord Chancellor may from time to time refer to it or as the Committee itself, with the approval of the Lord Chancellor, decides to consider.

At the end of its report, the Committee commented:

> Our terms of reference make it clear that we were intended to be a stand-
> ing Committee. Having made our inquiry, however, we are inclined to
> think that the principal service we can render will be the submission of
> this Report . . . [and] that the work of the two bodies whose establishment
> we have recommended . . . could more appropriately be undertaken by
> differently constituted Committees rather than by us. We believe that
> once these two successor committees have been launched, as we hope
> they will be before long, there will be no need for a Committee like this
> one.

Another interesting case is provided by the Himsworth Committee on the
Medical and Toxicological Aspects of CS Gas (Cmnd. 4775), which was
originally appointed to assess the use of the gas in civil disturbances in
Londonderry in the summer of 1969 and recommended in its interim report
(Cmnd. 4173) that its size be increased from three to eight and that its
mandate be extended to an examination of the effect of the gas in general;
the recommendation was accepted.

Sometimes a minister or his officials may feel that they must take a more
definite stand on the terms of reference. This is not a common occurrence,
but when it does occur it may take several forms. A minister or a permanent
secretary may simply write to his committee outlining more clearly what is
expected; such a letter is reproduced in the report of the Stamp Committee
on the London Taxicab Trade (Cmnd. 4483). Or, in the case of more
important committees, a minister may decide to attend an early meeting of
the committee in person in order to clarify its mandate. Thus, the Secretary
of State for Scotland attended the first meeting of the Fisher Committee on
Local Government Law Consolidation in Scotland (Cmd. 6933) in order to
impress on the Committee that 'any amendment we recommended should be
such as would be unlikely to provoke controversy and would be capable of
being readily substantiated'. He also attended the first meeting of the
Maconochie Committee on a Close Season for Deer in Scotland (Cmd. 9273)
to explain that

1 our recommendations need not be bound by existing legislation; [and]
2 although our remit referred to the desirability of establishing a close
   season for deer, it would not be out of place for us to consider, *inter alia*,
   control on the wholesale and retail disposal of venison.

There are also other less direct methods for a minister to convey his expectations. The Russell Committee on the Law of Succession in relation to Illegitimate Persons (Cmnd. 3051) reported that it was their 'understanding' that
they were not to deal with succession to dignities and titles of honour. It was
the minister's Parliamentary Private Secretary who made clear to the
Wilson Investigation into Caravans as Homes (Cmnd. 872) that 'what you
[the Minister of Housing and Local Government] had in mind was caravan-

living by ordinary people, rather than the special problems of gypsies or vagrants'.

Normally, though, the departmental attitude is one of *laissez faire*. No committee ever reported being rebuked for either exceeding or failing to fulfil its terms of reference; but a committee is unlikely not to convey its intentions to officials, who can then make clear what is acceptable and what is not. The Northumberland Committee on Recruitment for the Veterinary Profession (Cmnd. 2430) explained that 'our investigations have led us to place a somewhat broad interpretation on our terms of reference', including Northern Ireland and undergraduate studies, even though neither of these was specified in the terms of reference. However, the Committee report goes on,

> We were informed that our terms of reference should not be construed in the sense that we should express an opinion whether the number of under-graduate or postgraduate places in any particular school should be increased, whether a completely new school should be established or where veterinary schools should be located.

On the other hand, a committee may look as though it is going to leave out something important; thus, the Hopkins Committee on the Census of Distribution (Cmd. 6764) reported that

> It was indicated to us on our appointment that we should interpret the term 'Census of Distribution' in a wider sense than as applying only to the distribution of goods. We were informed that 'service' trades such as catering, hairdressing and laundries might also be considered as falling within the scope of our enquiries.

This all adds up to the fact that royal commissions and departmental committees enjoy a certain amount of discretion in the interpretation of their terms of reference. Departmental officials keep a watchful eye on events, but do not normally intervene unless their advice is requested. This is partly because committees, for their part, are more likely to want to refine rather than to expand their mandates. Moreover, committees will normally be fully aware of what is expected of them and will ordinarily keep officials fully informed of their intentions. Given a relationship of mutual confidence between departments and their committees, therefore, the latter are likely to find themselves relatively free to interpret their terms of reference to fit the precise situation which they themselves perceive. Without this mutual confidence, such flexibility is unlikely. Without flexibility, therefore, a committee does not serve a department as effectively as it can.

Arranging Meetings

Committees normally meet at their offices in London, but occasionally it may be felt desirable to hold meetings during visits to regional or local centres. To some extent, regional or local meetings may be intended merely to assuage special interests or feelings of neglect, but they can also facilitate the gathering of evidence. Information about a particular area of the country may be essential for a committee, and so it goes there to get it. Thus, the Oliver Committee on Electoral Registration (Cmd. 7004) held one of its twelve meetings in Belfast 'for the purpose of ascertaining the views of the registration officials and political parties on certain questions concerning electoral registration in Northern Ireland', which works under a slightly different system from that in the rest of the country. Or there may be good reason to expect significant regional or even local differences of opinion. For example, the Robson Committee on Coal Distribution Costs (Cmnd. 446) found regional differences and so held meetings in England, Northern Ireland, Scotland and Wales; and the Maconochie Committee on a Close Season for Deer in Scotland (Cmd. 9273) found local differences and so held fourteen meetings during a tour of the Highlands. But the most obvious case of all arises for committees investigating local disasters, when the evidence is bound to be on the spot, not in London.[5] There are several other reasons, too, for holding inquiries 'on site'.[6] Nevertheless, most committees have offices provided in London, and they normally hold all their meetings there.

Meetings customarily last for a whole day, but some committees occasionally meet for several days in succession or for less than a day at a time. The Crook Committee on the Statutory Registration of Opticians (Cmd. 8531), for example, had four two-day meetings and twenty single-day meetings.[7] Meetings of more than one day at a time are normally held to hear large blocks of evidence at one time or for deliberations leading up to the writing of a report. A few committees also held half-day meetings; these are usually scheduled to permit the hearing of some special bit of evidence. The Percy Royal Commission on Mental Illness and Mental Deficiency (Cmnd. 169), for example, met on forty four whole days and thirteen half-days, with all but one of the latter for hearing evidence. Most meetings, however, last for a single day.

Flexibility in committee procedures comes from the fact that there is a great deal of variation in the number of times a committee meets. Precise information on this point can be obtained from an analysis of the major postwar royal commissions and departmental committees; but before examining this, it is important to draw attention to two factors.

First of all, simply counting the number of full days of meetings recorded

---

5 See, for example, the reports of the three inquiries into fires at Cardiff, Worthing and Richmond (Surrey): Cmd. 6877, Cmd. 7048 and Cmd. 7440 respectively.

6 For example, the Crawford and Balcarres Committee on the Preservation of Downing Street (Cmnd. 457) held some of its meetings in the buildings on Downing Street!

7 Similarly, the Faversham Committee on Human Artificial Insemination (Cmnd. 1105) spread 18 meetings over 37 days, and the Mackenzie Committee on Electricity in Scotland (Cmnd. 1859) had 26 meetings in 46 days.

by each committee in its report does not take into account the possible occurrence of informal meetings. The Caine Committee on Grassland Utilisation (Cmnd. 547), for example, reported that it met 'formally' on twenty six days and 'informally in the course of visits' on fourteen other days.[8] Secondly, it is always very difficult to estimate the number of meetings of a committee of one. The number of times such a committee sits to hear evidence is clear, but it must also spend some time studying the evidence. This the chairman can do at any time and in any place; he does not need to discuss it with anyone except perhaps the committee secretary, but then this often involves quite informal meetings. For example, the chairman of the Henderson Inquiry (Cmd. 8896) reported that he spent several days at work on the papers related to the Timothy John Evans case before calling the first meeting (or 'conference', as he described it) between himself, his secretary and his assistant; two days later the oral hearings proper began. Subject to these two reservations precise information can be obtained about the number of meetings held by the major postwar royal commissions and departmental committees.

Committees have met anywhere from three or four to over two hundred times each, but the average among the major postwar committees is just over thirty (see Table 7.1). Royal commissions alone tend to meet much more frequently than departmental committees – which is the first really significant practical difference between them identified so far.

The smallest number of meetings was recorded by the Somervell Committee on State Immunities (Cmd. 8460) and by the McCarthy Committee on the Durham Education Dispute (Cmnd. 4150), which both had only three formal meetings. Another, the Upjohn Committee on the Court of Record for the Hundred of Salford, met only five times. The most efficient royal commission, the Tedder Royal Commission on University Education in Dundee (Cmd. 8514), had only twenty one meetings. Next came the Salmon Royal Commission on Tribunals of Inquiry (Cmnd. 3121) with twenty two meetings, but the average number of meetings for a royal commission was no less than eighty six. The largest number of meetings by a single committee was probably achieved by the Dow Royal Commission on East Africa (Cmd. 9457), which met 150 times in London and spent a total of seven months on tour in East Africa hearing evidence. Other busy royal commissions have been the Maud Royal Commission on Local Government in England (Cmnd. 4150) with 181 meetings and the Cohen-Radcliffe Royal Commission on the Taxation of Profits and Income (Cmd. 9474) with 173 meetings. The departmental committees which met most frequently were the Duncan Com-

8 The former secretary of the Geddes Inquiry on Shipbuilding (Cmnd. 2938) indicated in a private communication that the committee met formally on 38 occasions; then he went on to say, 'this is not a particularly meaningful figure, however, since there were numerous less formal occasions when the Committee, or some members of it, were able to discuss matters among themselves and receive information from third parties.'

Table 7.1 Major royal commissions and departmental committees, 1945–69, by number of meetings

number of meetings	royal commissions only	all committees
0–9	0	47
10–19	0	73
20–29	2	57
30–39	2	38
40–49	2	26
50–59	1	24
60–69	5	20
70–79	0	9
80–89	1	5
90–99	1	2
100 or more	9	15
no information	1	42
total	24	358
mean number of meetings	89	33

Notes: Informal meetings, meetings in the course of visits, and meetings of sub-committees are not included in these figures. Each full day is counted as one meeting; thus, two separate half-day sessions are counted as only one meeting.
Source: See Appendix B, p. 239.

mittee on Overseas Representation (Cmnd. 4107) with 153 meetings and the Robbins Committee on Higher Education (Cmnd. 2154) with 111. The average number of meetings for all committees was just over thirty.

Naturally, the usefulness of all these meetings depends at least in part on the degree of attendance by committee members. With this in mind, the Treasury advises that

> a committee which has a regular flow of work to deal with should, if possible, choose, and keep to, a regular meeting date and it should be understood that this date will not be changed, save in the most exceptional circumstances. The business will then be made ready for the committee, instead of the committee having to wait until the business is ready. Many committees do not have such a flow of work and need meet only irregularly. In these cases, the chairman and the secretary have a special responsibility for seeing that a good momentum is maintained and that when there is business to be done the meeting is fixed as early as circumstances allow.[9]

All the same, it is difficult to know how conscientiously members actually attend the meetings of their committees.

What evidence there is from the major postwar committees suggests that

9 *Committee Procedure, op. cit.*, Paragraph 7.

attendance is probably good in most cases but equally that there can be problems. Obviously, it will tend to be better for small committees (which can more easily adjust their dates for the convenience of individual members) and for committees which hold relatively few meetings. Even the seven-man Gorell Committee on the Regent's Park Terraces (Cmd. 7094) was obviously pleased to be able to report that it had held a total of seventeen meetings 'at which all members have been present, except on a very few occasions'. This is quite understandable, since service on a committee is entirely voluntary and it would be unlikely for it never to conflict with the ordinary full-time employment of at least some members.

Absenteeism causes more difficulty when it involves persistent offenders, for it is the persistent absentee who loses track of the committee's work – and is then, as many of those who have been connected with committees will relate, often the most insistent on having his particular views reflected in the final report! Trade unionists and Members of Parliament are sometimes presented as two kinds of members who are likely to prove recalcitrant, but it is difficult to say how much justice there is to this allegation. Undoubtedly, the problem is not confined to such members.[10] Royal commissions have quorums stipulated in their royal warrants, but these quorums are usually only a small fraction of the total membership and there is no indication of the extent to which they are actually observed. Attendance must present certain problems for committees, therefore, especially for those which are relatively large or meet relatively frequently.

When extended and unavoidable absences are anticipated, a member will often try to keep in touch with the work of the committee. Elaborate measures may be taken to facilitate his doing so; for example, Rear-Admiral Norris, a member of the Montagu Committee on Cadet Entry into the Royal Navy (Cmd. 8845), was posted to the Mediterranean but managed to keep 'in constant touch with the work of the Committee and transmitted his views and comments as it progressed'. Where the absentee is the chairman, another member will normally deputise for him. Sometimes the position of deputy chairman is formalised either by the appointing department at the time of appointment or by the committee itself when the need arises. For example, during the temporary absence of the chairman of the Committee on Crown Lands (Cmd. 9483), Sir Malcolm Trustram Eve, the Committee decided that another member, Sir Edward Gillett, should chair meetings held in London and a Scottish member, Hugh Watson, should chair meetings held in Edinburgh. For ordinary members, however, there is no evidence of committees going to the extent of 'pairing' or assigning proxies in the event of unavoidable absences.

One way of trying to reduce the burden of frequent attendance is to divide the work of the committee in some way. For example, the Cohen-Radcliffe

10 One former secretary told of a member who turned up for only two meetings out of fourteen – the first and the last!

Royal Commission on the Taxation of Profits and Income (Cmd. 9474) divided its meetings into meetings 'in committee' (ninety seven) and meetings 'in full session' (seventy six), of which twenty one of the latter were specially for hearing oral evidence. In this way, different standards of attendance can be set for different kinds of meetings. Alternatively, the members of a committee can be assigned among several sub-committees, and this will reduce the number of meetings each member is expected to attend as well as giving more flexibility in the scheduling of meetings. These devices are aimed at making attendance easier for the ordinary member; they will not be able to prevent or even discourage the determined absentee. In the final analysis, a recalcitrant member can be invited to resign from the committee, and some of the resignations 'for reasons of health' may in fact cover some such solutions to the problem of poor attendance.

Individual Responsibilities

The performance of a royal commission or a departmental committee is fundamentally the result of teamwork, and this depends to a considerable extent on how successfully the chairman, members and secretary work out a division of responsibilities among themselves. There are no hard-and-fast rules governing who does what in committee work; committees do not have constitutions and rules of procedure. Moreover, the way any committee works is primarily a function of what it has been asked to do. But there are certain expectations and accepted practices derived from the way royal commissions and departmental committees have worked in the past.[11]

The key man in a committee is its chairman, and that is why he is normally the first person to be selected.

> The chairman sets the pace and tone of the proceedings, and the general level of the members' aspirations. He must refrain from taking sides on contentious issues until other members' views are known. Otherwise he may destroy consensus instead of creating it. A really good chairman can create an effective committee against heavy odds, but even a good committee is unlikely to be effective if it has a poor chairman.[12]

The chairman is responsible for the conduct of the committee's meetings, both individually and as a whole. He must ensure that sufficient information has been gathered to enable the committee to carry out its mandate. Ulti-

---

11 There is a growing interest among sociologists and psychologists in the determinants of the behaviour of people in small groups such as committees. These aspects lie largely beyond the scope of this study, but see the classic studies by R. T. Golembiewski, *The Small Group* (University of Chicago Press, 1962); Dorwin Cartwright and Alvin Zander (eds.), *Group Dynamics*, 3rd ed. (New York: Harper and Row, 1968); and A. P. Hare (ed.), *Small Groups*, rev. ed. (New York; Knopf, 1966); two more recent studies are P. G. Herbst, *Autonomous Group Functioning* (London: Social Science Paperback, 1968), and T. M. Mills, *The Sociology of Small Groups* (Englewood Cliffs: Prentice-Hall, 1967).

12 David Donnison, 'Committees and Committeemen', *New Society* (18 April 1968), p. 560.

mately it is the chairman who is responsible for his committee to the minister or ministers who appointed it.

The Treasury provides very clear guidelines for committee chairmen in its notes on committee procedure. Before each meeting, the Treasury suggests, a chairman

> should have read his papers with special care . . . and have made a plan for drawing out the views of members in a reasonable order. In so far as he can foresee the views that will be expressed, he should have planned how he will regulate the subsequent discussion. If possible, he should have formed some view, but not a rigid one, of what the conclusion should be.
>
> He should introduce each item briefly so that there may be no doubt about the subject under discussion or the main points to be settled. He should ensure that all members who have a contribution to make are given an opportunity to speak, controlling the talkative and, where necessary, drawing out the silent. He should hold the thread of the discussion, summing it up at intervals if necessary, and should contribute to it helpfully but not too much. He should be able to seize upon any points which can serve as tentative conclusions. He should above all think in terms of the 'whole' so that the various 'parts' represented by the advice of different members of the committee can be fitted into a single framework and can appear as different sides of the same problem rather than as contradictions.
>
> Finally, he should ensure by his summing up that the conclusions reached are fully understood and accepted or, if there are reservations or disagreement, that these have been fully appreciated by all the committee.[13]

Besides preparing for and conducting each meeting in this way, a chairman should also keep in mind the overall progress of his committee. Each meeting should have some particular purpose in relation to a global plan of the committee's activities, and the chairman must be constantly evaluating and, if necessary, revising this plan. He must also assess whether the important witnesses are coming forward to present evidence to the committee and, if not, what can be done to encourage them to do so. If the committee is undertaking any research, the chairman should try to ensure that the research will indeed assist the committee to fulfil its terms of reference, that adequate resources are being made available for the research, and that agreed deadlines are being met. In short, the chairman is responsible for assuring the general progress of his committee from the moment when it is appointed to the time when it submits its final report.

The responsibility of a chairman is to the minister or ministers who appointed him. His responsibility is far more extensive than that of ordinary committee members, who are expected to do no more than contribute to the work of their committee. The chairman is responsible for planning and directing the execution of the work of the committee as a whole. Should he

13 *Committee Procedure, op. cit.*, Paragraphs 18–20.

fail, the committee will also fail unless the secretary or one or two members are exceptionally strong.

The secretary is a chairman's right-hand man; in fact, he can become the second most important man on a committee after the chairman. His regular duties include the arrangement of meetings, the preparation of an agenda and the briefing of the chairman before each meeting, drafting minutes and generally assuring the smooth operation of the committee. At the same time, the secretary often feels responsible in a special way to the department or departments which appointed the committee.

The secretary is normally responsible for arranging the details of each meeting. He will already have obtained from committee members some idea of the times which are convenient, and he will immediately set about finding a suitable place and adequate facilities in which the committee may conduct its meetings and (if required) hold its hearings.[14] Then, before each meeting,

> an agenda setting out the main headings for discussion should also be prepared. The agenda and supporting papers should reach members in time for them to be able to give adequate thought to the problems to be discussed. Even in the case of committees which meet regularly and discuss topics within a narrow field, papers should reach members at least 48 hours before the meeting. For other committees a week or more of notice may be desirable. Papers which require consideration may of course be circulated before the agenda, and on the other hand it may be necessary for the agenda to indicate that a paper will be circulated later. It may sometimes be desirable to check by telephone, before the agenda is issued, that all the members whose presence is essential for the discussion proposed can attend at the time stated.[15]

Similarly, officials or departments not regularly represented at committee meetings but having a special interest in the items on the agenda may be invited to attend. Finally, if witnesses are to attend the proposed meeting, the secretary will make a last-minute check with them.

In most cases, the secretary is also expected to provide his chairman with a briefing prior to each meeting.

> The amount of briefing which the chairman needs will depend upon circumstances. Sometimes the secretary need do no more than pass on any recent relevant information, e.g. that certain members will not be present; sometimes the chairman will need a brief which will summarise the main points he should make and help him in planning the meeting. It may

---

14 'A long table, and a square table . . . seem things of form, but are things of substance; for at a long table, a few at the upper end in effect sway all the business; but in the other form, there is more use of the Counsellors' opinions that sit lower.' (Sir Francis Bacon, 'Of Counsel'; quoted in *Committee Procedure, op. cit.*, Paragraph 16n.)

15 *Committee Procedure, op. cit.*, Paragraph 11.

usefully include notes about the views particular members are likely to express.[16]

For the benefit of chairman and members alike, the secretary will also keep notes of what transpires at each meeting and produce concise minutes of the points covered. During meetings, the Treasury instructs,

> the secretary must follow the progress made against the agenda or the chairman's brief, make notes and draw the chairman's attention to any point of substance that has been missed or to any point where it seems that members may be left in doubt as to the decision reached on the responsibility for execution. Apart from this, he should normally not take an active part in the discussion.[17]

Following each meeting, the secretary should circulate minutes of what transpired.

Between meetings, the secretary is expected to assure the smooth operation of the committee. He will prepare and maintain a circulation list of committee papers. He will write and circulate summaries of committee correspondence. He will organise an up-to-date index of all the important points discussed by the committee and its witnesses. He will also keep a record of questions which remain outstanding and remind the people concerned as necessary. For example, some of the committee's decisions may call for action by individuals or departments.

> In this case the secretary, even if he is not responsible for seeing that the action is taken, may quite properly keep an eye on the progress made and report difficulties or delays to the chairman. It is often convenient simply to keep a list of such outstanding items, new ones being added after each meeting and old ones being struck off as they are disposed of.[18]

Finally, if the committee consists of members of widely differing views, it may sometimes be a good idea for the secretary to arrange before or after meetings for the members to lunch or dine together; as the Treasury puts it, this is 'likely to help the development of a friendly spirit'.[19]

The secretary of a committee may also enjoy a special relationship with officials of the department or departments which appointed the committee. For one thing, the secretary is much more their own nominee than are the chairman and members, whose appointment is usually contingent on various factors such as satisfying certain interest groups, balancing one interest with another, and so on. For another thing, if he is a civil servant, his career is

---

16 *Committee Procedure, op. cit.*, Paragraph 13.

17 *ibid.*, Paragraph 21.

18 *ibid.*, Paragraph 49.

19 *ibid.*, Paragraph 50.

probably just beginning and he will hope to earn the respect of his superiors and his colleagues through the success of 'his' committee. These factors combine to bind the secretary in a special relationship with the officials who appointed him. It is not so much that the secretary will act simply as a pipe-line for information to and from departmental officials, nor that he will represent the views of the department to the committee and vice versa – though he may indeed do all this. Rather it is the more fundamental fact that the secretary is usually the only 'insider', or at least (if there are some civil servants among the committee's members) the most closely involved 'insider', who is connected with what is essentially a committee of 'outsiders'. This is the basic source of a secretary's strength and responsibility.

The members of a committee can play varying parts in its activities. They can help to assess evidence and examine witnesses. They can go on visits on behalf of the committee or undertake special tasks at its request, reporting back on the results of their endeavours. And they can take part in all the deliberations of the committee, from discussions of its mandate right up to the framing of its final report. They may do a great deal, rivalling the chairman himself in the significance of their contributions to the work of the committee.[20] Or they may do very little, content to be carried along by the chairman and other members.

Part of the folklore about royal commissions and departmental committees is that they produce a variety of standard 'characters', and this is as good a way as any of describing the responsibilities of members. Professor K. C. Wheare, for example, has described several such characters, including the expert, the layman, the official, the party man and the interested party.[21] Professor David Donnison has a slightly different list; he mentions the expert, the representative of an interest, the 'fuse box', the advocate of a particular philosophy, the consensus-builder, and the 'genial host'.[22] Other people have proposed other lists, but there is a good deal of overlap among them.

Some members, whatever the reasons for their original appointment, become the committee's resident experts on certain aspects of the terms of reference. For example, a member who is a lawyer may always be looked to by the committee for advice on the legal aspects of their mandate. If the member responds by limiting his contributions more or less to his acknow-

20 As an example of the important part which a single member can play, see an article in the *Sunday Times* (30 June 1968) about the influence of Dr Norman Hunt on the outcome of the Fulton Committee, entitled 'How Dr Hunt (aided and abetted by Harold Wilson) took over Fulton'. Even though it is very unusual to single out the efforts of any one member of a committee, Dr Hunt's colleagues expressed their appreciation of his efforts in a formal acknowledgement in their report (Cmnd. 3638). Hugh Clegg is reputed to have played a similar leading part in the Donovan Royal Commission on Trade Unions and Employers' Associations (Cmnd. 3623).

21 K. C. Wheare, *Government by Committee* (London: Oxford University Press, 1955), Chapter 2; see also Chapter 5 above.

22 Donnison, *op. cit.*, pp. 560–1.

ledged area of expertise, he will help to maintain his status. If his expertise is central to the committee's mandate, he may become, albeit unwillingly, a sort of committee 'guru':

> Every major issue awaits his comment before a decision can be reached · the decisions may not accord with his [own] views, but progress is slow on days when he is absent. He won't be away much, however, and he will be trusted and respected by his colleagues – otherwise he would not be accorded this role.[23]

Similar to the expert is the representative of an interest. His expertise consists of special knowledge of the attitudes or opinions held by certain sections of society.

> He, or she, knows exactly how the average nursery school teacher, or the average architect, or the average medical officer of health would feel about particular arguments, proposals and phrases. . . . He worries more than most [members], for he – like the secretary – will have to live with the report among his colleagues for years to come.[24]

An extreme variant of the representativ of an interest may be called a 'fuse box' – someone who can be relied upon to 'blow' if the committee strays too far beyond what is acceptable to the people directly concerned. For example, trade union officials may be invited to sit on committees for this purpose. Partisan and even tiresome though representatives and 'fuse boxes' may be, they can help a committee to keep its collective feet on the ground during the process of formulating recommendations, and also help to provide recommendations with an aura of credibility at least among the interests represented on the committee.

Special cases of both the expert and the representative may be provided by the official and the party man. Occasionally, as was shown in Chapter 5 above, civil servants and Members of Parliament are appointed to sit on royal commissions and departmental committees. They may be appointed as experts if, for example, the committee is dealing with a question in which they have become specialised through their official duties and political activities. Or they may be appointed more as representatives than as experts if, for example, the committee is dealing with a subject in which the aims of policy seem to be at odds with the realities of politics. As Professor Wheare has demonstrated, both the official and the party man can contribute very effectively to the proceedings of some royal commissions and departmental committees.[25]

Another, quite different, kind of character who may emerge in a com-

---

23 Donnison, *op cit.*, p. 560.

24 *ibid.*, p. 561.

25 Wheare, *op. cit.*, especially Chapter 4.

mittee is the advocate of a particular philosophy. This man is neither an expert nor a representative. Rather he is a generalist:

> he thinks in terms of general principles derived from a frame of reference that extends well beyond the task in hand. . . . He applies a system of thought derived from general assumptions about people, their rights and the character of the future society the committee is helping to create. . . . He can help a committee to reason about its proposals and convey a sense that it is making history as well as getting through the agenda.[26]

Where other members may be concerned with the technical accuracy or the political viability of a certain proposal, this man is concerned with the principle of the thing. Is it right? is it fair? is it just? he asks and forces the committee to face these questions too.

The consensus-builder is quite different again. He is a man who tempers his principles with the art of the possible. He is not really regarded as an expert by his fellow-members, nor does he feel bound to present the views of any particular sections of society. Instead he looks for opportunities to resolve conflicts and build consensus, cor ent to reach the best possible situation rather than committed to achievi g the ideal. This is his strength and his weakness. As Professor Donnison has pointed out, 'A committee with too few consensus-builders is liable to disintegrate altogether; a committee with too many will relapse into cosy unanimity which fails to penetrate beyond the superficial.'[27] The presence of one or more consensus-builders among the members of a committee is a necessary but not a sufficient condition of its success, and an overdose can be deadly.

Finally, many committees have their self-appointed 'genial hosts', without whom an added burden must fall on the chairman and the secretary. 'Genial hosts' are the members who realise, consciously or unconsciously, that committees are ultimately groups of men and women, each with his individual likes and dislikes, each with certain abilities and certain prejudices, and each with his pride and his vanity.

> [They] are the people who remember that it is time the committee had a party and arrange this with a minimum of fuss and the maximum of innocent enjoyment; they remember who has just become a grandfather, or been awarded a C.B.E., or been promoted, and ensure that proper note is taken of these events.[28]

They will also help the chairman to ensure that the less articulate and the less distinguished members do not feel left out but are encouraged to contri-

---

26 Donnison, *op. cit.*, p. 561.
27 *loc. cit.*
28 *loc. cit.*

bute to the work of the committee to the full extent of their abilities. The 'genial host' may also be an expert or the representative of an interest as well, but his social contribution to the friendly and co-operative spirit in which members of the committee work together is no less important for its ultimate success.

8
Taking Evidence

Royal commissions and departmental committees need information. Virtually every major committee since the war, it was argued in Chapter 6, was appointed at least partly for the purpose of obtaining facts and opinions about the subject of its mandate. Information is, in short, the life-blood of royal commissions and departmental committees.

Few committees are so expert or so representative that they cannot profit from the views of others. Royal commissions and departmental committees are not just discussion groups, to which each member contributes to the best of his personal knowledge and experience. They are expected to do more than this. They are expected to take all reasonable steps to ensure that their deliberations reflect all the significant and relevant information bearing on their terms of reference. Most committees, therefore, try to encourage people with special knowledge of the question to give evidence.

The most important thing about the way in which royal commissions and departmental committees gather evidence is that the process itself is in most cases such an open one. By systematically taking evidence on a specific problem from almost anyone who wants to give it, these committees provide a unique opportunity for the views of the various interests in society to be injected efficiently into the decision-making process. An average committee hears more than one hundred different individuals or organisations in the course of its work; the average royal commission has more than two hundred witnesses. These witnesses usually present an enormous quantity and variety of evidence, some of it written and some of it oral. Furthermore, in having to manage this mass of evidence, royal commissions and departmental committees have over the years developed a highly pragmatic approach to the question of what sort of procedures to use and how to cope with problems such as reluctant witnesses, the absence of certain interests and the need for legal safeguards. In short, royal commissions and departmental committees offer an illuminating case-study of the mechanics of public participation in government.

Invitations

At one of their earliest meetings, most committees will decide whether and what sort of invitations should be issued to solicit evidence on some or all aspects of their terms of reference. In principle, royal commissions and departmental committees are free to take whatever steps they wish, from none at all to a national canvass. For the procedures of committees, like the activities of nationalised industries, are not matters on which ministers can be questioned in Parliament.[1] In practice, of course, ministers and their officials can and do convey their views about what a committee should do; how much influence they have will vary from committee to committee. In one case, a committee investigating the abuse of social security benefits (Cmnd. 5228) reported that it had intended to issue a public invitation to give evidence about such abuse, but that their minister had dissuaded them from doing so on the grounds that 'the public would get the impression that they were being invited to tell tales and act as informers against their neighbours'. So instead the Committee wrote to all Members of Parliament and editors of the leading national newspapers asking them to give evidence on whatever they knew.

Essentially, a committee has three options in issuing invitations to give evidence. The traditional method is to publish a statement of invitation in the general press (chiefly the large daily newspapers). Secondly, committees may choose to publish a statement in the more specialised press (such as technical journals) or, thirdly, to send invitations directly to individuals or bodies thought likely to have valuable evidence to present. Some committees have relied on one of these methods of invitation alone; others have made use of two or all three methods. It might be thought odd that all committees which genuinely desired evidence did not simply adopt all three methods; however, each method has its own peculiar utility.

Among the major postwar royal commissions and departmental committees, the most popular form of invitation has been the general invitation soliciting evidence from any source. Such an invitation can be published in the national press and may even be broadcast over the radio and television, as it was (for instance) by the Hughes Parry Committee on the Legal Status of the Welsh Language (Cmnd. 2785). One committee decided to rely on nothing more than the announcement of its appointment in the press to attract evidence; but, when this produced 'little response' from the general public, the chairman wrote to the editors of four national newspapers inviting anyone to give evidence.[2] Special advertisements were inserted in the press on behalf of the Peppiatt Committee on a Levy on Betting on Race Horses (Cmnd. 1003) because the Committee felt that this was the best way 'to invite any persons or organisations interested in racing to submit evidence'.

1 D. N. Chester and Nona Bowring, *Questions in Parliament* (London: Oxford University Press, 1962), pp. 296ff.

2 Reference is to the Russell Committee on Illegitimate Persons (Cmnd. 3051). The four newspapers chosen were the *Daily Telegraph*, the *Guardian*, the *Glasgow Herald*, and the *Scotsman*.

Similarly, the Robbins Committee on a New Queen's Hall (Cmd. 9467) decided that

> in order that all possible shades of public opinion on this matter should come under our review, we have twice caused a notice to be inserted in public journals inviting the submission of evidence.

Most committees have relied on a combination of this form of general invitation plus direct invitations to individuals or bodies believed to have especially valuable evidence. The Mocatta Committee on Cheque Endorsement (Cmnd. 3), for example, issued two notices in the general press, one soon after its appointment and the other halfway through its hearings, and also sent out a series of individual invitations.[3] The Pritchard Committee on the Rating of Charities (Cmnd. 831) also sent out letters of invitation to individuals and one to the editor of *The Times* announcing the committee's willingness to receive evidence from any quarter.[4] In general, the objective of this double-barrelled strategy is to be both democratic – willing in general to receive evidence from any quarter – and effective – seeking evidence in particular from those best able to provide it.

In some cases, the combination of general and individual invitations is carefully managed so that each kind is used most effectively. For example, the Macmillan Committee on Land Registration in Scotland (Cmd. 7451) issued a general invitation through the press soon after its appointment and then was able to concentrate on a single aspect of its terms of reference in its letters of direct invitation.[5] Similarly, the Radcliffe Committee on the Working of Monetary System (Cmnd. 827) began by hearing some limited expert and official testimony on specific invitation. In addition, at its first meeting, the Committee wrote to 'some 30 associations representing the financial, industrial and commercial activity in this country'. Next, invitations were sent to a number of economists and then to others with special qualifications. Finally, as a last step, the Committee issued a general invitation in the press to anyone to present evidence.

Occasionally, a committee uses all three forms of invitation. The Grant Committee on the Sheriff Court (Cmnd. 3248) inserted a general invitation in the daily press and in several legal journals and then sent invitations to various individuals and organisations. Another interesting example is provided by the activities of the Pilcher Committee on Naval Discipline (Cmd. 8119), which sought to get in touch with officers and men, either still serving or discharged, who had been punished according to the laws of naval

---

3 Note that government officials are among those who may receive individual invitations; see Marjorie Ogilvy-Webb, *The Government Explains* (London: Allen and Unwin, 1965), pp. 30–3.

4 See also the 'Letters to the Editor' in *The Times* on 14 March 1958.

5 Direct invitations related only to the registration of writs in the Sasines Office.

discipline. To this end, the Committee asked the Admiralty to publicise an invitation to all officers and men to give evidence in confidence. The Committee also issued an invitation in the press and even went on the air to invite discharged personnel to give evidence.

Other procedures are less common. At first sight, for example, it might seem surprising that more use is not made of the technical press. The reason for this is probably that the technical press can be an unhappy compromise between the other two kinds of invitation, lacking both the generality of an open invitation in the general press and the personal appeal of a direct individual invitation. Secondly, direct individual invitations have rarely been used alone. This is probably because it would leave a committee open to charges of having deliberately selected its evidence to support some predetermined views. Occasionally, the use of direct individual invitations has been rejected altogether for this reason, as it was by the Pilkington Committee on Broadcasting (Cmnd. 1753).

On the other hand, a few committees decide not to bother with general invitations at all. In their particular cases, such an invitation seems unnecessary or inappropriate. One committee (Cmnd. 262) decided not to invite evidence through the press because 'sufficient publicity had already been given to this enquiry and . . . anyone interested would know that it was permissible to make representations, as indeed some have done.' Similarly, even the Milner Holland Committee on Housing in Greater London (Cmnd. 2605) relied entirely on questionnaires and felt it was unnecessary to make any special efforts to solicit general evidence: 'We think our appointment and our wish for information was [*sic*] sufficiently publicised and generally known. . . .' The Committee's judgement was apparently sound: it reported receiving 'a great mass of unsolicited evidence' all the same. For other committees, it just did not seem appropriate to issue general invitations. The Kennet Committee (Cmd. 8543), which was appointed to assess a draft Customs and Excise Bill, decided only to issue notices in the trade journals and letters of invitation to one hundred and forty interested organisations. The Strutt Committee (Cmd. 8009), appointed 'to review the regulations made under Section 7 of the Cremation Act, 1902', decided to invite evidence only 'from various national bodies . . . and certain persons who could help us on certain special aspects of the inquiry.' For a few committees, therefore, general public invitations were not used.

It is, of course, perfectly natural that committees will want, and desirable that they be able, to adapt their invitations for information to the needs of their particular mandates. Some subjects by their nature imply wide public discussion, which is likely to be stimulated by general public invitations to give evidence. Other subjects deserve more restrained, technical examination, which is more likely to be produced by direct individual invitations. Similarly, expert and especially representative committees are less likely than impartial committees to need to canvas public opinion by issuing general invitations and correspondingly more likely to need specialist advice obtained by issuing direct individual invitations. For these and other reasons, royal commissions and departmental committees show a certain amount of flexibility in the way in which they issue invitations to give evidence. Nevertheless, it was only a minority of the major postwar committees which did not issue, either alone or in conjunction with other kinds of invitations, a general call to the public to present evidence.

Witnesses and Their Evidence

The objective in issuing invitations for evidence is, of course, to induce experts and interested parties to come forward and present their views to the committee concerned. Such witnesses may be individuals appearing on their own behalf as private citizens, or they may appear as representatives of vast organisations such as business groups, trade unions, churches, government departments, universities, pressure groups of all kinds, and so on. The variety of witnesses who have appeared before royal commissions and departmental committees is almost without limit.

Not all witnesses present equally valuable information. Some witnesses provide expert information, while others present the opinions and attitudes of certain sectors of society. Some are well organised, while others are not. Some deal exhaustively with every aspect of the mandate, while others choose to concentrate on particular points. Drawing on his experience of several committees in the fields of housing and education, a former member has concluded:

> In a well developed sphere of professional knowledge, many organisations will be equipped to prepare evidence. The stronger they are, the less original their ideas are likely to be. Their evidence will usually be prepared by a group, representing various branches of the profession, whose draft must then be submitted to a larger body. By the time it is approved there will seldom be anything new left in it. But what powerful groups such as the BMA [British Medical Association] or the Association of Education Committees have to say about developments in their own field must always command attention.
>
> Other groups represent more specialised or ephemeral interests – the Comprehensive Schools Committee, for instance. Consumer groups, such as those representing parents of school children or tenants of rented housing, play an increasingly important part; university research groups (still contributing too rarely to such inquiries), political parties (at a local or national level) and individuals of all kinds (from the most expert to the arrant cranks) also contribute information and views.[6]

In short, witnesses are as varied as the society from which they come – and for which each often claims to speak!

6 David Donnison, 'Committees and Committeemen', *New Society* (18 April 1963), p. 559.

Table 8.1 Major royal commissions and departmental committees, 1945–69, by number of witnesses

number of witnesses	royal commissions only	all committees
fewer than 50	0	122
fewer than 10	0	17
10–19	0	17
20–29	0	36
30–39	0	29
40–49	0	23
from 50–99	4	73
50–59	1	20
60–69	1	20
70–79	0	14
80–89	2	12
90–99	0	7
100 or more	16	132
100–149	4	56
150–199	1	27
200–249	2	16
250–299	3	14
300 or more	7	19
no information	3	31
total	24	358
approximate mean number of witnesses	200	100

Note: These data refer to the total number of individuals submitting evidence to a committee, whether the evidence is written or oral or both. Organisations are counted as single witnesses, unless more than one individual representative thereof is referred to by the committee as having given written evidence.

Source: See Appendix B.

The number of witnesses appearing before a committee to present evidence tends to be either fairly restrained or very large. It may vary all the way from less than half a dozen to well over a thousand, but it is likely to be either less than fifty or more than a hundred. Among the major postwar committees, four committees in every five fell into these two categories, roughly half in each (see Table 8.1). Among royal commissions alone, all but four heard from more than one hundred witnesses each.

The largest number of witnesses ever heard by a single major committee since the war was 2,156. This record was achieved by the Maud Royal Commission on Local Government in England (Cmnd. 4040). It is an impressive record, too, since only three other committees heard from more than five hundred witnesses.[7] At the other end of the scale, several committees heard from a very small number of witnesses, including the Woods Committee on the Transfer of Certain Civil Servants to Other Duties (Cmd. 9220) which heard from six witnesses and the Thomson Committee on Criminal Statistics in Scotland (Cmnd. 3705) which heard from seven witnesses. One committee considered the opinions of only two witnesses; it decided to rely principally on

> its own experience and did not invite evidence from outside. The Home Secretary [who had appointed the Committee], however, put before the Committee a letter from Mr R. W. S. Pollard, a magistrate, and another from Mr Glen Craske, a metropolitan magistrate. . . . The remit was not to canvass public opinion but to produce a workable [draft] bill.[8]

One way of interpreting the data in Table 8.1 is to say that committees either do or do not regard the systematic canvassing of opinion as forming part of their duties. Although there are exceptions, committees which do not feel bound to survey opinion are likely to hear from fewer than fifty witnesses, while committees which do survey opinion are likely to hear from more than a hundred. The fact that few major postwar committees fell between these categories suggests that the distinction is indeed the result of a deliberate decision by each committee.

Witnesses may be asked to present evidence in either written or oral form. The kind of written evidence which a committee receives can vary all the way from a hand-written letter to a handsomely bound document in several volumes.[9] One committee even received a petition signed by over three thousand people![10] Another committee, the Molony Committee on Consumer Protection (Cmnd. 1781), announced in the press that

> anyone wishing to suggest classes of consumer goods to which accidents had been attributed, to inform us as to the frequency and severity of such accidents, to make observations for or against the principle of further control, or to record an interest in the subject, should do so in writing . . .

The result was nearly three hundred witnesses who produced '472 written statements, representations, proposals, expressions of opinion and com-

---

7 Reference is to the Verdon Smith Committee on the Censuses of Production and Distribution (Cmd. 9276), the Pilkington Committee on Broadcasting (Cmnd. 1753) and the Robbins Committee on Higher Education (Cmnd. 2154). The data do not include unsolicited letters.

8 Reference is to the Davies Committee on Matrimonial Proceedings in Magistrates' Courts (Cmnd. 638); the quotation is from a private communication from the former secretary of the Committee.

9 See, for example, Ivor Gowan and Leon Gibson, 'The Royal Commission on Local Government in England [Cmnd. 4040]: A Survey of Some of the Written Evidence', *Public Administration*, 46 (1968), pp. 13–24.

10 Reference is to the Morton Committee on Intestate Succession (Cmd. 8310) and a petition which urged several changes in the law to favour the widow of an intestate.

plaints' plus 1,918 letters from members of the public. A number of committees provoked spates of letter-writing, including the Weir Committee on Scottish Electricity and Gas Boards (Cmnd. 695), which received over 150 letters, 'mainly from housewives'.[11] Another committee (Cmd. 8116) reported receiving from just over 100 witnesses '223 memoranda which, with other papers circulated to the Committee, amount in total to 368 different papers, . . . [as well as] a large number of suggestions from members of the public.' Written evidence, therefore, can come in numerous and varied forms.

Somewhat more than half of the major postwar committees chose to rely on written evidence alone. They did not feel that it was necessary or even useful to take oral evidence as well. The Simonds Committee on the Subpoena Powers of Disciplinary Tribunals (Cmnd. 1033), for example, issued a press notice asking for written submissions from any member of the general public and sent individual invitations to each of the departments of government. Then,

> Having considered the written evidence which has been put before us we decided not to call for oral evidence because the views of interested parties appeared to us to have been stated sufficiently clearly and forcefully.

Representative committees, in particular, may feel that they do not need to bother taking oral as well as written evidence; in the words of one such committee (Cmnd. 2066), 'because there were on the Committee representatives of the main interested bodies, we did not deem it necessary to obtain oral evidence'.

Nevertheless, a lot of committees, including all the postwar royal commissions, have taken oral evidence. Sometimes oral evidence is intended merely to amplify written submissions. Or at least committees require that oral evidence follow a written presentation of views. In another case, oral evidence was required only for 'assistance on historical aspects' of the inquiry.[12] On the other hand, some committees feel that oral evidence is sufficient and even preferable by itself. Sometimes it is the nature of a committee's mandate which dictates the most appropriate kind of evidence. For example, many of the committees appointed to inquire into particular events, such as fires, accidents, allegations of misconduct of various kinds, and so on, decided to take only oral evidence.[13] Or a committee may simply feel that formal

11 See also the reports of the Morris Committee on the Selling Price of Houses (Cmd. 6670) and of the Brambell Committee on the Welfare of Animals (Cmnd. 2836) which received over 250 letters each.

12 Reference is to the Hughes Parry Committee on the Legal Status of the Welsh Language (Cmnd. 2785).

13 As did the Skelhorn Inquiry into the Case of Herman Woolf (Cmnd. 2319); however, both the Inquiries into the Case of Timothy John Evans (Cmd. 8896 under J. Scott Henderson and Cmnd. 3101 under Mr Justice James Brabin) took written evidence as well as oral.

written submissions are not suitable for its particular needs. A committee appointed to advise on the records and files kept by government departments (Cmd. 9163) explained that

> we have not asked for formal statements of evidence. There can be no representative body entitled to speak on behalf of all users of the records, nor is it possible to focus the needs of any considerable number of them. We have therefore felt it preferable to consult a number of individuals who make use of the records, relying on the diversity of our own interests and experience to ensure that all points of view were adequately represented.

Still, these examples are all exceptions. In the majority of cases when oral evidence was heard, it was used to supplement rather than to replace written submissions. Thus, most of the evidence which is presented to a committee is presented in written form.

Hearings

If committees choose to hear oral evidence as well as or (rarely) in place of written evidence, they will almost invariably set aside a number of their meetings especially for that purpose. Only when a very small number of witnesses is invited to give oral evidence is it likely to be integrated into the ordinary meetings of a committee. Not all of the major postwar committees which heard oral evidence gave details of how many of their meetings were given over to this purpose, but indications are that most of them spent fewer than twenty sessions. Royal commissions – all of which did hold special hearings – devoted an average of thirty four days to hearing oral evidence. The Dow Royal Commission on East Africa (Cmd. 9475) probably held as many hearings as any committee in the course of the seven months its members spent on tour in East Africa. Of the other major committees which reported the exact number of days spent in hearing oral evidence, the Duncan Committee on Overseas Representation (Cmnd. 4107) and the Herbert Royal Commission on Local Government in Greater London (Cmnd. 1164) held more hearings (seventy three and seventy respectively) than any other.

Legal counsel are not normally permitted to appear at these hearings on behalf of witnesses. The only exceptions have occurred in the case of some of the departmental committees appointed to examine particular events. For example, the chairman of the Inquiry into the Boarding Out of the O'Neill Boys (Cmd. 6636) allowed all twenty two witnesses who appeared before him to be represented by counsel. The Treasury Solicitor may be represented by counsel if he appears before such a committee.[14]

When witnesses request permission to be represented by counsel, the decision is normally made by the committee concerned. For example, the

14 As he was before the Durand Inquiry into Carlton Approved School (Cmnd. 937) and the Gibbens Inquiry into the Administration of Punishment at Court Lees Approved School (Cmnd. 3367).

chairman of one Inquiry (Cmnd. 2526) reported simply that 'Certain interested parties applied to be legally represented at the Inquiry and those applications I granted'. There is no report of there ever having been an appeal against a committee's decision. On occasion, a minister may make certain commitments in connection with a committee he is about to appoint. For example, the chairman of the second Inquiry into the Case of Timothy John Evans (Cmnd. 3101) reported that 'Before the Inquiry began, I was informed that the right to representation had been granted [by the Home Secretary] to [the mother and two sisters of] Evans'. Subsequently, there were five more applications for permission to be represented by counsel, and these were all dealt with by the chairman (who granted three of them). This is the way in which most requests for legal representation have been settled.

There is both more and less to this question than meets the eye. On the one hand, refusal by a committee to permit legal representation does not mean that people with legal training will not help to present the views of certain organisations to that committee. Relatively wealthy interest groups, for example, are likely to have legal advice in the preparation and even the presentation of their evidence. On the other hand, approval by a committee of the principle of legal representation inevitably entails the adoption of more formal procedures than are commonly employed by royal commissions and departmental committees. Committees admitting legal counsel may also have to resolve questions of contempt, perjury, intimidation of witnesses, and so on.[15] The admission of counsel to committee hearings is, therefore, a fairly complicated issue – and one which royal commissions and departmental committees have been understandably reluctant even to raise.

Committee meetings are normally held *in camera*, but an exception may be made when the committee is hearing oral evidence. Indeed, the tradition and the presumption is that such hearings should be in public unless there are exceptional circumstances which justify holding them in private. The standard position was stated by the Franks Committee on Administrative Tribunals and Inquiries (Cmnd. 218) when it reported that 'we decided to hear evidence in public unless there were special reasons for hearing any witnesses in private. We never found it necessary to hear evidence in private.' Nevertheless, among the major postwar committees, there is a considerable number of cases in which private hearings have occurred. The Ross Royal Commission on the Press (Cmd. 7700), for example, heard all of its oral evidence in private; subsequently only some of it was published since 'over a third of the witnesses asked us to treat some part of their evidence as confidential.' Another Committee (Cmnd. 2641) which took all of its oral evidence in

---

15 There is some protection for witnesses from intimidation and attempts at intimidation, but the witness before a committee does not enjoy the security of a witness in a court of law; see the Witnesses (Public Inquiries) Protection Act, 1892 (55 and 56 Vict., Chapter 64) as amended by the Magistrates' Courts Act, 1952 (15 and 16 Geo. VI and I Eliz. II, Chapter 55), Section 127 (2).

private agreed to allow witnesses to publish their remarks if they wished to do so but asked that they wait until after the committee had published its own report. Thus, the practice of opening or closing hearings for oral evidence is fairly divided.

Not even the archetypal one-man Inquiry follows any strict rules in this connection. Some – such as those into the disaster at the Bolton Wanderers' football ground, the disposal of land at Crichel Down, and local objections to Gatwick Airport – did hear oral evidence in public, since a public airing of opinion was probably implicit in their terms of reference.[16] But there are contrary examples. The Benson Inquiry into the Disposal of Scrap Cable (Cmnd. 605) began its procedure with a series of visits and private interviews. The chairman then wrote to the executive of the major interest group concerned (the National Association of Non-Ferrous Scrap Metal Merchants) to explain

> that I would be glad to meet for discussion in private any member who felt that he could assist me in my inquiries. I asked a representative number of scrap metal merchants who have submitted tenders for scrap during the last four years to see me. I have ascertained the methods of disposal of scrap cable adopted by [other branches of government, including] six other Electricity Boards. . . . I am not aware of any other steps which I could usefully have taken to help me in establishing the facts or in arriving at fair conclusions. The nature of the investigations I had to undertake made it impracticable to hold the inquiry in public.

On the other hand, both the Ince Committee on Allegations of Bias in Welsh Broadcasting (Cmnd. 1139) and the Ingleby Committee on Children and Young Persons (Cmnd. 1191) reported that 'We decided to meet in private', and offered no explanations at all. Where it is deemed advisable therefore, inquiries can and do hold their hearings for oral evidence in private.

Committees have normally justified a decision to hold private hearings by one or more six basic reasons. First of all, there is the possibility that a committee can obtain more information from witnesses who feel they can speak more freely and openly in private than they could do in public. As one committee explained,

> [we] decided at our first meeting that, despite many requests we had received to the contrary, we would not admit the public to our meetings or publish the evidence which we received. We fully realised that there might be advantages in giving full publicity to our proceedings, but it was apparent at the outset that it would not be easy to ascertain all the facts

16 See the reports of these three committees (Cmd. 6846, Cmd. 9176 and Cmd. 9215 respectively). Even the Tucker Inquiry into Proceedings before Seven Justices of the Aberayron Division, Cardigan (Cmd. 7061), which might not be thought to be of much public interest, held its two days of hearings in public.

essential to a proper consideration of the matters referred to us, particularly of those which had been the subject of acute public controversy. We came to the conclusion, therefore, that witnesses would be more likely to speak freely if their evidence was not to be published. We have found that our decision has in fact been welcomed by most of those who have appeared before us and that it has facilitated our inquiry.[17]

Similarly, the Faversham Committee on Human Artificial Insemination (Cmnd. 1105) reported that it held all its hearings in private in order to encourage 'frank discussions':

> We had a verbatim record made of our oral examination of witnesses, but this was purely for the convenience of members of the committee. We made it clear to those who gave evidence that the record would never be published, and in this way we found that our witnesses readily agreed to discuss with us fully and freely the intimate details of the practice into which we were enquiring.

Some subjects are obviously of such a nature that they can be treated more effectively in private discussions than in public debate.

Secondly, it may be the purpose of the committee rather than its subject matter which justifies hearing oral evidence in private. The Leggett Committee on Unofficial Stoppages in the London Docks (Cmd. 8236), for example, reported that it held all its meetings in private because the committee had been appointed to provide a suitable environment

> for the many sections of this complex industry [the port transport industry] to give expression to their views to an impartial body, and we have deliberately spread our inquiry over a sufficient period to permit various matters to be reexamined and discussed. There is no simple solution to the difficult problems created by the circumstances of the industry and while we have made certain recommendations, we feel that the greatest hope lies in the close co-operation of all concerned for the constructive development of the human affairs of the industry, looking to the future rather than to the past.

Subsequently, the Devlin Committee on the Port Transport Industry (Cmnd. 2734) echoed these sentiments and held 'a number of meetings, all in private, mainly with the representatives of the associations and unions but also with individuals'. This kind of committee can obviously work better in private.

A third advantage of the private hearing is that it tends to make the evidence less formal and therefore less of a burden both for witnesses to prepare

17 Reference is to the Henderson Committee on Cruelty to Wild Animals (Cmd. 8266). The Committee went on to say that 'In order to keep the public informed of our progress, we issued brief statements to the Press after all [ten] meetings at which oral evidence was heard'. Another committee arranged to have some of its hearings televised: namely, the Crowther-Kilbrandon Royal Commission on the Constitution (Cmnd. 5460).

and for committee members to absorb. This argument was used by the Bowes Committee on Inland Waterways (Cmnd. 486), for example, which had issued both general and individual requests for evidence.

Fourthly, the identity of witnesses cannot be kept secret if their evidence is given in public. For some particularly delicate inquiries, it may be desirable to preserve the anonymity of witnesses, at least until the committee can make known its findings, in order to avoid any attempts to prejudge the issues before the committee. This argument was used by the Denning Inquiry into the Security Service and Mr J. D. Profumo (Cmnd. 2152), whose witnesses included the then Prime Minister and several journalists, to explain its decision to hear evidence in private.

Fifthly, some committees feel bound by what they regard as a 'tradition' established by previous inquiries into the same subject. For example, the Beveridge Committee on Broadcasting decided to hold its hearings in private because this had been the practice adopted by committees on broadcasting in 1923, 1925–6 and 1935–6.[18] The logic of this argument is perhaps harder to follow than that of some of the other justifications which have been offered.

Finally, some committees do not hold public hearings because they have previously decided not to hear any oral evidence at all. As one committee explained (Cmd. 9063),

> The written evidence we received so amply covered what seemed to us every possible matter that could arise within our terms of reference that we decided that it was not necessary to seek elucidation or supplementation of the written representation by any oral evidence in public. . . . we indicated that if they [witnesses] so wished we were prepared to see them in private on any particular points they themselves might wish to elaborate. Only a few witnesses availed themselves of this offer . . .

To conclude, it is normally up to each committee to decide for itself whether to hear oral evidence in public or private. In only one case was a committee required to hold its hearings in public and that was the second Inquiry into the case of Timothy John Evans (Cmnd. 3101). According to the chairman,

> I was informed that the Inquiry should be conducted in public, except in so far as I in my discretion might decide that it was desirable to conduct part of the Inquiry in private.

Interestingly enough, this procedure was in complete contrast to that adopted at the first Inquiry into the same case (Cmd. 8946), which held all its hearings in private and advanced a number of valuable arguments in support of its

---

18 Reference is to the Beveridge Committee (Cmd. 8116), the Sykes Committee (Cmd. 1951), the Crawford and Balcarres Committee (Cmd. 2599) and the Ullswater Committee (Cmd. 5091) on Broadcasting. The Pilkington Committee on Broadcasting (Cmnd. 1753) also held its hearings in private, but did not offer this or any other justification.

decision: namely, the life of a condemned man was at stake; the mass of evidence put before the Inquiry required careful study, not forensic presentation and debate; confidential police reports were involved; and it was particularly important that witnesses should not be at all apprehensive about speaking the truth. In spite of this precedent, the second Inquiry found it necessary to sit in private on only two occasions: once to respect the confidence of the first Inquiry (two of its witnesses could not be traced and so their evidence to the first Inquiry was re-examined in private) and a second time to hear four other witnesses (two of whom also testified at the first Inquiry). Apart from this exception, all the major committees since the war have been free to hear evidence in public or in private as they wished.

Some committees resolve the dilemma by deciding to hear some of their oral evidence in public and some in private. The Brabin Inquiry just mentioned is one example of a committee which heard most of its evidence in public but on occasion went into private session. Other committees did just the opposite, holding most of their hearings in private but coming out into public sessions for some special pieces of evidence. The Henderson Committee on Security at Broadmoor (Cmd. 8594) held its hearings in private when they concerned the prison itself, but went into public session when it came to hearing from local authorities in the area. The Herbert Committee on the Electricity Supply Industry (Cmd. 9672) reported that

> All our meetings have been held in private with one exception. We received memoranda from various Welsh societies . . . [which] were of a character somewhat different from others in that they raised very general questions which appeared to us to be suitable for public inquiry. We therefore held a [special] two-day public meeting at Cardiff . . .

These mixtures of public and private hearings are the exception rather than the rule. Most committees decide to hear all of their oral evidence either in public or in private.

Problems of Taking Evidence

Taking evidence is a vital stage in the life of almost every royal commission and departmental committee, but it does pose certain difficulties. For one thing, evidence is not always the most efficient source of information. Not all of the evidence which a committee receives turns out to be useful; much of it can be repetitive, and some may even seem ludicrous. Evidence is, moreover, often presented by interested parties who are (quite legitimately, of course) anxious to promote certain particular ideas, and these preferences are bound to be reflected in the information presented. As a former committee member has testified,

> The first evidence submitted will be studied carefully. But after a year or so, the committee becomes so submerged in paper and so familiar with its

witnesses' views that only the most cogent statements will make much impact.[19]

In short, evidence can become almost overwhelming.

As a result, general public invitations to give evidence are sometimes as much for form's sake as out of a genuine desire to hear the views of the masses. The Devlin Committee on the Working of the Dock Workers' Scheme (Cmd. 9813) issued a general notice to the press about its willingness to receive evidence from any quarter, but it is quite clear from the report of the Committee that 'we have been chiefly concerned with the views of the Employers' Association on the one side and those of the Trade Unions on the other', and that the views of any other parties were quite incidental.

On the other hand, a more serious problem is presented by the fact that evidence may turn up too little rather than too much. There is nothing to ensure that all the information which could be useful to a committee is actually put before it in the evidence of the various witnesses who come forward. Some evidence, including commercial or industrial information, is secret and thus will not be put before a committee. There is no way even to ensure that all the relevant interests are represented. Organised interests are often in a better position than individuals to present their cases, since organisations usually have greater resources at their disposal for collecting data and preparing briefs. Some committees prefer quite frankly to deal with organisations, arguing that they tend to be more informed and more responsible than individuals, as did the Taylor Committee on the Tenure of Shop Premises in Scotland (Cmd. 7285). Thus, committees may invite the general public to give evidence, but to do so through various organisations; or the invitation itself may only be issued to individuals at the discretion of certain organisations. For example, the Plowden Committee on the Aircraft Industry (Cmnd. 2853) issued all its invitations through the Society of British Aerospace Companies. Finally, reliance on evidence from organised interests can obscure the fact that certain interests – including the 'public' interest, the interests of the poor, and so on – may not always have organised spokesmen. Thus, although interested organisations are normally easier to identify and deal with than individuals, committees run risks in relying too heavily on such sources of information.

Another difficulty lies in the fact that committees have to set deadlines for receiving evidence, and these deadlines tend to reflect the demands of committees' own timetables rather than the needs of those presenting evidence. For example, the Beveridge Committee on Broadcasting (Cmd. 8116) allowed only three months for receiving 'representations from all persons interested', although direct invitations were subsequently extended to a number of specific organisations and individuals. Similarly, the Ince Committee on Welsh Broadcasting (Cmnd. 39) invited evidence 'from any

19 Donnison, *op. cit.*, p. 599.

interested member of the public' to be presented within the space of only thirty three days, although the date was subsequently extended by more than twice this length of time. Other committees are more generous but, even so, may have to extend the deadlines they have set.[20] In spite of extensions, however, the need to impose a timetable on the taking of evidence inevitably imposes another limitation upon its value.

Another problem is that invitations to present evidence may fall on deaf ears, especially among the general public. The Guthrie Committee on Scottish Leases (Cmd. 8657) arranged for press releases by the Scottish Office and placed advertisements in the press; nevertheless,

> only two bodies representative of limited groups of tenants submitted evidence. Letters about personal or local difficulties were received from or on behalf of only six private individuals. The dearth of spontaneous evidence and paucity of specific complaints suggest [ironically] that in matters involved in our terms of reference there is in Scotland no acute and widespread sense of hardship or grievance.

Another Guthrie Committee, this one on Legal Aid in Criminal Proceedings in Scotland (Cmnd. 1015), reported that 'We received no evidence from private individuals in response to our announcement in the press'. Even direct invitations by this Committee produced disappointing results, since 'many of the bodies whom we approached individually felt that they were not in a position to offer us useful evidence'. Some committees, it is true, deal with matters which are just too esoteric to attract a large number of witnesses. Thus, a committee like the Fleck Committee on Windscale Piles and the Controlled Release of Wigner Energy (Cmnd. 471) is hardly likely to attract many witnesses from among the general public. On the other hand, there are some paradoxical cases, like the Maxwell Inquiry into the Need for a Central Criminal Court in South Lancashire (Cmd. 8955) which heard from no fewer than sixty three witnesses. Moreover, even a committee dealing with a question which, because it effects the daily life of thousands of people, might be expected to arouse widespread public interest and involvement does not always manage to do so. For example, the Burt Inquiry (Cmnd. 168) into allegations that public-house managers in the Carlisle and District State Management Scheme had been short-changing their customers complained that it had been unable to elicit a single witness from the general public!

In some cases, potential witnesses are openly hostile to a committee and have to be placated before they will agree to submit any evidence. This is most likely to occur in the case of committees dealing with matters of immediate and direct concern to certain interests, as was the Pilkington

---

20 For example, the Willink Royal Commission on the Police (Cmnd. 1728) set the end of June 1960 as a deadline for hearing evidence on subhead (4) of their terms of reference and then extended the deadline by a fortnight; even so, 'supplementary evidence' had to be heard into September and October.

Royal Commission on Doctors' and Dentists' Remuneration (Cmnd. 939). But there may also be more fundamental reasons for non-co-operation. As one committee (Cmnd. 5228) reported, 'Others whom we have approached have declined to co-operate with us on the ground that the institution of the inquiry reveals a social philosophy or an attitude ... of which they disapprove.'[21]

One proposal for dealing with the problem of lack of evidence has been that royal commissions and departmental committees be given the power – by having their requests enforced through the courts – to compel the attendance of witnesses before them or the production of papers for their examination. Royal commissions, it is true, already have such powers written into the royal warrants by means of which they are appointed:

> And for the better effecting of the purposes of this Our Commission, We do by these Presents give and grant unto you ... full power to call before you such persons as you shall judge likely to afford you any information upon the subject of this our Commission; to call for information in writing; and also to call for, have access to and examine all such books, documents, registers and records as may afford you the fullest information on the subject and to inquire of and concerning the premises by all other lawful ways and means whatsoever.[22]

No royal commission in this century has ever made use of these powers, and it is doubtful if the courts would sustain any attempts to do so.[23] On the one occasion when it was felt that a royal commission really needed powers of subpoena, they were granted not by virtue of the above clause in the royal warrant, but under the provisions of the Tribunals of Inquiry (Evidence)

21 The Committee goes on to add that it particularly regretted the reaction of one potential witness who 'we thought ... [was] in a position to tell us of the impact which measures currently adopted have, and which any proposed changes would have ...' The Committee continues rather drily: 'The reply which we received to our invitation ... was, however, couched in the following terms, and we did not, therefore, feel that we should press them further for assistance:

Sir,
I am in receipt of your letter ... and as minutes Secretary ... have been asked to reply. I have been asked to say that we completely disassociate ourselves from any process or findings of [the Committee], and would like to go on record that the whole thing is bullshit, repeat bullshit.

Yours very sincerely
Minutes Secretary

22 From the warrant of the Salmon Royal Commission on Tribunals of Inquiry (Cmnd. 3121), but this is typical.

23 R. M. Jackson, 'Royal Commissions and Committees of Inquiry', *The Listener*, LV, 1411 (12 April 1956), pp. 388–9, argues that, 'The Act of Parliament which abolished the Court of the Star Chamber in 1641 [16 Chas. I, Chapter 10] prohibited the Crown from setting up any jurisdiction of this kind. The Crown cannot, by issuing a document of this sort, give a royal commission powers akin to those of a law court.'

Act, 1921.[24] As far as departmental committees are concerned, none has ever been granted subpoena powers in its document of appointment; however, no less than fifteen tribunals of inquiry have been appointed under the Tribunals of Inquiry (Evidence) Act, 1921. There is no reason in principle why similar powers could not be given to all royal commissions and departmental committees, but there are several factors which make it inadvisable.

Some committees would certainly have found subpoena powers useful. The Vick Inquiry into Allegations of Ill-treatment of Prisoners in Liverpool Prison (Cmnd. 503), for example, reported that

> the fact that an inquiry was to be held was given wide publicity and this produced communications from a number of persons ... Nobody, of course, was in any way a compellable witness, nor did I think it right to exclude anyone who wished to come merely on the grounds that his evidence seemed from his preliminary communication likely to be irrelevant. Written statements were, however, taken by a representative of the Treasury Solicitor from most of those who volunteered to give evidence ...'

Nevertheless, some of the key witnesses, 'the prison officers, on their counsel's advice, declined to give evidence' to the Inquiry. In addition, several other committees have complained of the failure of some witnesses to respond to invitations to give evidence. The Jolly Inquiry into the Case of John Elliott (who was alleged to have been maltreated in Manchester Prison) found that one key witness had resigned from the Prison Commission since the incidents in question had occurred. This witness asked to be excused from attending the Inquiry, and the chairman commented in the report (Cmd. 6933), 'There is no power under which I could have compelled his attendance ...' Similarly, only six out of the seven Justices of the Aberayron Division of Cardigan implicated in the Tucker Inquiry (Cmd. 7061) into the hearing of two informations on behalf of the Minister of Food actually agreed to attend the Inquiry. Committees faced with this kind of lack of co-operation could clearly have profited from subpoena powers.

There are other committees, too, which suffer from a lack of response to their invitations to give evidence, but the case for granting subpoena powers is obviously stronger in some cases than others. It is stronger for committees dealing with particular events, for example, than for those dealing with more general problems, since specific witnesses may be essential to the former but one witness may well be as good as another for the latter. Even for committees on particular events, however, the case for granting subpoena powers is debatable.

For one thing, the granting of such powers would probably also mean

24 11 Geo. V, Chapter 7. Reference is to the Macmillan Royal Commission on Lunacy and Mental Disorder (Cmd. 2700). See also Chapter 2 above. Other statutory committees (Type III) have been given subpoena powers; see Denys Munby, 'The Procedure of Public Inquiries', *Public Administration* XXXIV (1956), pp. 175–85.

adopting other legal paraphernalia, including the right to legal representation and provisions for the protection of witnesses. Witnesses do already
have some statutory protection, and their anonymity can always be preserved
by *in camera* hearings.[25] Nevertheless, as Mr Justice Brabin indicated in his
report on the Case of Timothy John Evans (Cmnd. 3101), 'Those who gave
evidence at the Inquiry did not have the absolute protection which is given
to persons appearing in a Court of Law.'

For another thing, very few committees have in fact found that they had
to do without vital evidence because of a lack of powers for compelling it.
The earlier Henderson Inquiry into the Case of Timothy John Evans (Cmd.
8846), which 'had, of course, no power to compel any person to appear'
before it, found that only one witness refused to attend. She had already
given a statement to the police; so this was read out at the Inquiry. The
Gibbens Committee on Court Lees Approved School (Cmnd. 3367), 'had no
power to compel the attendance of witnesses or to require evidence to be
given on oath, but only one person (a former pupil at Court Lees) failed to
respond to an invitation to make a statement and all the witnesses gave
evidence on oath'. The Tribunal of Inquiry into the Accident to the Drilling
Rig *Sea Gem* (Cmnd. 3409) noted:

> The Tribunal was without statutory authority, had no power to compel
> the attendance of witnesses, nor was it empowered to administer oaths. So
> generous, however, was the contribution of all concerned that there can
> hardly ever have been an investigation better served by those who
> offered evidence.

Finally, Lord Denning – who, for his Inquiry into the Security Service and
Mr J. D. Profumo (Cmnd. 2152), came very close to having subpoena powers
– reported

> You [the Prime Minister] were good enough to say that, if I needed further
> powers I was to ask for them. I have not felt the need. Every witness whom
> I asked to come, has come without being subpoenaed. Every witness has
> answered the questions I put to him, without being threatened with
> contempt. I have been told as much truth without an oath as if it were on
> oath. It was not the lack of powers which handicapped me. It was the very
> nature of the inquiry with which I was entrusted.

In other words, you can lead a horse to water, but you cannot make it drink.

Thus, there is little that a committee can do to encourage the presentation
of evidence beyond issuing invitations to do so. One committee (Cmd. 9548)

25 It has long been an offence to intimidate or to attempt to intimidate witnesses before royal
commissions or departmental committees (see p. 135 n. 15 above). For an example of a
committee guarding the anonymity of its witnesses, see the practice adopted by the
Gibbens Inquiry for the protection of boys still at Court Lees Approved School (Cmnd.
3367).

reported that it adopted the practice of sending with its requests for evidence copies of its mandate and of all the statutes and orders relevant to it. Committees which are considering draft bills can send copies of the bill in confidence to potential witnesses. Terms of reference can be simplified for the purposes of hearing evidence. The Oaksey Committee on Police Conditions of Service (Cmd. 7831) reported that

> To accelerate progress, we divided our field of inquiry into sections [pay, allowances, hours of duty, and pensions] and asked the witnesses to send us their material on each group of subjects [i.e. section] as soon as it was ready.

Similarly, a Committee on Bankruptcy Law (Cmnd. 221) tried to draw out evidence by referring in its invitations to an 'embryonic' scheme which the Board of Trade had already proposed as one way of rectifying the weaknesses in the existing law. Beyond these sorts of tactics and ruses, there is really little that a committee can do to ensure that enough witnesses come forward to make the evidence balanced and representative of all the interests involved.

Royal commissions and departmental committees, therefore, face two fundamental problems in the taking of evidence. On the one hand, there may be too much evidence. Witnesses troop before the committee one after another, each to say much the same as the previous witness. Yet there is normally little a committee can do to select its evidence – especially if it wants to canvass public opinion – without distorting the overall effect or raising howls of protest. On the other hand, there may be too little evidence; and there is not much that a committee can do about this problem either, except to issue repeated invitations and pleas. Even so, there may simply be some interests in society – those of generations unborn are the classic examples – which simply have no organised representative who could come forward and give evidence. But the main difficulty is that royal commissions and departmental committees enjoy relatively little discretion in taking evidence. They are largely at the mercy of their potential witnesses, and there is not much that a committee can do to influence their decisions about whether and how they present their cases. It is not surprising, therefore, that committees have not always been ready to accept such a powerless position and have in fact taken more active steps of their own to obtain the information they require. The result is that many committees carry out research in addition to or even instead of listening to evidence.

9
Conducting Research

Broadly speaking, the methods adopted by royal commissions and departmental committees to obtain information about the subject of their mandates may be characterised as either active or passive. The passive methods, which were described in the previous chapter, depend upon organisations and individuals outside the committee coming forward to present evidence to the committee. There are, however, certain difficulties entailed in gathering information exclusively by this method. Committees may, therefore, decide to take more active steps to inform their deliberations. Rather than rely on piecing together the evidence selected and presented by others, whose purposes and objectives are often narrower or more partisan than its own, a committee may choose to seek out answers for itself under conditions whose objectivity can be assured and for purposes which can be tailored more closely to the needs of the committee. These more active efforts to obtain information can take several forms, but they may all be referred to collectively as research.

In most cases research does not replace but supplements evidence presented by witnesses. As the Herbert Royal Commission on Local Government in Greater London explained (Cmnd. 1164),

> Our inquiry was not one of those in which a conclusion can be reached solely by weighing up and evaluating what witnesses have said or written ... in which it is appropriate to follow the long accepted practice of requiring promoters to prove their case after running the gauntlet of opposition by [counter] petitioners ... The nature of our inquiry has been much wider than this. As we see it, we are required to consider the problems of the [Greater London] Area as a whole and to advise what form of local government is adequate to meet them. We have therefore conceived it our duty to inform ourselves upon these questions to the best of our ability by any means available to us, and to form our conclusions accordingly.

Thus, the Commission undertook extensive research into the problems of local government in London, but it did not neglect to hear evidence from witnesses as well. Its report went on to add:

We need hardly say that we have paid the most careful attention to all the evidence [from witnesses], which both in quality and quantity has been very weighty; but that study has been only part of the process of informing ourselves. We have collected much other material . . .

The Nature of Committee Research

Research can take many forms, of course, but it is useful to distinguish at least three main steps which a committee can take to further its objective of gathering information in an active manner. The first and probably most venerable device is the 'visit of inspection'. That is, a committee visits a place, an organisation or an event, either in Britain or overseas, with a view to learning about what goes on in the field or in 'real life'. The second device is the survey or questionnaire, which may be used as a means of gathering information about both matters of fact (e.g. a survey of the existing literature on a subject) and public opinion (e.g. an attitude survey). Thirdly, a committee may reflect its commitment to research through the existence of a special research subcommittee or research staff.

Using these criteria, it appears that royal commissions are a good deal more likely than departmental committees to have undertaken some kind of research. An analysis of the major committees since the war (see Table 9.1) reveals that about four out of five royal commissions have made use of at least one kind of research, whereas fewer than half the departmental committees have done so. There is also a difference in the pattern of research undertaken. Royal commissions have tended to undertake more than just one kind of research, whereas most departmental committees have been content to rely on a single kind of research. Moreover, departmental committees have tended to rely more heavily than royal commissions on visits of inspection, which are probably the simplest kind of research.

Table 9.1 Major royal commissions and departmental committees, 1945–69, by kind of research undertaken

kind of research	royal commissions only	all committees
visits of inspection	15	109
questionnaires and surveys	13	64
subcommittees, research staffs, etc.	14	89
one of the above	6	98
two of the above	7	58
all of the above	7	17
total committees reporting some kind of research	20	173
committees not reporting any research at all	4	185
total	24	358

Source: Reports of committees listed in Appendix B.

Although the data in Table 9.1 indicate that more than half the major postwar royal commissions and departmental committees have not undertaken any kind of research at all, this conclusion is a bit misleading. This is because, for some committees, research is neither necessary nor expected. For example, committees appointed to examine a unique and non-recurring event (such as a fire, a disaster or an allegation of some kind) are obviously not expected to do any research. Even in the case of committees such as the Tedder Royal Commission on University Education in Dundee (Cmd. 8514) or the Willis Committee on Licensing Planning (Cmnd. 2709), it is possible to understand (as was claimed) that research was unnecessary or inappropriate. It is hard to say just how many of the major committees since the war would fall into a category of those for which research was inappropriate – the lack of research by the Cohen-Radcliffe Royal Commission on the Taxation of Profits and Income (Cmd. 9474), for example, is not so easy to explain on these grounds – but they must number at least fifty and possibly as many as a hundred. On this basis, the proportion of committees actually undertaking research (with respect to committees which did or might reasonably have done so) could be as high as two thirds instead of less than one half.

The most common single kind of research by royal commissions and departmental committees is the visit of inspection. The practice dates from at least 1834, when 'ten roving barristers . . . visited, in pairs, the twelve hundred parishes' on behalf of the Royal Commission on Irish Church Revenues.[1] Among the major committees since 1945, half of all those which reported undertaking some kind of research made visits.

> A committee often makes visits to 'see for itself'. This can be fruitful, often in unforeseen ways (in public relations, or by enabling members to explore each others' views and reactions in the field), but it is expensive in time and money – particularly if the committee travels to foreign countries. Foreign visits will not help much unless the committee understands its field thoroughly, meets the right people and is well briefed.[2]

Most of the visits made by committees have been within the United Kingdom, and to a wide variety of different places, organisations or events. Some idea of this diversity can be gained from the select list of visits shown in Table 9.2. One of the most exacting 'visitors' must have been the Geddes Committee on Shipbuilding (Cmnd. 2937) which began its work by travelling to all twenty seven dockyards coming within its terms of reference. The Committee met and talked to management people and shops stewards in each yard, arranged for accountants to examine the books of each of the firms visited, 'and the principal [officer] of each firm has been seen privately to discuss his future plans'.

1 William Cory, *A Guide to Modern English History*, Part II (London: Kegan Paul, French, 1882), pp. 378ff.

2 David Donnison, 'Committees and Committeemen', *New Society* (18 April 1968), p. 559.

Table 9.2 Domestic visits of inspection by selected major royal commissions and departmental committees, 1945–69

nature of visit	number of visits	number of days	command number of source
children's homes, foster homes, etc.	451	—	6922
local authorities (in 41 counties)	58	—	
premises where celluloid stored	8	4	7929
bakeries	10	6	8378
Scottish museums	9	5	8604
publishers' premises	2	2	8662
slaughterhouses in Scotland	25	—	9376
boys' units in the Army	11	—	9433
small-scale horticultural producers	164	—	61
Army, Navy and Air Force units	49	—	35
Liverpool Prison	1	3	503
establishments exporting live cattle for slaughter	9	—	154
institutions providing further education in agriculture	(7)	(4)	614
salmon and freshwater fisheries	(12)	8	1350
Atomic Energy Authority establishments	(6)	—	342
ports and fish marketing centres	—	—	1266
centres of electricity production and distribution in Scotland	2	—	1859
ports	—	(12)	1824
security systems in museums	4	—	1750
geology and mining concerns	4	—	2351
headquarters of the Security Service	2	—	2152
smallholdings and smallholding authorities	16	13	3303
shipyards, and their managements and shop stewards	27	—	2937

Notes: A dash indicates that there is no information available, and numbers in parentheses are only approximate. The 'command number of source' is a reference to the report of the committee which made each of the visits described.

Source: See the reports of the committees indicated.

Visits may be announced in advance or they may deliberately not be. Most are announced in advance as a matter of courtesy or, if the committee plans to use the visit as an opportunity to 'show the flag', as a matter of policy. But surprise visits also have their uses. The Northumberland Committee on the Slaughter of Horses (Cmd. 8925), for example, recorded that many of its forty nine visits to slaughterhouses and knackers' yards were deliberately unannounced so that nothing could be done to affect the things it might see. On the other hand, a somewhat similar Committee on the Welfare of Animals (Cmnd. 2836) made visits to establishments where animals were kept but always gave notice of its intentions, arguing that the visits were intended for 'learning' and not for 'inspecting'. In any event the ordinary practice is for visits to be announced in advance.

Only twenty two of the major postwar committees have made visits abroad, and most of these have been to the closer countries of Europe. Quite often only some of the members of a committee will take part in visits, and this is especially true of visits abroad. Thus, the de la Warr Committee on Further Education for Agriculture (Cmnd. 614), for example, despatched three of its twelve members to Holland and another three to Sweden to study the policies and practices in those countries. Sometimes the visits are to specific cities: the Stone Committee on Hallmarking (Cmnd. 633) visited Berne, Amsterdam, Paris and Rome; while the Rochdale Committee on the Major Ports of Britain (Cmnd. 1859) visited the ports of Antwerp, Rotterdam and Hamburg. The very few committees that do travel outside Europe are likely to have special reasons for doing so; for example, the Gowers Committee on Foot-and-Mouth Disease (Cmd. 9214) went to Brazil and Argentina where the disease was thought to have originated, and the chairman and secretary of the Wilson Committee on Immigration Appeals (Cmnd. 3387) visited Pakistan and India to see where many of the immigrants had come from.

Besides the sort of formal or 'official' visits discussed so far, committees have also undertaken what may be called 'informal' visits. Informal visits tend to be more the result of chance than of any carefully conceived plan. Ordinarily they involve only one or two members, who may be on business of their own at the time, and very rarely the whole committee at once. But the Wheare Committee on Children and the Cinema (Cmd. 7945) regarded the informal visits of its members (to over one hundred children's cinema clubs) as important enough to warrant devising a standard reporting form so that the results of the different visits might be more easily compared. Informal visits may even follow from formal ones, as when the Wolfenden Committee on the Employment of National Service Men (Cmnd. 35) took advantage of some of their formal visits to units in the Forces to go informally into the barracks after hours to talk to the officers and men. Thus, informal visits can provide a valuable addition to the more formal ones.

Visits are normally undertaken relatively early in the life of a committee, and this suggests that they must often be used by a committee for developing an initial familiarity with the subject of their mandate. Certainly visits are, for some committees, an indispensable means for seeing how things work in practice. For this reason, visits are as useful as they are popular devices for committees to get a 'feel' for their subjects.

There has been one other recent development or elaboration of the idea of a visit of inspection and that is the pilot project. Naturally, such a device is by no means appropriate for every committee; all the same, it is remarkable that committees have made so little use of it to date. Among the major postwar committees, only two departmental committees have launched pilot projects. The Thomson Committee on Criminal Statistics in Scotland (Cmnd. 3705) reported that it had

> set up a working group of police officers and officials of the Scottish Home and Health Department . . . [who] assisted in the organisation of a pilot experiment. This experiment involved the co-operation of police, sheriff clerks and procurators fiscal, in Edinburgh, Glasgow, Paisley and Stirling, on certain crime recording and reporting procedures . . .

Similarly, the Henry Committee (Cmnd. 4137) was appointed to prepare (in the light of the recommendations of a previous committee) 'a detailed scheme for the introduction and operation of registration of title to land in Scotland . . . ' So what the Committee did was to set up a pilot scheme in Renfrew, 'putting our ideas to the hard test of practice and raising those questions which have not so far occurred to us but which will undoubtedly arise when the scheme is in operation'. The pilot project was also intended to provide valuable training for those who would eventually have to operate a registration scheme. But these are the only cases since 1945 of major committees which have reported conducting pilot experiments.

Another popular form of committee research is the questionnaire or survey. Its value is described in the following terms by one committee (Cmd. 9273) which made use of a questionnaire:

> We were anxious to secure as much evidence and information as possible concerning the problems confronting us and in particular to obtain the views of persons who might be materially affected by any recommendation we might make. Accordingly, we devised a form of questionnaire which we felt would not only facilitate the collection of evidence but would be of assistance to individuals or bodies desiring to submit their views to us in writing.

On the other hand, the Herbert Royal Commission on Local Government in Greater London (Cmnd. 1164) considered the undertaking of a survey of public opinion and rejected the idea:

> In collaboration with the Social Survey Division of the Central Office of Information we considered but decided against a survey of [public] opinion. We felt that a survey would not be a suitable instrument in view of the variety and complexity of the questions which we wanted to ask.

Of the major postwar committees which undertook research of some kind, roughly one in three made use of a questionnaire or survey.

Committees send questionnaires to a wide variety of respondents, and the examples in Table 9.3 will give some idea of their various purposes. Most of them are intended to produce information about facts; few are attitude or opinion surveys. One of the most frequent users of questionnaires was the Robbins Committee on Higher Education (Cmnd. 2154) which spent about

Table 9.3 Questionnaires administered by selected major royal commissions and departmental committees, 1945–69

respondents	subject	command number of source
British Dental Association and other professional groups	remuneration	7402
multiple retailers	resale prices	7696
industry and government	remuneration	7635
the general public	weights and measures	8219
various experts	cruelty to animals	8266
all prisoners' aid societies prison governors	prisoners' aid	8879
all local authorities (1,699) all slaughterhouses (285) all knackers (430)	slaughter of horses	8925
all Chief Constables		
all home commands	army organisation	9523
retail traders (1,968)	horticultural marketing	61
all Courts of Quarter Sessions	criminal business	1289
local authorities and 219 other bodies	social services	3703
all judges of County Courts	judgement debts	3909
consumer organisations	consumer credit	4596
various experts	adoption	5107

Notes: The list does not include any commissioned questionnaires carried out by other bodies on behalf of committees. Figures in parentheses indicate the total number of respondents. The 'command number of source' is a reference to the report of the committee which administered each of the questionnaires described.

Source: See the reports of the committees indicated.

£45,000 on a series of sample surveys between 1961 and 1963. Some committees reported profiting a great deal from the results of their surveys. The Runciman Committee on Horticultural Marketing (Cmnd. 61), for example, reported that it had found very little statistical information available when it was appointed. Accordingly, it sent out questionnaires to 1,968 retail traders and got 796 replies, resulting in more than 19,000 separate items of information. Sometimes the response rate is even better: the Northumberland Committee on the Slaughter of Horses (Cmd. 8925) heard from all but a dozen of 1,699 local authorities, all 285 slaughterhouses, three quarters of 430 knackers, and all but one Chief Constable in the whole country. But there have also been some disappointing results. The Chorley Committee on Higher Civil Service Remuneration (Cmd. 7635), for example, was not so fortunate; only twenty three replies resulted from a large mailing which it had undertaken.

Committees do not always feel that they can conduct their own surveys;

so they have other organisations undertake specific pieces of research for them. A favourite source of help has been the Social Survey Division of the Central Office of Information.[3] Immediately after the war, the Social Survey Division undertook an investigation into public shopping habits and opinions on the closing hours of shops for the Gowers Committee (Cmd. 7664). More recently the Division carried out an inquiry among five hundred doctors in Britain for the Sainsbury Committee on the Pharmaceutical Industry (Cmnd. 3410). For the Allen Committee on the Impact of Rates on Households (Cmnd. 2582), the Division carried out a survey of regular family expenditures at the Committee's request and it was already doing a Family Expenditure Survey which the Committee was able to use. For the Holland Committee (Cmnd. 2605), the Division undertook a number of surveys of housing in Greater London and in other cities. The Social Survey Division has been a constant source of help for committees in the postwar period.

Committees may also ask their appointing departments and others to supply information to them. The Appleton Committee on Mathematics and Science Teachers in Scotland (Cmd. 9419), for example, asked the Scottish Education Department (which had appointed the Committee) to prepare a series of 'factual statements' for them on particular topics indicated by the Committee. One Committee (Cmd. 8310) appointed by the Home Office reported making use of statistics supplied to them by the Senior Registrar of the Principal Probate Registry, and another Committee (Cmd. 8784) that it was 'indebted to the Customs and Excise Department for the factual information which they placed at our disposal, and to the Board of Trade for the statistical information which they provided'. Finally, the Oaksey Committee on Police Conditions of Service (Cmd. 7831) called upon the assistance of the Central Statistical Office and the Government Actuary. Thus, several government departments have been willing to come to the aid of their own committees and committees appointed by other departments.

There is also a slowly growing tendency to use private consultants on a contractual basis to do research for committees. The earliest postwar example was the Spens Committee on the Remuneration of General Practitioners (Cmd. 6810), which made use of a set of statistical tables which had been prepared for the Committee by a private individual (Professor Bradford Hill), but he was working not for the Committee but at the request of the British Medical Association. For the Phillips Committee on the Problems of Provision for Old Age (Cmd. 9333), the Institute of Actuaries and the Faculty of Actuaries agreed to carry out a special inquiry gratis. Both the Fleck Committee on the Fishing Industry (Cmnd. 1266) and the Rochdale Committee on Shipping (Cmnd. 4337) commissioned firms of accountants to advise them on some of the evidence submitted by firms in the fishing industry, and both Royal Commissions on the Press (Cmd. 7700 and Cmnd. 1811) retained a

3 Marjorie Ogilvy-Webb, *The Government Explains* (London: Allen and Unwin, 1965), pp. 133–7. The Social Survey Division was transferred to the General Registry Office in 1970.

firm of financial consultants to help in the analysis of the state of the companies in the industry. More recently, the Latey Committee on the Age of Majority (Cmnd. 3342) and the Crowther Committee on Consumer Credit (Cmnd. 4596) both commissioned surveys by National Opinion Poll (N.O.P.) Limited.[4] In the last few years, committees have also begun gradually to hire part-time individual 'consultants' (often from universities) and to commission more substantial external research studies (again, often from university bodies). The Fulton Committee on the Civil Service (Cmnd. 3638) and the Robens Committee on Safety and Health at Work (Cmnd. 5034) both employed individual academic consultants; and the Francis Committee on the Rent Acts (Cmnd. 4609) paid for three major research papers, including one from the Centre for Environmental Studies in London.[5] If experience in other countries is any guide, these practices are likely to become more common.

Research Subcommittees

Much the most common device included in the third kind of research described above has been the formal appointment of subcommittees to assist in the gathering of information.[6] For example, the Briggs Committee on Nursing (Cmnd. 5115) appointed nineteen subcommittees for various tasks from among its sixteen members. On several occasions, the use of subcommittees by a committee has not been entirely a matter of free choice. In fact, one of the most extensive uses of subcommittees was made by a committee appointed with subcommittees already attached. This Committee (Cmd. 8188), consisting of a chairman from outside the Civil Service plus two members who were civil servants, was asked to advise on 'the supply and demand, training and qualifications of certain medical auxiliaries'. When the committee was appointed, eight subcommittees were appointed simultaneously, one for each of eight different kinds of medical auxiliaries, and the three members of the committee proper were all members *ex officio* of each of the subcommittees. Two other major postwar committees reported receiving suggestions about subcommittees from their appointing departments. The Jones Committee on County Court Procedures (Cmnd. 7688) appointed by the Lord Chancellor explained that

---

4 The Phelps Brown Committee on Labour in Building and Civil Engineering (Cmnd. 3714) commissioned a survey by Research Services Ltd in 1967; the results were published as a 'Research Supplement' (Cmnd. 3714-I) to the report.

5 The Fulton Committee also set up what it called a 'Management Consultancy Group', but this did not really involve private consultants as such. It was rather a subcommittee of the main Committee (a device discussed below) by means of which one member (Dr Norman Hunt) co-opted a Treasury Official and two businessmen to help him make some detailed work studies in the Civil Service.

6 The Grigg Committee on Departmental Records (Cmd. 9163) observes a distinction between formal subcommittees and 'informal meetings among groups of members'.

In accordance with Your Lordship's letter to the chairman, dated 23 April 1947 [the day following the Committee's appointment], we appointed at our first meeting eight of our number [fifteen] to undertake detailed surveys of particular aspects of our work.

The Evershed Committee on Supreme Court Practice and Procedure (Cmd. 8878), which was also appointed by the Lord Chancellor in April 1947, reported doing the same thing 'in accordance with the expressed suggestion' of the Lord Chancellor. Normally, however, committees have been free to appoint subcommittees or not as they saw fit.

Committees which did decide to appoint subcommittees to help them in their research seem to have done so for several reasons, some merely to facilitate their own activities and others for reasons more closely related to the nature of their mandates.

To facilitate their activities, committees, especially large ones, may appoint subcommittees to hear evidence or to undertake visits. For example, the first major committee appointed in 1945 (Cmd. 6673) established 'a subcommittee under the presidency of the Chairman . . . for interviewing and consulting' some of its nineteen witnesses. Similarly, the Birsay Committee on General Medical Services in the Highlands and Islands (Cmnd. 3257) appointed a subcommittee to spend a week in Norway examining the situation there. A particularly interesting example of the administrative uses of a subcommittee is provided by the Crick Committee on the Form of Government Accounts (Cmnd. 7969). In order to conduct their detailed examinations of some of the various departmental forms of accounts and accounting, the Crick Committee set up several subcommittees or

> 'fact-finding teams', consisting of members of the Treasury Organisation and Methods Divisions and professional accountants from outside the Government service well versed in commercial accounting practice . . . In selecting the Departments for such special inquiry we aimed at securing the widest practicable range of functions, and those whose accounting systems have been reported upon are the Home Office, Admiralty, Board of Trade, Inland Revenue and Ministry of Works.

Some of these essentially administrative subcommittees may be very flexible. In one case, according to the former secretary,

> What happened was that the main Committee frequently asked two or three of its members with special knowledge of a particular subject to go into it, or to do a particular piece of drafting, or research, with or without a member of the secretariat or the research staff. They would report back to the main committee in whatever way seemed appropriate according to the nature of the specific job they were doing.[7]

7 In a letter from the former secretary of the Milner Holland Committee on Housing in Greater London (Cmnd. 2605).

R.C.—6

In all these cases, subcommittees were used essentially to facilitate the organisation of the work of the parent committee.

Subcommittees may, however, have a more substantial purpose. For one thing, a committee may find its mandate so broad that it can be dealt with only by dividing the whole committee into subcommittees and sharing the work among them. As the Wilson Committee on Noise (Cmnd. 2056) explained,

> The subject [of the mandate] is so wide, and the sources of noise so varied, that we have often found it necessary to divide into subcommittees. The three main subcommittees were those appointed to examine noise from aircraft, [noise] from industry and [noise] from surface transport.

Similarly, the Plowden Committee on the Aircraft Industry (Cmnd. 2853) appointed three subcommittees (on technology, economics and organisation, and international co-operation) plus a small working group (on civil aircraft) to gather most of its information. In cases such as these, the task of the parent committee is confined largely to co-ordinating the activities of its various sub-committees.

Secondly, a committee may appoint subcommittees for the purpose of dealing with aspects of their mandate which are too technical in nature for most of its members to understand. For example, the McCorquodale Committee on the Assessment of Disablement (Cmnd. 2847) appointed a sub-committee of its six medical members to deal with the medical aspects of disablement, and the Allen Committee on the Impact of Rates on House-holds (Cmnd. 2528) appointed a subcommittee 'to deal with technical questions' generally.

Thirdly, a committee may appoint a subcommittee to deal exclusively with some distinct aspect of its mandate, so that the full committee does not have to bother with it (except to formally approve the subcommittee report). For example, the Curtis Committee on the Care of Children (Cmd. 6922) appointed a subcommittee on 'Training in Child Care' as a result of the findings of a preliminary survey by the Committee that 'large sections of the staff caring for such children [as came within the Committee's terms of reference] were without any special training for the task'. This problem was clearly a distinct and, to some extent, more urgent aspect of the Com-mittee's mandate; so it was turned over to a subcommittee (whose findings were published as a separate interim report). Again, the Oliver Committee on Electoral Registration (Cmd. 7004) appointed a subcommittee 'to examine and advise us, at our request, on the machinery of registration and on the registration of members of the Forces', problems which must have appeared immediately separable from and independent of the rest of its mandate. Such aspects are conveniently dealt with by subcommittees.

Whenever subcommittees were appointed by the major postwar royal commissions and departmental committees, they usually did a good deal for the parent committee. One of the most extensive uses of subcommittees was reported by the Evershed Committee on Supreme Court Practice and Procedure (Cmd. 8878). This Committee sat for forty days as a full committee between its appointment in April 1947 and its final report in May 1953; during this same period, its subcommittees met on a total of no less than four hundred days. The subcommittees were set up to consider 'the various and very numerous questions (many of them of a highly technical nature)' which faced the Committee, and to deal with the special case of the Chancery Court of the County Palatine of Durham.[8] The similar and contemporaneous Jones Committee on County Court Procedure (Cmd. 7668) appointed an eight-man subcommittee which held sixty meetings (nearly three times as many as its parent Committee), and subcommittees of the Beaver Committee on Air Pollution (Cmd. 9322) held seventy four meetings compared with fifty nine for the Committee as a whole. Perhaps there is a natural tendency in any small group (such as a committee) for its work to be carried out *de facto* by a smaller subgroup, so that when a committee appoints a subcommittee it is merely institutionalising such a tendency. Nevertheless, not all subcommittees met more often than their parent committees: for example, subcommittees of the Allen Committee on the Impact of Rates of Households (Cmnd. 2582) and of the Plowden Committee on the Aircraft Industry (Cmnd. 2853) met on eighteen and twenty nine occasions respectively compared to twenty eight and forty eight for their parent committees.

Finally, subcommittees have made it easier for committees to co-opt additional people to assist them in specific matters. For example, the Crick Committee (Cmd. 7969) mentioned earlier was able to staff its 'fact-finding teams' with experts from the Treasury and from outside the Civil Service. The Lang Inquiry into the Pricing of Ministry of Aviation Contracts (Cmnd. 2581) similarly made use of an 'investigating team' led by the Secretary of the Committee and composed of three 'technical specialists' (one seconded from the Royal Ordnance Factories and two from the appointing Ministry of Aviation) and two accountants (one from each of the same two sources). The Fleck Committee on the Windscale Piles (Cmnd. 471) set up five 'Working Parties', four of which were chaired by co-opted experts who all signed the final report of the main committee along with the members. The Halsbury Committee on Decimal Coinage (Cmnd. 2145) formed a 'Working Party' which included five local authority Treasurers. The Maclean-Amery Committee on the Army Cadet Force (Cmnd. 268) set up five 'Working Parties', some of them including members co-opted from the Army Cadet Force and from the Regular Army. The Waverley Committee on Coastal Flooding (Cmd. 9165) set up a

---

8 Subcommittees were urged upon the Committee by the Lord Chancellor when he appointed it (see above). The report of the three-man subcommittee on the Durham Court was published as the Third Interim Report (Cmnd. 8617). The terms of reference were extended to include Durham in April 1951, four years after the Committee had originally been appointed.

subcommittee on oceanography which consisted of four of the members of the main committee but which also worked 'in close consultation' with the Director of the National Institute of Oceanography and a member of the Hydrographic Department of the Admiralty. Finally, the 'Management Consultancy Group' of the Fulton Committee on the Civil Service co-opted two businessmen to serve as members of a subcommittee appointed 'to examine a number of blocks of Civil Service work' in twelve government departments.[9]

This freedom to co-opt additional people for special needs is very precious, for it provides an important additional element of flexibility for committees. The Plowden Group on the Control of Public Expenditure (Cmnd. 1432) provides a particularly good example of the value of subcommittees. Lord Plowden was appointed 'to undertake a review of the principles and practice which govern the control by the executive of public expenditure'. In this task, he was 'aided by a Group of persons drawn from outside the Government service and senior officials drawn from Departments including the Treasury'. Later on, Lord Plowden was joined by three other full members, Sir Sam Brown, Sir Jeremy Raisman and J. E. Wall. In general, the full committee concentrated on the central problem of controlling public expenditure, while smaller subcommittees studied particular aspects and areas of concern. According to the published report of the Group, no less than thirty four Permanent Secretaries were co-opted from various departments at various times to serve on these subcommittees. In some cases, subcommittees also sought specialist advice from outside the Civil Service, although the Group decided against formally seeking evidence from outside bodies.[10] Thus, by making clever and extensive use of subcommittees, the Plowden Group was able to adapt ordinary committee procedures to its own particular needs.

Research Staff

Over the last few years, there has been an increasing willingness to provide royal commissions and departmental committees with full-time independent research staff of their own. In itself, this is not a new phenomenon nor even a very significant one. For one thing, committees have been undertaking research on a sustained and organised basis at least since the time of the well-known Hamilton Royal Commission on the Poor Laws in 1905–9, and probably before.[11] In the 1940's, the Simon-Henderson Royal Commission spent more than £100,000 on research into the growth and distribution of popula-

---

9 See the report of the Committee (Cmnd. 3638), especially Volume II (Non-Parliamentary Paper, 1968) which reproduces the findings of the subcommittee.

10 From a private communication from Treasury officials; see also the series of articles by D. N. Chester, R. W. B. Clarke, W. W. Morton and J. E. Wall in 'The Plowden Report' *Public Administration*, 41 (1963), pp. 1–50.

11 See the report of the Commission (Cd. 4498). See also Sidney and Beatrice Webb, *Methods of Social Study* (London: Longmans, Green, 1932).

tion in Britain.[12] Secondly, while many committees have not had formal research staff as such, secretaries and the more enterprising members must on occasion have undertaken studies on behalf of their committees which amounted to much the same as those which might have been carried out by formally appointed research staff. Lack of research staff obviously does not necessarily mean lack of research. Nevertheless, there is a limit to what one or two untrained part-timers can do even with the best will in the world; so the formal existence of full-time committee research staff does indicate at least a new level of importance attached to research activities. Moreover, what is significant about the events over the past few years is the growing frequency with which departments seem prepared to provide committees with such staff.

Among the major postwar committees, research staffs prior to 1965 were relatively modest. The Ross Royal Commission on the Press (Cmd. 7700) was granted the services of several civil servants as a 'research staff' and commissioned them 'to carry out systematic studies of the contents of newspapers'. Several other committees had what they described as 'large staffs' ready to prepare memoranda on specific topics as directed, but the only other major committee prior to 1965 to have what it called a 'research staff' was the Milner Holland Committee on Housing in Greater London. As the Committee explained,

> The collection and analysis of the new material on the current situation . . . required the services of a research staff of our own . . . This work was undertaken by a research staff [of seconded civil servants] under the direction of a Senior Research Officer of the Ministry [of Housing and Local Government].[13]

Thus, committee research staffs remained relatively modest until recently.[14]

With the appointment of three royal commissions in 1965 and 1966, however, a new era seems to have begun. For the first time, committees were assisted by independent research staffs recruited and appointed *ad hoc* from inside and outside the Civil Service. The breakthrough was achieved by the

12 See the report of the Commission (Cmd. 7695), as well as criticism of this expenditure in *House of Commons Debates*, 418 (4 February 1946), Columns 1439–47. Committee costs are discussed in Chapter 11 below.

13 See the report of the Committee (Cmnd. 2605). Research staff should be distinguished from assessors (mentioned in Chapter 5 above), who are appointed to give advice and assistance but not (at least in principle) to carry out research at the direction of the committee.

14 In fact, the lack of adequate research facilities for committees and other government bodies has been a common criticism of British government; see, for example, W. A. Robson, 'The Reform of Government', *Political Quarterly*, XXV, 2 (1964), pp. 200–1. The use of research staff by royal commissions is far more common in Canada, where it dates at least from the time of the Royal Commission on Dominion-Provincial Relations (1937) and is now the rule rather than the exception: see J. C. Courtney, 'Canadian Royal Commissions, 1946 to 1962', unpublished Ph.D. thesis (Durham, N.C.: Duke University, 1964), pp. 81ff.

Donovan Royal Commission on Trade Unions and Employers' Associations (Cmnd. 3623), which appointed a full-time research staff with a university lecturer in industrial relations as Research Director. Under the direction of this research staff, eleven research papers were published on a variety of topics related to the mandate of the Commission. Significantly, these studies appeared independently of the Commission's own report and as Non-Parliamentary Papers.

Still more ambitious steps were taken with the appointment of the Royal Commissions on Local Government in England (Cmnd. 4040) and in Scotland (Cmnd. 4150). Each was authorised to set up its own 'Intelligence Unit' headed by a 'Director of Intelligence', who (in the case of the English Commission) was also given the status of 'Assistant Commissioner' so that he could participate in all the meetings of the Commission. According to the report of the English Commission, the research staff made

> an indispensable contribution to our thinking. A vast amount of work was done . . . including the analysis and assessment of the mass of information available about economic, social and geographical conditions in all parts of the country.

In addition, the research staff of the English Commission organised a series of ten research studies by outside persons and organisations similar to those produced by the Donovan Commission. The Scottish Commission followed much the same procedure:

> We recognised from the start that we should need to build up a background of comprehensive facts about local government, as well as analysis and interpretation of these facts, to complement the evidence received from other quarters. It was with this object in mind that we set up an Intelligence Unit . . . The programme arranged by the Unit . . . comprised studies commissioned from members of the staff of the University of Strathclyde and from the Government, as well as exercises carried out by the staff of the Unit.

There can be little doubt that these efforts represent a new departure for royal commissions and departmental committees. Since the middle of the '60's, several other committees – not just royal commissions – have been granted research staffs. The Bolton Committee on Small Firms (Cmnd. 4811), for example, had a seven-man 'Research Unit' headed by a Research Director. Another (Cmnd. 4952) had a five-man 'Technical Support Group'. The Secretary of the Briggs Committee on Nursing (Cmnd. 5115) was given seven assistants, two advisers and four research assistants to help him organize and support the research activities of his Committee. Committees are also becoming a good deal more research-conscious, more at pains to describe what they have done and the kind of methodology it reflects. It remains to be seen, of course, whether these precedents will serve as the basis for a general expansion of the research activities of this kind of committee in the remainder of the 1970s.

The use of research staff, however, does create a situation of potential conflict. A committee and its research staff may have slightly different objectives: the committee to make recommendations and the research staff to discover truth. As Professor David Donnison has clearly explained, research staff

> are generally interested in particular aspects of the committee's work, in teasing out particular problems and discovering the truth about them. Often they are less concerned than the committee – sometimes scarcely concerned at all – about the final recommendations to be made. They are most unlikely to have a grasp of all features of the situation which the committee must consider before framing its recommendations.[15]

Without close co-ordination, therefore, there is a risk that research will do little to help a committee in framing its recommendations.

Finally, it should be noted that there are limits to what committees can do in the way of research of any kind. Royal commissions and departmental committees are, after all, essentially temporary bodies appointed for a specific purpose. They cannot always expect to be able to embark on a full-scale programme of research in the limited time which their activities can reasonably be expected to take. Besides, research is rarely an end in itself for committees; it is rather a means to enable them to produce more informed recommendations for policy or action. Thus, committees may well feel that their efforts can more usefully be spent in trying to profit from research already under way and to encourage further research by other people. The Todd Royal Commission on Medical Education (Cmnd. 3569), for example, reported having realised that:

> On some important matters the information available to us was far from adequate, but we could not ourselves organise research into medical education on a big scale. We have been conscious throughout of the urgency of our task and there would have been no possibility of planning and carrying out any major research project, and having the results available for full consideration, within the time we thought our work should take. We have had to accept, for our purposes, the virtual absence of systematic factual information about the practical processes of medical teaching in Britain and their effectiveness; we have recommended that provision be made for proper study of the aims and methods of medical teachers, as part of a substantial research effort in medical education in coming years.

Faced with this situation, the Royal Commission did what it could to obtain information.

15 Donnison, *op. cit.*, p. 559.

We were able in various ways to expedite the completion of research already in progress. We also arranged for support to be provided from public funds for several short surveys . . . of topics of special importance on which evidence might not otherwise have been adequate . . . One of our members . . . made a survey of undergraduate teaching in psychiatry. A survey of the organisation and administration of medical schools, undertaken by [the] Secretary of the Middlesex Hospital Medical School . . . provided a great deal of valuable factual information . . . We are indebted to . . . the many organisations and individuals who made available to us research findings in advance of publication, or at our invitation contributed memoranda on subjects on which they speak with particular authority.

Another committee, the Thorpe Committee on Allotments (Cmnd. 1466), even went so far as to encourage graduate students in appropriate fields to devote their theses to specific allotments. The Committee reported that it had been able to make use of theses on no less than forty nine different allotments scattered throughout the country.

Some Specific Examples

This section is designed to provide concrete illustrations of how individual committees have in practice organised their activities and especially how some of them have combined both passive and active efforts to obtain information. There is first a summary description of the various steps taken by all of the postwar royal commissions. Secondly, there are brief case-studies of the procedures adopted by five especially interesting departmental committees.

The efforts of the twenty four postwar royal commissions may conveniently be summarised by means of a list such as that in Table 9.4. There are some interesting variations among these royal commissions, but certain of the tendencies mentioned in this and earlier chapters will be clear. Royal commissions met relatively frequently, averaging over eighty meetings each. All of them held hearings for oral evidence, although not all of them reported exactly how many days these hearings occupied. Most royal commissions heard from more than one hundred different witnesses. Almost all of them carried out some kind of research and some of them broke new ground in so far as their development of the device of a research staff was concerned. In all of these respects, royal commissions differed from departmental committees; however, the differences were differences of degree rather than kind.

Departmental committees have managed to develop just as varied and imaginative sets of procedures as royal commissions, even if not always on quite the same scale. The next few pages give a brief description of the procedures adopted by five different committees: namely, the Lindsay Committee on the Expenses of Members of Local Authorities, the Wheare Committee on Children and the Cinema, the Lawrence Committee on the Remuneration of Ministers and Members of Parliament, the Heyworth Com-

Table 9.4 Selected aspects of the activities of royal commissions, 1945–69

Royal Commission on	total number of meetings	number of hearings	number of witnesses	research
Justices of the Peace (7463)	30	23	—	none
The Press (7700)	61	38	201	five questionnaires research staff
Betting, Lotteries and Gaming (8190)	42	25	141+	two visits to Eire 'obtained information' on foreign practices
Capital Punishment (8932)	63	31	117	visits to prisons, etc., 'Consulted experts' visits to Europe (2 months) and U.S.A. (3 weeks) questionnaire to governments in Europe and U.S.A.
The Taxation of Profits and Income (9474)	173	21	478	none
East Africa (9475)	150	many	700+	{ subcommittees { 7 months in Africa
University Education in Dundee (8154)	21	—	120	none
Marriage and Divorce (9678)	102	41	253	'obtained information' and consulted experts (some foreign) members took specific jobs functional sub-committees
Scottish Affairs (9212)	40	—	84	local and regional meetings visits to Ulster
The Civil Service (9613)	66	28	80	consulted experts visits to departments three questionnaires
Mental Illness and Mental Deficiency (169)	51	26	110	informal visits to institutions 'large staff' prepared memoranda as directed
Common Land (462)	69	31	395	visits and regional hearings commissioned surveys 'special reports' prepared by chairman and two others
Doctors' and Dentists' Remuneration (939)	80	23	167+	questionnaire statistical adviser 'lent by Ministry of Health' three subcommittees
Local Government in Greater London (1164)	114	70	—	visits to 79 of 117 local authorities 'commissioned certain special inquiries' research officer undertook certain 'research studies'

Table 9.4 (*continued*)

Royal Commission on	total number of meetings	number of hearings	number of witnesses	research
The Police (1728)	93	51	235	visits attitude survey by Social Survey Division (C.O.I.)
The Press (1811)	63	—	—	visits to newspaper offices questionnaires
The Penal System	30	6	—	none
Tribunals of Inquiry (3121)	22	16	67	questionnaire information on foreign practices
Trade Unions and Employers' Associations (3623)	128	58	430	questionnaire visits (domestic and foreign) surveys by Social Survey Division series of commissioned research studies research staff
Medical Education (3569)	100+	—	400+	visits (domestic and foreign) 'encouraged research'
Local Government in England (4040)	181	—	2,156	research staff series of research studies
Local Government in Scotland (4150)	148	19	344	visits (domestic and foreign) (59 days) research staff series of research studies
Assizes and Quarter Sessions (4153)	'frequent'	—	273	'special statistical survey' visits
The Constitution (5460)	163	24	263	some hearings televised 12 Assistant Commissioners to help evaluate evidence several research papers published

Notes: Numbers in parentheses are the Command numbers of the final reports of the respective royal commissions; the Royal Commission on the Penal System was dissolved before a report was issued (see Chapter 11 below), and information pertaining to it is taken from published records of evidence and a private communication from the former secretary. A dash indicates that there is no information available, and a plus sign that the figure given is a minimum estimate.

Source: See the reports of the Commissions indicated and Appendix B.

mittee on Social Studies, and the Fulton Committee on the Civil Service. These particular committees were chosen for the novelty of their procedures and for the interesting way in which each combined, adapted or invented various procedural devices to suit its particular needs.

The Lindsay Committee on the Expenses of Members of Local Authorities (Cmd. 7126) described its dozen meetings in the following way. There was a preliminary meeting eight days after the appointment of the Committee by a Minute of Appointment dated 23 July 1946. After a suitable delay to allow interests to prepare their memoranda, the Committee held two meetings in October in order to consider the written evidence. In November, the Committee journeyed to Edinburgh and Glasgow (12 and 13 November) in order to hear oral evidence from Scottish local government associations and local authorities. Similar evidence regarding England and Wales was heard in London at three meetings (21 and 28 November and 11 December) over the next four weeks. Five more meetings were necessary to discuss written evidence, to formulate committee policy and to draft the report. The meetings took place in December, January (on two occasions), February and April. The report was signed at the last meeting, on 24 April 1947.

The Wheare Committee on Children and the Cinema (Cmd. 7945) undertook a variety of different forms of research. It began by asking the Social Survey Division to make a study of 'the main features of the attendance of children at the cinema'. Next the Committee requested the Home Office and the Scottish Home Department to gather information on its behalf about the nature and extent of exhibitions of children's films (from Chief Constables throughout the country) and about local authorities' licensing practices. It also sent a questionnaire of its own dealing with cinemas and juvenile delinquency 'to all chairmen of juvenile courts, principal probation officers, directors of child guidance clinics, Chief Constables, heads and welfare officers of approved schools, superintendents of local authority remand homes, and superintendents of probation homes and hostels' in England and the corresponding Scottish authorities. The Committee also made a large number of visits to children's cinema clubs, and took advantage of the visits to make informal inquiries among the children attending children's cinema clubs. In addition, women's organisations were asked to present the views of mothers and the Commonwealth Relations Office to provide information on the situation and practice in foreign countries. In short, the Wheare Committee provides a fine example of the extent of research possible by a committee not deliberately equipped to carry out a large-scale programme of research.

The Lawrence Committee on the Remuneration of Ministers and Members of Parliament (Cmnd. 2516) realised soon after its appointment that the standard procedure of calling for evidence and holding oral hearings was not entirely appropriate. It 'would delay proceedings and might hamper freedom of discussion', the Committee reported. Accordingly a questionnaire was sent to all Members of Parliament, and 520 of them responded. The Committee then arranged to meet some of the members of both Houses of Parliament (including some of the leading peers, the leaders of the three parties, various officers of Parliament and some current and former ministers), officials of the Board of Inland Revenue and the Treasury, and the Government Actuary. The Foreign Office and the Commonwealth Relations Office were asked to provide information about the standards of remuneration in other countries. Finally, the Committee reported receiving a number of unsolicited letters from Members of Parliament and from private individuals.

The activities of the Heyworth Committee on Social Studies (Cmnd. 2660) are particularly interesting. The Committee issued a public invitation to give evidence. Then, in July 1963, one month after the appointment of the Committee, a questionnaire was sent out to all universities and colleges of technology asking them about the extent of their existing and planned research on social studies. The evidence concerning social studies which had been presented to the Committee on Higher Education (Cmnd. 2154) was reviewed. Then a second questionnaire was sent to all relevant research institutes, professional bodies, voluntary agencies, learned societies, and other organisations. At the same time as both these questionnaires were sent out, two others were sent to various departments of the central government.

But the really novel feature of the Committee's procedure was a series of five informal seminars which the Committee convened at various points around the country. The results of these seminars were, according to the Committee, 'extremely illuminating'. The first seminar was held in Kingston-upon-Thames in January 1964 and involved fourteen participants; it discussed the state of research in the social sciences generally and the formation of appropriate priorities. The second seminar was held in Manchester in April and was attended by more than nineteen people; it dealt with research into problems of regional and urban development. The third seminar, held at Cardiff in May for nineteen participants, discussed the research function of university departments of social science in Wales, with particular reference to the problems faced by relatively small departments. The fourth seminar considered 'fields of common interest to Government (central and local) and universities'; it was held in Glasgow in July and brought together twenty three experts. Finally, in London in November, twenty three people discussed the application of social sciences to social problems. The Committee also heard from over three hundred others both orally and in writing.

Finally, there is the Fulton Committee on the Civil Service (Cmnd. 3638).[16] The Fulton Committee sat for longer (nearly two and a half years) than most committees, and met far more frequently (eighty nine times). It received a great deal of evidence, both written and oral, with all of the oral evidence being presented at private hearings. The evidence was presented by eleven government departments, eighteen civil servant staff associations, twenty three schools or colleges, sixty two other organisations

16 See my more extensive description, 'The Fulton Committee on the Civil Service in Britain', in *Canadian Public Administration* XII (1969), pp. 89–107.

and thirty eight private individuals: a total of 152 submissions. Nearly 250 individuals appeared before the Committee to give oral evidence. In addition, various members of the Committee visited France, Sweden and the United States.

The Fulton Committee also set up what it called a Management Consultancy Group. This subcommittee consisted of a member of the parent Committee as chairman (Dr Norman Hunt), plus a Treasury official and two businessmen co-opted specially for the purpose. The Group conducted a series of studies of twenty three 'blocks' of Civil Service work in twelve different departments. In particular the Group examined:

a the amount and kind of responsibility held by each officer within the block

b the actual tasks performed by members of the various classes

c the qualities and skills which the work called for

d the relationship between administrators (including members of the Executive Class) and specialists (e.g. architects, engineers, scientists, etc.)

e whether the pattern of responsibilities and expertise was best designed to secure the efficient achievement of the block's objectives.

The Group's findings were published as Volume II of the Committee report.

The Fulton Committee commissioned five other surveys and investigations on various subjects pertaining to the Civil Service. There was a survey by questionnaire, conducted by Dr A. H. Halsey and I. M. Crewe, designed to provide the outline of a sociological portrait of the main general classes of the Civil Service. Dr R. A. Chapman undertook a survey by questionnaire and interview of the men and women who entered the Administrative Class as Assistant Principals in 1956, while Dr J. F. Pickering studied the subsequent careers of unsuccessful candidates for the Administrative Class in 1951. An official in the Civil Service Commission made a survey of the relative progress and performance of different types of entrant to the Administrative Class in order to test the validity of the selection procedures, and a Ministry of Defence official made a study of the work of the main committees which had previously examined the Civil Service. Finally, the Fulton Committee reported that it was able to benefit from five other studies undertaken for different purposes but having a bearing on its mandate.[17]

All these specific examples serve to underline the fundamental point about committee activities: that their procedures, including their manner of taking evidence and their conduct of research, are flexible enough to allow committees to adapt their activities to the specific needs of their mandates. It is this flexibility and adaptability which explains the extraordinary diversity which is to be found in the operations of this single institution of government.

17 The results of all the surveys and investigations mentioned in this paragraph were published in Volume III of the report (Non-Parliamentary Paper, 1968). Volumes IV and V reproduce some of the written evidence received by the Committee.

10
Writing the Report

The immediate, practical result of a committee's labours is a report. Royal commissions and departmental committees issue reports which, in effect, explain what they have done to discharge their terms of reference. Reports are the official testaments to the activities of these committees.

It is not always appreciated what a delicate and complicated job the writing of a committee report can be. The popular view seems to be that a committee report usually reflects its lowest common denominator or worse. (A camel, it has been said, is a horse designed by a committee![1]) But this hardly does justice to the subtleties that are often involved in writing committee reports. Among these problems are at least four that sooner or later confront almost all royal commissions and departmental committees. These are: the strategy and tactics of reporting itself, the use of interim reports and other devices, the mechanics of drafting, and the pursuit of unanimity. Each committee has to find its own way of resolving these problems and, once again, the overwhelming impression is of the flexibility with which committees have responded.

Strategy and Tactics

Before all the evidence has been received and before the results of all the research have become available, most committees will already have begun to hold meetings to assess the general directions indicated by the information already obtained and to discuss the shape of their reports. As time goes by, the proportion of meetings devoted to this purpose will increase until finally a committee is considering a draft report.[2]

---

1 There is also a story about an international committee appointed to look into the declining numbers of elephants in the world. The committee decided that each of its members would make some inquiries of his own and then report back to the full committee. The French member, so the story goes, returned with a slim document on the amatory habits of the elephant and the German with a three-volume study entitled, 'The Life-History of the Elephant'. The British representative had written a brief piece on 'Elephants I Have Known', while the Canadian had a study entitled, 'The Elephant: a Federal-Provincial Problem'! Additional nationals and their corresponding reports can, of course, be added to suit the audience for the story.

2 The only major committee since the war which did not issue a report of any kind was the Amory Royal Commission on Penal Reform in England and Wales. The Commission was

The first step in this process is for a committee to adopt, either consciously or unconsciously, a certain strategy for the presentation of its findings. Like any institution of government, a royal commission or a departmental committee is but one actor among many, in a process in which the effect of the actions of any one depends on the responses of others. For example, a committee may feel that a certain recommendation is desirable but realise at the same time that, for various reasons, a bald statement of the recommendation is not the most effective way of promoting it. In other words, a committee reflects certain tactical decisions in the manner in which it presents its conclusions.

Some committees reflect very simple strategies, while others develop quite sophisticated ones; but one tactic at least is likely to figure in most. This is a solution to the problem of reconciling what is desirable with what is feasible. On the one hand, a committee may choose to ignore political realities. It may feel that its report will be most valuable if it stands as an uncompromising landmark, outlining a set of goals against which can be measured the gradual evolution of the actual state of affairs. On the other hand, a committee may decide to propose only what it can realistically expect to have accepted by the government and the other interests concerned. This means sacrificing what the committee believes to be best in the hope of improving the chances for acceptance of what it believes to be attainable. There are also various ways of achieving a compromise between these two extremes. A committee may decide, for example, to propose a minimum programme of change, hoping thereby to provoke as little controversy as possible, but then add a few other recommendations as sacrifices or 'loss-leaders' knowing they will be rejected but hoping that they will draw the teeth of the critics. These more sophisticated strategies are delicate games to play, however, and can easily go awry.

Another tactical problem is the question of advocacy: to what extent should a committee plead its own case? On the one hand, a committee can decide to present the results of its work in as disinterested a fashion as possible, drawing only those conclusions which emerge clearly from its findings and deprecating anything which does not. On the other hand, a committee can examine the facts in no less disinterested a fashion, draw the same conclusions as before, but then argue the case in its report with all the persuasion and even passion it can muster. In other words, there are various ways in which a committee can argue or advocate its case. There is no simple rule about this, and committees have to work out their own ways of dealing with it.[3]

'dissolved' before its work was completed, according to a private communication from the former secretary. See also a statement by the Prime Minister in *House of Commons Debates* (27 April 1966), columns 703–5. See also the next chapter below.

3 This particular problem is also discussed in connection with the Fulton Committee on the Civil Service (Cmnd. 3638) in my article in *Canadian Public Administration*, XII (1969), pp. 89–107.

A third dilemma arises from the differences between appearance and reality, from the different attitudes which people may have towards the same phenomena. Royal commissions and departmental committees, by their very nature, work much more in the public eye than many of the ordinary processes of public administration. Thus, their recommendations must not only do justice to the problem put before them, but must also appear to do it justice.[4] This dilemma may be reflected in differences between the weight of public opinion as manifested in the evidence received and the opinions eventually reached by the committee itself. In short, a discrepancy arises between the evidence and the proposed conclusions. There is no simple rule about the legitimate or reasonable degree of discretion which a royal commission or departmental committee may exercise in accepting or disregarding the evidence presented to it. Alternatively, the same dilemma may be reflected in the kind of recommendations to be proposed. Should these be aimed at removing the symptoms of discontent or should they strike at the root causes? Again there is no simple answer to this question, and each committee has to work out some sort of response of its own.

Fourthly, a committee may have to choose between a long-term and a short-term perspective, and between a broad view and a narrow one. These are perhaps more differences of emphasis than of kind, but committees may often find tactical problems here all the same. For example, a committee may have to choose between trying to remedy existing injustices and trying to prevent future ones. Or it may have to choose between concentrating exclusively on the problems put before it or also taking into account all the important implications of what it proposes. Again each committee must develop its own strategy in response to the particular situation it perceives.

There may be still other tactical problems. Committees may have to decide whether to take into account some of the personalities involved in the problem, whether to consider the prospects of a change in government at the next general election, whether to learn from the fate of the recommendations of earlier committees on similar or related matters, whether to take into account the current state of the national economy, and so on. There are no general answers to any of these problems, and each committee must do its best to resolve them in the best way it can. How it does so constitutes a committee's strategy of reporting.

Timing may also be a crucial element in the writing of reports. Theoretically, royal commissions and departmental committees are free to set their own deadlines, although it seems to be inevitable that they are under pressure from some quarter to produce a report before they actually do! There may be irate Questions in Parliament asking the appropriate minister how much longer he expects the committee to take before its report is submitted, or

4 An amusing criticism of the excessive caution of some committee reports can be found in W. J. M. Mackenzie, 'The Plowden Report: Translation', *The Guardian* (25 May 1963), and reprinted in Richard Rose (ed.), *Policy-Making in Britain* (London: Macmillan, 1969), pp. 273–82.

there may be embarrassing editorials in the press suggesting that the evidence presented to the committee will be out of date before any report based on it is ever produced. Occasionally, officials may stress the need for haste when they appoint a committee; for example, the Geddes Committee on Shipbuilding (Cmnd. 2937) was directed 'to report within about a year', which it did. Similarly, the Minister of Housing and Local Government attended the first meeting of one of his committees (Cmnd. 2605) and

> pressed for the production of a report at the earliest possible moment. There has at no time been any relaxation of this pressure; and the Committee has throughout its work been conscious of a sense of urgency.

Or there may be a public statement when the committee is announced, as in the case of the Lawrence Committee on the Remuneration of Ministers and M.P.'s (Cmnd. 2516), whose appointment in December 1963 was accompanied by an announcement that 'the Committee should be asked to report as soon as possible after the General Election and that whatever action seems appropriate in the light of its report should then be taken without delay'.

Sometimes it is the committee itself which recognises that the nature of the subject imposes a need for haste. The Sharpe Committee on the Summary Trial of Minor Offences (Cmd. 9524) reported that it realised 'at once the urgency of the problem [and so] decided to press on with our deliberations with all possible speed'.[5] The Albemarle Committee on the Youth Services (Cmnd. 929) considered that it was 'meeting in conditions of unusual urgency and with a sense of working against time' because of the injustices which were then occurring. Thus the subject, as well as the minister, may demand prompt action.

Alternatively, committees know that certain times of the Parliamentary and administrative years are likely to be more propitious than others. For one thing, a committee report which appears during a Parliamentary recess is on balance less likely to attract public attention than if it had appeared while Parliament was in session. Similarly, recommendations which would affect departmental estimates are obviously better presented before these estimates are drawn up rather than just afterwards. As one Committee reported,

> It was clear to us from the outset that the sooner we could report the better, and in particular that any recommendations we might make on fiscal matters should be with you [the Chancellor of the Exchequer] early [in the year] if they were to receive consideration in time for your next Budget.[6]

5 The urgency of the problem arose out of the fact that it included things such as common traffic offences, nearly ninety-five per cent of which are admitted by the alleged offender without trial.

6 From the report of the Runciman Committee on the Taxicab Service (Cmd. 8804). The Committee in fact reported only six months after its appointment; it received written evidence over two months, held hearings for two more months and took a further two months to write a report.

It may even be wise for a committee to keep an eye on the progress of other royal commissions or departmental committees in existence, so that it does not find its report overshadowed by the simultaneous presentation of other reports all demanding the attention of government, Parliament and the general public.

Interim Reports and Other Devices

Royal commissions and departmental committees are not entirely defenceless in the face of these dilemmas. They have several devices which they can exploit to help them present their reports in the most effective way possible. The most important of these devices is probably the interim report.

Among the major postwar committees, approximately one committee in ten actually issued one or more interim reports, including two royal commissions.[7] Most of the committees which issued interim reports issued only one, although there was one case of three interim reports.[8]

A few of these interim reports are the result of frank suggestions by departmental officials. Royal commissions, for example, are invariably assured in their royal warrants of their 'liberty to report proceedings under this Our Commission from time to time if you shall judge it expedient so to do', and a few departmental committees are given similarly explicit assurances. But most committees decide on their own initiative whether and when to issue interim reports. The Baker Committee on the Mechanical Recording of Court Proceedings (Cmnd. 3096) produced an interim report (Cmnd. 2733), 'as it will be several months before we are able to reach some of our conclusions'. Similarly, the Lang Inquiry decided to issue two reports: an interim report (Cmnd. 2428) on the circumstances leading up to the taking of excess profits by Ferranti Limited on some forty contracts with the Bloodhound missile, followed by a second report (Cmnd. 2581) on the general problem of preventing further cases of excess profits in defence contracts.

Committees give various reasons for deciding to issue interim reports, but the two most common are described in the following extract from the terms of reference of several committees:[9]

> to make interim reports on any matter or matters arising out of their terms of reference as may from time to time appear to the Committee to merit *immediate* attention or warrant *separate* attention.

7 Reference is to the Willink Royal Commission on the Police (Cmnd. 1728), which issued one interim report (Cmnd. 1222), and the Cohen-Radcliffe Royal Commission on the Taxation of Profits and Income (Cmd. 9474), which issued two (Cmd. 8761 and Cmd. 9105).

8 Reference is to the Evershed Committee on Supreme Court Practice and Procedure (Cmd 8878) with its three interim reports (Cmnd. 7764, Cmd. 8176 and Cmd. 8617).

9 See, for example, the terms of reference of the Uthwatt-Jenkins Committee on Leasehold (Cmd. 7982 (7706)) or those of the Evershed Committee on Supreme Court Practice and Procedure (Cmd. 8878 (7764, 8176, 8617)); the italics are added.

In other words, either the subject of the committee falls into two or more parts which are more conveniently considered separately, or some aspect of the subject requires more urgent attention than the rest of it. The Crick Committee on the Form of Government Accounts (Cmd. 7969) issued two interim reports, one for each of these two reasons. Urgency prompted an interim 'Memorandum on the Financial Statement' as a result of which 'several proposals contained therein were adopted in the Financial Statement, 1949–50'. To give the matter separate attention was the purpose of the second interim report on the establishment of a Food Trading Fund. Neither interim report, however, was published except as an appendix to the final report.

Interim reports to deal with a conveniently separable or independent part of a committee's terms of reference may arise out of a ministerial request. The Committee on Further Education for Agriculture (Cmnd. 614) produced an interim report at the express request of the Minister of Agriculture, Fisheries and Food on a specific aspect of its mandate: namely, ministerial responsibility for the agricultural education provided by local authorities.[10] The Hunter Committee on Salmon and Trout Fisheries in Scotland (Cmnd. 2691) explained its interim report (Cmnd. 2096) by noting that the Secretary of State for Scotland had asked the Committee to 'give priority to that part of our remit which dealt with the regulation of fishing for salmon and migratory trout, and if possible to submit an interim report'.

Alternatively, a committee may decide to divide its findings among two or more reports on its own initiative. The Fisher Committee on Scottish Local Government Law Consolidation issued three separate reports because their terms of reference appeared to cover three readily distinguishable areas of law. The three reports dealt with public order (Cmd. 8729), public health (Cmd. 8751) and the police (Cmd. 8993). The Morison Committee on the Probation Service presented two reports for much the same reason. The terms of reference of the Committee seemed to fall explicitly into two (unequal) parts: the Probation Service as such and the approved probation hostel system. The first and major report (Cmnd. 1650) dealt with the Probation Service and was signed more than two years after the appointment of the Committee, while the second report (Cmnd. 1800) examined the approved hostel system and appeared six months later.

Sometimes the convenient division in the terms of reference lies not so much in the subject matter as in the existing departmental divisions of responsibilities. The Franklin Committee on Punishments in Prisons, Borstal Institutions, Approved Schools and Remand Homes divided its report into two (Cmd. 8256 and Cmd. 8429), since prisons and borstal institutions are administered and inspected by the Prison Commissioners while approved

---

10 The interim report was unpublished except as Chapter VIII of the final report because 'we had in any case intended to deal with this subject'.

schools and remand homes are administered and inspected by the Children's Department of the Home Office. Similarly, the Pilcher Committee on Naval Discipline issued a first report (Cmd. 8094) for the following reason:

> As we understand that decisions with regard to the Army and Air Force system await our report on the naval court-martial system, we have concentrated in the first place on the court-martial aspect of our terms of reference. In this our first report we therefore submit those recommendations on the naval court-martial system which it appears to us can safely be made without full consideration of the summary system.

Then, in its second report (Cmd. 8119), the Committee proceeded to deal chiefly with the powers of summary jurisdiction conferred by the Naval Discipline Act on officers in command of H.M. ships.

A special use for the 'separate attention' interim report is as a vehicle for the report of a subcommittee. The Curtis Committee on the Care of Children (Cmd. 6922) set up a subcommittee to deal with the question of suitable training for staff caring for children deprived of a normal home life; its report, 'Training in Child Care', was published as an interim report (Cmd. 6760) of the whole committee. The Wilson Committee on the Problem of Noise similarly produced two reports. The interim report, 'Noise from Motor Vehicles' (Cmnd. 1780), grew out of a subcommittee report and was signed by the Chairman alone 'on behalf of the Committee'. The final report, 'Noise' (Cmnd. 2056), appeared a year later and 'includes the substance of our interim report on noise from motor vehicles'.

The second major purpose of interim reports is to deal with matters of urgency. In some cases, the appropriate minister will draw the attention of the committee to the fact that part of its mandate is of more urgent concern than the rest. The Waverley Committee on Coastal Flooding (Cmd. 9165) reported that

> Shortly after we were appointed, we were asked by the Home Secretary to make a report [Cmd. 8923] on the third of our Terms of Reference [which concerned the need for further measures, including a warning system, to prevent further damage and loss of life] in the hope that it may be possible to put it into effect before the next warning period.

A sudden accident prompted the Home Secretary to write to the Molony Committee on Consumer Protection (Cmnd. 1781) to 'indicate that he would welcome the assistance of an interim report by this Committee on the general issue of the safety of consumer goods', and an interim report (Cmnd. 1011) was issued within less than nine months. Similarly, the Guthrie Committee on the Tenure of Shops and Business Premises in Scotland, the Guest Committee on Scottish Licensing Law, and the Cohen-Radcliffe Royal Commission on the Taxation of Profits and Income produced interim reports on parts of their terms of reference as the result of a request by the appointing minister to do so as a matter of urgency.[11]

In other cases, committees themselves issue interim reports following their own assessment of the urgency of the situation. The interim report of the Beaver Committee on Air Pollution (Cmd. 9322) was prompted by a feeling on the part of the Committee that there was a need for 'immediate ameliorative action' following the serious damage and loss of life caused by smog in London in December 1952. Accordingly, its interim report (Cmd. 9011) was devoted entirely to a discussion of various possible anti-pollutants, although recognising that in this direction lay only short-term palliatives. The Devlin Committee on the Port Transport Industry (Cmnd. 2734) produced a first report (Cmnd. 2523) only nineteen days after its appointment because it felt that the first of its three remits – an inquiry into the causes of 'the present dispute' – was more 'a matter of urgency' than the other two – decasualisation and labour efficiency in the docks. The Denning Committee on Procedure in Matrimonial Causes (Cmd. 7024) issued two interim reports (Cmd. 6881 and Cmd. 6945) during its seven months of existence because 'the need for action appears so urgent and so plain'. Similarly, the Jones Committee on County Court Procedure (Cmd. 9542) explained,

> We have now completed the taking of evidence but it may be some time before we are in a position to submit our final report. The impression left by the evidence is that in general those who resort to the county courts are satisfied with their working and appreciate the help and consideration which they received from the judges, registrars and officers of the courts. We have received a large number of suggestions for minor improvements of the procedure, but only upon one point has there been serious criticism, namely, the arrangements made for the hearing of actions which are tried by the judge. It seemed to us desirable that any suggestions we could make to meet this criticism (so far as it is well-founded) should be submitted to those concerned as soon as possible. We have therefore thought it best to deal with the problem in an interim report [Cmd. 7468].

Another interesting use of interim reports resulted from two Committees on Slaughterhouses. Both were invited 'to prepare a [long-term] plan' for slaughterhouses, one for England and Wales and the other for Scotland. Some months after their appointment in 1953, the government issued a White Paper (Cmd. 8989) announcing a major change in policy: the decontrol of meat marketing. The Herbert Committee on Slaughterhouses in England and Wales (Cmd. 9542) was informed by the Minister of Food that it would be

> helpful to the Agriculture Ministers and to myself if the Committee would consider the form which, with due regard to the long-term policy, interim

11 See the reports of these three Committees (Cmd. 7903 (7603), Cmnd. 2021 (1217), and Cmd. 9474 (8761, 9105) respectively).

arrangements might take to ensure that meat distribution is satisfactorily carried out when free marketing is resumed next summer.

The Committee reported that this point had already occurred to it and that it had decided to make the matter the subject of an interim report (Cmd. 9060), which duly appeared. In the meantime, the Committee decided that it should not continue its inquiries until the situation had stabilised into its new form: 'We considered it necessary to defer until after decontrol [of meat distribution] further enquiries relating to our original terms of reference.' The Committee accordingly adjourned for a period of about ten months following production of the interim report. The same problem faced the Handford Committee on Slaughterhouses in Scotland (Cmd. 9376). Following announcement of the change in government policy, the chairman of the Committee wrote to the Secretary of State for Scotland to ask for guidance. Although the Committee had nearly finished hearing oral evidence and although it had originally intended to deal with both long-term policy and the transitional period in a single report, the Committee eventually decided to submit an interim report (Cmd. 9061) along with that of the English Committee; however, the relatively more advanced stage of its procedures seems to have persuaded the Scottish Committee not to delay its final report as the English Committee did.

To summarise, there are two major reasons for issuing interim reports: to give separate treatment to some distinct aspect of a committee's mandate or to deal with a matter of urgency. Both reasons may be invoked either by ministers to persuade their committees to issue interim reports or by committees to justify their own decisions.

Interim reports can serve other purposes, but they have not often been justified on other grounds. For example, if interim reports are issued, their impact can then be examined and commented on in a subsequent report. Thus, the final reports of the two Slaughterhouse Committees just mentioned noted that 'all but one' of the prior recommendations of the English Committee and all the prior recommendations 'in general' of the Scottish Committee had been implemented in recent legislation.[12] Similarly, the Guest Committee on Scottish Licensing Law reported in a second report (Cmnd. 2021) that many of the recommendations of its first report (Cmnd. 1217) had been implemented in the Licensing (Scotland) Act, 1962.[13] Nevertheless, not many of the major postwar committees have in fact exploited this use of multiple reports. Only one of them has ever reported issuing a report exclusively for the purpose of commenting on reaction to its previous report: this was the 'Supplementary Report' (Cmd. 8946) by the chairman of the second Inquiry into the Case of Timothy John Evans, which was written to com-

12 Reference is to the Slaughterhouses Act, 1954 (2 and 3 Eliz. II Chapter 42).

13 The statutory reference is to 10 and 11 Eliz. II, Chapter 51.

ment on Parliamentary reaction to the findings of the Inquiry as set out in the main report (Cmd. 8896).[14]

There are, of course, less formal means available to royal commissions and departmental committees for floating 'trial balloons', and this may explain the relative disuse of interim reports for that purpose. Witnesses giving oral evidence to a committee can be queried directly for their reactions to various proposals. Draft recommendations can be circulated informally for discussion and suggestions from selected experts and interest groups alike; for example, the Adams Committee on Civil Judicial Statistics (Cmnd. 3684) reported that, 'We submitted a summary of the main recommendations proposed by us to [five senior judges], all of whom expressed their general approval.' The committee secretary can usually be relied on to keep departmental officials apprised of proposals for the main recommendations, so that comments, queries and objections are likely to reach the committee from that quarter as well.

One last area in which a royal commission or a departmental committee may exercise a certain amount of tactical flexibility is in its relations with the mass media. If a committee wants to launch its proposals on a flood tide of popular and expert discussion, then the media can do a lot to help create this state of affairs. Apart from periodic press releases describing the general progress of a committee's various activities, confidential information may also occasionally be leaked. Leaks may come from disgruntled committee members trying to promote their own views or from witnesses trying to achieve publicity. Sometimes, however, a committee may deliberately 'arrange' a leak to further its own ends. Leaks to the media are often a nuisance, as they will waste a good deal of a chairman's and a secretary's time by provoking investigations and even Parliamentary Questions about the sources of the leak. But leaks, whether accidental or deliberate, can be useful as well if they serve to keep alive public interest, to focus discussion on important issues or to dispel unfounded suspicions and anxieties. According to a former member of the Milner Holland Committee on Housing in Greater London, for example,

> Before the . . . report was published a leak to the *Sun* (not from the committee) provoked widespread speculation in the Sunday newspapers and helped to achieve the excellent coverage the report was given when it appeared.[15]

Similar leaks from the recent Donovan and Maud Royal Commissions also helped to promote discussion of their reports when they appeared.[16] In fact,

14 See also the Parliamentary reaction in *House of Commons Debates* (29 July 1953).

15 David Donnison, 'Committees and Committeemen', *New Society* (18 April 1968), p. 560; the report of the Committee was published as Cmnd. 2605.

16 Reference is to the Royal Commissions on Trade Unions and Employers' Associations (Cmnd. 3623) and on Local Government in England (Cmnd. 4040) respectively, and to various reports in the *Sunday Times* and other newspapers which appeared during the

if a committee persists in keeping the mass media at arm's length, it may find that they are relying on other, less scrupulous and less accurate sources of information. Far from helping a committee to sell its proposals, this may make the task a good deal more difficult.

The Mechanics of Drafting

The process of actually drafting a committee report is much more than merely a clerical job. It can have a strong influence on the substance as well as the form of the final recommendations. In theory, it is true, the draft of a report put before a committee is open to virtually unrestricted amendment by the committee; but in practice, radical changes are probably rare. For one thing, a draft report is to some extent a *fait accompli*. Members do not normally face a choice among several alternatives of more or less equal merit but a choice between an existing draft which can be modified and the prospect of starting from scratch again. It would be difficult to argue against working from the existing draft. Secondly, the existing draft is bound to embody certain features which cannot easily be changed by the piecemeal amendment of a few of its parts. The draft will have a theme, an order of presentation and argument, and a set of concepts and priorities which cannot easily be changed without revising the draft in a fairly fundamental way. A draft report will also have a certain persuasive power of its own, quite apart from the merits of the case it argues, due to the logic of its construction and the comprehensiveness of its scope. Especially if some members of a committee are still somewhat ambivalent, therefore, the job of preparing a first draft of the report can have a considerable influence on its ultimate form.

The normal practice is for the secretary of a committee to prepare its first draft. He will have attended all the meetings of the committee, he will have read and listened to all of the evidence, and he will have seen the results of any research undertaken by the committee. Moreover, he will have listened to all the discussions within the committee, and will have a good idea of the consensus that has grown up among the members. Finally, the secretary will probably be as well aware as any of the members of the various political and administrative constraints which exist. If he is asked to prepare a first draft of the report, the secretary will probably work largely on his own, making periodic reports to the chairman or the committee as a whole. When the draft is complete, it is laid before the committee for discussion and amendment.[17]

---

spring of 1968 and 1969 respectively. The fact that the research staff of both these royal commissions were busily publishing the findings of their research also helped to fan the flames of discussion.

17 This was the practice adopted by, for instance, the Heyworth Committee on the Gas Industry (Cmd. 6699), according to a private communication from the chairman. See also *Committee Procedure*, Treasury Notes on Government Procedure, No. 20 (London: HMSO, 1958), paragraphs 51–8.

On the other hand, the chairman, some of the members or even the whole committee may decide to take much more of a hand in the preparation of the draft of the report. The chairman may take the initiative and prepare the first draft entirely on his own. Lord Radcliffe, for example, is understood to like to take a large part in the drafting of the reports of his committees. The chairman may work in close co-operation with the secretary and perhaps one or two members who happen to be available. Sir John Masterman, when he was chairman of the Committee on the Political Activities of Civil Servants (Cmd. 7718), summoned his secretary to Oxford for a few days, and they wrote the report together.[18] Sometimes a committee will decide to appoint a subcommittee specially for the purpose of preparing a draft report.[19] Finally, a committee may even manage to prepare at least an outline of a draft report in plenary meetings of the whole committee. The Herbert Royal Commission on Local Government in Greater London (Cmnd. 1164), for example, described its procedure thus:

> The first occasion on which these matters [of a draft report] were discussed was at a weekend spent in Cambridge where we sat throughout Saturday 13th and Sunday 14th February 1960 and considered exhaustively all that we had heard and read. . . . We . . . met again in London during the weekend of 26th and 27th March and again sat throughout Saturday and Sunday. We have since met on a number of occasions to settle various questions and to agree on the form of our Report.

Each committee is free to arrange for the preparation of a draft in whatever way it sees fit. Ultimately, it will depend largely on the preference and the convenience of the particular people involved. If a chairman has already emerged as the leading member of the committee, the chances are that he will play a strong part in the preparation of a draft report. If, on the other hand, the members have constantly held the chairman in check, they are unlikely to allow him to prepare the draft on his own. If the committee has reason to fear departmental interference, it will probably not be prepared to give the secretary too much of a free hand. Each committee, in short, will find its own way in response to its own particular requirements.

The nub of the draft report will almost invariably be a series of fairly specific recommendations, but the number and nature of these recommendations can vary enormously. As the data in Table 10.1 indicate, royal commissions and departmental committees make an average of about forty recom-

---

18 From a private communication from the chairman. Sir John Masterman was then Provost of Worcester College, Oxford, and other members of the Committee who happened to be Oxford dons also took part in the drafting.

19 Drafting subcommittees were reported by, for example, the Lewis Committee on Army and Air Force Courts-Martial (Cmd. 7608), the Pilcher Committee on Naval Discipline (Cmd. 8119), the Nathan Committee on Charitable Trusts (Cmd. 8710) and the Anderson Committee on Grants to Students (Cmnd. 1051). These subcommittees reported twelve, ten, nine and six sessions respectively.

Table 10.1 Major royal commissions and departmental committees, 1945–69, by number of recommendations

number of recommendations	royal commissions only	all committees
fewer than 20	1	140
20–39	2	73
40–59	5	42
60–79	4	22
80–99	3	17
100–149	4	17
150–199	1	7
200 or more	1	7
no information	3	33
total	24	*358*
mean number of recommendations	82	40

Notes: The data refer to all reports (except reservations and dissents) issued by each committee, including final and interim reports. Individual recommendations are defined as presented in the report of the committee which proposed them. Where 'conclusions' can be distinguished from 'recommendations', only the latter are included.

Source: See Appendix B.

mendations each, although the average among royal commissions alone is nearly twice that number. Most committees clearly confine themselves to a relatively modest number of recommendations, and really long lists of one hundred or more are rare. The most prolific committees were the Grant Committee on the Sheriff Court in Scotland (Cmnd. 3248) with 375 recommendations, the Evershed Committee on Supreme Court Practice and Procedures (Cmd. 8878) with 353 recommendations, and the Jenkins Committee on Company Law (Cmnd. 1749) with 334 recommendations. At the other extreme, the Cunningham Committee on the Vassall Case (Cmnd. 1781) produced a report with only one single recommendation.[20]

Beyond this, there are few generalisations that can be made with much confidence. Some recommendations may be broad injunctions, while others may call for minute changes in the law. In response to the purpose for which the committee was originally appointed, some recommendations will merely convey information, others will propose policies and still others will suggest specific actions to implement policies. Some recommendations will be directed towards the government, but others may be aimed at other organisations and individuals outside the public sector. Some committees will recommend that action is urgent and others that it should be gradual. Some will even seem to do both: the Henry Committee (Cmnd. 4137) suggested that implementation

20 The report was actually intended as only an interim report, but it was superseded by a statutory Tribunal of Inquiry before it could finish its work (see the next chapter).

of their draft scheme for the registration of title to land in Scotland should proceed bit by bit but ought 'not to be too gradual'! Some committees will be quite clear on the need for radical change – the Maconochie Committee on Poaching and Illegal Fishing for Trout in Scotland (Cmd. 7917), for example, declared, 'We are satisfied that the problem calls for drastic action' – while others will urge caution in introducing any change at all. Some committees will praise the government for its actions so far, while others will be highly critical. For example, the Streatfield Committee on the Business of Criminal Courts (Cmnd. 1289) recorded in its report 'a considerable body of opinion' in favour of reform, and criticised the failure to implement even the moderate changes proposed by an earlier Committee. Perhaps the most important generalisation about committee recommendations, therefore, is that they do not follow any rules. A royal commission or a departmental committee is under virtually no constraints at all as to the sorts of things it recommends. This is a freedom which committees must be anxious to retain.

Once a draft report is completed, it will be submitted for consideration by the whole committee. There will be discussions, amendments will be proposed, and the draft may have to be revised several times. In the last analysis, though, there are only two possible outcomes: either the committee will agree upon a final draft or it will agree to disagree, and the result is a report which is either unanimous or divided.

In Pursuit of Unanimity

Most committees do manage to achieve unanimous agreement on a final report. Given the nature, the subject matter and the membership of some committees, it may seem surprising that unanimity has in fact been the rule rather than the exception. As the Willink Royal Commission on Betting, Lotteries and Gaming (Cmd. 8190) pointed out in its report,

> The subject of gambling is one on which there are many conflicting and strongly held opinions, and we do not expect that any single proposal which we make will be without its critics. Throughout the course of our inquiry we have tried to consider the problem as a whole, and we are glad to be able to say that we have reached unanimous conclusions both on the general principles on which the law should be based and on their application.[21]

21 Actually, the Commission had to resort to some fairly obvious circumlocutions in order to reach this state of unanimity. In this connection, Sir Alan Herbert has drawn sarcastic attention to the following sentences in the Commission report: 'We think it would be difficult to prove that in any of the types of football pools conducted by the larger firms skill is wholly unimportant . . . Nevertheless . . . the difficulty of forecasting correctly the result of a large number of matches is so great that the number of prize-winners is determined more by the laws of probability than the skill of the competitor.' (From 'Anything but Action?' in Ralph Harris (ed.), *Radical Reaction*, 2nd ed. (London: Hutchinson, 1961), p. 297.)

In particular, the diverse backgrounds and professions of committee members must make unanimity a considerable feat in some cases. The Crook Committee on the Statutory Registration of Opticians (Cmd. 8531) recorded that

> We are glad that the Committee, including as it does personnel representative of the medical profession, ophthalmic opticians and dispensing opticians as well as educationists, is able to present a unanimous Report and recommendations for action.

Not all committees have in fact been so fortunate, as the following press report reveals:[22]

COHEN OVER

Peter Walker, the new-style Minister of Housing, has ended two years of unhappiness and frustration for members of the Cohen committee on housing associations and societies. He has decided that their work should be considered complete, and the considerable material they had collected is to be processed at the Ministry.

Some members of the committee feel that Walker had no other course. Before the election the committee had just called a third halt to their proceedings. They were demanding an appointment with the Minister, and were determined to go no farther without the services of a civil servant competent to write up their report (which lack had handicapped them from the outset).

The other difficulty was the running warfare which developed between the chairman, Sir Karl Cohen, and the majority of his members. Sir Karl, formerly Labour's chairman of the Leeds housing committee, was in his colleagues' view wedded to the notion that housing was essentially a local authority concern and that voluntary housing associations and societies could never play a significant part.

Walker, from the Opposition benches, had already proved himself a friend of those on the committee who championed a more important role for the voluntary housing movement. Some, however, suspected his motives: there has been a marked Conservative tendency of late to promote housing associations as an alternative to council housing.

The committee members will be keen to see that their report, as drafted for them at the Ministry, faithfully represents the Majority view – that housing associations should be allowed to make a greater contribution, but not be used for getting local authorities 'off the hook'.

Indeed, as another Committee (Cmnd. 2066) pointed out, its own ability to reach agreement held out hopes for much broader agreement:

> The majority of our members represent a number of . . . bodies which might well have been thought to have conflicting interests, and while there

were inevitably differences of opinion we consider that the measure of agreement we have reached on the major contentious issues facing us has shown that a solution acceptable to a cross-section of . . . opinion can be produced.

To some extent this surprising degree of apparent unanimity is due to the fact that committees must sometimes simply avoid issues on which they are irreconcilably divided, especially if the point is only peripheral to the mandate. The Ridley Committee on a National Policy for the Use of Fuel and Power Resources (Cmd. 8647) explained in its report, 'We do not include any recommendation on the price level for coal since we are equally divided on this question.'[23] Or a committee may simply note disagreements as they occur in the report, and not go to the lengths of attaching a formal rider to the report. The Morton Royal Commission on Marriage and Divorce (Cmd. 9678) pointed out:

We have not been able to reach agreement on all the questions which were before us. This is not, perhaps, surprising when regard is had to the nature of the matters under discussion and to the wide differences of opinion revealed among those who gave evidence. In general, differences of view within the Commission have been set out in the body of the Report. It seemed to us that this would enable us to present more fairly the two sides of questions raising issues of wide social and moral significance.

But for some royal commissions and departmental committees, nothing can be done to avert open disagreement when the time comes to sign the report. The Treasury has provided the following advice:

Where a committee has failed to reach agreement on certain points, one of two courses should be taken. The opposing views may be set out in the body of the report without saying which members held them, thus: 'Some of us think . . ., others however think . . .', or the dissenting members may sign the report subject to reservations which are appended to the report and signed. The essential point is that agreement should be reached if possible, but if not, differences of view should not be obscured.[24]

In other words, the price of unanimity is compromise. If this means a significant watering-down of a committee's proposed conclusions, then the price is not worth paying and the chairman should not allow himself to be pressured into trying to pay it. In any case, the evidence shows that approximately one quarter of the major postwar committees have produced reports which were less than unanimous (see Table 10.2). Among royal commissions alone, indeed, disagreement has been more common than unanimity.

23 See also the various comments on the report of the Radcliffe Committee on the Working of the Monetary System (Cmnd. 827) in Arthur Seldon (ed.), *Not Unanimous* (London: Institute of Economic Affairs, 1960).

24 *Committee Procedure, op. cit.,* Paragraph 60.

Table 10.2 Major royal commissions and departmental committees, 1945–69, by extent of agreement in final report

extent of agreement		royal commissions only	all committees
unanimous (excluding one-man committees and committees not reporting)		11	241
divided		11	82
reservations only	5		55
dissents only	2		17
reservations and dissents	5		9
one-man committees		0	34
committees not reporting		1	1
total		24	358

Note: Reservations are disagreements by signatories of the main report, while dissents are disagreements by members who did not sign the main report. Interim reports are not considered.

Source: See Appendix B.

Formal disagreement can be registered in a variety of ways: there have been 'reservations', 'dissents', 'minority reports', 'memoranda of dissent', 'alternative recommendations' and so on. But they all fall into one of two groups according to the seriousness of the disagreement. First of all, there have been disagreements over points of detail which have not prevented their authors from signing the main report as well; such disagreements may be called *reservations*. Secondly, there have been disagreements of so funda-mental a nature as to lead their authors to feel that they could not in good conscience sign the main report as well; such disagreements may be called *dissents*.[25] Table 10.2 shows that, although there has been a considerable number of less-than-unanimous reports among the major postwar committees, most of the disagreements have not been very serious. Most of the disagree-ments have been merely matters of reservation, not dissent.

In fact, serious disagreement (i.e. dissent) has occurred in only twenty six major committees in the past twenty five years, although seven of them were recorded by royal commissions. When dissent has occurred, it has sometimes produced deep divisions within a committee. The Montagu Committee on Cadet Entry into the Royal Navy (Cmd. 8845), for example, reported that one of its members had discovered in the middle of the Committee's proceed-ings that

his views had diverged so far from those of the remainder of the Committee that it would be necessary for him to submit a Minority Report. Except

25 These terms are not always used this way in practice. 'Reservations' usually are just reservations, but 'dissents' may turn out to be either reservations or dissents (cf. Cmd. 9783 and Cmnd. 842). A so-called 'minority report' may be either a reservation or a dissent (cf. Cmnd. 547 and Cmnd. 851).

when additional evidence was being considered, he withdrew from further discussions until the final draft of our Report and the contents of his Minority Report were being discussed.

Another committee, the Maconochie Committee on Close Seasons for Deer in Scotland (Cmd. 9273), became seriously divided into two separate camps. The minority (three members) explained their relations with the majority (six members) in the following terms:

> We collaborated with our colleagues in preparing much of what is contained in the first four sections of their report, but, after careful consideration of all the evidence submitted and from our own practical experience, the conclusions which we have reached are in many respects so different from those of our colleagues that we have been unable to subscribe our names to the report of the majority of the committee. We kept our colleagues fully advised of the matters on which we differed from them and we refrained from attending their final meetings in order to afford them greater facilities for discussion and in the hope that differences might have been resolved. Events unfortunately proved otherwise.

The result was in effect two separate committees making opposite recommendations on the same evidence about the same subject!

Another indication that dissents represent fairly fundamental disagreement is reflected in the fact that there must often be considerable pressure on a minority to go along with the majority, or at least to turn a proposed dissent into merely a reservation. One member of the Nathan Committee on Charitable Trusts (Cmd. 8710) wrote a twenty-page dissent rather than sign the main report. He explained that he had thought very carefully about taking such a step, taking into account all the evidence presented to the Committee as well as his discussions with other members. Nevertheless,

> I still feel it my duty to qualify and supplement the recommendations, conclusions and reasons [of the main report], and to suggest alternatives in certain respects which seem to me by no means the least important. This I do with the greatest respect and deference ... more especially since where divergences on any other aspects have cropped up and not been fully reconciled certain of the members have been content to note in the Main Report an absence of unanimity whereas these present observations are by way of a Minority Report [i.e. a dissent] and must in the result stand over my name alone and with all the more diffidence accordingly.[26]

26 Normally reservations and dissents are completed at the same time as the main report, but in this case, the dissent followed the main report by two months (although both were eventually published together). The delay was due to the dissenting member wanting to see proofs of the main report before starting to write his own dissent. See also the report of the Crowther-Kilbrandon Royal Commission on the Constitution (Cmnd. 5460, paras. 31 and 32) for a somewhat less satisfactory relationship between majority and minority.

Too much should not be made of reservations. Some chairmen are not unwilling to allow reservations when they reflect a difference of opinion in the evidence put before a committee. This may be felt to make a committee's report more true-to-life. In other cases, though, reservations have weakened the impact of a committee's report. For instance, disagreement may be over precisely the issue or issues which the committee was expected to help resolve. Naturally, if a minister plans to take the initiative in any case, a divided committee report may actually strengthen his position by paving the way for leadership.

Disagreement may involve anywhere from one member of a committee to every member, and may affect interim as well as final reports. One of the most thoroughly divided committees was the Uthwatt-Jenkins Committee on Leasehold. Its interim report (Cmd. 7706) was accompanied by two dissents; there was also a retrospective disagreement with the interim report by Lord Justice Jenkins, who replaced Lord Justice Uthwatt as chairman after the interim report had been completed and who feared that 'my signature of the [final report] might in the absence of any indication to the contrary be taken as implying my tacit approval of the [interim report]'. The final report of the Committee (Cmd. 7982) was signed subject to two reservations and one dissent. Another significant case was the report of the Beveridge Committee on Broadcasting (Cmd. 8116), which was accompanied by ten reservations, of which the chairman and every member signed at least one each! Moreover, one member (Selwyn Lloyd M.P.) wrote a dissenting Minority Report in favour of commercial broadcasting – which in fact became more significant than the corresponding majority recommendation in favour of a continuing monopoly.[27] On the other hand, Lord Simey wrote a reservation to the report of the Fulton Committee on the Civil Service (Cmnd. 3638) which amounted to a disagreement about only the diagnosis and not the proposed cure.

There is little to indicate what sort of royal commissions and departmental committees have been prone to disagreement. In spite of what might be expected, representative and expert committees have not given rise to more reservations and dissents than have impartial committees. If anything, the opposite is the case. Smaller committees, though, are naturally less likely to end in disagreement than are larger ones. Oddly enough, committees failing to reach unanimous agreement have been more likely than other committees to have had women members and academic members, but less likely to have had civil servant members. It would be rash indeed to attempt an explanation of phenomena like these![28]

27 The Minority Report (written largely by Sidney and Beatrice Webb) of the Hamilton Royal Commission on the Poor Laws (Cd. 4498) similarly gained greater fame than its majority report. See Margaret Cole (ed.), *The Webbs and Their Work* (London: Frederick Muller, 1949).

28 The politics of decision-making within committees and similar small groups is a fascinating subject in itself. Clearly some members of a committee have dominated others – as Dr

Agreement on a final report, whether unanimous or divided, marks the end for a royal commission or a departmental committee. The committee has done as instructed in its terms of reference and produced a report about it. The last act is for the chairman, on behalf of the committee, to forward the report to the minister or ministers who appointed the committee. Once this has been done, the royal commission or departmental committee *de facto* ceases to exist.

Norman Hunt did on the Fulton Committee on the Civil Service (Cmnd. 3638) and as Derek Senior did on the Maud Royal Commission on Local Government in England (Cmnd. 4040) – but a precise explanation of how committees make decisions is more difficult. For example, mathematics and game-theory have been used to try to explain the strategies of voting and the formation of coalitions in committees: see Duncan Black and R. A. Newing, *Committee Decisions with Complementary Valuation* (London: William Hodge, 1951), and Duncan Black, *The Theory of Committees and Elections* (Cambridge University Press, 1958); but these theories have not had much practical application as yet.

11
Adjournment and Aftermath

The last act of a royal commission or a departmental committee is the transmission of its report to the minister or ministers who appointed it. This done, an *ad hoc* committee like a royal commission or a departmental committee *de facto* ceases to exist. Some committees, of course, take much longer than others to finish their work, and this is reflected in the varying duration for which committees exist. Similarly, some committees can mobilise much more resources than others, and this is reflected in their varying costs. Once again, the overwhelming impression gained from an analysis of these committees is of their enormous flexibility in the face of widely differing tasks.

Once transmitted to the appropriate ministers, committee reports are usually published as official government documents and released to the general public. Reports, of course, reflect the activities of the committees which write them; so the range of their concerns, the flexibility of their procedures and the importance of public participation in their deliberations are all apparent to the reader of committee reports. But whatever its form, a committee report is only one event among many in government. There is no guarantee at all that its intended effects are realised or even that it have any effect at all. Thus, committee members – or former committees members as they now are – can only sit back and watch to see what kind of fate awaits their report at the hands of government and the public.

Duration

Unlike the manner in which it is appointed, the way in which a royal commission or a departmental committee comes to an end is not entirely clear. A committee normally adjourns itself *sine die* when it has signed what it regards as its final report. Strictly speaking, however, a committee cannot disband itself since it did not appoint itself. Ministers who appoint committees, on the other hand, normally do not bother to formally dissolve them when they have finished their work. Thus, the Fisher Committee on Scottish Local Government Law Consolidation, which was appointed over twenty years ago and signed its last report (Cmd. 8993) in October 1953, was 'never formally disbanded . . . [but] has been inactive for about ten years [i.e. since 1957]'.[1]

Occasionally, a committee feels it is desirable to remove any doubts by indicating that, for its part, it considers its mandate to have been discharged. This could be important in some cases, as when a committee has been asked to determine responsibility or blame for something. For example, the Courtney Committee appointed to examine the development and production of Tudor aircraft for British Airways Corporation explained in its final report (Cmd. 7478) that it had dealt with only certain marks of the aircraft and added,

> We are not aware of any matters affecting the other marks which require examination and we propose to regard the submission of this report as discharging our task. We understand that you [the Minister of Supply, who had appointed the Committee] concur in this view.

In only a few cases have committees actually had to be suspended by their appointing departments. The Amory Royal Commission on the Penal System in England and Wales was 'dissolved' before it could issue any report at all. This is reputed to have been due to irreconcilable differences of opinion among its members.[2] The former secretary of the Macmillan Committee on Land Registration in Scotland (Cmd. 7451) explained that his Committee was suspended for the following reasons:

> After the publication of its interim report the Committee was enlarged in September 1948 to consider the second head of its remit . . . In December 1948, however, the Chairman, Lord Macmillan, resigned his appointment because of ill health. No successor was appointed as Chairman and the inquiry was suspended. In reply to a Parliamentary Question in the House of Commons on 21st April 1953 the Joint Under-Secretary of State for Scotland said that the Secretary of State had encountered no desire on the part of the profession for any immediate changes . . . The Committee did not meet again after December 1948.

Finally, there is the interesting case of the Cunningham Committee on the Vassall Case, which issued what was intended to be only an interim report (Cmnd. 1871) just two weeks after its appointment because

> it will clearly take us some further time to complete our investigation of the facts of this case. In the meantime, you [the Prime Minister, who had

---

1 According to a private communication from an official in the Scottish Development Department.

2 According to a private communication from the former secretary; there is also a statement by the Prime Minister in *House of Commons Debates* (27 April 1966), Columns 703–5. See also the press report in the previous chapter, p. 182.

3 According to a private communication from the former secretary.

Table 11.1 Major royal commissions and departmental committees, 1945–69, by duration

duration	royal commissions only	all committees
less than 6 months	0	69
6 months–1 year	2	71
1–1½ years	0	62
1½–2 years	6	63
2–2½ years	3	33
2½–3 years	6	24
3–4 years	3	24
4–5 years	4	7
more than 5 years	0	5
total	24	358
approximate mean duration	2½ years	1½ years

Source: See Appendix B.

appointed the Committee] have directed us, in view of the nature of public comment about the relationship between Vassall and those for whom he had worked, to submit an interim report on this aspect of the case.

This interim report provoked an immediate debate in the House of Commons, and it was decided to appoint a statutory Tribunal of Inquiry to look into the whole affair. Thus, the activities of the original Cunningham Committee were 'overtaken' by the appointment of the Tribunal, and the Committee disbanded.[4]

For all practical purposes, a royal commission or a departmental committee may be regarded as having come to an end on the date on which its final report is signed. In most cases, this is within two years of the date of its appointment, but detailed information about the major postwar committees is given in Table 11.1. The average duration of a committee has been about a year and a half, although more than half of the committees actually took less time than this. Royal commissions alone took an average of one year more than departmental committees; they also varied less, none ever having taken as little or as much time as did some departmental committees.

One of the quickest committees to report was the Brook Inquiry into certain allegations about the misuse of official facilities for the circulation of private documents: the report (Cmnd. 583) appeared six days after the Inquiry had been appointed. Similarly, it took Sir Edwin Herbert only thirteen days to complete his investigations into the damages and casualties arising out of the attack on Port Said in 1956. Sir Edwin, who was appointed

4 According to a private communication from an official in the Treasury; see also the report of the Radcliffe Tribunal of Inquiry (Cmnd. 2009).

by virtue of his being President of the Law Society, flew out to Cyprus and the Middle East for a week's investigations on the spot and then submitted a report (Cmnd. 47) during the following week. Both these, however, were one-man committees. Among the bigger committees, the quickest took three weeks to complete its report, while the quickest royal commission took nine months.[5] At the other extreme, five of the major postwar committees – none of them, incidentally, a royal commission – lasted for more than five years. Slowest of all was the Black-Sheil Committee on the Supreme Court of Northern Ireland (Cmnd. 227), which needed more than eight years.

Perhaps the oddest case of all concerns a committee appointed by the Home Secretary in February 1946 which did not report until April 1968, more than twenty two years later! The Robertson-Austin Committee on Gas Cylinders and Containers had twelve members (half of them civil servants) and was appointed

> to examine matters relating to the manufacture and use of cylinders and containers and analogous vessels for compressed gases, and to advise on scientific and administrative questions arising thereon.

According to the Committee's report, the cause of the delay lay in 'the comprehensiveness of the Committee's work and the extensive nature of their report' as well as the fact that

> the postwar years have seen constant and rapid – indeed, unparalleled development in the methods and techniques of conveying substances under pressure. Time and again the Committee, having come within measurable distance of completing their report, have found themselves obliged to postpone its submission pending the study of some new aspect of their field of reference.[6]

Moreover, when (according to an official in the Home Office) the Committee circulated the first draft of its report for comment in 1961,

> the volume of comment from industry was so great that the whole report was thought to need further consideration, and a whole number of industrial representatives have attended all meetings of the Committee since 1961.[7]

Once a royal commission or a departmental committee has signed its final report, it is forwarded to the minister or ministers who originally appointed

---

5 Reference is to the McCarthy Committee of Inquiry into an Educational Dispute in Durham (Cmnd. 4152) and the Salmon Royal Commission on Tribunals of Inquiry (Cmnd. 3121) respectively.

6 The report was published (in mimeographed form) by the Fire Department of the Home Office in 1969.

7 From a private communication; see also the report in the *Sunday Times* (29 January 1967).

the committee. Reports of royal commissions are sent to the Home Secretary (or the Secretary of State for Scotland) who in turn sends a copy to the Queen. In cases where the appointing ministers no longer exercise the appropriate responsibilities or even no longer exist at all, reports are forwarded to other ministers who have taken over the relevant jurisdictions. Thus, for example, the Thorpe Committee on Allotments (Cmnd. 4166) was appointed by the Minister of Lands and Natural Resources in August 1965; but, when it reported in June 1969, the Committee pointed out that

> on the dissolution of the Ministry of Land and Natural Resources on 16 February 1967, the administration of the current allotments legislation in England passed to the Minister of Housing and Local Government while the Secretary of State assumed responsibility for allotments in Wales,

and submitted its report to the latter two ministers accordingly.

Published Reports

When the report is received by the appropriate minister or ministers, the immediate problem is whether to publish the report. It is difficult to know how many committee reports are not published, since the only reliable evidence for the existence of a committee is often the existence of its report. But it would presumably require some special circumstances to convince a committee that the fruits of its labours should not be published when those of so many others are. Nevertheless, there is some evidence of committee reports which were not published. Only one report of the Barlow Committee on Scientific Man-Power (Cmd. 6824), for example, was ever published; yet apparently there was also a second report. According to one of the former secretaries,

> the Committee went on after the [first] report of 27th May [1946] (my diary records) to a total of twenty two meetings, [i.e. seven more following the first report]. The later meetings were addressed to the idea of a further report about Engineering Man-Power and a draft report was seen by the Committee at their last meeting on 23rd July. However, this report never saw the light of day . . .[8]

Another example is given by Sir Alan Herbert:

> In 1943 Mr Attlee sent the late Lord Ammon, Sir Derrick Gunston and my humble self to prowl about Newfoundland and Labrador. We did not all entirely agree. The government, I believe, had made up their mind already what they intended to do, and were not very pleased when I recommended something else. We wrote three different reports: and none of them was published.[9]

8 From a private communication; see also Lord Morrison, *Government and Parliament*, 2nd ed. (London: Oxford University Press, 1959), pp. 330–1.

9 'Anything but Action?' in Ralph Harris (ed.), *Radical Reaction*, 2nd ed. (London: Hutchinson, 1961), p. 265n.

But such cases are probably most exceptional. Where reports may occasionally not be published, however, is when they are relatively minor interim reports. For example, the Fleck Committee on Windscale Piles (Cmnd. 471) produced 'a brief interim report . . . shortly before Christmas [1957]', but neither the report nor any indication of its purpose was ever published. But this too is unusual: most unpublished interim reports do subsequently appear as appendices to the final reports, as in the report of the Williams Committee on Milk Distribution (Cmd. 7414), for example. In one case where not even this procedure was adopted, the explanation offered seems somewhat bizarre:

> Our Interim Report was not published. The reasons for this we understand were that the financial position of the country [in 1949] precluded the immediate adoption of some of our recommendations which might have involved fresh Exchequer expenditure, and that another committee set up by your predecessor [as Minister] was still actively examining [a closely related matter]. . . .[10]

If these standards were applied to the interim or final reports of every committee, however, a lot of them would probably never be published!

A more common procedure, adopted for committees whose reports it is felt to be not in the public interest to publish, is abridgement or censorship of the report. The report of the Radcliffe Committee on Security Procedures in the Public Service (Cmnd. 1861), for example, was published but not in full, since 'it would be right to publish the Committee's recommendations, with their supporting argument, to the maximum extent compatible with the public interest and the requirements of security.'[11] Similarly, the Plowden Committee on the Aircraft Industry (Cmnd. 2583) was censored

> in the interests of military and commercial security. These omissions were made on the recommendation of the Committee, which received all evidence on a confidential basis. They are of minor significance in the context of the report as a whole and do not affect its substance.

The Plowden Group on Public Expenditure (Cmnd. 1732) sent a series of confidential reports to the Chancellor of the Exchequer as the investigation proceeded; the published report represents a consolidation of the non-confidential aspects of the Group's interim reports. The reports of the Vick Inquiry on Evasions of Petrol Rationing (Cmd. 7372) and the Bridges Committee on Security at the National Gallery (Cmnd. 1750) were not published in full for fear of what the reports might reveal of the various

10 Reference is to the Mackintosh Committee on Social Workers in the Mental Health Services (Cmd. 8260). Compare these principles with the argument put forward by Peter Shore, *Entitled to Know* (London: MacGibbon and Kee, 1966).

11 See also the report of the Salisbury Committee on Security (Cmd. 9715) as well as D. G. T. Williams, *Not in the Public Interest: the Problem of Security in a Democracy* (London: Hutchinson, 1965).

methods of evasion and security respectively involved.[12] Finally, the recent Radcliffe Committee on 'D' Notice Matters (Cmnd. 3309) had its report published because it had the foresight to draft it with publication in mind: with its report to the Prime Minister went 'a special Annex, which is not intended for publication', which dealt with the confidential aspects of the mandate (i.e. the question of cable vetting).

There seems little disposition to publish reports dealing particularly with Wales in Welsh. Only two major committees, the Ready Committee on Welsh Language Publishing (Cmd. 8661) and the Bowen Committee on Bilingual Traffic Signs (Cmnd. 5110), had their reports published in both English and Welsh; both reports appeared as single 'parallel-text' publications. Other committees have not had their reports published in Welsh, even other committees dealing with peculiarly Welsh matters like the Hughes Parry Committee on the Legal Status of the Welsh Language (Cmnd. 2785).

Most committee reports are published within a month or two of their submission to ministers. But about a quarter of the major postwar committees have had to wait at least three months, some of them a good deal longer. Sometimes these delays are understandable, as when the report is highly controversial or when some question of security is involved. In the case of the Vick Inquiry into Evasions of Petrol Rationing (Cmnd. 503), for example, it was announced to the press that *prima facie* evidence of evasion had been uncovered in the course of the Inquiry and this was to be investigated; the report did not appear (even in a suitably censored form) for another year and then only as an appendix to a government policy statement. In other cases, delays in publication are less easy to understand, as the following press report reveals:

PROCRASTINATION PIQUES PAGE

Sir Harry Page is getting rather fed up about the non-appearance of his report on National Savings. It is of little consolation to him that we are all equally fed up with the Government's high-handed suppression of the report and the inadequacy of the Treasury briefing – 'I'm sorry, we know nothing about it' – on the subject.

'It's not all that earth-shaking that it needs all this palaver', said Sir Harry in a rare moment of bitterness. He has cause to feel more annoyed than he reveals. The last-minute decision to withdraw publication Maundy Thursday (April 19) came after Sir Harry was already en route for London and the press briefing.

---

12 In the same way, there was a feeling at the time of the assassination of Dr Martin Luther King in Memphis, Tennessee, in April 1968 that would-be assassins had obtained a wealth of information about the techniques of a law-enforcement agency (the Federal Bureau of Investigation) from the report of the Warren Commission which investigated the assassination of President Kennedy (*Report of the President's Commission on the Assassination of President John F. Kennedy* [Washington: Government Printing Office, 1964]).

Table 11.2 Major royal commissions and departmental committees, 1945–69, by size of report(s)

number of pages in report(s)	royal commissions only	all committees
0–50	0	145
50–99	2	78
100–149	2	45
150–199	2	23
200–249	2	16
250–299	2	16
300–349	1	6
350–399	4	7
400 or more	8	20
no information or no report	1	2
total	24	*358*
mean size (approximate)	330 pages	110 pages

Note: Data do not include separately published volumes of oral or written evidence or of research papers; but do include interim reports, reservations and dissents.

Source: See Appendix B.

The wasted train journey from Manchester was irritating; even more irritating is the singular lack of communication there has been between Sir Harry and the powers that be which appointed him and his committee.

He has received no reason for nearly two months' delay; the Government has made 'no effort to contact me to find out what's wrong'; and his letter to the Chancellor inquiring for details, was merely acknowledged, albeit courteously.

'I don't see what's biting them', says Sir Harry. 'It's not all that contentious.' He went on: 'There's nothing that couldn't have been settled in half an hour's discussion.' His last note of asperity was: 'They've got to take the decision to publish some time. You can't govern without making up your mind.'[13]

The reports of postwar royal commissions, however, have never been subjected to delays of more than three months; their publication can thus be regarded as virtually automatic.

The reports of royal commissions and departmental committees in their published form vary widely in size but little in form. Table 11.2 shows the variations in size among the major postwar committees. The most obvious point is that royal commission reports have averaged approximately three times the average length of departmental committee reports. On the other hand, a significant number of committees have in fact produced

13 *The Times*, 12 June 1973. The report of the committee was published by the end of June 1973.

very short reports of only a few pages each: one in four departmental committee reports is less than thirty pages in length. The longest report was that of the Maud Royal Commission on Local Government in England (Cmnd. 4040) which came to more than one thousand pages in three volumes.[14] In at least one case, however, great length was perceived as being counter-productive since it would discourage those for whom it was intended from reading it: as the Geddes Committee on Shipbuilding (Cmnd. 2937) noted in its two-hundred-page report,

> We realise that our own conclusions and recommendations are likely to lead to widespread discussion in the industry and we think it important that everybody concerned should have access to a short summary of what we have in mind. We shall therefore be submitting separately a short summary of our report and we hope that arrangements can be made for a copy to be provided to everyone in shipbuilding.

The reports are rarely best-sellers even among government publications, although a number have done well: the report of the Denning Inquiry into The Security Service and Mr J. D. Profumo (Cmnd. 2152) sold 145,000 copies, and the report of the Robbins Committee on Higher Education (Cmnd. 2154) sold 50,000 copies.[15]

Committee reports follow a fairly standard form.[16] They may be published as Command Papers or as Non-Parliamentary Papers, except that the reports of royal commissions are invariably published as Command Papers.[17] The reports normally begin with a copy of the document by means of which the committee was appointed and a list of the chairman and members of the committee. The first chapter almost always describes the appointment and procedures of the committee. The body of the report discusses the evidence the committee has received, including any research it may have done, and

14 Separately published volumes of appendices, evidence or research are not included in these figures: see the note to Table 11.2.

15 The report of the Beveridge Committee on Social Insurance and Allied Services (Cmd. 6404) seems to have been the best-selling White Paper ever (280,000 copies). (Information supplied by HMSO and published in the *Sunday Times*, 4 March 1968.) Occasionally the price of a committee report is set deliberately low to encourage sales and public discussion of the report; for example, the report of the Samuel Royal Commission on the Coal Industry (Cmd. 2600) was 295 pages long and sold for just one shilling.

16 A nice illustration of this occurred a few years ago in the United States with the appearance of an apocryphal committee report entitled, *Report from Iron Mountain on the Possibility and Desirability of Peace*, ed. L. C. Lewin (New York: Delta, 1967). Its major claim to credibility lay in the impeccably official style in which it was written!

17 Because they are technically papers of the Crown and so must be presented to Parliament 'by Command'. See Chapter 3 above for a discussion of the differences between and significance of Command and Non-Parliamentary Papers. One disadvantage of Command Papers is that they are rarely illustrated – although the report of the Jennings Royal Commission on Common Land (Cmnd. 462) was exceptional – whereas Non-Parliamentary Papers often are. See also F. M. G. Willson, 'Departmental Reports' *Public Administration*, XXX (1952), pp. 163–73.

(if it is appropriate) sets out its reasons for favouring one course of action or one set of recommendations over the others proposed to it. The last chapter usually includes a summary of all the committee's views and its recommendations, plus a paragraph of fulsome thanks to the secretary and his staff.[18] The reports are normally signed by the chairman and members, although sometimes (especially in the case of interim reports) the chairman alone may sign.[19] Finally, there is often an appendix listing the witnesses from whom evidence has been received; and there may also be other appendices giving details about the evidence and other research, about the practice in foreign countries, about previous committees on the same or related subjects, and various other peripheral matters.

Some committees also have some or all of their evidence and research published along with or even before publication of the final report. This is true of most but not all royal commissions. The Maud Royal Commission on Local Government in England (Cmnd. 4040), for example, published its research papers and the evidence presented to it long before its final report was published.[20] On the other hand, not many departmental committees have had their evidence published, and even then it may only be in the body of the final report. The Beveridge Committee on Broadcasting (Cmd. 8116) had some of its evidence published, for example, and so did the Fulton Committee on the Civil Service (Cmnd. 3638); but most did not.[21] The Radcliffe Committee on the Working of the Monetary System (Cmnd. 827) published the written evidence which had been 'of substantial assistance to us' and all of its oral testimony. The Robbins Committee on Higher Educa-

18 It is not clear if there is an informal scale among committees, whereby a secretary described as merely 'conscientious' has not done as good a job as one described as 'indispensable', and so on! But one or two committees have not said anything at all about their secretaries e.g. the Franklin Committee on Punishments (Cmd. 8429). Moreover, it appears that Lord Denning, in his report on the Security and Mr J. D. Profumo (Cmnd. 2151), simply copied a paragraph of thanks verbatim from the final report of the Willink Royal Commission on the Police (Cmnd. 1728)!

19 The Report of the Ince Committee on the Legal Status of the Welsh Language (Cmnd. 2785) was not signed at all. The interim report of the Waverley Committee on Coastal Flooding was signed by the chairman alone (Cmd. 9165).

20 Unlike the evidence of some pre-war royal commissions, none of the evidence of postwar royal commissions was ever published as a Command Paper, although the Pilkington Commission on Doctors' and Dentists' Remuneration (Cmnd. 939) did publish a 'Statistical Supplement' as a Command Paper (Cmnd. 1064). The Tedder Royal Commission on University Education in Dundee (Cmd. 8514), for example, did not have its evidence published at all.

21 The evidence of the Beveridge Committee was in fact published twice, once as an appendix to the main report and once separately as Cmnd. 8117 – the only time since the war that evidence has been published as a separate Command Paper. The Radcliffe Committee on 'D' Notice Matters (Cmnd. 3309) also had its evidence published as part of its report. Recently, the practice has developed of publishing evidence as a supplement to the report; thus, the evidence of the Phelps Brown Committee on Labour in Building and Civil Engineering (Cmnd. 3714) appeared as Cmnd. 3714-I.

tion (Cmnd. 2154) was promised that

> Records of the oral evidence we took, the written evidence on which our discussions were based and a number of other memoranda are to be published. Arrangements are being made for most of the rest of the written evidence we received to be available for public inspection [deposited in six] libraries and other places in various parts of the country.

Naturally, the publication of evidence given originally in confidence requires the approval of its authors. Where publication is intended, permission is normally secured at the time of presentation. Another alternative is to do as the Littlewood Committee on Experiments on Animals (Cmnd. 2641) did, and to permit witnesses to publish their own evidence if they so desire as long as they wait until the committee has submitted its own report. Most committees, however, do not have their evidence published.

When the report of a committee is published, there may be a formal statement in Parliament about the government's attitude towards the report and its conclusions. Such a statement may endorse the committee's recommendations and promise immediate action to implement them. Or the statement may be noncommittal, indicating that the government has not yet made its mind up about the committee's findings – or that it rejects them completely! Occasionally, the government may make quite clear that it does not accept a committee's report, but ministers are understandably unwilling to repudiate committee recommendations outright, since their own decisions are almost bound to appear more politically motivated in comparison. In fact, the more common practice is for no formal Parliamentary statement to be made at all. This does not, of course, prevent the report of a committee being brought up in debate or by means of a Question. The tendency is for ministers to formally announce in Parliament the more important and the more contentious committee reports and to deal with the others if and when they are brought up.

Costs

Royal commissions and departmental committees also vary a great deal in their cost. Committees may incur expenses for office accommodation, research, fees for accountants or consultants, travelling, special secretarial services (such as shorthand transcriptions of oral evidence), postage and telephone charges, and so on. They may also be charged for the salaries and wages of full-time staff, but not normally for those of civil servants on part-time duty on the grounds that the expense of such permanent officials would be incurred anyway regardless of their particular work for a committee.[22] Finally, there are the inevitable costs of printing and publishing the report

22 See the comments of the Ross Royal Commission on the Press (Cmd. 7700) on the nature of its expenses.

Table 11.3 Major royal commissions and departmental committees, 1945–69, by net cost

net cost	royal commissions only	all committees
less than £100	0	38
£100–£500	0	73
£500–£1,000	0	40
£1,000–£5,000	1	54
£5,000–£10,000	1	8
£10,000–£50,000	15	35
£50,000–£100,000	4	7
over £100,000	1	3
no information	1	95
total	23	353

Notes: Net costs are in real pounds and do not include the costs of printing and publishing nor any revenue derived from sales of the reports, evidence or research reports. Of the committees for which there was no information, it should be recognised that many of these probably did not report costs because their net costs amounted to very little or even nothing at all.

Source: See Appendix B.

of the committee and possibly some of its evidence or research. Only a small fraction of all these costs will be recouped from sales of the report.

Leaving aside the expenses of printing and publishing, the costs of major committees in the period since the war have ranged from nothing at all to nearly half a million pounds (see Table 11.3). The Harman Committee on Chancery Chambers (Cmnd. 967), for example, incurred no expenses at all and the Howitt Committee on Unpatented Inventions (Cmd. 9788) reported expenses of only one pound seventeen shillings! On the other hand, the Crowther-Kilbrandon Royal Commission on the Constitution (Cmnd. 5460) cost the public purse over £430,000 before it had finished. The most expensive departmental committee since the war was the Robbins Committee on Higher Education (Cmnd. 2154), which cost £128,700. In general, royal commissions are likely to cost between £10,000 and £50,000 each, whereas departmental committees are likely to cost less than £5,000 each. These costs are by no means exorbitant. Committees appointed prior to 1945 have cost as much as or more than many postwar committees: for example, the Simon-Henderson Royal Commission on Population (Cmd. 7695) appointed in 1944 cost £201,371. British committees also compare favourably in cost terms with similar committees in other countries: the Royal Commission on Bilingualism and Biculturalism is reported to have cost the Canadian Government nearly $10,000,000. Many of the major postwar committees in Britain have cost really very little. Some of them must rank among the best bargains the taxpayer ever gets from his government!

The costs of royal commissions are always voted in a distinct Vote in the Civil Appropriation Accounts entitled 'Royal Commissions, Etc.' (or, as it was called prior to 1928, 'Temporary Commissions'). This Vote is described as the 'Account of the sum expended . . . for the salaries and other expenses of Royal Commissions, committees, special inquiries, etc. . . .' It includes the costs of salaries, shorthand, travelling and incidental expenses, advertising and other publicity and special surveys; but it does not include certain overhead costs, such as accommodation and the use of official postal facilities. The Vote also includes a lot of other items which are not royal commissions, including statutory and standing committees and other bodies (and even the 'Treasury Pool of Shorthand Writers' at times!). The costs of departmental committees may also be provided for in this same Vote, or they may just be included in the regular Votes of their appointing departments. In the latter case, a committee may be itemised explicitly or it may be paid for out of an appropriate item or items in the Accounts at the discretion of the department or departments concerned.[23]

It is partly this variety of procedures which makes it difficult to determine the degree of independence enjoyed by royal commissions and departmental committees with respect to their expenditures. Some committees seem to have had almost a free hand and an unlimited budget, whereas other committees have had to justify the need for every pound. In general, committees must work out their own relationships with their respective officials. Although committees are nominally free to dispose of the funds allocated to them in whatever ways they see fit, their actual behaviour is bound to affect the level of funds made available to them. Relatively costly committees will, therefore, probably have had to justify their need for and demonstrated their ability to make effective use of above-average levels of funding. Financial control of royal commissions and departmental committees is thus largely the result of informal agreement between chairman and departmental officials. Here no doubt is one area in which an experienced chairman can be useful to a committee!

It is interesting to aggregate the annual net costs of the major postwar royal commissions and departmental committees to see how much has actually been spent on them. The results of such calculations are shown in Table 11.4 and illustrated in the accompanying figure. Although relatively much less numerous, royal commissions can be seen to have accounted for over half of the more than two million pounds which have been spent on committees during the past quarter of a century. Moreover, more has been spent on the last six royal commissions as on the previous eighteen together.

23 Sir Herbert Brittain, *The British Budgetary Process* (London: Allen and Unwin, 1959), Chapter 12, discusses departmental discretion in the spending of public money. See also the Treasury's guide, *Government Accounting* (London: HMSO, 1969).

Table 11.4 Total net costs of major royal commissions and departmental committees, 1945–69, by financial years

financial year	royal commissions only (£ thousands)	all committees (£ thousands)	total public expenditure (£ millions)	index of expenditure
1944–5	39.6	42.9	761.5	59.9
1945–6	39.6	45.3	815.9	55.5
1946–7	48.1	54.5	1,208.0	45.1
1947–8	58.7	63.8	1,367.5	46.7
1948–9	57.1	64.7	1,712.1	37.8
1949–50	18.6	32.5	1,904.4	17.1
1950–1	19.9	34.4	1,920.9	17.9
1951–2	21.2	26.2	3,237.0	8.1
1952–3	31.5	39.6	2,909.8	13.6
1953–4	43.3	58.5	2,916.0	20.1
1954–5	47.3	57.0	2,909.1	19.6
1955–6	29.8	42.5	3,364.7	12.6
1956–7	29.9	44.5	3,366.8	13.2
1957–8	27.4	52.6	3,625.4	14.5
1958–9	26.3	61.0	3,857.7	15.8
1959–60	15.6	48.8	4,075.2	12.0
1960–1	29.7	81.7	4,457.4	18.3
1961–2	32.4	146.1	4,387.9	33.3
1962–3	6.7	96.5	4,640.6	20.8
1963–4	0	75.9	5,147.2	14.7
1964–5	0	57.6	5,613.5	10.3
1965–6	46.3	125.1	6,126.9	20.4
1966–7	167.3	202.9	7,157.6	28.3
1967–8	197.2	288.8	8,855.3	32.6
1968–9	147.5	288.2	9,868.5	29.2
1969–70	0	252.0	11,065.3	22.7
total	1,324.4	2,439.4		
mean	53.0	97.6		

Notes: (1) financial years are from 1 April to 31 March.
(2) net costs are total costs in real pounds less the costs of printing and publishing reports and any revenue derived from their sale.
(3) annual net costs are calculated by allocating individual committee net costs according to the number of months of the respective financial years during which each committee was in existence. Totals do not add due to rounding. Committees reporting no net costs are ignored (see Table 11.3).
(4) total public expenditure is derived from the annual Civil Appropriations Accounts.
(5) the index of expenditure is designed to allow for changes in the value of the pound and in the general level of government activities. The index is obtained by dividing the net costs of all committees by total public expenditure and multiplying the quotient by one million. The early part of this index is of dubious value owing to the gradual postwar re-integration of classified wartime appropriations into the Civil Appropriation Accounts.

Source: For data on committees, see Appendix B, p. 239.

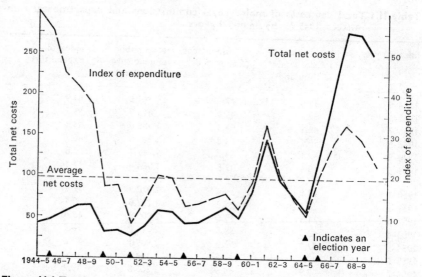

Figure 11.1 Total net costs and index of expenditures of major royal commissions and departmental committees, 1945-69, by financial years

Both these facts reflect the trend towards greater emphasis on research (see Chapter 9 above), especially by the most recent royal commissions.

Taking royal commissions and departmental committees together, the data reveal at least two important tendencies. First of all, there appears to have been a definite although still gradual increase in the amount of money spent annually on these committees. The average annual net cost of major royal commissions and departmental committees over the past quarter-century has been about £98,000, but this is roughly twice what it was in the 1950s. To some extent, this increase is due merely to inflation: committee costs are recorded in real (not constant) pounds. But it also reflects rising levels of public expenditure generally: total government spending has increased well over ten times since the years immediately after the war. By constructing an 'index' of public expenditure on royal commissions and departmental committees, however, it is possible to examine the rate of spending independently of both inflation and the changing role of government. Even so, the overall gradual growth in spending is still apparent (see Figure 11.1). Leaving aside the years immediately following the war (when the figures on total public expenditure are not really comparable due to the gradual re-integration of classified defence appropriations), annual spending on royal commissions and departmental committees has roughly doubled over the past two decades. Governments, therefore, are paying more for the use of advisory committees, and most of this increase is probably a reflection of more extensive efforts to carry out research.

The other tendency suggested by the data in Table 11.4 is a fairly definite cyclical pattern. Committee costs, it seems, build up to a peak, fall off and then rise to another peak roughly four to six years later. This same cycle appears in both the unadjusted and the adjusted cost figures. The most plausible explanation for this phenomenon is that committees are, after all, part of the political as well as the administrative scene in Britain. Every one of the six 'low' points in both the graphs in Figure 11.1 – i.e. the points of minimum expenditure – corresponds to an election year. Governments, it seems, like to appoint committees early on in their political lives in order to have them complete their reports in time for the next election – not only so that the activities of the committees can reflect favourably on the government but also so that public expenditure in an election year can be slightly reduced!

The Fate of Committee Reports

At first glance, it might be thought that, since royal commissions and departmental committees are officially appointed by the government and since public money is used to pay for their activities, their recommendations would, at least in most cases, be automatically accepted and implemented as soon as practicable. But there is another point to be considered. Royal commissions and departmental committees are and must remain advisory in nature. Governments cannot abdicate their responsibility under the constitution to make and implement policies, regardless of the merits of any advice they may receive from any source. Whatever a royal commission or a departmental committee may recommend, it is still the government which must govern. Accordingly, a government has complete discretion in its treatment of committee reports and recommendations.

The more popular belief seems actually to be that committee recommendations are, if anything, automatically ignored. Forty years ago the typical reception of a royal commission report was described in the following terms:

> On the day of publication [of the report], *The Times* would print a good summary and an appreciative leading article. The less Olympian papers would be content with slogans . . . with inset portrait of the Chairman (if a peer). There would be a few letters in the Sunday papers, a few questions in the House; possibly a debate on the motion for adjournment. Then the report would die . . . gently die, to rise again (fractionally) in professorial lectures or in answers to questions . . . in university examinations.[24]

Many people would probably suspect that this is still a fairly accurate description of what happens to the reports of most committees.

24 See the contribution by Major Greenwood in Lord Kennet, 'On the Value of Royal Commissions in Sociological Research', *Journal of the Royal Statistical Society*, New Series, C. III (1937), p. 400.

In fact, the fate of a committee's report can range all the way from the kind of total disregard described above to wholesale acceptance and implementation of its recommendations. To give an example, the recommendations of the du Parcq Royal Commission on Justices of the Peace were accepted in large measure and formed the basis of broad and sweeping legislative changes.[25] On the other hand, the recommendations of the Willink Royal Commission on Betting, Lotteries and Gaming were ignored, at least for the next decade following the Commission's report.[26] These examples could be multiplied, and illustrations could be provided of a whole range of fates between these two extremes.[27] But the meaning of all these examples would be open to question in a fundamental way. How can it be proved in any particular case that a committee's recommendations really *caused* the specified changes which are discovered to have followed the publication of its report?

For one thing, there is the problem of the lapse of time. It is a matter of popular belief that the recommendations of royal commissions and departmental committees normally take a fairly long time to be implemented even when they are not totally disregarded. Professor Harold Laski once estimated that,

> On the average, in our system of government, it takes nineteen years for the recommendations of a unanimous report of a Royal Commission to assume statutory reform [*sic*]; and if the Commission is divided in its opinion, it takes, again on the average, about thirty years for some of its recommendations to become statutes.[28]

Laski does not explain how he arrived at this conclusion, but that it is widely shared is revealed in an amusing exchange which once took place in the House of Commons:

> *Mr Leslie Hale:* I have always taken the view that the period of gestation which goes between the conception of an idea and its realisation is not the

---

25 See the report of the Commission (Cmd. 7463) and the subsequent Justices of the Peace Act, 1949 (12, 13 and 14 Geo. VI, Chapter 101). Similarly, the government announced that it would accept the recommendations of the Maud Royal Commission on Local Government in England on the same day as it published the Commission report (Cmnd. 4040) – although the subsequent change of government made this statement rather academic.

26 See the discussion of this and several other cases of neglect in Sir Alan Herbert, 'Anything but Action?', in Ralph Harris (ed.), *Radical Reaction*, 2nd rev. ed. (London: Hutchinson, 1961), pp. 269–79.

27 For example, Professor Victor Wiseman says that the government adopted exactly seventy of the ninety five recommendations of the Franks Committee on Administrative Tribunals and Inquiries (Cmnd. 218); see H. V. Wiseman, *Politics in Everyday Life* (Oxford: Blackwell, 1966), p. 75. See also Sir Ivor Jennings, *Parliament*, 2nd ed. (Cambridge University Press, 1957), pp. 211–20, for a number of earlier examples.

28 H. J. Laski, *Parliamentary Government in England* (London: Allen and Unwin, 1938), p. 117.

period for argument about the precise appearance of the child which is to be born. Once the idea is conceived we should let it develop without trying to limit it too much . . .

Mr James Griffiths: . . . Mrs Beatrice Webb used to say and deplore that from the beginning of an idea until its adoption in this country the average period was thirty years.

Mr Hale: I forget the period of gestation of an elephant. One of my hon. Friends says that it is eighteen months . . .

Mr Wedgwood Benn: I remember, because it is ten percent of the period that it takes for the recommendations of a royal commission to be implemented.

Mr Hale: My hon. Friend is generous to Royal Commissions.[29]

At a distance of thirty or even fifteen years, however, it becomes very dubious whether the relationship between the recommendations of a committee and the eventual reforms is in fact a causal one.

Secondly, there is the problem of assessing how close must be the similarity between a committee's recommendations and subsequent changes in official policy and actions in order for there to be a causal connection between the two. On the one hand, there are cases of committee recommendations appearing word for word in statutory form.[30] On the other hand, it could be argued in some cases that any official action where none was planned is largely the result of a committee's recommendations even if quite different recommendations – such as those of a dissenting minority report – are actually adopted.[31]

Thirdly, even in cases where there is some acceptable degree of similarity between a committee's recommendations and subsequent reforms and even where the time-lag between the two events is deemed to be without significance – even so, there need not be any causal connection involved. Recommendations by a committee may merely confirm official decisions made before its appointment or on the basis of quite different considerations from those produced by the committee. In other words, the reforms apparently caused by the committee's recommendations might have been undertaken even if the committee had made contrary proposals or even if it had never been appointed at all.

The difficulty is that the effects of a committee's recommendations do not lie wholly or even largely in its own hands. There are some tactics and devices which a committee may use to help 'sell' their recommendations, but their

---

29 *House of Commons Debates*, 548 (27 January 1956), Columns 547–8.

30 For example, compare the recommendations of the Reading Committee on Highway Law Consolidation (Cmnd. 630) with the provisions of the Highways Act, 1959 (7 and 8 Eliz. II, Chapter 25).

31 See, for example, Selwyn Lloyd's dissent to the report of the Beveridge Committee on Broadcasting (Cmd. 8116).

effectiveness still depends on a great many factors beyond its control and even beyond its powers of influence. Royal commissions and departmental committees are above all advisory committees. They have no powers of execution. The fate of their recommendations lies in hands other than their own.

No doubt the acceptance of their recommendations must be a source of considerable satisfaction to members of a committee, just as rejection or (perhaps worse) complete disregard must be a bitter disappointment. But these feelings need not be entirely justified. A royal commission or a departmental committee should not really be praised or blamed simply on the basis of the apparent fate of its recommendations. As the next chapter tries to show, evaluating the role of these committees in British government is far from easy.

12
Conclusion and Assessment

It is widely recognised that the 'golden age' of royal commissions is a thing of the nineteenth-century past.[1] What is not so universally appreciated is that, taken together, royal commissions and departmental committees are still, and have been throughout the twentieth century, a major institution of government. The proposition advanced in this study (see Chapter 1) is essentially that this popularity is due to two things: the flexibility and adaptiveness of royal commissions and departmental committees in the face of the different kinds of challenges they face, and their role as mechanisms for facilitating public participation in government. This in turn derives from a special ability to reflect both the 'art' and the 'science' of government.

A Major Institution of Government

The appointment of royal commissions and departmental committees has remained above a fairly substantial annual level almost continuously since records began. Throughout the seven decades since the turn of the present century, the number of committees in existence each year has only once (during the Second World War) fallen below the level set in 1900. It is true that royal commissions represent a declining proportion of the total number of committees, but this proportion has never been a large part of the total number. It is also true that the total number of committees has gone down slightly at certain times (as it did in the 1930s, for example), but these changes can always be related to contemporary economic and political events. It is fair to conclude that, throughout this century, royal commissions and departmental committees have been a constant feature of government in Britain.

In the quarter-century since 1945, there have been (on average) sixty royal commissions and departmental committees in existence every year. It is estimated that there have been over six hundred new committees appointed within this same period. (This means that roughly one third of the com-

1 H. M. Clokie and J. W. Robinson, *Royal Commissions of Inquiry* (Stanford University Press, 1937).

mittees in existence each year were appointed during that year.) Looked at in another way, these figures show that, on average, a new royal commission or departmental committee has been appointed every fortnight since 1945. There is no disputing their popularity.

Nor is it any longer possible to raise any serious questions about the constitutional legitimacy of royal commissions and departmental committees.[2] Quite apart from theoretical arguments on both sides, the vast number of precedents must now surely be regarded as conclusive. In any case, it is a well-established constitutional convention that ministers may seek whatever advice is necessary to enable them to carry out their responsibilities, and there is nothing about royal commissions and departmental committees to make them an exception to this general rule. The appointment of such committees may be criticised on various grounds, but it is no longer credible to make a case against them on constitutional grounds.

At the same time, it has to be admitted that not every detail of the constitutional position of royal commissions and departmental committees is entirely clear. There is still some doubt on at least three points: namely, their accountability to Parliament, their powers of *subpoena* and their status following a change of government.

Ministers are clearly not accountable to Parliament for the activities of royal commissions and departmental committees in the same way as they are for the activities of their own departments and civil servants. Rather, royal commissions and departmental committees are, in this respect, in somewhat the same position as nationalised industries.[3] On the other hand, royal commissions and departmental committees spend public monies voted by Parliament in departmental or other appropriations, and ministers are, of course, responsible to Parliament for the expenditure of these appropriations.

Secondly, there is the question of the power of royal commissions and departmental committees to compel the attendance of witnesses and the production of papers. Royal commissions are invariably granted just such powers in their warrants of appointment; however, these warrants and the powers in them are conferred by the Crown and not by Parliament, so that it is very doubtful that the courts would enforce these powers if called upon to do so. On the other hand, royal commissions as well as departmental committees may be granted subpoena powers by an Act of Parliament – the Tribunals of Inquiry (Evidence) Act, 1921 – and a special procedure has

---

2 Even the most determined of modern critics, Sir Alan Herbert, does not make this accusation; see his 'Anything but Action?' in Ralph Harris (ed.), *Radical Reaction*, 2nd ed. (London: Hutchinson, 1961).

3 See D. N. Chester and Nona Bowring, *Questions in Parliament* (London: Oxford University Press, 1962), p. 296; and D. N. Chester, 'Public Corporations and the Classification of Administrative Bodies', *Political Studies*, 1 (1953), pp. 34–52. On the accountability of nationalised industries in general, see Lord Morrison of Lambeth, *Government and Parliament* (London: Oxford University Press, 1959), Chapter 12.

been established for this purpose; however, the results have not been found altogether satisfactory.[4]

Thirdly, there is the question of the status of a departmental committee following a change of government. A royal commission is nominally appointed by the Crown and so is not affected by a change of government; but a departmental committee could be held to be the adviser of a specific government or minister, whose defeat or departure would mean *ipso facto* the termination of the committee's mandate. In fact, there seems never to have been any misunderstanding on this point, and no committee has reported being brought to a premature end for this reason; however, the strict legal position is not clear.

There is little sign of much desire to clarify any of these matters. In all probability clarification will not occur unless and until some serious dispute arises. It has been suggested, however, that one way of resolving some of these doubts would be to make the appointment of each separate royal commission or departmental committee subject to approval by Parliament.[5] Such a procedure would presumably clarify the direct accountability of these committees to Parliament, facilitate the granting of subpoena powers (if desired), and remove any doubts about their status following a change of government or minister. The main weakness of this proposal is that it would probably also lead to a fairly drastic reduction in the number of royal commissions and departmental committees actually appointed – and to the corresponding growth of a similar but less formal and less open kind of committee appointed without recourse to Parliamentary sanction. Ministers would find it intolerable to have their advisers vetted by Parliament every time they wanted to appoint a group of them to be a committee, and it would clearly be impossible for Parliament to forbid ministerial resort to any form of collective advice except that which it had specifically approved.

It seems probable, therefore, that the precise constitutional position of royal commissions and departmental committees will remain unclear until specific difficulties arise requiring a decision or a precedent one way or the other. But this area of vagueness should not be construed as raising any question about the constitutional legitimacy *per se* of royal commissions and departmental committees. On the latter point, there can no longer be any doubt. The sheer numbers of these committees appointed during the present century alone leave no other conclusion possible but that they are a legitimate and significant institution of government.

Committee 'Abuses'

In spite of (or perhaps because of) their widespread popularity, the appointment of royal commissions and departmental committees has always had its

4 (II Geo. V., Chapter 7). See also Chapters 2 and 8 above and the reports of the Salmon Royal Commission on Tribunals of Inquiry (Cmnd. 3121) and the Salmon Committee on Contempt of Tribunals of Inquiry (Cmnd. 4078).

5 Sir Alan Herbert, *op. cit.*, p. 293.

critics. Most such critics nowadays base their case on a distinction similar to the one advanced in Chapter 6 above: namely, that between the *substantial* and the *political* reasons for appointing committees. Critics contend that committees are appointed primarily for political rather than substantial reasons, and that appointment for political reasons is an 'abuse' of the institution.

Critics who maintain that governments abuse royal commissions and departmental committees have three principal lines of attack. First of all, it is argued, royal commissions and departmental committees are – or ought to be – unnecessary. If they are appointed, therefore, it must be as a substitute for any more positive action. Secondly, even if they are not intended as a substitute for action, they are designed to get the government 'off the hook' by postponing the need for any more positive action. Finally, even if neither of these charges can be proved, critics argue that in any case the findings of royal commissions and departmental committees usually have no effect on any subsequent action by the government. Thus, Joshua Toulmin Smith was persuaded to brand these committees as 'pernicious' institutions of government.[6]

The difficulty with all these charges of 'abuse' is not that they are wrong, for in fact there is some truth to them. Rather it is that the criticisms are misdirected. Other institutions of government are similarly 'abused', and there is no evidence that royal commissions and departmental committees suffer more than others. Besides, what is 'abuse' from one point of view may quite well be good tactics from another: abuse is in the eye of the beholder. In any case, the fact that an institution is abused is surely at least as much an indictment of the political system which abuses it as it is of the institution itself.

Royal commissions and departmental committees are unnecessary, it is argued; their appointment is *prima facie* evidence of a failure to govern.[7] Parliament and the Civil Service, it is maintained, possess or ought to possess whatever expertise is necessary for governing the country. Except in a few special cases, therefore, resort to groups of outside advisers is unnecessary. This argument is based on a rather ingenuous view of government. If government were simply a matter of expertise, there might be some justice to this charge – although Parliament could similarly be declared unnecessary beside an expert Civil Service! In fact, of course, government is far more than merely a matter of expertise. And the argument that royal commissions and departmental committees can or should contribute nothing to it suggests a failure to understand the process of government.

Nevertheless, the appointment of a royal commission or a departmental

6 Joshua Toulmin Smith, *Government by Commissions Illegal and Pernicious* (London: Sweet, 1849).

7 This is Sir Alan Herbert's main criticism of royal commissions and departmental committees in *op. cit.*, pp. 263–5 and *passim*. See also Brian Chapman, *British Government Observed* (London: Allen and Unwin, 1963), p. 32.

committee sometimes does serve as a substitute for action. A committee may well find that further action is not justified: that, in spite of initial impressions or in spite of pressures from certain segments of society, the public interest does not demand any significant change in the status quo. It can be argued that the bound volumes of a committee's report, especially when they present comprehensive plans for change, can have a kind of vicarious effect. Once the committee has reported, there is a tendency to feel the problem has been adequately dealt with and that nothing further need be done. Examination-and-publicity-by-committee is equated with solution. If, however, enough people feel this way, then perhaps the public interest has been well served by the removal of what was a false problem. If not, then proponents of change will have been given a valuable new weapon in their struggle for improvements. In other words, to say that a royal commission or a departmental committee has served as a substitute for action is not necessarily to prove abuse. There may well be times when no further action is justified, or times when the substitute strengthens the case for the real thing.

The second main line of attack is that, even if royal commissions and departmental committees are useful, the fact remains that they often have the effect of postponing more positive steps to deal with the problem at issue. In this connection, critics like to draw attention to the fact that the average length of ministerial tenure of office is very close to the average duration of a committee, so that a minister is likely to have changed departments before his committees produce any reports! Thus, William Cory, a nineteenth-century historian, described royal commissions as 'evasion through pretence of sceptical docility'.[8] Harold Wilson is reported to have once remarked that royal commissions and departmental committees 'take minutes and waste years'.[9] The most colourful formulation of this criticism was made by Lord Kennet in a discussion before the Royal Statistical Society in 1937; according to the minutes of that meeting,[10]

He [Lord Kennet] would like to detain the meeting with a few remarks on the natural history of Royal Commissions. It was known to all that the functions of the Governors of a democracy were largely the functions of a medicine man. They had to distract the attention of democracy as a whole from really vital matters by displays calculated to keep them happily occupied – a function in which they received the greatest and most constant assistance from the press. Anyone who, like himself, was a superficial student of anthropology, would know that one of the favourite devices of

8 William Cory, *A Guide to Modern English History*, Part II (London: Kegan Paul, Trench, 1882), p. 379, with reference to the 1834 Royal Commission on Irish Church Revenues.

9 Quoted by Eric Lubbock, 'Have Royal Commissions Had Their Day?', *The Times* (13 December 1966).

10 As reported in Lord Kennet, chairman, 'On the Value of Royal Commissions in Sociological Research', *Journal of the Royal Statistical Society*, New Series, C. III (1937), p. 408.

the medicine man was a tribal dance, and in order to persuade his tribe that something very important was going on in the way of activity, he would put up a dance in the middle of the tribal circle. That was the first function of a Royal Commission – a tribal dance to persuade the general public to believe that something very active was in progress. A continued study of the ways of the medicine man would bring out another device – the medicine hut. This was a hut shrouded by curtains into which he retired for a long period with the object of persuading the tribe that something very important was going on and that it was essential that they should wait for his emergence. This was the second function [of a royal commission], and both were totally illegitimate.

There was a third function, even more illegitimate, and that was the promotion of the dog-fight. When a Government finds itself extremely hard put to it to distract the attention of the public from one of the fundamental ills for which the public expects a remedy from the Government, and for which the Government is sorry it can find no remedy, it promotes a dog-fight between the people with different views, and for starting a dog-fight there is no method so valuable as that of a Royal Commission.

He would make one further observation upon the natural history of a Royal Commission. Like other drugs (if he might be allowed to change the metaphor), if it were to be used efficiently, it must be used sparingly, or it became exhausted in its effect. He had known Governments, of which he had himself been a humble member, which had made too great a use of the dope of a Royal Commission with the consequence that it lost its effect. He had indeed known a time when a self-denying ordinance had to be passed by a succeeding Government that no further Royal Commissions should be set up because the name had become a matter for derision. No Government more deserved the hatred of its successors than one which exhausted the use of this valuable method of distracting the attention of the public.

If royal commissions and departmental committees are used for postponing action, then they are symptoms of a tactical requirement of government. Governments determined to postpone action on some matter can find other ways of achieving the same result without appointing a royal commission or a departmental committee. Even Parliament may be used by a government to help postpone the need for action. Nor is it clear that royal commissions and departmental committees are more frequently used to gain time than are other institutions of government. In fact, it is questionable whether the use of royal commissions and departmental committees as a delaying device is really very sound tactics. These committees are bodies over which the government has relatively little control. The result is that they may well turn out to have the effect of keeping alive interest in a problem which, left on its own,

would have died a natural death. A committee may also lend new respect-
ability to fringe views by appearing to give them an official hearing. When
eventually it reports, moreover, a committee may have the effect of redoub-
ling pressures for action.[11] Thus, to the extent that royal commissions and
departmental committees are used as delaying devices, they are not alone in
this use. Moreover, they are not even an especially 'safe' way of causing
delay.

Nor is the use of royal commissions and departmental committees in this
way necessarily an abuse. Delay can be a legitimate political and administrative tactic. Few people would insist that democratic principles require that
a government be immediately responsive to every interest which clamours for
attention. A government has a mandate to govern, which means balancing
its own conception of what is the best policy with the various expressions of
public opinion, not just reacting automatically to the latter. Thus, delay can
be both legitimate and useful. It can provide a test of staying-power: is the
pressure for change more than a passing whim? Delay can also provide time
for officials to prepare suitable legislation. Delay can allow for hearing from
other, less vocal but no less legitimate interests, and so on. Of course, delay
can also be the result of incompetence, party-political interference, and other
less desirable causes; but delay is not necessarily an illegitimate tactic of
government. Thus, to show that a particular royal commission or departmental committee has had the effect of postponing action is not to prove that
the government has abused either the committee or the public interest. More
than twenty years ago, Professor V. C. Fowke wrote:

> As for the use of royal commissions to enable governments to postpone
> action, this purpose is held to be reprehensible and is always concealed as
> carefully as possible from the taxpayer. Realism, however, should lead the
> taxpayer to admit that at times he forces governments to exactly this kind
> of procedure. With our modern cult of progress and of activism we
> apparently can never admit the possibility that under certain circum-
> stances the best action can be no action at all. Governments consequently
> are driven to carry on all sorts of ostentatious and elaborate 'busy work'
> of which the appointment of a royal commission may be as harmless and
> as economical as any.[12]

The third major line of attack on royal commissions and departmental
committees is that, even if they are not 'abused' as substitutes for further
action or at least to postpone the need for it, their recommendations are in
any case unlikely to have any significant effect on whatever further action is
eventually taken. Even if royal commissions and departmental committees

11 See Norman Wilson, *The British System of Government* (Oxford: Blackwell, 1963), pp. 54–6.
12 V. C. Fowke, 'Royal Commissions and Canadian Agricultural Policy', *Canadian Journal of Economics and Political Science*, XIV (May 1948), pp. 165–6.

are actually necessary and not merely diversionary, the argument goes, they are still ineffectual and irrelevant. As John Bright wrote to a friend in 1879,

> Some people still have faith in Parliamentary Committees and Royal Commissions . . . I confess that I have none . . . If an inquiry, such as you refer to [a royal commission on agricultural distress], is granted, I hope it may do some good if it only shows once more how useless such inquiries are.[13]

Reference has already been made (in the previous chapter) to some estimates of how long it is thought to take for the recommendations of any committee to be put into effect: the consensus seemed to be either fifteen or thirty years! The appointment of royal commissions and departmental committees under such circumstances, the argument concludes, is an abuse of the institution. Either more attention should be paid to their findings, or they should not be appointed at all.

This argument is more persuasive than the previous two. Undoubtedly, there have been cases in which the recommendations of a royal commission or a departmental committee have been ignored. On the other hand, there is also an impressive weight of opinion to support the contrary view. Professor A. H. Birch, for example, has stated flatly that the importance of royal commissions and departmental committees 'can hardly be exaggerated, since most major legislative changes are preceded by this kind of enquiry'.[14] Similarly, Professor H. M. Stout has written that 'the practice [of appointing royal commissions and departmental committees] on the whole is highly commendable'. Even though their reports may lead to no immediate action, he argues, they nevertheless stand as milestones; one way or another, royal commissions and departmental committees are 'the source of a substantial amount of parliamentary legislation'.[15] The main reason for this disagreement is probably that, ironically, critics are prepared to recognise all sorts of political reasons for the appointment of a committee but not to accept that a committee may have political effects of its own. In other words, critics tend to see the value of committees only in terms of the direct translation of their recommendations into legislation, whereas committees can also serve many other purposes.

Another difficulty, of course, is the whole problem of cause and effect discussed in the previous chapter. How long must a committee wait for its

---

13 In a letter to Frederick Blood (26 June 1879), quoted in H. J. Hanham, *The Nineteenth-Century Constitution* (Cambridge University Press, 1969), pp. 313–14. See also Sir Alan Herbert, *op. cit.*, *passim*.

14 A. H. Birch, *Representative and Responsible Government* (London: Allen and Unwin, 1964), p. 203.

15 H. M. Stout, *British Government* (London: Oxford University Press, 1953), p. 130. Five case-studies are provided in R. A. Chapman (ed.), *The Role of Commissions in Policy-Making* (London: Allen and Unwin, 1973).

recommendations to be translated into action for it not to have been abused? How close must be the connection between the details of its recommendations and the actions actually taken? Is a committee not abused anyway, even if its recommendations are implemented, when a decision has already been taken long before the committee was appointed?

The real difficulty in dealing with all these allegations of 'abuse' is that they depend on statements about royal commissions and departmental committees which are very difficult to prove or disprove. They are essentially political arguments. If, for example, one is inclined to agree with the findings of a particular committee and the government does nothing to implement those findings, then one will also be inclined to argue that the government has 'abused' that committee. If, on the other hand, one regards the government attitude of inaction as essentially correct, then one will be more likely to say that the committee has served a useful purpose in providing a forum for interests to say their piece. It is true that there might be a wide measure of agreement that, in some cases, committees have been redundant, have been designed to gain time for party-political ends, or have been largely ineffectual and irrelevant; but there will always be an opposing view.

Committee Uses

Nothing said so far explains why there have been so many royal commissions and departmental committees appointed in so many areas of public policy. It is quite clear that these committees must enjoy a number of characteristics which make them highly attractive to government. The key to what these characteristics might be lies in two of the main themes of this study: that royal commissions and departmental committees are a flexible and adaptive institution of government, and that they provide an effective mechanism for public participation. The precise appeal of a committee probably varies from one case to another, but it is possible to describe at least ten features of committees which may make them attractive. Thus, royal commissions and departmental committees are: 1 flexible, 2 adaptive, 3 *ad hoc*, 4 impartial, 5 made up of 'outsiders', 6 open, 7 participatory, 8 research-oriented, 9 advisory, and 10 relatively inexpensive. Few if any of these characteristics are peculiar to royal commissions and departmental committees, of course, but their combination in a single institution of government is unique.

Throughout this study and especially in Chapter 6, it has been argued that a royal commission or a departmental committee is sufficiently flexible to make it an appropriate vehicle for dealing with almost any kind of subject. It may be a major issue or a minor one, a simple problem or a complex one, a local matter or a national one, a technical question or a practical one, a public matter or a confidential one. Any aspect of government may be examined by one of these committees, and even some which hardly seem to concern government at all! In fact, royal commissions and departmental committees are often granted a certain amount of discretion in applying and interpreting their terms of reference in order to allow the maximum degree of flexibility (see Chapter 7). One reason for their popularity, therefore, is their ability to deal with almost any kind of problem.

Secondly, it has been argued that royal commissions and departmental committees are extraordinarily adaptive to the specific requirements of their mandate. In particular, the formal organisation of their structure and procedures (see Chapters 8 and 9) can be made to correspond to the precise nature of their task. This is a very useful organisational characteristic, since the problems which beset a government do not always observe the niceties of its formal organisation. Government is divided into departments, departments into divisions, and so on in such a way as to enable it to respond to certain kinds of demands – ideally the most common or the most important demands. Similarly, within each of these jurisdictions, standard procedures are developed to ensure an efficient and equitable response. Inevitably, though, there are problems which cut across the established jurisdictions and call into question the standard procedures. Royal commissions and departmental committees permit a tailor-made response to such problems without upsetting the existing structure of government. As Wilhelm Dibelius put it, royal commissions and departmental committees constitute a 'typically English device . . . for making self-government effective over topics for which there are as yet no self-governing organs'.[16]

Third, royal commissions and departmental committees are *ad hoc* or problem-oriented. That is, they are appointed specifically for the job they are intended to carry out, and not for any more general purpose (see Chapter 2). This means that a committee's membership, mandate, activities and report can all be designed in relation to the specific problem which the committee has been appointed to deal with. No compromise is necessary on this point, for if a committee is found to have overlooked some related question, then a second committee can readily be appointed to repair the omission! Royal commissions and departmental committees, therefore, permit a relatively rapid institutional response to immediate demands on government. Thus it is that, over a period of time, a study of these committees is bound to be a study of virtually all the major issues of public policy.

In the view of some observers, institutions which, like royal commissions and departmental committees, are adaptive, flexible and *ad hoc* represent the organisational wave of the future. Professor Warren Bennis, for example, has written,[17]

The social structure of organisations of the future will have some unique characteristics. The key word will be 'temporary'. There will be adaptive,

16 Wilhelm Dibelius, *England* (London: Jonathan Cape, 1930), p. 253.

17 Warren Bennis, 'Beyond Bureaucracy', in Bennis and P. E. Slater, *The Temporary Society* (New York: Harper Colophon, 1968), pp. 73–4. See also Bennis, 'Post-Bureaucratic Leadership', *Trans-Action*, 6.9 (1969), pp. 44–51 and 61.

rapidly changing *temporary* systems. These will be task forces organised around problems to be solved by groups of relative strangers with diverse professional skills. The group will be arranged on an organic rather than mechanical model; it will evolve in response to a problem rather than to programmed role expectations . . . Adaptive, problem-solving, temporary systems of diverse specialists, linked together by co-ordinating and task-evaluating executive specialists in an organic flux – this is the organisation form that will gradually replace bureaucracy as we [now] know it. As no catchy phrase comes to mind, I call these new-style organisations '*adaptive structures*'.

Royal commissions and departmental committees in Britain are 'adaptive structures' *par excellence*. From the standpoint of anticipated organisational developments, therefore, the future of these committees seems assured.

Royal commissions and departmental committees possess other advantages. One of these (fourth in the list set out above) is that they are normally considered to have no vested interests. They seem to possess a degree of impartiality to which few other institutions of government can lay claim. Royal commissions and departmental committees can go where ministers and their officials might hesitate to tread. They can criticise government departments, non-departmental organisations and local authorities without causing offence; they can adjudicate salaries and set out conditions of employment within the government or outside; they can carry out quasi-judicial jobs such as assessing the causes of accidents or examining allegations of misconduct; and so on (see Chapter 6). This is another feature which makes royal commissions and departmental committees attractive to government.

Fifth, royal commissions and departmental committees are composed mainly of people from outside the full-time public service. In fact, an average of roughly five hundred people are brought into contact with Whitehall via these committees every year (see Chapter 5). They come from different backgrounds, different jobs and different professions. They may be experts in the subject under study by the committee or they may simply be people of sound judgement. In either case, the co-opting of manpower on this scale and of this quality represents a significant infusion into the public service. Would-be reformers of the Civil Service have often urged greater contact between civil servants and the outside world as one way of making government more effective.[18] Royal commissions and departmental committees provide a simple and direct means of achieving this kind of interaction.

Sixth, the activities of royal commissions and departmental committees are normally quite open.[19] The existence of each committee is usually made

18 See, for example, the Fabian Society pamphlet, *The Reform of the Higher Civil Service* (London: Gollancz, 1947), and the report of the Fulton Committee on the Civil Service (Cmnd. 3638).

19 Although there has never actually been a test-case, the provisions of the Official Secrets Act, 1911 (1 and 2 Geo. V, Chapter 28) would probably not be held to apply to the

public along with its membership and its terms of reference. It may take oral evidence at meetings which are open to the public and reported in the press, and it will probably publish some of its evidence or at least deposit it for public consultation in a library or some other suitable place. When a royal commission or departmental committee has completed its study, it publishes its conclusions as well as the arguments supporting them in a report which is freely available to the general public. Decision-making *en clair* like this is not characteristic of the ordinary operations of Whitehall. Thus, in cases where it is desirable that good government not only be done but also be seen to be done, a royal commission or a departmental committee is a very useful device.

Seventh, royal commissions and departmental committees provide a direct link between government departments and the general public, or at least the interested part of it. The voice of the ordinary citizen in government is theoretically his Member of Parliament, but in practice he has a number of other links with Whitehall. In particular, various interest groups of which he is a member may have close, if informal, connections with the Civil Service and with ministers.[20] Rarely, however, is the participation of interest groups as openly solicited or as faithfully recorded in Whitehall as it is by most royal commissions and departmental committees (see Chapter 8). This, in turn, permits these committees to play a part in educating public opinion to the existence and the complexity of a problem and focussing concern on it. Moreover, as Ian Gilmour has pointed out, 'the alerting of public opinion may induce contending interests to soften their demands . . .'[21] Finally, the close contact between government and governed through royal commissions and departmental committees makes of them what may be termed administrative 'outposts' or sounding-boards of public opinion.[22] All these factors contribute to the usefulness of these committees.

Eighth, royal commissions and departmental committees can be used to promote research in any area where it is thought desirable by the government (see Chapter 9). A committee may actively encourage research and even effectively subsidise it. Or the mere fact of the committee's existence may be enough to awaken or reawaken interest in a particular subject through the 'spin-off' effect of its own interest and activities. The recent trend towards

---

activities of a royal commission or a departmental committee, unless classified information of some kind had been made available to the committee in the course of its work. See K. C. Wheare, *Government by Committee* (London: Oxford University Press, 1955), p. 65. Nevertheless, individual committee members traditionally do not divulge the opinions of the committee (until the final report appears) or of its individual members.

20 See, for example, Allen Potter, *Organised Groups in British National Politics* (London: Faber and Faber, 1961), Part IV; and S. E. Finer, *Anonymous Empire: a Study of the Lobby in Great Britain*, rev. ed. (London: Pall Mall Press, 1966), Chapter 41.

21 Ian Gilmour, *The Body Politic* (London: Hutchinson, 1969), p. 189.

22 Sir Ivor Jennings, *Cabinet Government*, 3rd ed. (Cambridge University Press, 1959), p. 84, argues for the value of such 'outposts'.

more extensive facilities for research by committees is likely to increase the tendency to appoint them for this reason.

Ninth, royal commissions and departmental committees are relatively independent of government. Appointing a committee does not bind the government or a department to accepting its recommendations, or indeed to doing anything at all. As government becomes more and more complex, it is very useful for officials to have ways of experimenting, of floating 'trial-balloons', of discovering new ideas, and so on, without committing their ministers. Royal commissions and departmental committees provide just such a mechanism through which these ends may be pursued with safety. Outside experts and ideas 'are kept safely in the kennel and do not have to be let into the house', as one observer has put it.[23]

Tenth, royal commissions and especially departmental committees are relatively inexpensive (see Chapter 11). Even now, it is still possible to finance a committee for under £500, and for most of them the cost is well under £5,000. This is an amount which most departments could reasonably hope to find somewhere in their budgets at almost any time. For these modest sums, the government benefits from an average of 250 man-days of work per committee.[24] The government would be hard put to get the same results as it can get from royal commissions and departmental committees from some other source for the same price.

Some Further Comments

Although they are both useful and popular, royal commissions and departmental committees should not, *pace* Charles J. Hanser and others, be regarded as having achieved a state of perfection.[25] It is quite reasonable to defend the use of these committees and, at the same time, to criticise some aspects of the way in which they function.

It must be stated immediately, however, that the reform of any institution of government needs to be approached with care. For one thing, the ultimate effects of any reform are not always obvious. Reforms may, in fact, turn out to have effects quite opposite to those which were intended, or the effects of one reform may conflict with those of another. Secondly, reforming any one institution of government may alter the balance between it and other parts of government. Thus, increasing the effectiveness of royal commissions and departmental committees may serve to strengthen the executive at the expense of Parliament, for example, and this may or may not be desirable – even to the extent of out-weighing all other considerations. The point of departure for the suggestions which follow, therefore, is that the implemen-

23 Ian Gilmour, *op. cit.*, p. 189.

24 Assuming an average eight-man committee (see Chapter 5) which meets an average of thirty-two times (see Chapter 7).

25 Reference is to C. J. Hanser, *Guide to Decision: the Royal Commis ion* (Totowa, N.J.: Bedminster Press, 1965), whose attitude is quoted in Chapter 2 above.

tation of any administrative reforms should be undertaken with caution and even diffidence.

Royal commissions and departmental committees are often criticised for their membership. It is argued that members and especially chairmen could be chosen from a broader section of the community than in practice they are.[26] There is perhaps a tendency to overdo this criticism; for example, the appointment of committees has been stigmatised as 'government by Radcliffery'.[27] Examination of the facts (see Chapter 5) shows that most of the chairmen and all but a few of the members of the major postwar committees were novices, and remarkably few of the others had served on more than two or three other committees each. Nevertheless, there is some justice on the side of the critics. Naturally, departments want to play it 'safe' in their choice of people to be chairmen and members of committees, but departments could probably afford to take greater risks than they normally seem to do.

For one thing, officials normally try to obtain the most eminent and most qualified people available, but these are not always the most suitable people for work on committees. The energies of highly qualified people will, in all probability, already be divided among several different responsibilities, and they will just not be able to spend as much time with a committee as they might like. Instead, then, departments should look for younger men and women who can be expected to reach a position of eminence in their respective fields in the future, rather than those who have already achieved it. This will mean people with a reputation to make, rather than people with a reputation to protect. Writing specifically about barristers on committees in the nineteenth century, William Cory made the same point:[28]

> Twenty or thirty years after being called to the bar an Englishman, it seems, thinks it beneath him to consider what ought to be the law, except when he has a chance of determining what is the law by deductive reasoning. If caught at the age of thirty, there is a fair hope of a barrister's being modestly legislative, ready to treat the author of a theoretical treatise as a possible ally and inclined to help a statesman as an engineer helps a general.

Departments could well seek to fill their committees more with people inclined to be 'modestly legislative' and less with people known simply to be good committeemen.

26 See, for example, Peter G. Richards, *Patronage in British Government* (London: Allen and Unwin, 1963).

27 See Sir Alan Herbert, *op. cit.* In fact, Lord Radcliffe has chaired one royal commission, three departmental committees and two other kinds of committees in the past thirty years; see Mary Morgan (ed.), *British Government Publications: an Index to Chairmen and Authors 1941–66* (London: The Library Association, 1969).

28 Cory, *op. cit.*, p. 367.

As for the backgrounds and occupations of members of royal commissions and departmental committees, it is difficult to generalise. Nevertheless, it does seem as though it might be useful to have more civil servants appointed as members. Traditionally, the committee secretary is relied upon to convey the 'official view', but there seems to be no reason why the practical problems of implementing any proposals which a committee might feel inclined to make should not be put before it more directly by a civil-servant member. Although there may be little that a committee can do to influence the fate of its recommendations, it should make every effort to be as practical as possible in framing them. Civil-servant members, on an equal footing with those from outside government, could be of assistance to a royal commission or departmental committee in this way.

Members of the judiciary have also figured fairly frequently among both the chairmen and members of royal commissions and departmental committees. Although their proven impartiality makes them ideal committeemen in one sense, this same impartiality may be put in jeopardy by their too frequent appointment to committees. Professor MacGregor Dawson wrote of the same practice in Canada in the following terms:[29]

> There would seem to be little purpose in taking elaborate care to separate the judge from politics and to render him quite independent of the executive, and then placing him in a position as a Royal Commissioner where his impartiality may be attacked and his findings – no matter how correct and judicial they may be – are liable to be interpreted as favouring one political party at the expense of the other.

Some committees are of such a nature that a member of the judiciary can clearly make a special contribution, even one which a practising lawyer could not as well provide; but committees falling in this class are not as numerous as the appointment of members of the judiciary would suggest.

The tendency to appoint members of the judiciary to serve on royal commissions and departmental committees is one reflection of the fact that such service is unpaid. There is unlikely to be much change in the composition of committees unless and until this practice is changed. To pay for service on committees would, in a sense, be more honest. Civil servants, Members of Parliament and members of the judiciary are in effect being paid for their services when they sit on committees. Besides, government is not a charity. It pays those who serve it on a full-time basis, and there is no reason in principle why it should not do the same for those who serve it part-time. Nor can it be argued that payment would provide the 'wrong' sort of motivation for public service, unless the same is held to be true of service in Parliament, the courts or the Civil Service. If members of royal commissions and departmental

29 R. M. Dawson, *The Government of Canada*, 3rd ed. rev. (University of Toronto Press, 1957), p. 482. See also John C. Courtney, 'In Defence of Royal Commissions', *Canadian Public Administration*, XII, 2 (1969), pp. 201–6.

committees were remunerated for their efforts, they could undoubtedly be drawn from a broader segment of society.[30]

The obvious argument against paying for committee service is that it would have the effect of increasing the cost of each committee.[31] In all probability, this would lead to a reduction in the total number of committees appointed. It might also mean smaller committees, fewer meetings and closer Treasury scrutiny. In some cases, these side-effects would be desirable but in other cases they might not be. Perhaps the most sensible solution would be simply to allow departments the discretion to pay committee members in cases where they feel it to be appropriate. Or the practice might be established of paying royal commissioners but only rarely members of departmental committees. Some such practice could go a long way towards broadening the source of recruitment for royal commissions and departmental committees.

Turning to the activities of royal commissions and departmental committees once they have been appointed, one of the most frequent criticisms has been that they take too long to report. In fact, royal commissions take an average of two and a half years and departmental committees an average of one and a half years (see Chapter 11). The duration of a committee depends on a number of factors. First, it must organise its programme of work. Next, if the committee decides to take evidence, it must first announce its intention to do so and then allow enough time for those interested to prepare their evidence. If the committee decides to undertake research, then this too has to be planned, organised and executed. Finally, the more successful all these activities turn out to be, the more time is required to digest the results. Thus, it is difficult to see how many committees could have drastically reduced the time they took. Committees are usually fully aware of the need for special haste when there is one, and can be expected to proceed as quickly as is reasonable. All the same, it would not be unreasonable to suppose that paid committeemen would be willing to meet more frequently and so (other things being equal) get through their programme of work more rapidly.

Other criticisms can be made of the activities of royal commissions and departmental committees. For one thing, the taking of evidence from all and sundry sometimes seems to take on the significance of a religious creed. In fact, committees could probably exercise more discretion than they normally do in this matter. As anyone who has sat through committee hearings or read through its written evidence will testify, a lot of it can be tedious and repetitive.[32] In some cases, committees do have a duty to hear from all interested

30 Incidentally, the problem of absenteeism (see chapter 7 above) would probably also be reduced.

31 An estimate of the amount of the increase in cost can be obtained easily enough by taking the number of man-days required by a committee and multiplying it by an appropriate *per diem* rate.

32 For a detailed analysis of the evidence put before one committee, see Ivor Gowan and Leon Gibson, 'The Royal Commission on Local Government in England [Cmnd. 4040]: a Survey of Some of the Written Evidence', *Public Administration*, XLVI (1968), pp. 13–24.

parties, but in many other cases, they could (and sometimes do) rely entirely on selected individual invitations to give evidence coupled with less formal methods such as interviewing. Hearings for oral evidence could more often be restricted to cases where the committee expects to profit from the testimony, and even then need not be attended by all members of the committee (especially if a transcript of the hearings is made). Larger secretariats could be appointed to assist members in summarising and assessing the evidence. Improved internal organisation, such as the greater use of subcommittees, could also help reduce the burden of taking evidence. Fundamentally, however, a committee should try to assess in very realistic terms the value of the evidence likely to be presented before it is solicited and be guided accordingly in their invitations.

Secondly, research methods could be improved. Except in a few cases, the techniques used – visits of inspection, surveys, questionnaires, statistical analyses, etc. – are relatively unsophisticated (see Chapter 9). Few royal commissions or departmental committees undertake and evaluate pilot programmes, for example, or other kinds of experiments. They should be encouraged to do so. Apart from the Social Survey Division and a few firms of chartered accountants or survey research experts, consultants are infrequently called upon to assist committees. There has been a slight tendency towards the wider use of consultants in recent years and this should be encouraged. In cases where committees are able to set up research staffs of their own – and the number of these cases should be increased – more attention should be paid to designing a clear and definite research strategy so that the findings inform the recommendations of the committee to the fullest possible extent. The practice of co-opting additional people from inside and outside government to serve on specialised subcommittees – as the Fulton Committee (Cmnd. 3638) did – or even just to take part in seminars could also be exploited to a greater extent than it has been. Finally, interim reports (see Chapter 10) could be used more effectively by committees as instruments of research to test ideas ('trial balloons') against public reaction. A number of committees have made effective use of all these devices, but many others have not.

Finally, in a more speculative vein, it is intriguing to wonder whether royal commissions and departmental committees might not perform some useful service even after submitting their final reports. As Wilhelm Dibelius pointed out many years ago, 'there is certainly much waste involved, when one thinks how all the talent thus assembled for some piece of legislative preparation is afterwards dispersed to the four winds'.[33] It would be interesting to see the effects of having a royal commission or a departmental committee mandated not only to make recommendations but also to advise government during the process of implementing those recommendations and

33 Dibelius, *op. cit.*, p. 254.

then to examine the results of their joint handiwork some time later. This would not mean that royal commissions and departmental committees were simply transformed into standing advisory committees, but rather that they should be 'recallable' *ad hoc* committees. They would not be expected to consider 'such matters as may from time to time be referred to them', as are most standing advisory committees. Instead, the idea is that royal commissions and departmental committees should not automatically disband as soon as their final reports are delivered to their appropriate ministers. In some cases, great benefit could be derived from continuing contact between a committee and the officials and departments implicated in its recommendations. In fact, even the prospect of a committee's persisting beyond its final report might have a salutary effect on both the attitude of departmental officials towards the committee and its own sense of what is politically feasible and practical. There is as yet no formal precedent for allowing a royal commission or departmental committee such an 'intimate' role, but it would seem to be an obvious possible innovation which could, in some cases, help to make the policy-making process more efficient and more effective.

Inquiries and Investigations

Possibly the most intriguing thing about royal commissions and departmental committees is that they reflect two quite different views of government. These two views are summarised in the concepts of an 'inquiry' and an 'investigation'.

An *inquiry* is based on the belief that truth is something which is revealed in free and open debate between opposing interests. Claim and counterclaim do battle before an impartial tribunal, which then reaches a conclusion on the basis of the evidence presented to it. The epitome of the inquiry is the court of law, in which a 'committee' of twelve 'good men and true' hears the evidence and renders a verdict on it. Few other kinds of inquiries operate under the same stringent rules as a court of law, but the principle of truth winning out in free and open debate is central to them all.

An *investigation*, on the other hand, is based on the assumption that truth is something which can best be discovered through diligent search. It does not normally emerge in free and open debate because debate rarely is free and open. Some interests in society are more powerful and more persuasive than others and none of them represents the so-called public interest. Thus, an investigation sets out with the objective of obtaining a balanced view of the whole matter, of finding the interests which are under-represented or even not represented at all, and of gathering facts as well as opinions. The epitome of the investigation is perhaps to be found in the scientific experiment. Not all investigations proceed with quite the same clinical detachment as the scientist tries to achieve, but the principle that truth is something obtainable through observation and measurement lies at the root of all investigations.

Neither one of these views is inherently superior to the other. The advantage of the inquiry is that it is more likely to be able to provide solutions to immediate practical problems; but, in so doing, it may unwittingly overlook important aspects which an investigation might have uncovered.[34] The advantage of the investigation is that it is more likely to produce results of long-term value, although it may lose sight of the immediate problem in the process.[35] An inquiry relies more on the inductive capacities of its members, while an investigation relies on their deductive capacities. Moreover, each reflects certain attitudes towards the nature of government. The assumption behind an inquiry is that government is essentially an art; the assumption behind an investigation is that government is essentially a science.[36]

Because they reflect fundamentally different conceptions of the nature of government, inquiries and investigations naturally imply quite different kinds of institutions and procedures to carry them out. As far as royal commissions and departmental committees are concerned, these differences are manifested most clearly in the selection of members for appointment to royal commissions and departmental committees and, secondly, in the efforts of committees to obtain information.

The membership of a committee will tend to reveal the assumptions and expectations of those who appointed it. Impartial committees, for example, imply a role of inquiry, whereas expert and representative committees imply one of investigation. Similarly, the appointment of judges and peers may indicate an inquiry, while the appointment of academics and civil servants may mean an investigation. A relatively small or low-ranking secretariat will be likely to mean an inquiry, whereas a large or high-ranking one suggests an investigation. It is difficult to draw any firm conclusions on these points, of course, since the particular circumstances of each committee may warrant exceptional measures; but there is a general tendency to build into a committee's membership certain assumptions about its role in government.

Similarly, the procedures adopted by a royal commission or a departmental committee in its efforts to obtain information will tend to reveal the assumptions of officials and the perceptions of the committee about its role. As Sir Arthur MacNalty is reported to have once explained,

> There were two kinds of Royal Commission, or two methods on which Royal Commissions worked. There were those which heard witnesses,

34 See, for example, Jennifer Hart's criticisms of the Willink Royal Commission on the Police (Cmnd. 1728), 'Some Reflection on the Report of the Royal Commission on the Police', *Public Law*, IX (1963), pp. 283–304.

35 See, for example, Professor Peter Self's criticism of the statutory (Type III) Roskill Commission on the Third London Airport, ' "Nonsense on Stilts": Cost-Benefit Analysis and the Roskill Commission', *Political Quarterly*, 41, 3 (1970), pp. 249–60.

36 The same two contrasting attitudes are reflected in two contemporary books on British public administration: for the government-as-an-art view, see C. H. Sisson, *The Spirit of British Administration*, 2nd ed. (London: Faber and Faber, 1966); and for the government-as-a-science view, see Max Nicholson, *The System: the Misgovernment of Modern Britain* (London: Hodder and Stoughton, 1967).

collated evidence and made recommendations based on the data considered; there was also the kind of Royal Commission that, besides acting on the lines already mentioned, initiated scientific research into the matter of their terms of reference.[37]

In general, then, committees which regard themselves as inquiries tend to rely on what were described as passive efforts to obtain information on which to base their findings (see Chapter 8), while committees which see their role as more one of investigation are likely to take active steps to obtain information (see Chapter 9). Again these tendencies cannot be regarded as universal, since each particular committee must juggle a variety of conflicting demands. Nevertheless, committee procedures are likely to reflect certain assumptions about its intended role.

Few royal commissions or departmental committees actually reflect either the inquiry or the investigation in its pure form. Under the influence of a variety of conflicting pressures, most reflect a compromise between the two, albeit a compromise in which one or the other may predominate. Moreover, this balance may change as the committee proceeds with its job. The expectations of its appointment, for example, may not be borne out in its procedures. The important thing, however, is to decide what kind of role – what combination of the inquiry and the investigation – a committee is to play, and to design it accordingly. Thus, all the various structural and procedural aspects of royal commissions and departmental committees examined in this study are not unrelated to one another: they are all part of the way in which a committee designs and plays its role in government. The better that relationship and that process are understood, the more useful and effective royal commissions and departmental committees can be in the years ahead.

37 Sir Arthur MacNalty in Lord Kennet, *op. cit.*, pp. 404–5.

Appendix A
Note on Historical Sources
for Chapter 3

Chapter 3 contains data on the number of royal commissions and departmental committees appointed and in existence since 1800. The purpose of this note is to describe how these data were obtained.

There are several possible primary sources of information about the appointment of committees, including instruments of appointment, departmental records, Treasury financial records, and the reports of the committees themselves. Over the long period of time in question, however, the most reliable source is committee reports. The problem that this poses is that any historical series based on published reports is only as complete as the various collections of official government documents on which it is based. Moreover, such a series must by definition leave out any committee which, for whatever reason, did not produce any published report. All the difficulties encountered in compiling time-series on royal commissions and departmental committees stem from these two basic problems.

Prior to 1800, the records of official papers are incomplete. As Professor and Mrs Ford have explained,

> Before the nineteenth century there was no systematic way of preserving the papers, so that the records and the collections which have come down to us cannot be regarded as complete. Many papers must have passed out of the custody of the House before efforts were made to preserve them.[1]

In fact, there are three possible sources of information about official papers before 1800. There are the Journals of Parliament themselves, to which other official papers were added from time to time on the recommendation of a committee of the Speaker; however, not all papers were deemed important enough to warrant inclusion. These omissions are only partly accounted for by two collections of pre-nineteenth century official papers, which are known as the 'First Series' and the 'Abbot Collection'. The First Series is in fifteen

---

1 P. Ford and G. Ford, *A Guide to Parliamentary Papers* (Oxford: Blackwell, 1955), p. 23. See also Hilda Jones, 'Parliamentary Papers', *Catalogue of Parliamentary Papers, 1801–1900* (London: King and Son, 1904), p. v.

volumes, and it covers the period from 1773 until 1801.[2] It has two main drawbacks: it includes only a selection of the reports of Parliamentary committees in that period, and it excludes papers which had already been published in the Journals. Luke Hansard repaired the second omission in 1835 by adding to an index to the First Series which he was compiling a list of all the papers which had been published in the Journals since 1696.[3] The bigger problem of the papers which had not been published in the Journals nor in the First Series was tackled by Mr Speaker Abbot in 1803. The Abbot Collection, as it became known, consists of one hundred and ten volumes (plus an index) of all the then available and hitherto unpublished official papers from 1731 until 1800; but the fact that there is only a handful of papers included for some years suggests that there must still be many omissions.[4] For the years before 1800, therefore, it is possible to talk only about particular committees and to give examples of their use; it is very difficult to say anything precise about even the number of committees appointed each year.

Since 1800, however, the collections of official papers are more reliable. Parliamentary Papers, which are papers arising directly from the activities of Parliament or papers actually presented to Parliament for its use, have all been preserved and bound in sets of Sessional Papers extending, with short interruptions during the two World Wars, from 1800 to the present day. From 1800 to 1836, some official papers selected by the Speaker continued to be published as appendices to (rather than inserted directly into) the Journals, but this practice was discontinued owing to the additional expense involved.[5]

Unfortunately, however, this does not mean that a record of every committee report can be found in the Sessional Papers. Some official papers were still left out of the Sessional Papers, and these included some departmental committee reports. Moreover, by 1882, the volume of official papers had reached a point where they could no longer all be bound in the sessional sets; so a distinction emerged between 'Parliamentary Papers' and 'Official Publications' or (as they are now called) 'Non-Parliamentary Papers'.[6] While all Parliamentary Papers continued to be bound in the Sessional Papers, Non-Parliamentary Papers did not. To this day, there are no official bound sets of

2 Four volumes appeared in 1793 and eleven in 1803.

3 Reprinted in P. Ford and G. Ford, *Hansard's Catalogue and Breviate of Parliamentary Papers, 1696–1834* (Oxford: Blackwell, 1953).

4 According to the Fords' *Guide* (*op. cit.*), the only sets now in existence are held by Parliament, the British Museum, and University College, London (incomplete). The catalogue to the collection was reprinted in 1954: *Catalogue of Papers Printed by Order of the House of Commons, 1731–1800* (London: HMSO, 1954).

5 Ford and Ford, *Guide, op. cit.*, p. 23 n. 2. It was only at this time that Parliamentary Papers began to be printed and made available to the general public on a systematic basis.

6 *ibid.*, pp. 28–9.

Non-Parliamentary Papers, and consolidated lists of these Papers were not formalised until 1922.[7]

As far as royal commissions are concerned, the situation is clear enough. Reports of royal commissions have invariably been published as Command Papers, which are Parliamentary Papers.[8] Therefore, if a royal commission has issued an official report since 1800, it will be included in the Sessional Papers of Parliament for the appropriate year and, of course, in the corresponding *General Index* to these Papers. It should be added, however, that royal commissions appear in the indices under subject headings and are not normally cross-referenced under any common institutional heading such as 'royal commissions' or 'committees'.[9]

As far as departmental committees are concerned, the situation is less clear. The reports of these committees may be published either as Command Papers (i.e. Parliamentary Papers) or as Non-Parliamentary Papers, and there does not seem to be any hard and fast rule about it.[10] This means that, if a departmental committee has issued an official report, it will probably be included in the Sessional Papers for the appropriate year if it appeared between 1800 and 1882. Between 1882 and 1922, its report may be listed in the appropriate departmental list of Official Publications; since 1922, its report will appear in the appropriate *Consolidated List*. It should be added that departmental committees, like royal commissions, are not normally cross-referenced under any common institutional heading.

These, then, are the most important primary sources for information about royal commissions and departmental committees. Based on these sources, several lists of committees have already been compiled.[11] None of these provides a complete and up-to-date list of either royal commissions or departmental committees for the period of time required. On the other hand, it would be foolish to duplicate work that has already been done. Accordingly, the available secondary sources have been drawn upon as far as possible.

7 *Consolidated List of Government Publications* (London: HMSO, annually from 1922). Since 1936, the *Lists* have been further consolidated into volumes covering successive five-year periods.

8 See Chapter 3 above for a discussion of the meaning and significance of Command Papers.

9 Three such indices cover the period from 1801 to 1948–9: *General Index . . ., 1801–1852* (London: HMSO, 1938); *General Index . . ., 1852–1899* (London, 1909); and *General Index . . ., 1900 to 1948–9* (London: HMSO, 1960).

10 See the discussion about the publication of departmental committee reports in Chapter 11 above.

11 There are even lists among the Sessional Papers themselves, as part of a Parliamentary Return. C. J. Hanser, *Guide to Decision: the Royal Commission* (Totowa, N.J.: Bedminster Press, 1965), pp. 240–1, cites some examples of such lists. See also *House of Commons Debates* (2 April 1963), Columns 237–42, for a recent example. All of these 'Official' lists are too limited in scope for our purposes.

The most important of these secondary sources are lists prepared by the following people:[12]

a for royal commissions: J. Toulmin Smith, A. H. Cole and the staff of the Harvard University Library, H. M. Clokie and J. W. Robinson, P. Ford and G. Ford, C. J. Hanser, and David Butler; and

b for departmental committees: R. V. Vernon and Nicholas Mansergh, and P. Ford and G. Ford

In the case of royal commissions, the first three lists provide information about the nineteenth century and all but the first provide information about the twentieth century. In the case of departmental committees, however, all the information relates to the present century; there is nothing at all about the nineteenth century.

The first list of royal commissions was prepared by Joshua Toulmin Smith in 1849, and it contained 161 entries for the period from 1832 to 1844.[13] These entries are not actually distinct royal commissions, but what he calls 'heads of reference to Commissioners' Reports in the index to Parliamentary Papers printed between 1832 and 1844'. (Toulmin Smith adds, 'It would be no easy matter to get a complete list of all the Commissions.') It is rather difficult to assess the implications of a list of 'heads of reference', since it could either under-estimate the number of actual commissions (if several appeared under a single heading) or over-estimate them (if there is much cross-referencing). Nor does the list appear to be complete: there is no head of reference under which, for example, the Durham report on British North America (1838–9) would be likely to appear.[14] At another point in his book, Toulmin Smith refers to a Parliamentary Return which states that 'no less than ninety one Commissions of Inquiry, *eo nomine*, had been constituted' in much the same period as he had originally selected.[15] At still another point, he talks of the 'more than one hundred cases [of royal commissions] within the last twenty years'.[16] At best, therefore, Toulmin Smith's figures are only an indication of the actual number of royal commissions appointed during the late 1820's, '30's and early '40's: the figures indicate an average of about five per year.

The other two lists of royal commissions in the nineteenth century were compiled by A. H. Cole and the staff of the Harvard University Library, and by H. M. Clokie and J. W. Robinson. The Harvard list is accurate and pre-

---

12 Mary Morgan has also compiled a useful list of *British Government Publications* indexed by chairmen and authors (London: the Library Association, 1969), but it covers only the period from 1941 to 1966.

13 J. Toulmin Smith, *Government by Commissions Illegal and Pernicious* (London: Sweet, 1849), pp. 22ff.

14 The report is printed in *Parliamentary Papers*, XVII, 3 (1839).

15 Toulmin Smith, *op. cit.*, p. 183. The period referred to in the Return was from 8 July 1831 to 15 February 1848.

16 *ibid.*, p. 176.

cise and contains detailed references to 198 royal commissions appointed between 1860 and 1899.[17] Clokie and Robinson list 449 royal commissions appointed during the whole century.[18] Their data seem to be accurate in most cases, although cross-checking with other sources did reveal a few errors and omissions. Unlike the Harvard list, Clokie and Robinson seem to have worked at least partly from other secondary sources, such as those compiled by Parliamentary staff.[19] Neither the Harvard list nor Clokie and Robinson attempt to exclude standing (Type II) or statutory (Type III) commissions, although Clokie and Robinson do make similar distinctions.[20]

Both the Harvard list and Clokie and Robinson also provide information on royal commissions in the twentieth century from 1900 to about 1935 in each case. To these sources can be added three others. First of all, Professor P. Ford and his wife, G. Ford, have compiled a magnificent, three-volume annotated catalogue of Parliamentary Papers from 1900 to 1954.[21] From the point of view of this study, the Fords' *Breviates* are complete except in one respect: their scope is restricted to Parliamentary Papers dealing with

> matters which have been, or might have been, the subject of legislation or have dealt with 'public policy' . . . With certain exceptions, we have tried to include all the reports [including reports of royal commissions and departmental committees] falling within our definition . . . The exceptions which have been omitted are . . . all reports relating to the internal affairs or constitutions of Dominions and Colonies, and . . . reports dealing exclusively with ecclesiastical questions and with military and naval matters, whether connected with operations or internal organisations.[22]

No such exceptions are made in Chapter 3 of this study. The other two lists of twentieth-century royal commissions are by C. J. Hanser (143 commissions

17 A. H. Cole, *A Finding-List of British Royal Commission Reports: 1860–1935* (Harvard University Press, 1935). The first impression of this list is discouraging: for a book in which details are important, the pagination in the table of contents is incorrect nine times out of twenty and, after a careful discussion of the different abbreviations of 'Command Paper', the same one (Cd.) is used throughout!

18 H. M. Clokie and J. W. Robinson, *Royal Commissions of Inquiry* (Stanford University Press, 1937), pp. 58–9, Table I, and pp. 76–8, Table II. The figure '388' on p. 75 must be a misprint for '389'.

19 See, for example, Clokie and Robinson, *op. cit.*, pp. 78–9 n. 23. Oddly enough, Clokie and Robinson make no reference to the Harvard list, which was published two years before their own book.

20 Clokie and Robinson, *op. cit.*, p. 202, Table V, and pp. 114ff. See Chapter 2 above for a discussion of the various types of advisory committees.

21 P. Ford and G. Ford: *A Breviate of Parliamentary Papers, 1900–1916, A Breviate of Parliamentary Papers, 1917–1939*, and *A Breviate of Parliamentary Papers, 1940–1954* (Oxford: Blackwell, 1957, 1951 and 1961 respectively). Reports of advisory committees seem to account for at least half the entries in each of the volumes.

22 *Breviate . . ., 1917–1939*, pp. ix–x. There seems to be an inconsistency on this point in listing (*ibid.*, p. 18) the report of the Dardanelles Commission (Cmd. 371) but not that of the Mesopotamia Commission (Cd. 8610).

up to 1964) and David Butler (144 commissions up to 1966).[23] Both lists, however, include some commissions which are really statutory and standing committees rather than royal commissions in the sense used here.

Turning now to departmental committees, there are only two secondary sources available: a set of lists prepared by R. V. Vernon and Nicholas Mansergh for the period from 1919 to 1939 and the Fords' three *Breviates* for the period from 1900 to 1954.[24]

Vernon and Mansergh have constructed fifteen separate lists of advisory bodies grouped (except in one case related to the reform of the machinery of government) according to the department which appointed them. There is a certain amount of duplication in the lists, since some committees were appointed by more than one department. There are also some significant omissions in that there are no lists of committees appointed by a number of departments, including the Home Office, the Scottish Office and the Lord Chancellor's Office. These particular omissions are particularly unfortunate since, at least in the postwar years, it is these three departments which have made most frequent use of departmental committees.[25] Finally, the lists are not always careful to distinguish standing advisory committees (Types I and II) and statutory committees (Type III) from departmental committees (Type IV). Subject to these reservations, Vernon and Mansergh offer a useful selection of departmental committees appointed between the wars.

The Fords' three *Breviates* are as valuable in connection with departmental committees as they were for royal commissions, but there is still the same problem of scope. The *Breviates* do not contain references to committee reports dealing with certain subjects, principally colonial, ecclesiastical and military matters. Moreover, although the data available go back as far as the beginning of the present century, they have not yet been brought beyond 1954.

For royal commissions, the list provided by Clokie and Robinson was used as a point of departure for the period from 1800 to 1831. The list was checked in its entirety with the official *General Index* of Parliamentary Papers.[26] The period from 1832 to 1859 was also based initially on the work of Clokie and

---

23 Hanser, *Guide to Decision, op. cit.*, p. 239ff; and David Butler, *British Political Facts, 1900–1968*, 3rd ed. (London: Macmillan, 1969), pp. 175–9.

24 R. V. Vernon and Nicholas Mansergh, *Advisory Bodies: A Study of Their Uses in Relation to Central Government, 1919–1939* (London: Allen and Unwin, 1940), pp. 443–500; and Ford and Ford, *Breviates, op. cit.*, Butler, *op. cit.*, pp. 180–2, also has a list of departmental committees, but it is a select list and was derived largely from the two secondary sources just mentioned.

25 See Chapter 4 above.

26 Fourteen changes were made in the Clokie and Robinson list: Nine commissions were omitted, four because they were standing commissions and five because they were not committees appointed by the Crown. Five royal commissions were added, four as a result of subdividing two entries into six different commissions and one because it was an entirely new one (the Royal Commission on the State of African Settlements appointed in 1812). There were also a number of minor corrections of dates.

Robinson. Again their work was checked against the official indices of Parliamentary Papers, although the fact that Clokie and Robinson list only the most important commissions by name meant that the checking was more difficult.[27] For the period from 1860 until the end of the century, the Harvard University list was checked against the figures presented by Clokie and Robinson and the appropriate official index. Finally, the twentieth-century part of the list is a composite of the information provided by all the appropriate secondary sources mentioned above, with adjustments to exclude standing and statutory commissions. For this part of the series, too, frequent reference was made to primary sources. Accordingly, it is possible to be confident that the data on royal commissions are quite accurate.

For departmental committees, the result is less satisfying. The Fords' *Breviates* provide a vital and almost always reliable source; data were compiled from that source and cross-checked against the lists prepared by Vernon and Mansergh, with the result that some additions were made. There is still, however, the possibility that some committees dealing with colonial, military and ecclesiastical matters have been overlooked. But the major difficulty is that the *Breviates* stop at the end of 1954, and there are no adequate secondary sources covering the subsequent period.[28] Short of examining every single official publication since 1954, the only thing to do is to try and estimate the number of departmental committees appointed and in existence each year.

One way of doing this is to extrapolate from the data which are available on departmental committees whose reports were issued as Command Papers. From 1921 (when the Treasury issued a Circular setting out what is still the basis for the use of Command Papers) until the early '50s, it is possible to compare the appointment of *all* departmental committees with the sample of those whose reports were published as Command Papers.[29] Assuming that the same approximate numerical relationship has persisted since then, it is possible to estimate the total number of departmental committees appointed and in existence each year from the data in Appendix B. Under the circumstances, this is the best that can be done.

27 No changes were found to be necessary beyond the exclusion of standing and statutory commissions.

28 Unfortunately, P. Ford, G. Ford and Diana Marshallsay, *Select List of British Parliamentary Papers, 1955–1964* (Shannon: Irish University Press, 1970) does not provide enough information to serve as a supplement to the *Breviates*.

29 Between 1900 (when the *Breviates* begin) and 1921 (the year of the Treasury Circular). fewer than forty departmental-committee reports were *not* published as Command Papers, In fact, the data have been estimated from 1953 onwards, beginning two years earlier than necessary in order to allow for 'overlapping' committees omitted from the *Breviates*. It has not been possible to allow for the Fords' omission of committees on colonial, military and ecclesiastical matters between 1945 and 1952.

Table A Royal commissions and departmental committees, 1800–1969, by numbers appointed and in existence annually

year	royal commissions only		all committees	
	number appointed	number in existence	number appointed	number in existence
1800	0			
1	0			
2	0			
3	1			
4	1			
5	1			
6	3			
7	1			
8	0			
9	4			
1800–9	11			
1810	1			
1	0			
2	6			
3	1			
4	0			
5	1			
6	2			
7	2			
8	1			
9	5			
1810–19	19			
1820	0			
1	6			
2	1			
3	1			
4	2			
5	3			
6	1			
7	3			
8	2			
9	1			
1820–9	20			
1830	4			
1	2			
2	3			
3	11			
4	4			
5	9			
6	8			
7	1			
8	3			
9	1			
1830–9	46			

Table A (*continued*)

year	royal commissions only		all committees	
	number appointed	*number in existence*	*number appointed*	*number in existence*
1840	2			
1	6			
2	5			
3	5			
4	1			
5	7			
6	5			
7	7			
8	6			
9	7			
1840–9	51			
1850	5			
1	3			
2	3			
3	9			
4	9			
5	8			
6	7			
7	8			
8	13			
9	10			
1850–9	75			
1860	3	10		
1	5	14		
2	7	12		
3	4	15		
4	8	17		
5	7	17		
6	5	18		
7	7	21		
8	8	24		
9	5	22		
1860–9	59	17 (mean)		
1870	3	21		
1	3	14		
2	4	12		
3	3	13		
4	4	15		
5	4	12		
6	4	11		
7	5	11		
8	7	16		
9	6	15		
1870–9	43	14 (mean)		

Table A (*continued*)

year	royal commissions only		all committees	
	number appointed	*number in existence*	*number appointed*	*number in existence*
1880	4	17		
1	5	15		
2	5	18		
3	2	12		
4	3	14		
5	2	10		
6	8	14		
7	3	14		
8	4	14		
9	4	13		
1880–9	40	14 (mean)		
1890	2	11		
1	4	8		
2	4	12		
3	6	17		
4	3	16		
5	2	13		
6	4	12		
7	3	11		
8	5	14		
9	2	12		
1890–9	35	13 (mean)		
1900	3	14	16	37
1	4	14	17	40
2	5	15	18	39
3	5	15	23	42
4	3	12	17	45
5	3	12	21	41
6	11	19	27	52
7	1	15	23	55
8	3	17	24	63
9	6	19	23	56
1900–9	44	15 (mean)	209	47 (mean)
1910	2	16	22	57
1	2	12	28	62
2	6	13	35	66
3	3	12	20	59
4	2	10	17	45
5	0	7	21	44
6	4	8	27	47
7	0	5	24	56
8	2	4	27	59
9	3	4	48	72
1910–19	24	9 (mean)	269	57 (mean)

Table A (*continued*)

year	royal commissions only		all committees	
	number appointed	*number in existence*	*number appointed*	*number in existence*
1920	1	4	34	62
1	3	4	27	54
2	1	4	23	43
3	3	5	29	51
4	3	6	28	54
5	2	7	24	58
6	3	9	15	55
7	3	7	21	51
8	2	6	14	46
9	4	8	24	45
1920–9	25	6 (mean)	239	52 (mean)
1930	1	7	16	51
1	1	6	18	46
2	1	3	14	40
3	1	2	12	34
4	3	3	21	39
5	4	6	20	42
6	1	5	21	49
7	1	4	16	42
8	3	5	19	42
9	0	4	10	30
1930–9	16	5 (mean)	167	42 (mean)
1940	0	1	6	17
1	0	1	12	22
2	0	1	18	35
3	0	1	20	42
4	2	3	29	61
5	0	2	26	65
6	1	3	34	63
7	1	3	38	71
8	0	3	42	88
9	2	4	27	80
1940–9	6	2 (mean)	252	54 (mean)
1950	0	2	18	66
1	3	5	29	66
2	1	5	25	66
3	2	6	29	73
4	1	6	25	73
5	1	6	25	62
6	0	2	16	40
7	2	4	44	71
8	0	3	31	70
9	0	2	27	66
1950–9	10	4 (mean)	269	65 (mean)

Table A (continued)

year	royal commissions only		all committees	
	number appointed	number in existence	number appointed	number in existence
1960	1	3	12	52
1	1	2	21	46
2	0	2	15	49
3	0	0	31	58
4	1	1	25	63
5	2	3	20	65
6	4	7	22	60
7	0	5	27	69
8	0	5	16	67
9	1	4	17	62
1960–9	10	3 (mean)	206	59 (mean)
1800–99	399			
1860–99	177	15 (mean)		
1900–69	135	6 (mean)	1,611	54 (mean)
1800–1969	534			

Notes: Data include committees appointed between 1800 and 1969. (Committees listed in Appendix C are not included.) Each committee is deemed to be 'in existence' each year from the year of its appointment to the year of its adjournment. Blanks indicate that no data are available. Data on departmental committees may omit some dealing with colonial, ecclesiastical and military matters and are only estimated for the period from 1953 onwards (see text).

Source: See text.

Appendix B
Major Postwar Royal Commissions and Departmental Committees

The following list provides detailed information on the 356 committees – 24 royal commissions and 332 departmental committees – contained in the sample described in Chapter 3. In general, they are listed in order of the Command number assigned to their final reports; royal commissions are specially marked with an asterisk. A fuller description of each of the column headings in the following list, as well as an explanation of the abbreviations used, is given at the end of the list.

The sources of this information are threefold. The major source is the published reports of each of the committees listed. This has been supplemented by information gathered in interviews and correspondence with former chairmen, members and secretaries of committees as well as present and former civil servants and politicians. Thirdly, information has been gathered from a variety of other sources, including statements and Questions in Parliament, the press, *Who's Who*, books and scholarly articles.

Table B Major postwar royal commissions and departmental committees

1 command number	2 short title and chairman	3 date of appt.	4 date of adjmnt.	5 apptg. depts.	6 purpose	7 size	8 member-ship	9 number of witnesses	10 number of meetings	11 recommendations	12 unanimity	13 net costs (real £)	14 interim reports
6636	The Boarding Out of the O'Neill Boys Sir Walter Monckton K.C.	28 Mar 45	8 Apr 45	c	I	1	I	29	4/—	(15)	u	—	
6670	The Selling Price of Houses John W Morris K.C.	19 Mar 45	19 Jul 45	gv	IA	7	I	18	16	—	U	129	
6673	Training for Business Administration Sir Frank Newson-Smith	Feb 45	7 Jun 45	j	IA	18	R	19	3/9	12	U	—	
6687	The Census of Production Sir George Nelson	12 Jun 45	26 Sep 45	c	IA	12	—	—	—	20	U	—	
6736	The Case of Arthur Clatworthy Tom Eastham K.C.	4 Jan 46	28 Jan 46	c	I	1	R	34	4/—	5	u	—	
6748	China Clay Professor W R Jones	11 Dec 45	10 Jan 46	f	IA	3	—	25	—	5	U	—	
6764	The Census of Distribution Sir Richard Hopkins	12 Jun 45	8 Mar 46	f	IPA	18	R	76	—	14	U	—	
6782	Exhibitions and Fairs Lord Ramsden	(Jun 45)	17 Dec 45		IPA	16	R	—	4	31	U	—	
6783	A Case Heard by Gilling East Justices Lord Justice Tucker	25 Feb 46	18 Mar 46	cd	I	1	E	9	2/—	—	u	—	
6810	The Remuneration of General Practitioners Sir Will Spens	Feb 45	26 Apr 46	gv	IA	9	E	45	32	7	1D	517	
[6824]	Scientific Man-Power Sir Alan Barlow	9 Dec 45	23 Jul 46	h	IP	7	E	—	7/22	32	U	—	[unpub. fin. rept.]
6846	The Disaster at Bolton Football Ground R Moelwyn Hughes K.C.	22 Mar 46	25 May 46	c	I	1	I	64	5/—	5	u	420	
6868	Social and Economic Research Sir John Clapham	(Jun 45)	3 Jun 46	bh	IP	8	E	26	—	3	U	—	
6876	New Towns Lord Reith of Stonehaven	19 Oct 45	25 Jul 46	kv	IP	13	I	128+	16	91	U	1,356	6759, 6794
6877	The Fire at Merthyr House, Cardiff John Flowers K.C.	7 May 46	5 Jul 46	c	I	1	I	29	2/—	6	u	288	
6911	Homeless Children (Scotland) James L Clyde K.C.	20 Apr 45	30 Jul 46	v	IPA	15	I	195	12	25	5R	—	

Ref	Subject / Chairman	Appointed	Reported											Notes
6922	Care of Children *Miss Myra Curtis*	8 Mar 45	Aug 46	cgh	IPA	17	I	260	64	62	7R	1,639	6760	
6925	Legal Aid and Legal Advice in Scotland *John Cameron K.C.*	23 Nov 45	21 May 46	v	IA	6	I	25	10/12	36	1D	90		
6933	The Case of John Elliott *J C Jolly K.C.*	31 Jul 46	16 Sep 46	c	I	1	I	23	2/—	3	u	—		
7004	Electoral Registration *G H Oliver M.P.*	29 Nov 45	Dec 46	cv	IPA	15	R	20	12	21	9R	391		
7024	Procedure in Matrimonial Causes *Mr Justice Denning*	26 Jun 46	21 Jan 47	d	IA	12	I	113	15/23	74	U	503	6881, 6945	
7048	The Fire at Ferring Grange Hotel *A P L Sullivan*	(Dec 46)	3 Feb 47	c	I	1	E	20	1/—	—	u	177		
7049	The Confession Made by David Ware *J C Jolly K.C.*	21 Feb 47	25 Feb 47	c	I	1	I	—	—	1	u	—		
7061	Proceedings before Aberayron Justices *Lord Justice Tucker*	15 Jan 47	21 Feb 47	cd	I	1	E	10	2/—	2	u	—		
7076	The Assessment of Disablement *Judge Ernest Hancock*	26 Mar 46	19 Dec 46	n	IA	10	E	7	11	—	U	30		
7094	The Regent's Park Terraces *Lord Gorell*	12 Jan 46	21 Jan 47	a	IPA	7	I	59	17	14	U	—		
7126	Expenses of Members of Local Authorities *Lord Lindsay of Birker*	23 Jul 46	24 Apr 47	gv	IPA	11	R	105	12	17	1D	392		
7147	Double Day-Shift Working *Professor J L Brierly*	20 Mar 45	Jan 47	j	IA	9	I	41	8/12	12	3R	304		
7150	Disturbances at Standon Farm Approved School *John C Maude K.C. M.P.*	2 Apr 47	21 May 47	c	I	2	I	22	3/—	22	U	285		
7285	The Tenure of Shop Premises in Scotland *Prof. T M Taylor*	28 Mar 47	28 Nov 47	v	IPA	8	R	52	10	9	U	155		
7361	The British Film Institute *Sir Cyril Radcliffe K.C.*	29 Dec 47	2 Mar 48	h	IA	6	I	43	10	9	U	—		
7372	Evasions of Petrol Rationing *G Russell Vick*	20 Jan 48	31 Mar 48	i	IA	3	I	35	27	19	U	502		
7402	The Remuneration of General Dental Practitioners *Sir Will Spens*	2 Sep 46	10 May 48	gv	IA	9	I	30	15	8	U	366		
7414	Milk Distribution *Maj-Gen W D A Williams*	14 Oct 46	21 Jan 48	e	IA	6	I	130+	30/47	41	3R	—		Pub. as appendix to final report

Table B (continued)

1 command number	2 short title and chairman	3 date of appt.	4 date of adjmnt.	5 apptg. depts.	6 purpose	7 size	8 member-ship	9 number of wit-nesses	10 number of meet-ings	11 recom-menda-tions	12 unani-mity	13 net costs (real £)	14 interim reports
7420	The Remuneration of Consultants and Specialists Sir Will Spens	May 47	19 May 48	gv	IA	11	E	35	16	10	U	384	
7440	The Fire at Townshend Terrace Alfred J Long K.C.	10 Dec 47	24 May 48	c	I	1	I	16	6/—	3	u	—	
[7451]	Land Registration in Scotland Lord Macmillan	4 Mar 48	—	v	IPA	5	I	18	3/—	8	U	140	[no final report]
7463	*Justices of the Peace Lord du Parcq	24 Jun 46	5 May 48	c	IPA	16	I	—	23/—	59	2R1D	5,605	
7464	The Electricity Peak Load Problem Sir Andrew Clow	Feb 48	25 May 48	i	I	10	R	—	22	7	U	548	
7478	Tudor Aircraft A/C/M Sir Christopher Courtney	27 Sept 47	23 Jun 48	l	I	4	I	67	20/30	37	U	—	7307
7557	Industrial Diseases Judge Edgar T Dale	31 Mar 47	19 Oct 48	n	IA	10	R	32	18	—	U	476	
7565	Medical Partnerships Mr Justice Slade	20 Apr 48	8 Nov 48	g	IA	5	I	23	5/15	30	U	173	
7566	Marriage Guidance Grants Sir Sidney Harris	14 Feb 48	19 Oct 48	c	IA	6	I	30	18	5	U	8	
7608	Army and Air Force Courts-Martial Mr Justice Lewis	4 Nov 46	13 Apr 48	m	IPA	8	E	183	49	94	1R	181	
7635	Higher Civil Service Remuneration Lord Chorley	Jan 48	21 Sep 48	b	IA	5	E	15	6/9	10	U	—	
7637	Mining Subsidence Theodore Turner K.C.	3 Jan 47	25 Jan 49	i	IA	9	I	90	31/—	19	U	—	
7639	Depositions Mr Justice Byrne	5 Mar 48	22 Dec 48	c	IA	12	I	48	15	13	U	131	
7664	Shops and Non-Industrial Employment Sir Ernest Gowers	1 Jan 46	5 Mar 49	cv	IPA	16	I	136	13/55	88+	U	1,372	7105
7668	County Court Procedure Mr Justice Jones	22 Apr 47	12 Apr 49	d	IA	15	I	87	21	92	U	349	7468
7696	Resale Price Maintenance G H Lloyd Jacob K.C.	7 Aug 47	25 Mar 49	f	IP	7	I	—	25/42	—	1R	—	

No.	Title / Author												
7700	*The Press — Sir David Ross	14 Apr 47	13 Jun 49	c	IP	17	I	201	38/61	26	2R	20,522	
7705	Civil Aircraft Certification — A/C W Helmore	22 Sep 47	3 Jun 48	l	IPA	14	E	45	26	20	U	15	
7718	The Political Activities of Civil Servants — J C Masterman	25 Feb 48	26 Apr 49	b	IA	10	E	80+	15	13	U	322	
7728	Taxation and Overseas Minerals — Sir Eric Bamford	21 Sep 48	8 Mar 49	b	IPA	6	E	10	7+	4	U	—	
7732	Mineral Development — Lord Westwood	2 Aug 46	29 Mar 49	i	IP	11	E	94	30/40	10	1R	1,830	
7740	The Limitation of Actions — Lord Justice Tucker	19 Jan 48	30 Jun 49	dv	IPA	11	E	27	9	7	U	205	
7746	Civil Aviation Personnel — G/C C A B Wilcock	22 Sep 47	8 Jun 48	l	IA	14	E	162	20	27	U	15	
7831	Police Conditions of Service — Lord Oaksey	12 May 48	31 Oct 49	cv	IA	6	E	157+	23/71	94	U	—	7674
7836	The Cost of the Home Information Services — Sir Henry French	(Oct 48)	13 Jul 49	b	IA	5	E	21+	22	22	U	—	
7837	The Distribution and Exhibition of Cinematograph Films — Viscount Portal//Professor Sir Arnold Plant	Dec 48	28 Nov 49	f	IA	7	E	74	21/43	24	1R	—	
7888	The Export and Slaughter of Horses — Earl of Rosebery	28 Apr 49	22 Dec 49	ev	IP	5	I	41	—	24	U	350	
7903	The Tenure of Shops and Business Premises in Scotland — Lord Guthrie K.C.	13 Nov 48	14 Nov 49	fv	IPA	7	I	47+	—	18	U	122	7603
7904	Intermediaries — Sir Edwin Herbert	15 Feb 49	21 Oct 49	a	IA	5	I	88	21	6	U	152	
7917	Illegal Fishing in Scotland — Robert H. Maconochie K.C.	25 Aug 48	27 Dec 49	v	IPA	9	I	165	2/7	14	U	150	
7929	Celluloid Storage — J I Wall	Jun 48	30 Jan 50	c	IP	9	E	23	31	8	U	236	
7945	Children and the Cinema — Professor K C Wheare	19 Dec 47	24 Mar 50	chv	IPA	21	I	270	34	31	1R	2,661	
7948	Land Drainage (Scotland) — Joseph F Duncan	Jul 47	21 Dec 49	v	IPA	7	I	15	13	8	2R	409	
7969	The Form of Government Accounts — W F Crick	Nov 47	24 Feb 50	b	IA	6	E	46	77	33	U	—	

Pub. as appendix to fin. rept.

Table B (continued)

1 command number	2 short title and chairman	3 date of appt.	4 date of adjmnt.	5 apptg. depts.	6 purpose	7 size	8 member-ship	9 number of witnesses	10 number of meetings	11 recommendations	12 unanimity	13 net costs (real £)	14 interim reports
7982	Leasehold in England and Wales Lord Uthwatt/Lord Justice Jenkins	20 Feb 48	7 Jun 50	d	IPA	10	I	108	10/60	31	4R2D	4,004	7706
8005	The Employment of Children in Entertainments Sir Maurice Holmes	28 May 48	12 Jun 50	c	IPA	8	I	96+	37	37	U	518	
8009	Cremation D L Bateson/H H L Strutt	1 May 47	19 Jul 50	c	IA	5	E	24	14	27	U	—	
8059	The Qualifications of Planners Sir George Schuster	May 48	19 Sep 50	kv	IP	9	E	94	21	42	U	543	
8116	Broadcasting Lord Radcliffe/Lord Beveridge	21 Jun 49	15 Dec 50	ho	IPA	11	I	125	62	100	10R1D	13,000	
8119	The Naval Discipline Act Mr Justice Pilcher	17 Feb 49	6 Nov 50	m	IPA	6	E	136+	51	79	1R	148	8094
8144	The Law of Succession in Scotland Lord Mackintosh	30 Jul 49	9 Dec 50	v	IPA	8	I	31	11	17	U	120	
8147	Aircraft Landing and Taking-Off Lord Brabazon of Tara	(Feb. 50)	18 Jan 51	l	I	1	E	40	10	15	u	—	
8170	The Industrial Health Services Judge Edgar T Dale	1 Jun 49	30 Nov 50	a	IA	11	R	109	27	—	U	941	
8188	Medical Auxiliaries Dr V Zachary Cope M.D.	May 49	1 Dec 50	gv	IP	8	E	199	104+	—	9R	1,950	
8189	The Taxation of Trading Profits James M Tucker K.C.	17 Jun 49	20 Feb 51	b	IPA	6	R	147	12/—	65	U	376	
8190	*Betting, Lotteries and Gaming Sir Henry Willink K.C.	28 Apr 49	16 Mar 51	c	IPA	13	I	141+	25/42	35	U	11,051	
8219	Weights and Measures Legislation Sir Edward Hodgson	18 Oct 48	13 Dec 50	f	IPA	15	I	189	48	50	U	2,746	
8236	Stoppages in the London Docks Sir Frederick Leggett	19 May 50	25 Apr 51	j	IA	5	I	14+	33	13	U	887	
8260	Social Workers in the Mental Health Services Professor J M Mackintosh	8 Jul 48	24 Jan 51	g	IP	10	E	77	—	20	U	64	unpub.
8266	Cruelty to Wild Animals J Scott Henderson K.C.	2 Jun 49	17 Apr 51	cv	IPA	8	I	128	10,18	62	U	661	

No.	Title / Author												
8310	The Law of Intestate Succession *Lord Morton of Henryton*	13 Oct 50	5 Jun 51	d	IPA	9	I	7+	0/6	13	U	60	
8364	The Court of Record for the Hundred of Salford *G R Upjohn K.C.*	11 Sep 50	10 Aug 51	s	IA	5	E	18	2/5	8	U	—	
8378	Night Baking *Sir Frederick Rees*	18 Sep 50	13 Aug 51	j	IP	5	I	79	17	6	U	2,257	
8429	Punishments in Prisons, Etc. *H W F Franklin*	5 Nov 48	24 May 51	c	IPA	6	I	109	26	68	U	697	8256
8440	Local Land Charges *Sir John Stainton K.C.*	18 Mar 49	20 Dec 51	d	IPA	13	I	39	43	16	2R	372	
8452	Purchase Tax/Utility *Sir William Douglas*	31 Jul 51	21 Dec 51	b	IA	7	I	59	16	4	U	—	
8453	A Draft Customs and Excise Bill *Lord Kennet of the Dene*	13 Jun 51	12 Dec 51	b	A	13	R	32	17	—	U	55	
8460	State Immunities *Lord Justice Somervell*	23 Nov 49	13 Jul 51	p	IA	10	E	30	0/3	—	U	—	
8470	Post Office Recognition *Sir Maurice Holmes/Lord Terrington*	15 Feb 51	17 Jan 52	o	IPA	5	I	13	(10)/14	8	U	127	
8510	Cotton Import *Sir Richard Hopkins*	5 Dec 51	28 Mar 52	fs	IA	14	E	24+	12	6	U	485	
8514	*University Education in Dundee *Lord Tedder*	3 Mar 51	24 Apr 52	v	IA	9	E	120	21	52	U	1,237	
8522	The Conviction of Devlin and Burns *Albert D. Gerrard Q.C.*	2 Apr 52	21 Apr 52	c	I	1	I	—	6	1	u	—	
8531	The Statutory Registration of Opticians *Lord Crook*	23 Sep 49	27 Mar 52	gv	IA	15	E	104	28	28	U	1,492	
8594	Security Arrangements at Broadmoor *J Scott Henderson Q.C.*	12 May 52	17 Jun 52	g	IP	4	I	109	1/7	15	U	—	
8604	The National Museum of Antiquities of Scotland *J R Philip Q.C.*	5 Apr 51	31 Jul 52	v	IA	3	E	45	5/6	13	U	92	
8609	Scottish Financial and Trade Statistics *Lord Catto*	4 Jul 50	May 52	v	IA	8	I	14+	21	14	U	1,272	
8647	The Use of Fuel and Power Resources *Viscount Ridley*	Jul 51	24 Jul 52	i	IP	8	I	87	12/40	40	U	399	
8657	Scottish Leases *Lord Guthrie*	9 Feb 52	29 Jul 52	v	IPA	9	E	45	13	19	U	132	
8661	Welsh Language Publishing *A W Reddy*	20 Oct 51	23 Jun 52	cq	IPA	3	I	24	2/6	7	U	130	

unpub.

Table B (continued)

1 command number	2 short title and chairman	3 date of appt.	4 date of adjmnt.	5 apptg. depts.	6 purpose	7 size	8 member-ship	9 number of witnesses	10 number of meetings	11 recommendations	12 unani-mity	13 net costs (real £)	14 interim reports
8662	Copyright *Marquess of Reading/H S Gregory*	9 Apr 51	31 Jul 52	f	IPA	9	R	143	57	67	U	278	
8710	Charitable Trusts *Lord Nathan*	Jan 50	Jul 52	a	IPA	13	I	142	40	40	1D	570	
8746	Liability for Damage Done by Animals *Lord Chief Justice Goddard*	1 Aug 51	24 Nov 52	d	IPA	8	E	5+	19	5	2R	52	
8784	Tax-Paid Stocks *Sir Maurice Hutton*	Jul 52	4 Feb 53	b	IPA	7	E	149	21	5	U	180	
8804	The Taxicab Service *Viscount Runciman of Doxford*	Aug 52	6 Feb 53	b	IA	8	I	19	—	12	U	—	
8830	Purchase Tax (Valuation) *Frederick Grant Q.C.*	24 Jul 52	18 Mar 53	b	IA	6	E	141	27	2	2R	311	
8845	Entry into Certain Branches of the Royal Navy *Ewen E S Montagu Q.C.*	Jul 52	2 Apr 53	m	IA	11	E	118	40	62	1D	455	
8861	Cotton Import (Review) *Sir Richard Hopkins*	10 Mar 53	18 May 53	f	IA	14	E	8+	10	9	U	270	
8878	Supreme Court Practice and Procedure *Lord Justice Evershed*	22 Apr 47	20 May 53	d	IA	24	E	347+	40	353	4R	502	7764, 8176, 8617
8879	Discharged Prisoners' Aid Societies *Sir Alexander Maxwell*	20 Mar 51	27 Mar 53	c	IPA	7	R	62	15	7	U	61	
8896	The Case of Timothy John Evans *J Scott Henderson Q.C.*	6 Jul 53	13 Jul 53	c	I	1		23	3/4	3	u	—	8946 (sup. report)
8925	The Slaughter of Horses *Duke of Northumberland*	15 Oct 52	1 Aug 53	ev	IA	7	I	71	9	23	U	859	
8932	*Capital Punishment *Sir Ernest Gowers*	4 May 49	5 Sep 53	c	IPA	12	I	117	31/63	89	4R	18,494	
8955	A New Criminal Court in South Lancashire *Sir Alexander Maxwell*	16 Dec 52	31 Aug 53	cd	IPA	10	E	63	8	8	U	203	
8993	Scottish Local Government Law Consolidation *Professor Matthew G Fisher Q.C.*	9 Jun 48	Oct 53	v	A	14	I	0	53	—	U	339	8729, 8751

Ref	Title / Author	Date 1	Date 2										
9063	The Taxation of Provisions for Retirement *James M Tucker K.C.*	3 Aug 50	23 Dec 53	b	IPA	6	E	160	0/16	65	2R	164	
9091	Crofting Conditions *Principal Thomas Murray K.C.*	6 Jun 51	19 Jan 54	v	IP	11	I	65	38/—	42	1D	2,202	
9112	Shares of No Par Value *Montagu L Gedge Q.C.*	29 Dec 52	14 Jan 54	f	IPA	8	E	56	9/18	11	1D	296	
9117	Drainage of Trade Premises *Lord Hill Watson Q.C.*	Jun 51	28 Jan 54	v	IPA	9	E	39	4/13	—	3R	—	
9131	Recruitment and Publicity for Civil Defence *William Mabane*	31 Jul 52	3 Mar 54	cgqv	IA	16	I	28+	21	23+	U	—	8708
9138	The Overseas Information Services *Earl of Drogheda*	Oct 52	Apr 54	p	IP	8	I	59+	67	47	U	—	
9150	New Trials in Criminal Cases *Lord Tucker*	16 Dec 52	10 Apr 54	cd	IPA	8	I	53	10	8	U	4	
9163	Departmental Records *Sir James Grigg*	18 Jun 52	31 May 54	bu	IA	7	I	78	24	58	U	525	
9165	Coastal Flooding *Viscount Waverley*	28 Apr 53	21 Apr 54	cekv	IPA	14	I	121	26	35	U	—	8923
9176	The Disposal of Land at Crichel Down *Sir Andrew Clark Q.C.*	6 Nov 53	13 May 54	e	I	1	I	28	7/—	25	u	—	
9212	*Scottish Affairs *Earl of Balfour*	25 Jul 52	21 Jul 54	v	IP	15	I	84	40	61	U	15,647	
9214	Foot-and-Mouth Disease *Sir Ernest Gowers*	11 Sep 52	13 Jul 54	e	IPA	8	I	255	39	65	U	11,850	
9215	Local Objections to Gatwick Airport *Sir Colin Campbell*	29 Jan 54	24 Jun 54	k	I	1	I	38	15/—	—	u	—	
9220	The Transfer of Certain Civil Servants *J H Woods*	(Jun 54)	14 Jul 54	a	P	3	E	6	—	6	U	—	
9244	Scottish Valuation and Rating *Lord Sorn*	20 May 53	17 Aug 54	v	IPA	8	I	49+	11/18	39	U	484	
9248	The Adoption of Children *Sir Gerald Hurst Q.C.*	26 Jan 53	Apr 54	cv	IPA	9	I	152	19/35	48	U	617	
9273	Close Seasons for Deer in Scotland *Robert H Maconochie Q.C.*	7 Jul 52	11 Jun 54	v	IPA	9	E	120	(40/49)	24	3D	1,665	
9276	The Censuses of Production and Distribution *Sir Reginald Verdon-Smith*	4 May 53	1 Jul 54	f	IP	14	I	564	4/20	25	U	—	

Table B (continued)

1 command number	2 short title and chairman	3 date of appt.	4 date of adjmnt.	5 apptg. depts.	6 purpose	7 size	8 member-ship	9 number of witnesses	10 number of meetings	11 recommendations	12 unanimity	13 net costs (real £)	14 interim reports
9322	Air Pollution *Sir Hugh Beaver*	21 Jul 53	10 Nov 54	ikv	IA	11	E	121	59	41	U	1,109	9011
9333	The Problems of Providing for Old Age *Sir Thomas Phillips*	Jul 53	27 Nov 54	b	IP	10	I	72	18/35	(26)	5R	1,271	
9376	Slaughterhouses (Scotland) *Sir John Handford*	12 Mar 53	30 Dec 54	v	IPA	6	I	115	15/30	4+	U	282	9061
9419	Mathematics and Science Teachers in Scotland *Sir Edward Appleton*	10 Oct 53	9 Mar 55	v	IP	12	R	55	32	48	U	221	
9433	Boys' Units in the Army *B L Hallward*	20 Dec 54	28 Feb 55	m	I	3	I	—	0	—	U	140	
9467	A New Queen's Hall *Professor Lionel Robbins*	Oct 54	29 Apr 55	b	I	5	E	133	10/16	10	U	—	
9474	*The Taxation of Profits and Income *Sir Lionel Cohen/Lord Radcliffe*	2 Jan 51	20 May 55	c	IA	14	R	478	38/173	106	7R3D	26,577	8761, 9105
9475	*East Africa *Sir Hugh Dow*	1 Jan 53	16 May 55	c	IA	7	I	700+	—/150	—	U	27,526	
9483	Crown Lands *Sir Malcolm Trustram Eve*	Dec 54	17 May 55	a	IA	6	E	20	15	16	U	—	
9523	The Territorial Army *J R H Hutchison M.P./Fitzroy Maclean*	11 Mar 54	21 Apr 55	m	I	7	E	67	24	31	U	120	
9524	The Summary Trial of Minor Offences *Sir Reginald Sharpe Q.C.*	12 Oct 54	1 Jun 55	c	IA	11	I	50	10	13	U	181	
9542	Slaughterhouses (England and Wales) *R Herbert*	9 Feb 53	18 Jul 55	e	IPA	6	I	126	24/44	25	U	985	9060
9548	Statutory Provisions for Industrial Diseases *F W Beney Q.C.*	12 May 53	15 Jul 55	n	IA	12	E	66	21	6	3D	560	
9588	Pig Production *Sir Harold Howitt*	10 Jan 55	28 Sep 55	cev	IA	7	E	89	11/22	33	U	—	
9613	*The Civil Service *Sir Raymond Priestley*	16 Nov 53	10 Nov 55	c	IA	12	I	80	28/66	103	6R	15,844	
9663	The Cost of the National Health Service *C W Guillebaud*	May 53	16 Nov 55	gv	IA	5	E	113+	37/54	(91)	2R	633	

Ref	Title / Author	Date appointed	Date reported									
9672	The Electricity Supply Industry / *Sir Edwin Herbert*	9 Jul 54	9 Dec 55	i	IA	7	I	125+	63	125	U	539
9678	*Marriage and Divorce / Lord Morton of Henryton*	8 Sep 51	20 Dec 55	c	IPA	18	I	253	41/102	81	2R	30,755
9715	Security / *Marquess of Salisbury*	23 Nov 55	Mar 56	a	IA	7	E	—	—	—	U	—
9732	The Local Organisation of the Ministry of Agriculture, Fisheries and Food / *Sir Arton Wilson*	Dec 54	24 Jan 56	e	IA	5	E	(400)	(25)/46	78	U	(2,700)
[9734]	A Department of Scientific and Industrial Research / *Sir Harry Jephcott*	Apr 55	(Dec 55)	h	IA	5	E	66	—	5	U	— [unpub. fin. rept.]
9738	The Employment of Children in the Potato Harvest / *Sir Hugh Rose*	23 Sep 55	6 Mar 56	v	IP	9	E	58	8	2	1D	110
9755	The Office of the Public Trustee / *Sir Maurice Holmes*	Mar 54	28 Jul 55	d	IPA	5	I	22	18	7	U	22
9757	The Composition and Nutritive Value of Flour / *Professor Sir Henry Cohen*	May 55	10 Jan 56	egv	I	5	E	35	3/7	12	U	144
9788	Unpatented Inventions in Defence Contracts / *Sir Harold Howitt*	Nov 55	24 Jan 56	f	IPA	3	I	7	10	11	U	2
9813	The Dock Workers Scheme, 1947 / *Mr Justice Devlin*	27 Jul 55	12 Jun 56	j	IA	5	I	20+	17	11	U	—
9825	Land Charges / *Mr Justice Roxburgh*	1 Oct 54	19 Jul 56	d	IPA	5	E	22	11	—	U	32
9861	Recruitment to the Dental Profession / *Lord McNair Q.C.*	25 Mar 55	Aug 56	gv	IP	11	I	131	(0)/28+	17	1R	966
9883	Disabled Persons / *Lord Piercy*	12 Mar 53	24 Sep 56	giv	IA	13	E	172	54	46	U	216
3	Cheque Endorsement / *A A Mocatta Q.C.*	18 Apr 55	31 Aug 56	b	IPA	5	I	48	25	16	U	6
35	The Employment of National Service Men / *J F Wolfenden*	1 Mar 56	1 Oct 56	m	I	3	I	—	0	11	U	615
39	Welsh Broadcasting / *Sir Godfrey Ince*	29 Feb 56	9 Nov 56	o	I	3	I	30	2/9	6	U	210
47	Damage and Casualties in Port Said / *Sir Edwin Herbert*	7 Dec 56	19 Dec 56	m	I	1	I	24	(11)	8	u	500

Table B (continued)

1 command number	2 short title and chairman	3 data of appt.	4 date of adjmnt.	5 apptg. depts.	6 purpose	7 size	8 member-ship	9 number of wit-nesses	10 number of meet-ings	11 recom-menda-tions	12 unani-mity	13 net costs (real £)	14 interim reports
61	Horticultural Marketing *Viscount Runciman of Doxford*	31 Mar 55	20 Dec 56	cev	IPA	7	E	257	32	16	U	1,980	
154	The Export of Live Cattle for Slaughter *Lord Balfour of Burleigh*	6 Feb 57	15 Apr 57	ev	IPA	5		77	9	25	U	510	
168	The Carlisle State Management Scheme *C S S Burt Q.C.*	12 Feb 57	15 Apr 57	c	I	1	I	20+	3/—	7	u	66	
169	*Mental Illness and Mental Deficiency *Lord Percy of Newcastle*	20 Feb 54	7 May 57	c	IPA	11	E	110	26/51	62	U	22,175	
218	Administrative Tribunals and Inquiries *Sir Oliver Franks*	1 Nov 55	15 Jul 57	d	IA	16	I	226	27/61	95	1R	16,068	
221	Bankruptcy Law Amendment *Judge John B Blagden*	13 Oct 55	27 May 57	f	IPA	6	I	62+	25/103	58	U	255	
227	The Supreme Court of Northern Ireland *Lord Justice Black/Mr Justice Sheil*	1 Nov 49	19 Mar 57	d	IPA	7	E	—	0/51	7	U	275	
247	Homosexual Offences and Prostitution *Sir John Wolfenden*	24 Aug 54	12 Aug 57	cv	IPA	15	R	203+	32/62	30	6R	7,311	
251	The Cardiganshire Constabulary *H J Phillimore*	19 Mar 57	30 Apr 57	c	I	1	I	23	2/—	13	u	—	
262	The Purchasing Procedure of the British Transport Commission *Sir Harold Howitt*	24 Jul 57	12 Sep 57	l	I	1	I	40	—	—	u	4,600	
268	The Army Cadet Force *Fitzroy Maclean M.P./Julian Amery M.P.*	31 Aug 56	12 Jul 57	m	I	8	E	88	6	50	U	(100)	
269	Building Legislation in Scotland *C W Graham Guest Q.C.*	27 Jan 54	15 Jul 57	v	IA	10	E	44	30	69	U	590	
283	The Interception of Communications *Sir Norman Birkett*	29 Jun 57	18 Sep 57	a	IPA	3	E	—	12/29	16	1R	—	
338	The Organisation of the Atomic Energy Authority *Sir Alexander Fleck*	Oct 57	16 Dec 57	a	IA	3	E	8+	7	22	U	—	
342	Health and Safety in the Atomic Energy Authority *Sir Alexander Fleck*	Oct 57	19 Dec 57	a	IA	6	E	—	6	12	U	—	

unpub.

No.	Title / Author											
446	Coal Distribution Costs *Sir Thomas Robson*	16 Mar 56	28 Apr 58	i	IP	6	I	59+	9/36	—	U	952
456	Diligence *Sheriff Hector McKechnie Q.C.*	Jul 56	Jun 58	v	IA	10	E	46	7/21	96	U	358
457	The Preservation of Downing Street *Earl of Crawford and Balcarres*	Jul 57	1 Mar 58	a	IA	5	I	—	—	5	U	—
462	*Common Land *Sir Ivor Jennings Q.C.*	1 Dec 55	11 Jul 58	c	IA	12	E	395	31/69	70	U	30,376
471	The Windscale Piles *Sir Alexander Fleck*	Oct 57	17 Jun 58	a	I	7	E	—	—	8	U	—
472	The Tenancy of Shops (Scotland) Act, 1949 *Ian H Shearer Q.C.*	16 Jan 58	16 Jun 58	v	IP	5	I	57	—	1	U	22
473	The Rights of Light *Mr Justice Harman*	29 Mar 57	12 May 58	d	IPA	7	I	26	(2)/7	6	U	—
479	Proceedings before Examining Justices *Lord Tucker*	1 Jun 57	10 Jul 58	c	IP	12	E	125	21	8	U	338
486	Inland Waterways *H Leslie Bowes*	1 Feb 56	11 Jun 58	l	IA	8	I	121	12/24	55	4R	—
503	Ill-treatment of Prisoners in Liverpool Prison *Sir Godfrey Vick Q.C.*	16 Jul 56	6 Dec 56	c	I	1	I	—	20/—	—	u	—
544	Conditions in the Prison Services *Mr Justice Wynn-Parry*	8 Oct 57	11 Aug 58	cv	IA	6	I	34	11/20	48	1R	566
545	Recruiting for the Armed Forces *Sir James Grigg*	Dec 57	31 Jul 58	m	IP	7	I	—	2+	30	U	4,562
547	Grassland Utilisation *Sir Sydney Caine*	5 Sep 57	3 Oct 58	cev	IA	11	I	159	40	15	4R	2,701
583	The Misuse of Official Facilities *Sir Norman Brook*	5 Nov 58	11 Nov 58	a	I	1	E	20	—	4	u	—
605	The Disposal of Scrap Cable by the London Electricity Board *Henry Benson*	28 Jul 58	10 Nov 58	i	I	1	I	29+	—	9	u	—
614	Further Education for Agriculture *Earl De La Warr*	Mar 57	Nov 58	eh	IP	12	I	159	29	33	U	928
630	Highway Law Consolidation *Marquess of Reading*	25 Feb 58	25 Nov 58	klq	A	16	R	28	0/11	—	U	—
638	Matrimonial Proceedings in Magistrates' Courts *Mr Justice Arthian Davies*	5 Jul 58	18 Dec 58	c	A	11	I	0	8	5	U	36

Table B (continued)

1 command number	2 short title and chairman	3 date of appt.	4 date of adjmnt.	5 apptg. depts.	6 purpose	7 size	8 member-ship	9 number of wit-nesses	10 number of meet-ings	11 recom-menda-tions	12 unani-mity	13 net costs (real £)	14 interim reports
660	The Public Library Service / Sir Sydney Roberts	3 Sep 57	11 Dec 58	h	IA	16	I	105	20	28	2R	1,259	
663	Hallmarking and Assaying / Sir Leonard Stone	7 Dec 55	3 Sep 58	f	IPA	6	I	111	50	(36)	U	1,271	
695	Co-operation between Area and Scottish Electricity and Gas Boards / Sir Cecil Weir	17 Mar 58	13 Feb 59	iv	IA	8	E	140	16	11	U	311	
786	The Colonial Development Corporation / Lord Sinclair of Cleeve	8 Apr 59	22 Jul 59	p	IA	3	E	8	—	8	U	—	
812	London Roads / G R H Nugent M.P.	Nov 57	Jul 59	l	IA	12	R	5	8	6	6R	—	
818	Funds in Court / Mr Justice Pearson	14 Feb 58	11 May 59	d	IPA	10	E	42	13	29	U	100	
827	The Working of the Monetary System / Lord Radcliffe	3 May 57	30 Jul 59	b	IP	9	R	219+	59/88	5+	U	16,525	
831	The Rating of Charities / Sir Fred Pritchard	22 Jan 58	29 Jun 59	k	IP	5	I	165	29	33	U	1,731	
842	Conflicts of Jurisdiction Affecting Children / Lord Justice Hodson	5 Feb 58	3 Jul 59	d	IA	8	E	9	5	9	1R	218	
846	Anthrax / R F Levy Q.C.	4 Jun 57	18 Jun 59	j	IA	5	I	71	20	28	U	587	
851	Civil Jury Trial in Scotland / Lord Strachan	21 Nov 57	2 Jul 59	v	IPA	10	I	86	5/15	20	3D	246	
872	Caravans as Homes / Sir Arton Wilson	25 Nov 58	31 Jul 59	k	I	1	I	22+	45/71	(35)	u	938	
929	The Youth Service in England and Wales / Countess of Albemarle	Nov 58	22 Oct 59	h	IP	13	I	111	30	44	U	966	
937	Disturbances at Carlton Approved School / Victor Durand Q.C.	14 Sep 59	31 Dec 59	c	I	1	I	69	14/—	32	u	4,928	
939	*Doctors' and Dentists' Remuneration / Sir Harry Pilkington	27 Mar 57	10 Feb 60	c	IA	9	I	167+	23/80	47	1D	33,586	

No.	Subject / Chairman											
967	Chancery Chambers and the Chancery Registrar's Office *Lord Justice Harman*	4 Jul 58	5 Feb 60	d	IA	5	E	39	18	41	U	0
999	Solid Smokeless Fuels *N M Peech*	3 Apr 59	Mar 60	i	I	4	E	13	1/8	(18)	U	24
1003	A Levy on Betting on Horse Races *L E Peppiatt*	9 Nov 59	11 Apr 60	c	IPA	7	I	26	14	22	U	—
1015	Legal Aid in Criminal Proceedings *Lord Guthrie*	19 Dec 57	Feb 60	v	IA	12	I	54	12	34	1D	126
1033	Powers of Subpoena of Disciplinary Tribunals *Viscount Simonds*	5 Jan 60	11 May 60	cv	IP	3	E	32	0/15	4	U	41
1051	Grants to Students *Sir Colin Anderson*	Jun 58	26 Apr 60	hv	IPA	16	I	209	48	85	1R	3,879
1105	Human Artificial Insemination *Earl of Feversham*	3 Sept 58	27 Jun 60	cv	IPA	9	I	186	37	8	2D	1,591
1120	Coal Derivatives *A H Wilson*	23 Apr 59	7 Jul 60	i	IP	9	E	54	16	47	U	1,299
1140	The Importation of Charollais Cattle *Lord Terrington*	Jun 59	Jul 60	ev	IA	4	I	86	4/14	2	U	1,961
1147	Milk Composition *J W Cook*	May 58	28 Jul 60	cegv	IPA	16	I	70	27	23	U	2,662
1164	*Local Government in Greater London *Sir Edwin Herbert*	10 Dec 57	3 Oct 60	c	IPA	7	E	—	70/114	7+	U	37,177
1173	The Examination of Steam Boilers in Industry *G G Honeyman*	28 May 58	May 60	j	IA	5	E	39	10	12	1R	—
1191	Children and Young People *Viscount Ingleby*	3 Oct 56	5 Oct 60	c	IPA	15	I	151	49	125	3R	1,692
1255	Legal Education for African Students *Lord Denning*	25 Jul 60	16 Dec 60	d	IPA	21	I	44+	11	11	U	72
1266	The Fishing Industry *Sir Alexander Fleck*	27 Nov 57	13 Dec 60	cev	IP	8	I	101	53	50	2R	255
1289	The Business of the Criminal Courts *Mr Justice Streatfield*	17 Jun 58	30 Dec 60	cd	IA	9	E	156	15/50	34	U	1,197
1350	Salmon and Freshwater Fisheries *B L Bathurst*	7 Oct 57	1 Mar 61	e	IPA	12	I	189	36	151	U	3,505
1406	Compensation for Victims of Crimes of Violence [chairman unknown]	Feb 59	20 Dec 60	c	IA	—	—	—	17	(29)	—	—

Table B (continued)

1 command number	2 short title and chairman	3 date of appt.	4 date of adjmnt.	5 apptg. depts.	6 purpose	7 size	8 member-ship	9 number of witnesses	10 number of meetings	11 recommendations	12 unanimity	13 net costs (real £)	14 interim reports
1432	The Control of Public Expenditure *Lord Plowden*	30 Jul 59	9 Jun 61	b	IP	9	E	34	89	—	U	—	
1597	The Remuneration of Milk Distributors *Sir Guy Thorold*	Nov 59	16 Nov 61	ev	IA	6	I	36	33	29	U	1,030	
1606	Magistrates' Courts in London *Judge C D Aarvold*	28 Jul 60	20 Nov 61	cd	IA	8	I	49	13/33	56	U	31	
1664	Fowl Pest Policy *Professor Sir Arnold Plant*	Jul 60	Jan 62	ev	IPA	8	I	121+	33	29	U	15,335	
1681	Security in the Public Service *Lord Radcliffe*	11 May 61	21 Nov 61	a	IPA	5	I	70+	61	38	U	—	
1728	*The Police *Sir Henry Willink Q.C.*	25 Jan 60	24 May 62	c	IPA	15	I	235	51/93	146	6R1D	39,350	1222
1749	Company Law *Lord Jenkins*	10 Dec 59	30 May 62	f	IPA	14	I	154+	20/64	(334)	7R	22,840	
1750	Security at the National Gallery *Lord Bridges*	26 Sep 61	13 Feb 62	a	I	2	I	35	11	(8)	U	—	
1753	Broadcasting *Sir Harry Pilkington*	13 Jul 60	1 Jun 62	o	IPA	13	I	520	39/78	120	U	42,700	
1781	Consumer Protection *J T Molony Q.C.*	30 Jun 59	25 Apr 62	f	IPA	12	I	295	0/56	215	U	1,667	1011
1800	The Probation Service *Sir Ronald Morison Q.C.*	27 Mar 59	7 Jun 62	cv	IA	14	I	205	35/57	177	1R	3,305	1650
1808	Industrial Designs *Kenneth Johnston Q.C.*	11 May 59	14 May 62	f	IPA	8	I	109	22/48	59	U	654	
1811	*The Press *Lord Shawcross Q.C.*	4 Mar 61	5 Sep 62	c	I	5	I	—	63	55	U	27,900	
1824	The Major Ports of Great Britain *Viscount Rochdale*	29 Mar 61	26 Jul 62	l	IPA	5	I	206	42	—	U	6,874	
1829	The Limitation of Actions for Personal Injury *Mr Justice Edmund Davies*	27 Jan 61	Aug 62	dv	IPA	11	I	35	9	5	U	352	
1835	The Economy of Northern Ireland *Sir Herbert Brittain/Sir Robert Hall*	4 May 61	May 62	c	IPA	12	R	4+	22	30	U	—	

No.	Title / Chairman	Date 1	Date 2										
1859	Electricity in Scotland — C H Mackenzie	21 Mar 61	7 Sep 62	v	IP	7	E	67	46	28	U	1,764	
[1871]	The Vassall Case — Sir Charles Cunningham	22 Oct 62	7 Nov 62	a	I	3	E	0	4	1	U	—	[no final report]
2021	Scottish Licensing Law — Lord Guest	13 Aug 59	5 Apr 63	v	IPA	12	I	134	13/28	96	1R	(450)	1217
2032	The Registration of Title to Land in Scotland — Lord Reid	25 Sep 59	Mar 63	v	IPA	9	I	46	6/17	57	U	990	
2056	The Problem of Noise — Sir Alan Wilson	Apr 60	Mar 63	h	IA	13	R	226+	28	188	U	—	1780
2066	The Teaching Profession in Scotland — Lord Wheatley	9 Nov 61	23 May 63	v	IA	22	R	96	26	96	U	—	
2145	Decimal Currency — Earl of Halsbury	19 Dec 61	19 Jul 63	b	IA	6	I	290	57	—	2R	20,000	
2152	The Security Service and Mr Profumo — Lord Denning	21 Jun 63	16 Sep 63	a	I	1	E	(160)	69	—	U	—	
2154	Higher Education — Professor Lord Robbins	8 Feb 61	23 Sep 63	a	IPA	12	E	514	111	178	1R	120,000	
2171	The Organisation of Civil Science — Sir Burke Trend	Mar 62	23 Sep 63	a	IA	7	E	45	30/44	15	U	—	
2202	A Complaint by the National Union of Bank Employees — Lord Cameron Q.C.	9 Apr 63	7 Aug 63	j	I	1	I	28	8/—	1	u	—	
2276	Representational Services Overseas — Lord Plowden	30 Jul 62	2 Dec 63	a	IA	7	E	139	34	52	U	—	
2282	Meat Marketing and Distribution — Sir Reginald Verdon-Smith	18 Apr 62	16 Jan 64	cev	IPA	7	I	292	62	43	U	6,035	
2300	Turnover Taxation — Gordon Richardson	16 Apr 63	21 Feb 64	b	I	3	E	114	35	2	U	320	
2306	Children and Young Persons (Scotland) — Lord Kilbrandon	29 May 61	10 Jan 64	v	IPA	13	I	56	15/29	44	U	659	
2319	The Case of Mr Herman Woolf — Norman J Skelhorn	19 Dec 63	16 Mar 64	c	I	1	I	78	16/—	8	u	—	
2351	Overseas Geology and Mining — Sir Frederick Brundrett	Apr 62	30 Apr 63	p	IP	10	R	38	(3)/10	14	U	—	
2419	The Demand for Agricultural Graduates — C I C Bosanquet	Nov 62	30 Apr 64	cev	I	9	I	165	10/17	25	U	1,384	
2430	Recruitment for the Veterinary Profession — Duke of Northumberland	29 Oct 62	29 Jun 64	ev	IP	7	I	97	30	4	U	1,911	

Table B (continued)

1 command number	2 short title and chairman	3 date of appt.	4 date of adjmnt.	5 apptg. depts.	6 purpose	7 size	8 member-ship	9 number of wit-nesses	10 number of meet-ings	11 recom-menda-tions	12 unani-mity	13 net costs (real £)	14 interim reports
2516	The Remuneration of Ministers and M.P.s *Sir Geoffrey Lawrence*	19 Dec 63	20 Oct 64	a	IA	3	E	—	—	9	U	14,841	
2526	The Cases of Halloran and Cox and Others *W L Mars-Jones Q.C.*	31 Mar 64	16 Oct 64	c		1	I	68	46/—	18	u	—	
2528	The Law on Sunday Observance *Lord Crathorne*	11 Jul 61	16 Sep 64	c	IPA	8	I	151	34	31	U	75	
2581	Ministry of Aviation Contracts *Sir John Lang*	24 Jan 64	7 Jan 65	bl	IA	3	E	11+	72	60	U	4,040	2428
2582	The Impact of Rates on Households *Professor R G D Allen*	12 Jun 63	13 Nov 64	kv	I	6	E	114+	28	(32)	U	24,751	
2605	Housing in Greater London *Sir Milner Holland Q.C.*	24 Aug 63	11 Mar 65	k	I	12	I	279	60	—	U	31,380	
2627	Jury Service *Lord Morris of Borth-y-Gest*	23 May 63	29 Jan 65	c	IPA	11	I	206	12/27	58	U	444	
2641	Experiments on Animals *Sir Sydney Littlewood*	23 May 63	19 Feb 65	c	IPA	14	I	139	28	83	1R	1,606	
2660	Social Studies *Lord Heyworth*	Jun 63	23 Feb 65	h	IP	6	E	328	29	26	U	7,500	
2691	Scottish Salmon and Trout Fisheries *Lord Hunter*	12 Mar 62	24 May 65	v	IPA	7	I	192	90	155	U	2,398	2096
2709	Licensing Planning *J Ramsay Willis Q.C.*	15 Apr 64	21 May 65	c	IP	9	R	63	7	11	1R	157	
2719	Positive Covenants Affecting Land *Mr Justice Wilberforce*	Jul 63	13 Jul 65	d	IPA	10	I	25	0/15	14	U	249	
2734	The Port Transport Industry *Lord Devlin*	30 Oct 64	28 Jul 65	j	IA	4	E	—	3/(8)	10+	U	—	2523
2755	The Court of Criminal Appeal *Lord Donovan*	25 Feb 64	24 Jun 65	cd	IA	7	E	59	59	47	U	69	
2773	The Bossard and Allen Cases *Sir Henry Wilson Smith*	9 Aug 65	6 Sep 65	a	I	3	I	7	6/10	—	U	—	
2785	The Legal Status of the Welsh Language *Sir David Hughes Parry*	30 Jul 63	15 Jun 65	q	IP	3	E	244+	20+	31	U	9,489	

No.	Title / Chairman												
2836	The Welfare of Livestock *Professor F W R Brambell*	Jun 64	(Oct 65)	ev	IPA	9	E	115	15/33	28	U	1,720	
2847	The Assessment of Disablement *Lord McCorquodale of Newton*	26 Oct 64	10 Nov 65	n	IA	13	I	14+	11	13	U	261	
2853	The Aircraft Industry *Lord Plowden*	9 Dec 64	3 Dec 65	l	IPA	8	E	234+	(10)/50	48	1R	16,300	
2934	Legal Aid in Criminal Proceedings *Mr Justice Widgery*	25 Apr 64	31 Jan 66	c	IA	14	I	135	13/21	92	U	1,227	
2937	Shipbuilding *A R M Geddes*	16 Feb 65	24 Feb 66	f	IPA	7	E	120	38	120	U	55,213	
[ ]	*The Penal System *Viscount Amory**	28 Jul 64	(Apr 66)	c	IPA	16	I	—	6/30	0	—	—	[no report issued]
3051	The Law of Succession by Illegitimate Persons *Lord Justice Russell*	11 Feb 64	12 May 66	dv	IPA	9	I	51	0/6	12	1R	0	
3084	Legal Records *Lord Justice Russell*	4 Jan 63	16 May 66	d	IPA	7	E	—	(20)/27	—	U	4	
3096	The Mechanical Recording of Court Proceedings *Mr Justice Baker*	6 Oct 64	18 Jul 66	d	IA	6	E	22	0/19	22	U	1,114	2733
3101	The Case of Timothy John Evans *Mr Justice Brabin*	23 Aug 65	10 Aug 66	c	I	1	I	169	32/35	—	u	—	
3104	Pay for Dock Workers *Lord Devlin*	22 Apr 66	13 Aug 66	j	IA	3	E	—	—	3	U	—	
3118	Conveyancing Legislation and Practice *Professor J M Halliday*	16 Jun 64	26 Aug 66	v	IPA	5	E	38	54	65	U	593	
3121	*Tribunals of Inquiry *Lord Justice Salmon Q.C.**	28 Feb 66	1 Nov 66	c	IPA	7	E	67	16/22	50	U	12,800	
3175	Prison Escapes and Security *Earl Mountbatten of Burma*	24 Oct 66	21 Dec 66	c	IPA	1	I	200+	—	52	u	—	
3248	The Sheriff Court *Lord Grant*	8 Aug 63	13 Mar 67	v	IPA	14	I	133	13/40	375	4R	2,032	
3257	General Medical Services in the Highlands and Islands *Lord Birsay*	(Oct 64)	Mar 67	v	IP	9	I	139	12+	61	1R	—	
3303	Statutory Smallholdings *Professor M J Wise*	22 Jul 63	10 Apr 67	e	IPA	6	I	150+	33/70	106	U	3,084	2936
3309	'D' Notice Matters *Lord Radcliffe*	28 Feb 67	17 May 67	a	IA	3	E	24	11	16	U	—	

Table B (continued)

1 command number	2 short title and chairman	3 date of appt.	4 date of adjmnt.	5 apptg. depts.	6 purpose	7 size	8 member-ship	9 number of wit-nesses	10 number of meet-ings	11 recom-menda-tions	12 unani-mity	13 net costs (real £)	14 interim reports
3342	The Age of Majority *Mr Justice Latey*	30 Jul 65	5 Jun 67	d	IP	11	I	81	14/65	52	2D	—	
3367	Punishment at Court Lees Approved School *Edward B Gibbens Q.C.*	15 May 67	27 July 67	c	I	1	I	46	5/—	10	u	—	
3387	Immigration Appeals *Sir Roy Wilson Q.C.*	23 Feb 66	31 Jul 67	c	IPA	7	I	70	14/31	28	U	2,117	
3409	The Accident to the Drilling Rig Sea Gem *J Roland Adams Q.C.*	8 Feb 67	26 Jul 67	i	I	1	I	30	29/—	8	u	—	
3410	The Pharmaceutical Industry *Lord Sainsbury*	May 65	Aug 67	gv	IP	11	I	161	18/60	33	U	10,500	
3448	Criminal Statistics *Wilfrid Perks*	17 Jun 63	21 Sep 67	c	IA	13	E	64	33	14	U	661	
3516	Capital Projects Overseas *Earl of Cromer*	23 Mar 67	5 Jan 68	f	IPA	1	E	135	—	(7)	u	—	
3569	*Medical Education *Professor Lord Todd*	6 Aug 65	30 Mar 68	c	IPA	16	E	400+	100+	—	U	72,000	
3587	Statutory Maintenance Limits *Miss Jean Graham Hall*	26 Jun 66	11 Mar 68	c	IA	7	I	60	21	14	U	—	
3623	*Trade Unions and Employers' Associations *Lord Donovan Q.C.*	8 Apr 65	24 May 68	c	IPA	12	E	430	58/128	87	6R	85,335	
3638	The Civil Service *Lord Fulton*	8 Feb 66	19 Jun 68	ab	IPA	12	R	250	89	(158)	1R	45,000	
3684	Civil Judicial Statistics *Chief Master Paul Adams*	25 Mar 66	15 May 68	d	IA	9	E	48	26	14	U	—	
3691	Personal Injuries Litigation *Lord Justice Winn*	12 Jan 66	23 May 68	d	IA	7	E	245	54	117	5R1D	—	
3703	Local Authority Personal Social Services *Frederic Seebohm*	20 Dec 65	18 Jun 68	cghk	IPA	10	I	239	86	206	U	18,532	
3705	Criminal Statistics in Scotland *Alexander Thomson Q.C.*	5 Nov 63	1 May 68	v	IA	9	E	7	14	31	U	404	

Ref	Title / Chairman												
3714	Labour in Building and Civil Engineering *Professor E H Phelps Brown*	22 Mar 67	28 Jun 68	jr	IPA	6	E	74	30/55	25	U	—	
3748	Herbage Seed Supplies *C H M Wilcox/Lord Donaldson*	Nov 66	(Jul 68)	cev	I	16	R	36	17	91	U	2,561	
3904	The Protection of Field Monuments *Sir David Walsh*	26 Apr 66	(Jan 69)	r	IPA	9	I	31	27	44	U	—	
3909	The Enforcement of Judgment Debts *Mr Justice Payne*	3 Mar 65	21 Nov 68	d	IA	12	I	182	11/78	23	10R	—	
3960	Delays in CEGB Power Stations *Sir Alan Wilson*	Jul 68	21 Feb 69	i	IA	6	E	42	28/32+	6	U	174	
3998	Intermediate Areas *Sir Joseph Hunt*	21 Sep 67	20 Feb 69	b	IPA	10	R	330	30	27	4R	4,170	
4011	Marriage Law in Scotland *Lord Kilbrandon Q.C.*	9 May 67	21 Mar 69	v	IPA	10	I	66	2/12	45	U	671	
4018	Civil Air Transport *Professor Sir Ronald Edwards*	5 Nov 67	1 Apr 69	f	IPA	7	E	325	—	12	U	37,735	
4028	National Libraries *Dr F S Dainton*	Dec 67	27 Mar 69	h	IA	5	E	262	—	132	U	22,000	
4040	*Local Government in England *Sir John Maud*	31 May 66	28 May 69	c	IPA	11	E	2,156	181	115	4R	285,596	
4078	Contempt of Tribunals of Enquiry *Lord Justice Salmon Q.C.*	25 Jul 67	12 May 69	cv	IA	6	E	68	7/13	8	U	471	
4107	Overseas Representation *Sir Val Duncan*	7 Aug 68	Jun 69	p	IPA	3	E	61	73/153	102	U	—	
4114	Trawler Safety *Admiral Sir Derec Holland-Martin*	5 Mar 68	9 May 69	f	IPA	6	E	53	36	88	U	7,400	3773
4137	A Scheme for the Registration of Title to Land in Scotland *Professor G L F Henry*	5 Nov 65	May 69	v	IA	5	I	25	101	—	U	803	
4150	*Local Government in Scotland *Lord Wheatley Q.C.*	31 May 66	19 Sep 69	v	IPA	9	I	344	19/148	161	3R	91,487	
4152	An Education Dispute in Durham *Dr W E J McCarthy*	8 Jul 69	29 Jul 69	hj	I	3	I	31	2/3	4	U	—	
4153	*Assizes and Quarter Sessions *Lord Beeching*	7 Nov 66	4 Sep 69	c	IA	9	E	273	—	78	U	58,000	
4156	Method II Selection of Administrative Class Civil Servants *J G W Davies*	7 Oct 68	(Jul 69)	t	IA	5	E	62	34	23	U	4,800	
4166	Allotments *Professor H Thorpe*	2 Aug 65	16 Jun 69	kq	IPA	7	I	217	58	44	U	—	

Table B (continued)

1 command number	2 short title and chairman	3 date of appt.	4 date of adjmnt.	5 apptg. depts.	6 purpose	7 size	8 member-ship	9 number of witnesses	10 number of meetings	11 recommendations	12 unanimity	13 net costs (real £)	14 interim reports
4190	Antibiotics in Animal Husbandry and Veterinary Medicine *Professor Michael M Swann*	Jul 68	Sep 69	egnv	I	9	E	90	—	32	U	12,345	
4225	Foot-and-Mouth Disease *Duke of Northumberland*	28 Feb 68	3 Nov 69	e	IPA	7	I	504	48	116	U	16,453	3999
4292	The Supreme Court of Judicature of Northern Ireland *Lord MacDermott K.C.*	14 Mar 66	12 Dec 69	d	IA	8	E	12	58	97	2R	—	
4335	The Functions and Organisation of the Central Training Council *Frank Cousins*	27 Feb 69	9 Mar 70	j	IPA	7	R	69	16	9	U	—	
4337	Shipping *Viscount Rochdale*	22 Jul 67	4 Feb 70	f	IPA	6	E	235	—	94	U	94,466	
4366	Commercial Rating *Professor D S Anderson*	Aug 68	28 Apr 70	v	IPA	9	E	20	6/20	13	U	623	
4371	The Fire Service *Sir Ronald Holroyd*	2 Feb 67	11 May 70	cv	IPA	11	I	87	70+	108	1R	—	
4407	The Patent System and Patent Law *M A L Banks*	10 May 67	11 May 70	f	IPA	10	E	149	51	126	2R	37,700	
4453	Scottish Inshore Fisheries *Hon. Lord Cameron Q.C.*	8 Dec 67	May 70	v	IPA	6	E	115	25	22	U	1,816	
4483	The London Taxicab Trade *Hon. A Maxwell Stamp*	28 Oct 67	24 Jul 70	c	IPA	8	I	37	62	77	U	21,344	
4509	Boy Entrants and Young Servicemen *Lord Donaldson*	19 Dec 69	28 Aug 70	m	IPA	12	E	—	—	12	1R	—	
4595	Legal Education *Hon. Mr Justice Ormrod Q.C.*	19 Dec 67	25 Jan 71	d	IPA	14	E	109	26	43	U	—	
4596	Consumer Credit *Lord Crowther*	24 Sep 68	30 Dec 70	f	IPA	9	R	122	35	67	U	—	
4609	The Rent Acts *H E Francis Q.C.*	Oct 69	29 Jan 71	kqv	IA	5	E	264	18/41	36	1D	75,500	
4775	Medical and Toxicological Aspects of CS *Sir Harold Himsworth*	30 Aug 69	9 Jul 71	c	I	3	E	51+	13+	15	U	—	4173

4810	Death Certification and Coroners *Norman Brodrick Q.C.*	17 Mar 65	22 Sep 71	c	IPA	9	E	107	70	114	U	—
4811	Small Firms *J E Bolton*	23 Jul 69	21 Sep 71	f	IP	4	E	491	121	—	U	141,500
5107	Adoption of Children *Sir William Houghton/Judge F A Stockdale*	21 Jul 69	24 Jul 72	cv	IPA	17	E	191	48/—	92	U	5,805
5460	*The Constitution *Lord Crowther/Lord Kilbrandon*	15 Apr 69	10 Oct 73	c	IPA	16	I	263	24/163	233	2D	434,234
5629	One-Parent Families *Sir Morris Finer*	6 Nov 69	22 Mar 74	n	IA	13	E	216	8/78	230	U	180,380

Notes to Table B

Parentheses indicate approximate or estimated data, a dash indicates that there are no data available, and a plus-sign indicates that the figure to which it is appended is a minimum value. Other symbols and abbreviations are explained in the columns in which they are used.

1) This column gives the Command number of the final report of each committee. Where the report shown is not a final report, this is indicated by square brackets and is explained in column (14). In this column, all Command numbers below 6000 should be prefixed 'Cmnd.' and all those above 6000 'Cmd.' (see Chapter 3 above).

2) There is no official short title for a royal commission or a departmental committee (as there is for modern statutes, for example), so that the titles shown in this column may not always coincide with other usages. See P. Ford and G. Ford, *A Breviate of Parliamentary Papers*, 1940–1954 (Oxford: Blackwell, 1961), pp. ix–xi. Chairmen are listed as they were on the date of their appointment to the committee; for example, the chairman of the Royal Commission on Local Government in England (Cmnd. 4040) is listed as Sir John Maud, although he became Lord Redcliffe-Maud before the Royal Commission reported. Where a second chairman has been appointed to succeed the first, both are listed (in order).

3) The date of appointment is in most cases the date on which the document of appointment for the committee (see Chapter 4 above) was signed. Where this is not available, the date will usually be that of the official announcement of the committee's existence or of the first meeting of the committee, whichever is earlier.

4) The date of adjournment is the date on which the final report of the committee is signed. Where no final report is published, the date refers to the last known meeting of the committee or the official announcement of its adjournment or disbandment (see Chapter 11 above).

5) Departments are defined in accordance with the method devised in Chapter 4 above (see especially Table 4.2) and are indicated in this column as follows:

a	Prime Minister's Office	*l*	Transport
b	Treasury	*m*	Defence
c	Home Office	*n*	Social Services
d	Lord Chancellor's Department	*o*	Postmaster General
e	Agriculture, Fisheries and Food	*p*	Foreign Office
f	Board of Trade	*q*	Welsh Office
g	Health	*r*	Public Building and Works
h	Education and Science	*s*	Duchy of Lancaster
i	Power	*t*	Civil Service Department
j	Employment and Productivity	*u*	Master of the Rolls
k	Housing and Local Government	*v*	Scottish Office

6) Purpose is defined as in Chapter 6 above; the same abbreviations (I, IP, IA, IPA, etc.) are used.

7) The size of each committee is shown as of the date of appointment given in Column 4. Subsequent changes due to resignations and/or additional appointments are not shown.

8) Committee membership is characterised as impartial (I), expert (E) or representative (R), as in Chapter 5 above.

9) The number of witnesses includes all those who presented either oral or written evidence or both, regardless of whether the evidence was solicited or not (see Chapter 8 above). Institutions count as single witnesses unless more than one representative thereof is recorded by the committee as having sponsored the evidence or attended its hearings, in which case they are all counted.

10) Where one figure is given, this indicates the total number of full days during which the committee sat in full and plenary session. Informal meetings, visits and subcommittee meetings (except those of drafting subcommittes) are not included. Where two figures are given, the first indicates the number of full days devoted to hearing oral evidence and the second indicates the total number of days in which the committee was in session as defined above). See also Chapter 8 above.

11) The number of recommendations is based on each committee's own itemisation of its recommendations. Where 'conclusions' are distinguished by the committee from its 'recommendations', only the latter are inclined. Recommendations in all the reports of each committee are included (see Chapter 10 above).

12) Reservations (R) and dissents (D) (in the final report only) are characterised by the number of committee members subscribing to them, not by the number of points of disagreement at issue. Unanimous reports are denoted 'U' or 'u', the latter being used for one-man committees which are bound to be unanimous.

13) Reference to 'net costs' excludes costs of printing and publishing, as well as any revenue derived from the sale of reports (see Chapter 11).

14) The Command numbers of published interim reports are listed in order in this column. If interim reports were not published separately or even not published at all, this is indicated. If the report cited in Column 1 is not a final report – and this is indicated by square brackets – an explanation is given in this column.

Appendix C
Major Departmental
Committees since 1969

In Chapter 3, a selection was made of the more important of the six hundred or so royal commissions and departmental committees in the postwar period. Since the end of the period covered (1969), additional departmental committees have been appointed. Using the same criteria as were used in Chapter 3, the following table lists the major departmental committees which had issued final reports by the time of going to press.

In addition, three major departmental committees have issued interim reports: the Thomson Committee on Criminal Appeals in Scotland (Cmnd. 5038), the Lowry Committee on Civil and Criminal Jurisdiction in Northern Ireland (Cmnd. 5431) and the Faulks Committee on Defamation (Cmnd. 5571).

Furthermore, the appointment of a Royal Commission on the Press (chairman, Mr Justice Finer) was announced in the House of Commons, 2 May 1974. There was also discussion of the appointment of a Royal Commission (though it may be made into a standing royal commission) on corruption in business and public life (see *House of Commons Debates*, 29 April 1974). There have also been press reports of the appointment of Lord Annan to chair a departmental committee on the future of broadcasting.

Table C Major departmental committees since 1969

command number	short title	chairman	date of appointment	date of adjournment
4449	Industrial Relations at Heathrow Airport	Prof. D. J. Robertson/ W H Griffiths Q.C.	26 Mar 70	Jul 70
4641	Defence Procurement	D G Rayner	Oct 70	31 Mar 71
4696	Rabies	R Waterhouse Q.C.	6 Apr 70	10 May 71
4807	Work of the Fire Service	Sir Charles Cunningham	8 Mar 71	29 Oct 71
4823	Allegations of Brutality in N. Ireland	Sir Edmund Compton	31 Aug 71	3 Nov 71
4901	Interrogation of Terrorists	Lord Parker of Waddington	16 Nov 71	31 Jan 72
4913	Public Trustee Office	H R Hutton	May 71	Nov 71

Table C—*cont.*

command number	short title	chairman	date of appointment	date of adjournment
4952	Crowd Safety	Lord Wheatley	4 Feb 71	16 Mar 72
5012	Privacy	K Younger	13 May 70	25 May 72
5034	Safety and Health at Work	Lord Robens	29 May 70	9 Jun 72
5042	Lead Poisonings at Avonmouth Smelter	Sir Brian Windeyer	29 Feb 72	23 June 72
5076	Work and Pay of Probation Officers and Social Workers	J B Butterworth	24 Dec 71	31 Jul 72
5099	Contract Farming	Sir James Barker	9 Jun 71	30 Jun 72
5104	Section of the Official Secrets Act 1911	Lord Franks	20 Apr 71	1 Aug 72
5110	Bilingual Traffic Signs	Roderic Bowen Q.C.	17 Mar 71	30 Jun 72
5115	Nursing	Prof. Asa Briggs	2 Mar 70	(Aug 72)
5137	Penalties for Homicide	Lord Emslie	18 Nov 70	(Oct 72)
5154	Liquor Licensing	Lord Erroll of Hale	1 Apr 71	23 Oct 72
5185	Legal Procedures to Deal with Terrorists in N. Ireland	Lord Diplock	18 Oct 72	(Nov 72)
5191	Discharge and Supervision of Certain Psychiatric Patients	Sir Carl Aarvold	28 Jun 72	13 Nov 72
5228	Abuse of Social Security Benefits	Hon. Sir Henry Fisher	22 Mar 71	4 Oct 72
5243	Children's Footwear	Mrs Alison Munro	Jun 72	6 Dec 72
5273	National Savings	Sir Harry Page	5 Jun 71	6 Mar 73
5281	Property Bonds and Equity-linked Life Assurance	Sir Hilary Scott	10 Feb 71	19 Mar 73
5322	Dispersal of Government Work from London	Sir Henry Hardman	(Oct 70)	Feb 73
5354	Scottish Licensing Law	Dr C W Clayson	2 Apr 71	12 Jun 73
5506	Lotteries	K P Witney	20 Jan 71	Oct 73
5518	The Use of Valuers in the Public Service	R S Borner	72	(Dec 73)
5566	The Export of Animals for Slaughter	Lord O'Brien of Lothbury	26 Jul 73	6 Feb 74
5579	The Working of the Abortion Act	Mrs Justice Lane	Jun 71	(Apr 74)
5582	The Handling of Complaints against the Police (England and Wales)	A D Gordon-Brown	Apr 73	Dec 73
5583	The Handling of Complaints against the Police (Scotland)	W K Fraser	Apr 73	Dec 73
5601	British Trade Mark Law and Practice	H R Mathys	24 Jul 72	20 Dec 73
5636	Local Government Rules of Conduct	Lord Redcliffe-Maud	Oct 73	17 May 74

Bibliography

Anson, W. R. *Law and Custom of the Constitution.* Volume 1, fifth ed. by M. L. Gwyer. Volume 2, fourth ed. by A. B. Keith. Oxford University Press, 1922 and 1935.

Armstrong, Sir William. 'The Fulton Report: The Tasks of the Civil Service.' *Public Administration,* **47** (1969), pp. 1–11.

Aylmer, G. E. *The King's Servants: The Civil Service of Charles I, 1625–1642.* London: Routledge and Kegan Paul, 1961.

Bagehot, Walter. *The English Constitution.* Ed. R. H. S. Crossman. London: Collins, 1963.

Baron, Stanley Wade. *The Contact Man: the Story of Sidney Stanley and the Lynskey Tribunal.* London: Secker and Warburg, 1966.

Beer, Samuel H. *Modern British Politics: a Study of Politics and Pressure Groups.* London: Faber and Faber, 1965.

Bell, Kathleen. *Tribunals in the Social Services.* London: Routledge and Kegan Paul, 1969.

Beloff, Max. 'Another Plowden Report: The Foreign and Commonwealth Services.' *Public Administration,* **42** (1964), pp. 415–19.

Bennett, Gordon L. 'An Administrator Looks behind the Scenes of a Royal Commission.' M.A. thesis for Carleton University. Ottawa: mimeo, 1964.

Bennis, Warren G. 'Beyond Bureaucracy.' In Bennis and P. E. Slater. *The Temporary Society.* New York: Harper Colophon, 1968.

Bennis, Warren G. 'Post-Bureaucratic Leadership.' *Trans-Action,* **6,** 9 (1969), pp. 44–51, 61.

Birch, A. H. *Representative and Responsible Government: an Essay on the British Constitution.* London: Allen and Unwin, 1964.

Black, Duncan. *The Theory of Committees and Elections.* Cambridge University Press, 1958.

Black, Duncan, and R. A. Newing. *Committee Decisions with Complementary Valuation.* London: William Hodge, 1951.

Brady, Alexander. 'Royal Commissions in the Dominions: a Note on Current Political Practice.' *University of Toronto Quarterly,* **VIII** (1939), pp. 284–92.

Braybrooke, David, and Charles E. Lindblom. *A Strategy of Choice: Policy Evaluation as a Social Process.* New York: Free Press, 1963.

Bridges, Lord. 'Haldane and the Machinery of Government.' *Public Administration,* **XXXV** (1957), pp. 254–65.

Brittan, Samuel. *The Treasury under the Tories, 1951–1964.* Harmondsworth: Penguin, 1964.

Brittain, Sir Herbert. *The British Budgetary System*. London: Allen & Unwin, 1959.

Brown, A. J. 'The Use of Advisory Bodies by the Treasury.' In Vernon and Mansergh, *op. cit.*, pp. 86–125.

Brown, R. D. *The Battle of Crichel Down*. London: Bodley Head, 1955.

Brown, R. G. S. *The Administrative Process in Britain*. London: Methuen, 1970.

Browne, G. P. *The Judicial Committee and the British North America Act*. University of Toronto Press, 1967.

Callard, K. B. 'Commissions of Inquiry in Canada: 1867–1949.' Special Report prepared for the Privy Council. Ottawa: mimeo, 1950.

Campbell, G. C. *The Civil Service in Britain*. Harmondsworth: Penguin, 1955.

Campion, Lord. *An Introduction to the Procedure of the House of Commons*. Third ed. London: Macmillan, 1958.

Cartwright, Dorwin and Alvin Zander, eds. *Group Dynamics: Research and Theory*. Third ed. New York: Harper and Row, 1968.

Cartwright, T. J. 'The Fulton Committee on the Civil Service in Britain.' *Canadian Public Administration*, **XII** (1969), pp. 89–107.

Cartwright, T. J. Review of *Guide to Decision*. *Canadian Journal of Economics and Political Science*, **XXXIII** (1967), pp. 482–4.

Chapman, Brian. *British Government Observed: Some European Reflections*. London: Allen and Unwin, 1963.

Chapman, R. A. 'The Fulton Report: A Summary.' *Public Administration*, **46** (1968), pp. 443–51.

Chapman, R. A. ed., *The Role of Commissions in Policy-Making*. London: Allen and Unwin, 1973.

Chester, D. N. 'The Crichel Down Case.' *Public Administration*, **XXXII** (1954), pp. 389–401.

Chester, D. N. 'The Plowden Report: Nature and Significance.' *Public Administration*, **41** (1963), pp. 3–15.

Chester, D. N. 'Public Corporations and the Classification of Administrative Bodies.' *Political Studies*, **1** (1953), pp. 34–52.

Chester, D. N., and Nona Bowring. *Questions in Parliament*. Oxford University Press, 1962.

Chester, D. N., and F. M. G. Willson. *The Organisation of British Central Government, 1914–1964*. Second ed. London: Allen and Unwin, 1968.

Chester, T. E. 'The Guillebaud Report.' *Public Administration*, **XXXIV** (1956), pp. 199–210.

Clarke, R. W. B. 'The Plowden Report: the Formulation of Economic Policy.' *Public Administration*, **41** (1963), pp. 17–24.

Clokie, H. M., and J. W. Robinson. *Royal Commissions of Inquiry: The Significance of Investigations in British Politics*. Stanford University Press, 1937. Now reprinted (New York: Octagon Books, 1969).

Cohen, Emmeline. *The Growth of the British Civil Service, 1780–1939*. London: Allen and Unwin, 1941.

Cole, Arthur H. *A Finding-List of British Royal Commission Reports: 1860–1935*. Cambridge: Harvard University Press, 1935.

Cole, Arthur H. *A Finding-List of Royal Commission Reports in the British Dominions*. Cambridge: Harvard University Press, 1939.

Coombes, David. *The Member of Parliament and the Administration: the Case of the Select Committee on Nationalised Industries*. London: Allen and Unwin, 1966.

Cory, William. *A Guide to Modern English History*. Part II (MDCCCXXX–MDCCCXXXV). London: Kegan Paul, Trench, 1882.

Courtney, John C. 'Canadian Royal Commissions of Inquiry, 1946 to 1962: an Investigation of an Executive Instrument of Inquiry.' Ph.D. thesis for Duke University. Durham, N.C.: mimeo, 1964.

Courtney, John C. 'In Defence of Royal Commissions.' *Canadian Public Administration*, **XII,** 2 (1969), pp. 198–212.

Courtney, Leonard. *The Working Constitution of the United Kingdom and Its Outgrowths*. London: Dent and Company, 1901.

Crick, Bernard, ed. *Essays on Reform, 1967: a Centenary Tribute*. Oxford University Press, 1967.

Crick, Bernard, 'Parliament and the Matter of Britain.' In Crick, *Essays on Reform, op cit.*, pp. 203–22.

Crick, Bernard. *The Reform of Parliament*. London: Weidenfeld and Nicolson, 1964.

Critchley, T. A. *The Civil Service Today*. London: Gollancz, 1951.

Crozier, Michel. *The Bureaucratic Phenomenon*. London: Tavistock Publications, 1964.

Daalder, Hans. *Cabinet Reform in Britain, 1914–1963*. Stanford University Press, 1963.

Daalder, Hans. 'The Haldane Committee and the Cabinet.' *Public Administration*, **XLI** (1963), pp. 117–35.

Davis, H. W. C. *The Age of Grey and Peel*. Oxford University Press, 1929.

Dean, Sir Maurice. 'The Fulton Report: Accountable Management in the Civil Service.' *Public Administration*, **47** (1969), pp. 49–63.

Dibelius, Wilhelm. *England*. Trans. from the German by Mrs Mary Hamilton, M.P. Intro. by A. D. Lindsay. London: Jonathan Cape, 1930.

Doern, G. B. 'The Role of Royal Commissions in the General Policy Process and in Federal-Provincial Relations'. *Canadian Public Administration*, **X,** 4 (December 1967), pp. 415–28.

Donnison, D. V. 'Committees and Committeemen.' *New Society* (18 April 1968), pp. 558–61.

Dunnett, Sir James. 'The Fulton Report: Equipping the Civil Service for Its Tasks.' *Public Administration*, **47** (1969), pp. 13–31.

Elcock, H. J. *Administrative Justice*. London: Longman, 1969.

Fabian Society. *The Reform of the Higher Civil Service*. London: Gollancz, 1947.

Finer, S. E. *Anonymous Empire: a Study of the Lobby in Great Britain*. Rev. ed. London: Pall Mall Press, 1966.

Ford, P., and G. Ford. *A Breviate of Parliamentary Papers, 1900–1916*. Oxford: Blackwell, 1957

Ford, P., and G. Ford. *A Breviate of Parliamentary Papers, 1917–1939*. Oxford: Blackwell, 1951.

Ford, P., and G. Ford. *A Breviate of Parliamentary Papers, 1940–1954*. Oxford: Blackwell, 1961.

Ford, P., and G. Ford. *A Guide to Parliamentary Papers*. Oxford: Blackwell, 1955.

Ford, P., and G. Ford. *Hansard's Catalogue and Breviate of Parliamentary Papers, 1696–1834*. Oxford: Blackwell, 1953.

Ford, P., G. Ford and D. Marshallsay. *Select List of British Parliamentary Papers, 1955–1964*. Shannon: Irish University Press, 1970.

Fowke, V. C. 'Royal Commissions and Canadian Agricultural Policy.' *Canadian Journal of Economics and Political Science*, **XIV** (May 1948), pp. 163–75.

Gilmour, Ian. *The Body Politic*. London: Hutchinson, 1969.

Gladden, E. N. *British Public Service Administration*. London: Staples Press, 1961.

Golembiewski, R. T. *The Small Group: an Analysis of Research Concepts and Operations*. University of Chicago Press, 1962.

Gordon Walker, Patrick. *The Cabinet*. London: Jonathan Cape, 1970.

Gosnell, H. F. 'British Royal Commissions of Inquiry.' *Political Science Quarterly*, **XLIX** (March 1934), pp. 84–118.

Gowan, Ivor, and Leon Gibson. 'The Royal Commission on Local Government in England: A Survey of Some of the Written Evidence.' *Public Administration*, **XLVI** (1968), pp. 13–24.

Graves, John. 'The Use of Advisory Bodies by the Board of Education.' In Vernon and Mansergh, *op. cit.*, pp. 176–226.

Greenwood, R., A. L. Norton and J. D. Stewart. 'Recent Changes in the Internal Organisation of County Boroughs: Part I. Committees.' *Public Administration*, **47** (1970), pp 151–67.

Gretton, R. H. *The King's Government: a Study of the Growth of the Central Administration*. London: G. Bell and Sons, 1913.

Griffith, J. A. G. *Central Departments and Local Authorities*. London: Allen and Unwin, 1966.

Griffith, J. A. G. 'The Crichel Down Affair.' *Modern Law Review*, **XVII** (1955), pp. 557–70.

Grove, J. W. *Government and Industry in Britain*. London: Longmans, 1962.

Hagestadt, L. 'Local Advisory Committees'. *Public Administration*, **XXX** (1952), pp. 215–19.

Hamson, C. J. 'The Real Lesson of Crichel Down.' *Public Administration*, **XXXII** (1954), pp. 383–7.

Hanham, H. J. *The Nineteenth-Century Constitution, 1815–1914: Documents and Commentary*. Cambridge University Press, 1969.

Hanser, C. J. *Guide to Decision: the Royal Commission*. Totowa, N.J.: Bedminster Press, 1965.

Hanson, A. H. *Planning and the Politicians and Other Essays*. London: Routledge, 1969.

Hanson, Hugh R. 'Inside Royal Commissions'. *Canadian Public Administration*, **XII**, 3 (Fall 1969), pp. 356–64.

Hare, A. P., *et al.*, eds. *Small Groups: Studies in Social Interaction*. Rev. ed. New York: Knopf, 1966.

Harris, W. G. 'The Fulton Report: The Role of the Professional in the Civil Service'. *Public Administration*, **47** (1969), pp. 33–47.

Harrison, Enid. 'Local Advisory Committees'. *Public Administration*, **XXXI** (1953), pp. 65–75.

Hart, Jennifer. 'Some Reflections on the Report of the Royal Commission on the Police'. *Public Law*, **IX** (Autumn 1963), pp. 283–304.

Herbert, Sir Alan P. 'Anything but Action? A Study of the Uses and Abuses of Committees of Inquiry.' In Ralph Harris, ed. *Radical Reaction: Essays in Competition and Affluence*, second ed. (rev.). London: Hutchinson, 1961.

Herbert, A. P. 'Sad Fate of a Royal Commission.' *Mild and Bitter*. London: Methuen, 1936.

Herbst, P. G. *Autonomous Group Functioning*. London: Social Science Paperback for the Tavistock Institute, 1968.

Heuston, R. F. V. *Essays in Constitutional Law*. London: Stevens and Son, 1961.

Hicks, U. K. 'Plowden, Planning and Management in the Public Service.' *Public Administration*, **XXXIX** (1961), pp. 299–312.

Hodgetts, J. E. 'The Role of Royal Commissions in Canadian Government.' *Proceedings of the Third Annual Conference of the Institute of Public Administration of Canada*, Philip Clark (ed.). Toronto: mimeo, 1951, pp. 351–67.

Hodgetts, J. E. 'Royal Commissions of Inquiry in Canada.' *Public Administration Review*, **IX**, 1 (1949), pp. 22–9.

Hodgetts, J. E. 'Royal Commissions of Inquiry in Canada: a Study in Investigative Technique.' M.A. thesis for the University of Toronto. Toronto: typescript, 1940.

'How Dr Hunt (aided and abetted by Harold Wilson) took over Fulton.' *Sunday Times* (30 June 1968).

Hutchison, Peter. 'The Committee System in East Suffolk.' *Public Administration*, **XXXVII** (1959), pp. 393–402.

Irving, Clive, Ron Hall and Jeremy Wallington. *Scandal '63: a Study of the Profumo Affair*. London: Heinemann, 1963.

Jackson, R. M. *The Machinery of Local Government*. Second ed. London: Macmillan, 1965.

Jackson, R. M. 'Royal Commissions and Committees of Inquiry.' *The Listener*, **LV**, 1411 (12 April 1956), pp. 388–9.

Jackson, R. M. 'Tribunals and Inquiries.' *Public Administration*, **XXXIII** (1955), pp. 115–23.

Jennings, Sir Ivor. *Cabinet Government*. Third ed. Cambridge University Press, 1959.

Johnson, D. McI. *A Cassandra at Westminster*. London: Johnson, 1967.

Johnson, F. A. *Defence by Committee: the British Committee of Imperial Defence, 1885–1959*. Oxford University Press, 1960.

Johnson, Nevil. *Parliament and Administration: the Estimates Committee, 1945–65*. London: Allen and Unwin, 1966.

Jones, Hilda Vernon. *Catalogue of Parliamentary Papers, 1801–1900*. London: King and Son, 1904.

Keeton, G. W. *Trial by Tribunal*. London: Museum Press, 1960.

Keith, A. B. *The British Cabinet System*. Rev. ed. by N. H. Gibbs. London: Stevens and Sons, 1952.

Keith, A. B. *The King and the Imperial Crown*. London: Longmans, Green, 1938.

Kennet, Lord, chairman. 'On the Value of Royal Commissions in Sociological Research, with special Reference to the Birth-Rate.' Discussion with Lord Kennet in the Chair and Contributions by Major Greenwood *et al.*, *Journal of the Royal Statistical Society*, New Series, **C**, 3 (1937), pp. 396–414.

Koester, C. B. 'Standing Committees in the British House of Commons.' *The Parliamentarian*, **XLIX**, 2 (April 1968), pp. 64–72.

Laski, H. J. *Parliamentary Government in England: a Commentary*. London: Allen and Unwin, 1938.

Laski, H. J. Review of *Royal Commissions of Inquiry*. *New Statesman and Nation* (13 August 1938), p. 258.

Lewin, Leonard C. ed. *Report from Iron Mountain on the Possibility and Desirability of Peace.* New York: Delta, 1967.

Lolme, J. L. De. *The Constitution of England.* Ed. W. H. Hughes M.P. London: Hatchard, 1834.

Lubbock, Eric. 'Have Royal Commissions Had Their Day?' *The Times* (13 December 1966).

Lupton, Tom, and Shirley Wilson. 'The Social Background and Connections of "Top Decision Makers." ' In Rose, *Policy-Making in Britain, op. cit.,* pp. 5–25.

Mansergh, Nicholas. 'The Use of Advisory Bodies in the Reform of the Machinery of Government.' In Vernon and Mansergh, *op. cit.,* pp. 31–85.

March, James G., and H. A. Simon. *Organizations.* New York: Wiley, 1958.

Marshall, Geoffrey. 'The Franks Report on Administrative Tribunals and Enquiries.' *Public Administration,* **XXXV** (1957), pp. 347–58.

Marshall, Geoffrey. 'Tribunals and Inquiries: Developments Since the Franks Report.' *Public Administration,* **XXXVI** (1958), pp. 261–70.

Marshall, Geoffrey, and G. C. Moodie. *Some Problems of the Constitution.* Third ed. London: Hutchinson, 1964.

Martindale, Hilda. *Women Servants of the State, 1870–1938: a History of Women in the Civil Service.* London: Allen and Unwin, 1938.

May, Erskine. *The Law, Privileges, Proceedings and Usage of Parliament.* Seventeenth ed. London: Butterworth, 1964.

Medley, D. J. *English Constitutional History.* Third ed. Oxford: Blackwell, 1902.

Melville, H. *The Department of Scientific and Industrial Research.* New Whitehall Series. London: Allen and Unwin, 1962.

Mills, T. M. *The Sociology of Small Groups.* Englewood Cliffs: Prentice-Hall, 1967.

Milne, Sir David. *The Scottish Office.* New Whitehall Series. London: Allen and Unwin, 1957.

Mitchell, Harvey. 'To Commission or Not to Commission: Introduction.' *Canadian Public Administration,* **V,** 3 (1962), pp. 253–60.

Moore, W. H. 'Executive Commissions of Inquiry.' *Columbia Law Review,* **XIII** (June 1913), pp. 500–23.

Morgan, A. Mary. *British Government Publications: an Index to Chairmen and Authors, 1941–66.* London: Library Association, 1969.

Morrison of Lambeth, Lord. *Government and Parliament: a Survey from the Inside.* Oxford University Press, 1959.

Morton, W. W. 'The Plowden Report: The Management Functions of the Treasury'. *Public Administration,* **41** (1963), pp. 25–35.

Munby, Denys. 'The Procedure of Public Inquiries.' *Public Administration,* **XXXIV** (1956), pp. 175–85.

Murray, Sir Evelyn. *The Post Office.* Whitehall Series. London: Putnam, 1927.

Mackenzie, W. J. M. 'The Articulation of Pressure-Group Demands.' *British Journal of Sociology,* **IV,** 2 (1955), pp. 133–48. Reprinted in Richard Rose, ed. *Studies in British Politics: a Reader in Political Sociology.* London: Macmillan, 1966. Chapter IV, pp. 202–19.

Mackenzie, W. J. M. 'The Civil Service, the State and the Establishment.' In Crick, *Essays on Reform, op. cit.,* pp. 182–202.

Mackenzie, W. J. M. 'Committees in Administration'. *Public Administration,* **XXXI** (Autumn, 1953), pp. 235–44.

Mackenzie, W. J. M. 'The Plowden Report: A Translation'. *The Guardian* (25 May 1963). Reprinted in Richard Rose, *Policy-Making in Britain, op. cit.*, pp. 273–82.

Mackenzie, W. J. M. and J. W. Grove. *Central Administration in Britain*. London: Longmans, 1957.

Mackintosh, John P. *The British Cabinet*. Second ed. London: Stevens and Sons, 1968.

Mackintosh, John P. 'The Royal Commission on Local Government in Scotland, 1966–69.' *Public Administration*, **48** (1970), pp. 49–56.

Nelson, J. R. 'The Fleck Report and the Area Organisation of the National Coal Board.' *Public Administration*, **XLIII** (1965), pp. 41–57.

Newsam, Sir Frank. *The Home Office*. New Whitehall Series. London: Allen and Unwin, 1954.

Nicholson, Max. *The System: the Misgovernment of Modern Britain*. London: Hodder and Stoughton, 1967.

Ogilvy-Webb, Marjorie. *The Government Explains: A Study of the Information Services*. London: Allen and Unwin, 1965.

Pateman, Carole. *Participation and Democratic Theory*. Cambridge University Press, 1970.

Peterson, A. V. 'The Machinery for Economic Planning: III. Regional Economic Planning Councils and Boards.' *Public Administration*, **XLIV** (1966), pp. 29–41.

Plowden, William. 'An Anatomy of Commissions.' *New Society* (15 July 1971), pp. 104–7.

Political and Economic Planning. *Advisory Committees in British Government*. London: Allen and Unwin, 1960.

Political and Economic Planning. 'Government by Appointment'. *P.E.P.*, **XXVI**, 443 (25 July 1960), pp. 207–25. Reprinted in Stankiewicz, *op. cit.*, pp. 282–300.

Pollard, R. W. S. *Administrative Tribunals at Work*. London: Stevens, 1950.

Potter, Allen. *Organised Groups in British National Politics*. London: Faber and Faber, 1961.

Prouty, Roger. *The Transformation of the Board of Trade, 1830–1855*. London: Heinemann, 1957.

Redlich, Josef. *The Procedure of the House of Commons*. Two volumes. London: Constable, 1908.

Rhodes, Gerald. *Administrators in Action*. Volume Two. London: Allen and Unwin, 1965.

Richards, Peter G. *Patronage in British Government*. London: Allen and Unwin, 1963.

Richards, Peter G. 'The Tribunals of Inquiry (Evidence) Act, 1921.' *Public Administration*, **XXVII** (1949), pp. 123–8.

Robinson, K. E. 'Another Plowden Report: A Single Ministry?' *Public Administration*, **42** (1964), pp. 420–2.

Robshaw, Peter. 'Another View on the London Government Royal Commission.' *Public Administration*, **XXXIX** (1961), pp. 247–50.

Robson, William A. 'Public Inquiries as an Instrument of Government.' *British Journal of Administrative Law* [now *Public Law*], **I** (1954–5), pp. 71–92.

Robson, William A. 'The Reform of Government.' *Political Quarterly*, **XXV**, 2 (1964), pp. 193–211. Reprinted in part in Stankiewicz, *op. cit.*, pp. 150–1.

Robson, William A. 'The Reform of London Government.' *Public Administration*. **XXXIX** (1961), pp. 59–71.

'Royal Commissions as They Are and as They Should Be.' *The Spectator*, **74** (6 April 1895), pp. 457–8.

Rose, Richard, ed. *Policy-Making in Britain: a Reader in Government.* London: Macmillan, 1969.

Rose, Richard. *Politics in England: An Interpretation.* Boston: Little, Brown, 1964.

Salmon, Sir Cyril. *Tribunals of Inquiry.* Lionel Cohen Lecture to the Hebrew University of Jerusalem, 1967. Jerusalem: Magnes Press, 1967.

Seldon, Arthur, ed. *Not Unanimous: A Rival Verdict to Radcliffe's on Money.* London: Institute of Economic Affairs, 1960.

Self, Peter. 'The Herbert Report and the Values of Local Government.' *Political Studies,* **X** (1962), pp. 146–62.

Self, Peter. ' "Nonsense on Stilts": Cost-Benefit Analysis and the Roskill Commission.' *Political Quarterly,* **41,** 3 (July–September 1970), pp. 249–60.

Sellar, Watson. 'A Century of Commissions of Inquiry.' *Canadian Bar Review,* **XXV** (1947), pp. 1–28.

Sharpe, L. J. 'The Report of the Royal Commission on Local Government in Greater London.' *Public Administration,* **XXXIX** (1961), pp. 73–92.

Shore, Peter. *Entitled to Know.* London: Macgibbon & Kee, 1966.

Simon, Herbert A. *The Sciences of the Artificial.* Boston: M.I.T. Press, 1969.

Simon, Herbert A. *The Shape of Automation for Men and Management.* New York: Harper Torchbooks, 1965.

Sisson, C. H. *The Spirit of British Administration and Some European Comparisons.* Second ed. London: Faber and Faber, 1966.

Smellie, K. B. *A Hundred Years of English Government.* Second ed. rev. London: Duckworth, 1950.

Smith, Brian C. *Advising Ministers: a Case-Study of the South West Economic Planning Council.* London: Routledge and Kegan Paul, 1969.

Stankiewicz, W. J., ed. *Crisis in British Government: the Need for Reform.* London: Collier-Macmillan, 1967.

Stout, H. M., *British Government.* Oxford University Press, 1953.

Stubbs, William. *Select Charters and Other Illustrations of English Constitution History from the Earliest Times to the Reign of Edward the First.* Eighth ed. Oxford University Press, 1905.

Taylor, Eric. *The House of Commons at Work.* Sixth ed. Harmondsworth: Penguin, 1967.

Toulmin Smith, Joshua. *Government by Commissions Illegal and Pernicious: the Nature and Effects of All Commissions of Inquiry and Other Crown-Appointed Commissions; the Constitutional Principles of Taxation; and the Rights, Duties and Importance of Local Self-Government.* London: S. Sweet, 1849.

Tout, T. F. *Chapters in the Administrative History of Mediaeval England.* Six volumes. Manchester University Press, 1920–37.

Troup, Sir Edward. *The Home Office.* Whitehall Series. London: Putnam's, 1925.

Vandyck, N. D. *Tribunals and Inquiries: a Guide to Procedure.* London: Oyez Publications, 1965.

Vernon, R. V., and Nicholas Mansergh, eds. *Advisory Bodies: A Study of Their Uses in Relation to Central Government, 1919–1939.* London: Allen and Unwin, 1940.

Wade, H. W. R. *Administrative Law.* Second ed. Oxford University Press, 1967.

Wade, H. W. R. *Towards Administrative Justice.* Ann Arbor: University of Michigan Press, 1963.

Wall, J. E. 'The Plowden Report: Management Services in Industry'. *Public Administration,* **41** (1963), pp. 37–50.

Walls, C. E. S. 'Royal Commissions – Their Influence on Public Policy'. *Canadian Public Administration*, **XII**, 3 (Fall 1969), pp. 365–71.

Weber, Max. *The Theory of Social and Economic Organization*. Ed. A. M. Henderson and T. Parsons. New York: Free Press, 1947.

Wheare, K. C. *Government by Committee: an Essay on the British Constitution*. Oxford University Press, 1955.

Wheare, K. C. *Modern Constitutions*. Second ed. Oxford University Press, 1966.

Wilding, Norman and Philip Laundy. *An Encyclopaedia of Parliament*. Rev. ed. London: Cassell, 1961.

Wilensky, Harold. *Organizational Intelligence: Knowledge and Policy in Government and Industry*. New York: Basic Books, 1967.

Williams, D. G. T. *Not in the Public Interest: the Problem of Security in Democracy*. London: Hutchinson, 1965.

Willson, F. M. G. *Administrators in Action*. Volume One. London: Allen and Unwin, 1961.

Willson, F. M. G. 'Departmental Reports.' *Public Administration*, **XXX** (1952), pp. 163–73.

Wilson, Norman. *The British System of Government*. Oxford: Blackwell, 1963.

Wiseman, H. V. *Politics in Everyday Life*. Oxford: Blackwell, 1966.

Wraith, R. E., and S. B. Lamb. *Public Inquiries as an Instrument of Government*. London: Allen and Unwin, 1971.

Young, G. M. *The Colonial Office in the Early Nineteenth Century*. London: Longman, 1961.

Young, Wayland. *The Profumo Affair: Aspects of Conservatism*. Harmondsworth: Penguin, 1963.

Index